Television/Death

Television/Death

Helen Wheatley

Edinburgh University Press is one of the leading university presses in the UK. We publish academic books and journals in our selected subject areas across the humanities and social sciences, combining cutting-edge scholarship with high editorial and production values to produce academic works of lasting importance. For more information visit our website: edinburghuniversitypress.com

© Helen Wheatley 2024, 2025

Edinburgh University Press Ltd
13 Infirmary Street
Edinburgh EH1 1LT

First published in hardback by Edinburgh University Press 2024

Typeset in 12 on 14pt Arno Pro and Myriad Pro
by Cheshire Typesetting Ltd, Cuddington, Cheshire

A CIP record for this book is available from the British Library

ISBN 978 1 4744 5172 7 (hardback)
ISBN 978 1 4744 5173 4 (paperback)
ISBN 978 1 4744 5174 1 (webready PDF)
ISBN 978 1 4744 5175 8 (epub)

The right of Helen Wheatley to be identified as the author of this work has been asserted in accordance with the Copyright, Designs and Patents Act 1988, and the Copyright and Related Rights Regulations 2003 (SI No. 2498).

Contents

List of Illustrations   vii
Acknowledgements   ix

Introduction: Television/Death   1
     Death – live on TV . . .   1
     Death – intimate and close up   5
     Death and grief – complicated, slowly unfurling   9
     Life and death beyond the grave – posthumous television   13

Part I: Death and Dying on Television

1. **Everyday death: The early history of death on British television**   29
     Everyday autopathographies: facing death   35
     Making sense, working through: grief, bereavement and the business of the funeral   54
     Television autopathographies today   61

2. **Signs of care: Assisted suicide on television**   66
     A suitable case for television? The history of assisted dying on British television   68
     Caring through and in television production: contemporary autopathographies of assisted dying   78
     Caring for the viewer: the persistence of television as cultural forum   90

Part II: Dramas of Grief, Bereavement and the Television Afterlife

3. **A good death? Death and the afterlife in US television fiction**   95
     Death and the dead in American television   96

The persistence of the soul: television afterlives	108
'Uplifting views. Healthy pursuits. Timeless Americana'	115
4. Dramas of grief: Television and mourning	**130**
The narrative forms of grief and mourning	133
Emotional realism and the experience of grief, on and off screen	135
Watching others grieve: new ways of thinking about grief	139
5. Haunted houses, haunted landscapes: Grief and trauma in the television ghost story	**151**
Exploring haunted landscapes: the British television ghost story	154
Trauma, temporality and the haunted houses of post-broadcast television	165

Part III: Posthumous Television

6. Entering the mausoleum: Posthumous television	**187**
Television and memorialisation	195
Haunted television: trauma and the spectre in the archive	203
7. *Ghost town*: Posthumous television in the city	**222**
Activating the archive: memory, history and the uses of posthumous television	230
Ghost Town: exploring the city through posthumous television	232
Memory explosions and unlocking memory	241
Posthumous images and the haunting of the city	244
This is our history: remembering past lives through the television archive	250
Notes	258
References	266
Index	284

Illustrations

Figures

0.1	The death of Peter Smedley, *Terry Pratchett: Choosing to Die* (BBC2, tx. 13/06/11)	6
0.2	The funeral of Hayley Cropper, *Coronation Street* (Granada for ITV, 1960–)	10
0.3	Queen Elizabeth II – the posthumous archive re-broadcast (BBC1, tx. 8/9/22)	14
1.1	Tony Whiteley, close up, *Remember All The Good Things* (BBC1 North West region tx. 12/11/74)	44
1.2	Bill and Harriet looking bored, *Dying* (PBS, tx. 29/4/76)	49
1.3	The factory-like funeral home, *Death Today* (BBC1, tx. 13/6/69)	57
1.4	Lou comforts Andy, *My Last Summer* (Love Productions for Channel 4, 2014)	63
2.1	Studio trial set-up, *A Suitable Case for Killing* (BBC2, tx. 8/2/75)	73
2.2	Cees's death, *Dood op Verzoek/Death on Request* (Ikon, tx. 20/10/94)	77
2.3	Simon Nock, end of the voiceover, *How to Die: Simon's Choice* (BBC2, tx. 10/2/16)	83
2.4	Holding hands, *Terry Pratchett: Choosing to Die* (BBC2, tx. 13/06/11)	85
3.1	Ned Stark's daughters witness his death, 'Baelor' (S1, E9), *Game of Thrones* (HBO, 2011–2019)	97
3.2	Stoved-in head, 'Crossroads' (S1E8), *Six Feet Under* (HBO, 2001–2005)	105
3.3	The Accountant's office, 'Janet(s)' (S3, E9), *The Good Place* (NBC, 2016–2020)	119

3.4 The afterlife advertised, 'Welcome to Upload' (S1, E1), *Upload* (Amazon Studios, 2020–) 124
4.1 Leigh weighed down by grief, 'One Fun Thing' (S1, E1) *Sorry for Your Loss* (Facebook Watch, 2018–2019) 135
4.2 Jeff's trauma, 'Kintsugi' (S1, E7) *Kidding* (Showtime, 2018–2020) 139
4.3 Loved Ones: the reassembled dead, 'The Prodigal Son Returns Home' (S1, E10) *The Leftovers* (HBO 2014–2017) 144
5.1 The pastoral eerie in *The Living and The Dead* (BBC1, 2016) 158
5.2 Ruth in Alice's bedroom (E4), *Marchlands* (ITV1, 2011) 161
5.3 Nell and Olivia in the morgue, 'Open Casket' (E2), *The Haunting of Hill House* (Netflix, 2018) 170
5.4 Melody: 'Please find me!', 'Mystery Signals' (E1), *Archive 81* (Netflix, 2022) 177
6.1 Savile as spectre, *Jimmy Savile: Britain's Worst Crimes* (Channel 5, tx. 18/11/15) 208
6.2 Glitching, 'haunted' title sequence, *Jimmy Savile: A British Horror Story* (Netflix, 2022) 209
6.3 Watching the spectre, *Jimmy Savile: A British Horror Story* (Netflix, 2022) 211
7.1 Posthumous Coventry on television (tx. 1/9/65) *ATV Today* (ATV for ITV, 1964–1981) 223
7.2 Remembering Coventry (2018). Author's photograph 236
7.3 Coventry Cathedral (2018–2022). Author's photograph 238
7.4 Crowds at the dedication of the Chapel of Unity at Coventry Cathedral (tx. 12/6/62) *Midlands News* (ATV for ITV, 1956–1969) 247

Table

7.1 Ghost Town activities, 2018–2022 228

Acknowledgements

There are many people I would like to thank for their help in developing this book. Firstly, while much of the television programming discussed here is readily available to view, some of it was not. It is thanks to the hard work of following people that I was able to access the posthumous television archive so extensively: Mark Macey at the BBC who was extremely generous with his time and help; Clare Watson and Phil Leach and the entire team at the Media Archive of Central England whose dedication to public engagement and willingness to talk to me about my ideas enabled the *Ghost Town* project to come to life; Chris Perry and his team of dedicated volunteers at Kaleidoscope; and Massimo Moretti at Studio Canal. I am also extremely grateful to the people who gave up their time to talk to me about making programmes about death and dying, specifically Rowan Deacon, Charlie Russell and Vivien Whiteley-Toyn. Their honesty and insight about tackling the subject of dying on screen was absolutely critical at the start and end of this project. Many thanks, too, go to everyone who talked to me about their encounters with posthumous television during the *Ghost Town* project.

Books also grow out of conversations with others, and the long gestation period of this book has meant I have had *a lot* of conversations about this work with significant groups of people. I would like to thank my colleagues at the University of Warwick, particularly all the staff and students of the Department of Film and Television Studies and the Centre for Television Histories. Extra special thanks go to those colleagues who helped me organise and run the events I discuss in Chapter 7, particularly Katie Crosson, Joanne Garde-Hansen, Rachel Moseley, Kat Pearson and Rick Wallace. They have all been important interlocutors for this project along the way, especially Kat who wrote a brilliant doctoral thesis about television and UK Cities of Culture alongside this book and enriched my understanding of the relationship between television and place. Katie Klaassen, Emma Roberts,

Shantel Edwards and especially Tracey McVey all provided brilliant support which enabled bits of this research to happen.

The first part of the book was developed through exchanges with colleagues at the SCMS conference in Seattle (particularly Anna McCarthy and Mimi White); conversations with friends and colleagues who invited me to the Universities of East Anglia, Nottingham, Southampton and Sussex (particularly Emma Pett, Su Holmes, Cathy Johnson, Shelley Cobb, Andy Medhurst and Katherine Farrimond); and through the editorial insight of Amy Holdsworth, Karen Lury and Hannah Tweed when an earlier version of Chapter 2 appeared in their book *Discourses of Care: Media Practices and Cultures* (2020). Part II of the book was enriched by invitations to conferences at the University of Kent (and by conversations with Stacey Abbott at the conference), Aarhus University (with thanks to Anne Marit Waade and Kim Toft Hansen for the kind invitation and stimulating conversation) and Sheffield Hallam's Centre for Contemporary Legend (many thanks go to Diane Rodgers for conversations there and beyond). The final section of the book was informed by conversations with Rowan Aust, Karen Boyle, Jen VanderBurgh and Helen Wood, and others at SCMS in Toronto; John Ellis, Nick Hall and others at the Screen conference in Glasgow; colleagues at the University of Birmingham (particularly Cat Lester); Lynn Spigel at SCMS in Seattle; critical conversations all over Coventry with Nirmal Puwar and the folks from the Photo Archive Miners (especially Ben Kyneswood and Mark Cook); walking and talking in the woods with my friend Duncan Whitley (who also helped me wrangle my illustrations and read parts of the book to check they made sense); and most of all my friend and colleague John Wyver who invited me into his creative process for the documentary *Coventry Cathedral: Building for a New Britain* (BBC4, tx. 9/6/21) and has talked to me often about the importance of the television archive. My thanks also go to the editors and reviewers of the *Journal of Cinema and Media Studies* who helped to improve parts of Chapter 6, the editors of *Flow* who allowed me to preview bits of this book at a late stage in its development, and Bethan Michael-Fox and Renske Visser who invited me to contribute to the *Death Studies Podcast* and their special 'Death on Screen' issue of the journal *Revenant* at a critical moment of distillation for this work.

Writers need places to write, and I have been grateful to the people and organisations who gave me places to develop parts of the book. I wrote most of Chapter 1 and parts of Chapter 2 in my little bedroom in Angie Morgan's flat in Crete, in between trips to the beach and up into the mountains for fabulous food. Chapter 4 was written in libraries in Melbourne, alongside my dear friend Alastair Phillips and colleagues from the School of Media, Film and Journalism at Monash University, thanks to the generous support of the Warwick-Monash Alliance. I have also been lucky to work with forward-thinking venues and organisations in my home city of Coventry who have all opened their doors to archival television; special thanks go to friends at Coventry Cathedral (particularly the Very Reverend John Whitcombe, Asha Eade-Green, Dianne Morris and Martin Williams), the now sadly closed Shopfront Theatre (particularly Julia Negus and Chris O'Connell), Aaron Law and the members of the Coventry Society, Christine McNaught and the women of FWT, the organisers of the 'Humans at Work' project at Warwick Arts Centre (especially Kate Sayer and Lali Dangazele), and Jane Nellist at Coventry TUC.

Finally, I thank my friends and family for their patience and understanding. Completing a book has often meant not giving enough time to the people that matter the most, especially my children, Rudy, Dora and Kit. I'm looking forward to having our evenings and weekends back, and to getting out and living life again.

This book is dedicated to my friends who have all enriched my life in the years of writing it. Thank you, especially, to Susie Cowley-Haselden, Jo Gane, Katie Klaassen, Tracey McVey, Angie Morgan, Rachel Moseley, Becky Newbould, Claire Scott, Claire Thompson, Rob West, Shiam Wilcox and Helen Wood.

Introduction: Television/Death

This book begins with four deaths. Each of these deaths will reveal something about television's relationship to death, dying and bereavement. They will show us how death is represented on television, and also how television captures life (and death) posthumously.

Death – live on TV . . .

A tall man with a comedically rumpled-looking face stands on stage in front of red velvet curtains, dressed in a tuxedo and wearing a somewhat incongruous red Fez hat. As his glamorous blonde assistant adorns him with a 'magic' cloak, oversized and made of shot, orange silk, the live audience in the theatre auditorium laugh. He is, indeed, quite a sight. He mutters 'Thank you, love', his arms stretching out, almost, into his trademark gesture (splayed hands a kind of pantomime of a magical spell-casting movement) and then he crumples to the ground. His assistant and the audience laugh. He breathes heavily, not looking up, then falls further back into the curtain. His arms and legs rise and fall. He makes a strange, guttural, snoring sound. They laugh some more. Then, as a hand appears from behind the curtain to drag him backwards, the words 'Live from Her Majesty's' appear on screen and jaunty music begins to play.

The above is a description of the unexpected death from a heart attack of the British television performer, comedian and magician Tommy Cooper, broadcast live on the ITV variety show *Live from Her Majesty's* (LWT for ITV, 1983–1985) on 15 April 1984. It is a moment that reminded millions of British television viewers of the closeness of death to life, or of the fact that 'the live' on screen always carries with it the possibility of death. Everywhere that life is photographed, filmed, videoed, broadcast, *captured* in some way, so is death. Television, so firmly associated with the 'live' even after it was possible, more common, even, to broadcast pre-recorded programming, is the audio-visual medium which captures death most frequently. Death takes place in the midst of life and therefore it also takes place live on our television screens. Its occurrence isn't always immediately apparent to us – in the case of Cooper, his death looked like part of his regular act to both the diegetic audience and the viewer at home – but when it comes it always interrupts the regular flow of television broadcasting: advertising suddenly cuts in at an unexpected moment, screens go blank, cameras pan quickly away, television presenters and performers are left floundering in its wake.

We might recall a number of high-profile deaths on (or just off) screen during live broadcasts. For example, alongside the death of Tommy Cooper, viewers in the UK might remember the death just off camera of the actor Gareth Jones during the live teleplay 'Underground' (tx. 30/11/58), an episode of the anthology drama series *Armchair Theatre* (ABC/Thames for ITV, 1956–1974), which continued with the other actors improvising around the unexpected event of an actor dying of a heart attack just as he was about to step on screen. We might also think about the death of seven astronauts including the first civilian to be sent to space, teacher Christa McAuliffe, during the widely televised launch of the *Challenger* space shuttle on 28 January 1986. Because of the build-up of excitement about McAuliffe's inclusion in the mission, many schoolchildren were watching this disaster as it happened live on screen. In the US, school TV sets had been wheeled into classrooms and school halls for coverage of the launch, whereas in the UK many children raced home from school to watch the live broadcast on the children's news programme, *Newsround* (BBC1/BBC2/CBBC, 1972–).[1] We might also recall a number of deaths that occurred during live, televised sport, including the tragic, accidental death of racing driver Ayrton Senna during the coverage of the San Marino Grand Prix on 1 May 1994.[2] Similarly, viewers are regularly confronted with deaths that are captured and broadcast during news programming. Television news places death on our screens intentionally (as I have discussed previously (2016)), sometimes filmed during coverage of war, famine, natural disasters and so on, and, much less often, broadcast live (as in the harrowing images of people falling from the World Trade Center to their deaths during early news coverage of the terrorist attacks of 11 September 2001). While these deaths are the subject of television news coverage, there have also been incidents whereby those involved in delivering news programming have died live, and unexpectedly, on screen. The live on-air suicide of news reporter Christine Chubbuck during the local morning talk show *Suncoast Digest* (WXLT-TV,

1972–1974) on 15 July 1974 has become a source of fascination for some, and indeed two feature films were made about this TV death in 2016.³ Chubbuck shot herself in the head after announcing to the viewer:

> In keeping with the WXLT practice of presenting the most immediate and complete reports of local blood and guts news, TV 40 presents what is believed to be a television first. In living colour, an exclusive coverage of an attempted suicide.

The double murder in 2015 of news anchor Alison Parker and cameraman Adam Ward when presenting an item for *Mornin'* (WDBJ, 1969–), an early morning local news programme produced for CBS affiliate WDBJ in Virginia, is another case in point. Parker and Ward's murder happened live on screen at 6.46 am on 26 August 2015 while Parker was interviewing Vicki Gardner, executive director of the local chamber of commerce, at the edge of Smith Mountain Lake in Moneta. The gunman, 41-year-old Vester Lee Flanagan II, was a former reporter and disgruntled ex-employee of WDBJ.

While all the above deaths were broadcast on live television, many of them were also simultaneously recorded, either by the broadcasting company that made them or by the viewer at home. These and other live TV deaths therefore remain available to view, frequently circulating online on platforms such as YouTube as evidence of the fascination with this phenomenon. A search for 'television deaths' on YouTube will quickly produce compilations of two kinds of death: spectacular or poignant death scenes from TV dramas which Sue Tait describes as forming the 'necrophilic imaginary' of television (2006) and montages of people dying on live TV. This latter category is edited into packages that promise the '10 Most SHOCKING Deaths Caught on LIVE TV' or the '5 Times We Watched People Die on Live TV'. They lift these moments of everyday, live television out of broadcast obscurity and re-circulate them, making them familiar, reiterative and ubiquitous for those who seek them out. These are often pirated television deaths, captured live and recorded and re-recorded by those who have no claim to their rights ownership; they are copies of live TV which are not contained by an official broadcast archive and freely continue to circulate online. Typically, such compilations feature a musical soundtrack, voiceover narration and/or an in-screen presenter, and/or scrolling titles that contextualise the deaths at hand. They also usually lack diegetic sound and, in some instances, these extracts of historical programming are presented in still, rather than moving, images. In all these ways, the producers of these compilation videos seek to get around copyright claims that could be made by the television production companies behind each broadcast in order to remove the videos from circulation. These compilations can be seen as a more recent iteration of what critics have referred to as the 'death film' (Kerekes and Slater, 1993; Schaefer, 1999), that category of filmmaking which covers a variety of genres from early cinema coverage of public executions to the mondo film, snuff film and the death compilation film such as the *Faces of Death* and *Death Scenes* franchises. They produce a similar affective response, implicit in André Bazin's description of the screening of death as being akin to the 'the profanation of corpses and the desecration of tombs' (2003: 31). They are shocking, hard to watch, and intentionally so.

These YouTube compilations therefore capture the repeated disruption of television as a *live* medium and in doing so tell us something about the ontology of the medium as 'still live', even in a supposedly post-broadcast, post-live TV era. Though much of our television is not now broadcast or watched live, we still regularly watch live sporting events, live news broadcasts, even live light entertainment programming. As discussed at the start of this introduction, death is the ultimate interruption of the live, and therefore television's 'banal liveness' (see White, 1999) can swiftly be disrupted by the arrival of death in any and all contexts. Perhaps the most upsetting 'live TV death' compilation I watched during research for this book was one of on-screen heart attacks where a series of television performers in TV genres as diverse as news and sports broadcasting, home shopping programming and the television talent show suddenly slumped forward or fell to the floor as their hearts had gone into cardiac arrest, suffering that most ordinary and unspectacular of deaths. These compilations also challenge our perception of television as always only fleeting and impermanent. Television is both live enough to capture death in all its unexpected forms and locations, but recordable enough that these deaths can frequently be replayed by those who wish to see them, over and over again. Andy Parker, the father of Alison Parker whose on-screen murder was discussed above, has campaigned hard to have recordings of his daughter's murder removed from public circulation on the internet;[4] however, despite Parker's wishes, these recordings are still available on a variety of websites and within a number of these YouTube compilations, as are the on-screen deaths of Tommy Cooper, Ayrton Senna, Christa McAuliffe and others. In the case of Christine Chubbuck, there is a widely circulated 'recording' of her suicide which is believed to be faked footage of a hugely degraded piece of archival television. The actual recording made of this broadcast by the studio she worked for is believed to be lodged for safekeeping with a law firm appointed by the widow of Chubbuck's boss, Robert Nelson (see Riesman, 2016). Both the freely circulating live TV death compilations, the faked Chubbuck footage and the locked-away real footage of Chubbuck's death (if it still/ever existed) can be seen as further evidence of the television archive's ability to capture life and death posthumously. We will return to this idea below.

Death – intimate and close up

A man and a woman sit together on a sofa, filmed by a handheld camera positioned close to them. On the other side of the couple, another woman holds up liquid in a small, plastic cup and asks if the man wishes to drink it, sleep, and then die. The scene then cuts to a wobbly close-up of the cup being handed over. Zooming back out, we see that this is also being filmed by another man on a small digital camera. Affirming several times that he wishes to take the drink, the man seated on the sofa thanks the woman who gave it to him, and then thanks the television crew in the room, including the presenter who comes into shot to shake his hand. As he says, 'My wife's very good at putting me to sleep just by rubbing my hand', the camera pans down to focus on his hand, resting on her leg, as she strokes it tenderly. After drinking the contents of the cup, the man slips into unconsciousness, held by the two women beside him. The scene cuts between a tight shot of their embrace and a series of close-ups of the presenter as he looks on. The woman crouching beside the sofa explains to the other woman that the man is sleeping 'a very deep sleep' and soon his breathing and his heart will stop. As the sounds of the man's breathing are no longer heard on the soundtrack, close-ups of the woman's face, and her hand stroking his hand, are repeated.

What role do we expect television to play in our understanding of death and dying experiences? Beyond the shock of the unexpected deaths on live TV described in the first section of this introduction, how might we hope that television will handle death for us, prepare us for death's inevitable arrival, help us to anticipate our own deaths and those of the people we love? How will television enable us to face mortality? Much of this book will argue that as a medium of direct, intimate and domestic address, television seeks to bring us 'closer to death'. It does so in the sense that we might become more familiar with a variety of experiences of death, dying and bereavement through our everyday television viewing, and achieves this 'becoming intimate with death' via a range of formal strategies. As will

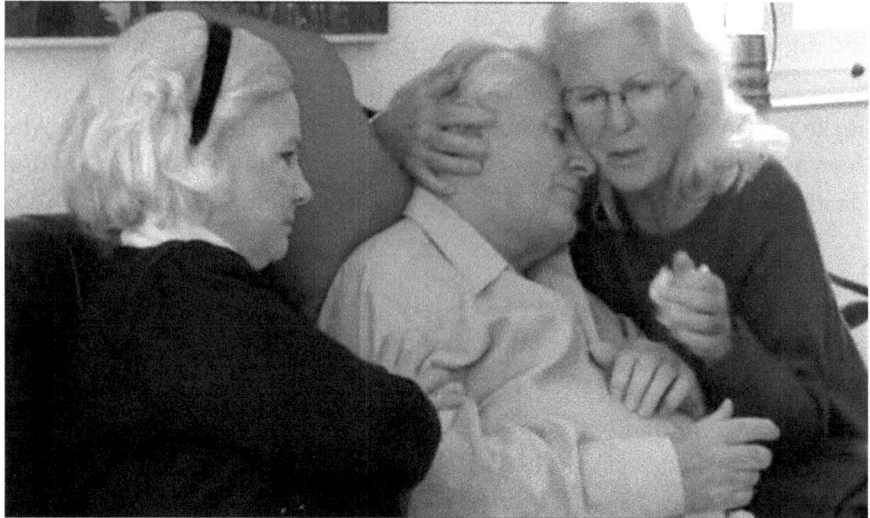

Figure 0.1 The death of Peter Smedley, *Terry Pratchett: Choosing to Die* (BBC2, tx. 13/06/11).

be explained throughout *Television/Death*, television documentaries and dramas can and have worked hard in a variety of different ways to make sense of death and dying for their audiences. In the case described above, a pivotal scene from the documentary *Terry Pratchett: Choosing to Die* (BBC2, tx. 13/06/11), the retired English businessman Peter Smedley has travelled to Dignitas in Switzerland to seek a legal assisted death following the decline of his health due to motor neurone disease. While the nature of his dying and its representation on TV is not without controversy, what this scene epitomises here is a sense of intimacy and a closeness to the dying subject which seems particularly 'at home' on television.[5]

The tight framing of Smedley, his wife Christine, the Dignitas staff, and the presenter of this documentary, the author Terry Pratchett, all seek to bring the viewer as close as is possible to the experience of this particular death. Several theorists have proposed that it is ultimately impossible to accurately portray the experience of death on screen: for example, in relation to the presentation of death in the film documentary, Vivian Sobchack argues that 'We do not see death on the screen, nor understand its visible momentum or contours ... It lies over the threshold of visibility and representation' (1984: 287). However, in this moment from *Terry Pratchett: Choosing to Die*, we see the television documentary working hard to acquaint us as intimately as possible with a particular experience of dying: it does so through the use of the close-up, through the revelation of the programme-making team as part of Smedley's death experience, positioning them in a physically close relationship with the subject at the moment of his death and therefore as witness to it, and via the inclusion of bits of sound and dialogue that stress the intimacy of this moment (the amiable chat of the people in the room at this extraordinary time in Smedley's life, the sound of his breathing ceasing).

There is also something particularly poignant about knowing that this sequence would be watched in people's homes. As I have argued elsewhere (see Wheatley 2006, 2016, 2020a, 2020b), television's sense of intimacy, its formation of a close, emotional connection between those on screen and those watching at home, is increased when we consider that it is received in the private spaces of people's houses, their living rooms, their bedrooms. These facts of television viewing have caused some anxieties in the history of television's representation of death and dying, from fears about children encountering large numbers of graphic, fictional death depictions on TV (as discussed in the introduction to Chapter 3) to concerns about people stumbling across upsetting scenes of 'real death' or troubling posthumous images on television during the course of an evening's viewing (as discussed in Chapters 1, 2 and 6 of this book). However, on the other hand, we might see the bringing of death into our homes via television as a reassuring 're-domestication' of death at a point in history when dying largely takes place in hospitals and hospices. As we will see throughout this book, this is an argument that has been made time and again in relation to television's handling of this subject. In *Television/Death*, the nature of television's intimacy and the medium's conversational, even confessional, address when dealing with matters relating to death, dying and bereavement will be examined. This is television that presupposes an intimate relationship between programme and viewer, and which sees the viewer as part of a community inclusive of those on screen as well as others watching at home. This argument mirrors that of Charlton D. McIlwain, who proposed in 2005 that the topic of death in US television drama was proof of television's construction of a collective viewing community:

> Individual and collective contemplation of death provides an impetus for collective identity, despite the varieties of otherness we encounter . . . That death is a topic of public discourse engaged in by members of a given community is . . . the most significant element of building and sustaining community itself. That is, our deliberations about death are more important than our knowing what follows; that we are able to speak about death supersedes our ability or need to provide an explanation for it. (8)

Theses such as McIlwain's bring us back to the proposals made in Stephen Heath and Gillian Skirrow's early writing about the power of television. Writing about the British current affairs series *World in Action* (Granada for ITV, 1963–1998), they define what they see as being fundamental about television, implicitly drawing a line between its address to a community and its powers of communication:

> Direct, and direct for me. Television is the institution of an *occupation*: it occupies the viewer as subject in a permanent arena of 'communicationality'... Little matter in this respect what is communicated, the crux is the creation and maintenance of the communicating situation and the realisation of the viewer as a subject in that situation. The subject of television is a citizen in a world of communication; he or she is called – and occupied – there, for that world. Immediacy, intimacy and mass communication: television here and now, for me personally, for me as the unity of everyone. (1977: 56)

What is central to this critical history of death, dying and bereavement on television, then, is the sense that those making television, whether they be participants in a death-related documentary or the creators of a dramedy about grief and bereavement, tell stories about death and dying to a group of viewers with whom they share a sense of unity, of community, perhaps a common sense of humanity. We can envisage this community in different ways, of course. In the UK, as Part I of this book will show, death-related programming has been produced under the impetus of a public service broadcasting system which envisages a national viewing public that might be informed and educated about death and dying, as well as entertained, by television. This book has led me to discuss the ways in which the tenets of public service broadcasting have continued into the post-broadcast moment and how, across the history of British television, they have also been enabled by the broadcast of the television of other nations. But beyond the public service context of British television, Part II of this book shows that producers, writers and directors of television within commercial broadcasting systems have more broadly sought to make sense of death, and to work through experiences of grief and bereavement, for their viewers. Programme makers in the US have done so with humour as well as horror, through the optics of humanist philosophy, via an engagement with complex debates about ethics and how to 'live well' and working through theories of death-related trauma. All the programming discussed in this book can therefore be seen as intelligent television when it comes to the handling of death, dying and bereavement, even if it might traditionally be placed on different parts of the 'Quality TV' scale or suggest different levels of seriousness in its intent.

Death and grief – complicated, slowly unfurling

A group of people gather in the chapel of a crematorium as men and women enter the room carrying a floral cardboard coffin, accompanied by the sound of Queen's 'Don't Stop Me Now'. As the pallbearers lower the coffin onto its resting place, we cut to a close-up of a sad-looking man, dressed in a beige jacket. He looks forlorn, lost. Following this, wider shots of the room reveal people of a variety of ages clutching at daffodils, supporting each other at the start of a funeral service. They all sit. The celebrant leading the funeral addresses the room: 'Welcome to a celebration of the life of Hayley Anne Cropper. That piece of music was her choice. She thought it would make you chuckle. Death is a very personal matter for those who know it in someone close to them. But we're all concerned, directly or indirectly, with the death of an individual because we're all part of one human community and no one of us is independent or separate.' As she recites these words, shots of the congregation's reactions are cut together. People laugh, cry, look lost in thought, comfort those around them. The celebrant continues: 'For those of us who believe that death brings the end of an individual's existence, life's significance lies in the experiences we achieve in that span of time. And life's permanence lies in the memories of those that knew us and the influence we've left behind. The love and laughter that filled Hayley's life will live in the memories of her family and friends far longer than the sadness caused by her leaving.'

The funeral described above is that of Hayley Cropper (Julie Hesmondhalgh), a long-standing character in the British soap opera *Coronation Street* (Granada for ITV, 1960–), broadcast on 31 January 2014. Hayley had been diagnosed with pancreatic cancer in July the previous year, and fans of the soap opera had followed her reaction to the terminal diagnosis, her treatment and her decision to take her own life (in an episode broadcast eleven days earlier), lying next to her husband, Roy (David Neilson), in their bedroom at home. After knowing Hayley through sixteen years of her life in the fictional town of Weatherfield, the congregation in this funeral scene is connected to the deceased in a whole variety of ways: as well as her beloved husband, it contains her foster daughter Fiz Brown (Jennie McAlpine) and her close friend and ex-boss Carla Barlow (Alison King), along with a variety of other friends, neighbours and ex-colleagues. Characters in this

Figure 0.2 The funeral of Hayley Cropper, *Coronation Street* (Granada for ITV, 1960–).

scene had been in the soap opera for varying lengths of time across what was then its fifty-four year run, and all would be well known to the audience of *Coronation Street*.[6] A wide-angle shot of the congregation from the perspective of Hayley's coffin during the celebrant's eulogy very deliberately shows all these people together, all at once (see Figure 0.2), demonstrating these complex connections visually and presenting this cast as a community.

It is, then, a room in which characters with long and complex histories with the deceased mourn her passing. They do this alongside an audience that has shared in the Croppers' story and followed the minutiae of their lives together as a couple since 1998. When Hayley died earlier in the month, she did so in another room stuffed full of memories, crammed with reminders of her life in the soap opera – familiar costumes, props and, particularly, photographs that brought to mind earlier moments in the soap's history (for example, photos of Hayley and Roy's wedding in 1999, their trip to Blackpool in 2013 following her diagnosis, and the arrival of Roy's mother, Sylvia Goodwin (Stephanie Cole), in 2011). During the funeral itself, we are once again reminded of these complex and long-standing relationships: for example, Roy describes his life before meeting Hayley as a 'dark corner', whereas Fiz recounts her first shopping trip with Hayley as her foster parent, offering committed viewers of *Coronation Street* an opportunity to think back and remember events that happened in the soap opera sixteen and thirteen years previously. Roy and Hayley's relationship had not always been a straightforward one: Roy was not initially aware that Hayley was a trans woman when he first met her, and, as with any soap couple, they had been through all kinds of difficulties together including the arrival in Weatherfield of Hayley's illegitimate child and Roy's suicide attempt. This television death, then, and the feelings of grief and bereavement that are felt by characters after it, is a messy and complicated one.

Coronation Street received high praise for its presentation of this complex storyline, and rightly so.[7] Its handling of the gradual progression of Hayley's illness towards her death across a period of six months, and then the ongoing, slowly unfurling grief experienced by the characters who loved her, demonstrate one of the specific ways in which television's extended serial forms lend themselves to the representation of death, dying and bereavement. This storyline not only shows us how complex character attachments develop over time, but also that television is better able than any other screen media to represent the long duration of dying and the lengthy emotional process of grieving.[8] The long duration of the soap opera means that characters' grieving does not end with this funeral; characters close to Hayley, particularly her friend Carla and husband Roy, continue to express their grief at her loss for years to come. For example, when Carla suffers a psychotic episode in an episode broadcast on 31 May 2019, her hallucinations initially manifest Hayley wearing her trademark red anorak, as Carla desperately seeks the security and comfort that her dead friend represented. In September 2022, eight years after Hayley's death, a storyline about Roy's trauma at the loss of this same coat when he begins to clear out some of Hayley's possessions from his house can be seen as evidence of his ongoing grief.

When we see characters grieving on screen – attending Hayley's funeral, talking through their feelings of loss with other characters in the soap opera – we might also suppose that the long-term viewer is being invited to vicariously grieve the loss of a beloved character, to experience what DeGroot and Leith refer to as the 'parasocial grief' (2015) of viewers for characters that die in continuing dramas. Indeed, the address given by the celebrant Suzie Forrester (Kate Rutter) recounted above implicitly acknowledges this, simultaneously addressing both viewers and characters when she explains 'we're all concerned, directly or indirectly, with the death of an individual because we're all part of one human community and no one of us is independent or separate'. The celebrant reassures us that 'life's permanence lies in the memories of those that knew us and the influence we've left behind'. Here this 'human community', those who remember Hayley, involves characters on screen *and* their viewers. In 1979, the director Norman Swallow produced the documentary 'Death on the Street' (tx. 26/7/79) for the series *This England*, which explored precisely this topic, following the death of Ernie Bishop (Stephen Hancock) on *Coronation Street*. The documentary saw Hancock visiting viewers in the North West of England to discuss their reactions to his character's death and its narrative focused on the messy entanglement of real life and soap opera life. For instance, as Hancock considers footage of the funeral of another *Coronation Street* character, Martha Longhurst (Lynne Carol), and the funeral cortège that led towards the first on-screen burial in the programme (tx. 20/5/64), he states:

> These were real Salford streets and the people on the pavement were real and whenever I look at sequences like this, I find myself wondering where fact ends and fiction begins. *Coronation Street* isn't a documentary, but for many people, myself included, it contains more fundamental truths than so called documentaries.

Hancock's musings here speak of the power of continuing drama to explore real-life – and death – experiences for its viewers.

While *Television/Death* does not focus on death in soap opera any further than this snapshot analysis of *Coronation Street*'s handling of dying and bereavement, this example stands in the book's introduction as a precursor for arguments made about contemporary television's long duration and serial form, along with its playfulness with narrative time (what Jason Mittell would call television's 'narrative complexity' (2006)), which all allow for a verisimilitudinous depiction of the emotional experiences of grief, bereavement and death-related trauma. If, as in the example above, the continuing bonds between ongoing characters, viewers and the deceased in British soap opera are invited by the unending narrative form of this genre, then the narrative forms of the dramas and dramedies analysed in Part II of this book, many of them produced in the US, all work in different ways to portray the complex emotions (grief, trauma) associated with bereavement. *Television/Death* will explain how. This book is perhaps unusual in its examination of television fictions alongside documentaries and other forms of factual programming; earlier studies of the topic of death on television have focused on one or other of these forms of programming. I place them side-by-side here in acknowledgement that the subjects of death, dying and bereavement permeate nearly all forms and genres of television. We will get a richer, fuller picture of television's relationship with death if we look at it more holistically, understanding how this topic shifts in different historical, national and generic contexts.

Introduction   13

Life and death beyond the grave – posthumous television

At 12.39 pm on 8 September 2022 an episode of the popular BBC daytime series Bargain Hunt (BBC1, 2000–) is interrupted by a sudden fade to black. Following this interruption of the fun and hubbub of the programme, a sombre-looking news presenter extends a welcome to the Bargain Hunt viewer and informs them that the Queen of the United Kingdom is 'under medical supervision'. After appearing on camera initially, the presenter then speaks over a photograph of the Queen taken earlier that week, talking to the viewer and the BBC's royal correspondent about this grave turn in events. Fifteen minutes later, as part of this rolling news coverage, archive footage is shown of the Queen visiting a hospice earlier in the summer. The Queen looks frail but very much alive. Over the course of the next six hours, news anchors, reporters and other royal experts digest the reports of the Queen's ailing health in a rolling news programme. They continue to do so in the studio, over the phone and, often, accompanied by archival images – still and moving – of the Queen. At 6.30 pm, ongoing speculation about the Queen's health over footage of crowds gathering at Buckingham Palace is interrupted by the announcement that the Queen has died. Another sombre news broadcaster appears on screen, dressed in a dark, pinstriped suit, white shirt and black tie, to read a statement about the Queen's death from the palace. As he begins to recap the Queen's age and achievements, archive footage of the Queen alive and well and undertaking her royal duties begins to roll.

While I was completing this book in the autumn of 2022, Queen Elizabeth II, longest-reigning monarch of the United Kingdom, died. Her death, lying-in-state, and funeral were unprecedented television events. Between 8 September, the day of her death, and the 19th day of the same month, when her state funeral took place, hundreds of hours of television were given over to the kind of rolling news broadcasting described above. The BBC played a particularly prominent role in the commemoration of the Queen's life and marking of her death, though all major broadcasters in the UK (and many beyond) provided their own coverage. For example, for the five days leading up to the Queen's funeral the BBC streamed constant coverage of her lying-in-state on their streaming platform BBC iPlayer, as an estimated 250,000 people filed past her coffin.[9] Broadcast coverage of her funeral itself was a day-long event: again, all major broadcasters produced special news coverage, with the BBC covering the funeral across television, radio, iPlayer and BBC Sounds from 8 am until 5 pm, followed by a news recap on their flagship channel, BBC1, and then a special episode of *The One Show* (BBC1, 2006–) called 'Our Queen Remembered'. In many ways, the Queen's death reaffirmed the place of television in our lives. Unlike the furore which had been caused by the wall-to-wall coverage of her husband's death the year before, as discussed in Chapter 6 of this book, the viewing public seemed largely resolute about the domination of 'Queen's death' coverage across the television schedule. If the Queen's death was a time of national mourning and introspection, it was certainly assumed that we turned to television to make sense of the days that followed.

The aspect of this coverage that was most striking to me in relation to the focus of this book was the speed and regularity with which television archive footage was incorporated into news programming about the Queen's death. As the description above shows, fifteen minutes after the announcement of the Queen's ailing health, we saw footage of her, elderly and with limited mobility but lively, during a visit to a hospice with her daughter, Princess Anne. When her death was announced just under six hours later, archive footage of the Queen in earlier times and in better health was immediately incorporated into the BBC's news coverage, and over the course of the next few hours, a much broader range of older footage was shown over expert commentary, incorporated into split-screen reporting, and edited into slick documentary packages looking back over the Queen's life (see Figure 0.3 for examples of this use of archive footage).

As Mhairi Brennan's work on the use of archive footage during television coverage of the Scottish Referendum has shown, those working at the

Figure 0.3 Queen Elizabeth II – the posthumous archive re-broadcast (BBC1, tx. 8/9/22).

'coal face' of the media archive work 'minute by minute' to 'catalogue and digitally archive . . . footage while simultaneously facilitating instant access to that material for programme makers . . . looking to re-use clips in news bulletins and programmes' (2020: 23). In the case of the Queen's death, this process enabled a wide array of archive television to be incorporated into news programming posthumously.

Seeing the Queen alive and well on screen just moments after her death had been announced reminds us that as well as capturing the moment of death (as the first two of our four examples in this introduction show), the television archive also preserves life before death. In doing so, I argue, television becomes the posthumous medium *par excellence*. As I will explain in greater detail in Part III of this book, the critical thinking that surrounds death and the recorded image has somehow, inexplicably, largely missed out television's posthumous possibilities. Part II explores the terrain of television dramas about life after death, dissecting the ways in which narratives of continuing life beyond the grave abound in television fiction, showing television to be a 'posthumous medium' in relation to its obsession with the afterlives of the characters it creates. However, as the example of the coverage of the Queen's death demonstrates very clearly, television might also be seen as posthumous in an entirely different context, as one of the photographic arts capable of 'embalming time' (Mulvey, 2006: 56). In this sense, television is ontologically posthumous, always and forever capturing life before death and capable of bringing the dead back to life, though this aspect of television's identity as a medium is distinctly under-explored in comparison to photography and film, for example. In the final section of this book, then, television's posthumousness will be examined at length. In doing so, it draws on Jeremy Tambling's proposal that the posthumous is 'a way of thinking about the pastness of the past, and about our own present' (2001: 8). *Television/Death* therefore considers television as an extension of photography's ability to present the posthumous, looking at how television brings the dead back to life in a variety of different ways and contexts, and at what is specific about watching the dead on television, extending the already extensive work on this in relation to film.

This book acknowledges that all images of the living on screen will also eventually be posthumous images, and when death or people who have died appear on screen, this fact is brought into sharp relief. To go back to our very first death, all footage of Tommy Cooper is now, of course, posthumous. In and out of the archive, the dead comedian comes back, posthumously, to entertain us. In 2022, for example, the Christmas edition of the UK

TV listings magazine *Radio Times* advertised potential engagements with posthumous performers under the heading 'Nostalgia', next to a large photograph of Cooper doing his trademark 'magic hands' gesture: 'There are chances to enjoy the work of the late Robbie Coltrane [this Christmas] . . . while Talking Pictures has *Tommy Cooper's Christmas* . . . from 1973 and festival specials from the *Carry On* crew' (Tate, 2022: 47). Cooper therefore continues to be a television performer nearly thirty-nine years after his death. His dying on screen is not entertaining. It is achingly sad. However, he is no more or less posthumous in this footage of *Live from Her Majesty's* than he is in any of his other screen performances.

Television/Death is divided into three sections. Part I, 'Death and dying on television', looks at the representation of death and dying in television documentary, across a range of national contexts and historical periods but with a particular focus on the UK example. Chapter 1, 'Everyday death: The early history of death on British television', charts the early history of the representation of death and dying on TV in the UK. It looks at the ways in which religious programming handled death in the mid- to late twentieth century, examines the death-focused output of the BBC's Community Programme Unit, as well as analysing several significant documentaries and panel shows on the subject. The chapter examines the development of the television 'autopathography' across all these forms of programming; that is, programming that is made through of the dying and/or bereaved subject's desire to tell their own story, to recount their own experiences for the viewing public. This chapter therefore considers the question of *why* people would get involved in making such programming. It does so firstly through a reconstructive history, analysing key programmes and the press interviews, previews and reviews that accompanied their broadcast. In order to answer the question of why people made such programming, I also interviewed one of the participants in two of the key autopathographies I examine in this chapter: Vivien Whiteley-Toyn, who made *Remember All The Good Things* (BBC1 North West region, tx. 12/11/74) before the death of her husband, Tony, and *Vivien Whiteley: On Her Own* (BBC1 North West, tx. 24/10/75) after it. Extracts from this interview are incorporated into this chapter and offer a rich insight into the process of making television documentaries at the end of life, as well as reflection on the decision to do so. While the history that is told in this chapter largely focuses on the television of the latter part of the twentieth century, the chapter closes with some analysis of more recent television autopathographies (*My Last Summer* (Love Productions for Channel 4, 2014) and *A Time to Live* (tx. 17/5/17)) and proposes that British television continues to provide a platform for the dying to speak: for themselves, to their loved ones and to the wider viewing public.

While the autopathographies examined in Chapter 1 are largely the stories of people dying a 'natural' death (from cancer, motor neurone disease, brain tumours, and so on) and who incorporate programme making into the patterns of their palliative care or their coming to terms with the death of loved ones, Chapter 2, 'Signs of care: Assisted suicide on television', focuses on the topic of an assisted death/suicide and looks at how this form of dying has been presented in factual television from around the world. As with Chapter 1, analysis in this chapter is concerned with questions of representation (how is assisted dying depicted in television documentary) and grapples with questions of intent: for whom is the assisted dying programme made? The chapter considers how this programming works though the complex moral and ethical questions raised for those who seek, those who watch, and those who film an assisted death. It opens with a consideration of the early history of this form of dying on British television: as with the broadcasting history told in Chapter 1, this is a history of religious broadcasting, current affairs programming, the output of the BBC's Community Programme Unit and the anthology documentary series. The chapter considers how this programming sought 'balance' in its representation of assisted dying, as well as analysing how television's intimate mode of address enabled an emotionally engaging presentation of this particular death experience. While this begins as a history of British television broadcasting, the programmes in this early history were not all made in the UK; for example, the most controversial programme discussed here, *Dood op Verzoek/Death on Request* (Ikon, tx. 20/10/94), was shown as part of the *Modern Times* (BBC2, 1995–2015) series in the UK, as well as being shown all around the world, but was initially made for Dutch television. The history of assisted dying on TV is therefore also a history of the international circulation of television documentary. In the latter part of this chapter, I look at some more recent, stand-alone documentaries made about assisted dying including *Terry Pratchett: Choosing to Die* (BBC2, tx. 13/06/11), *Dignitas – la mort sur ordonnance* (RTS, tx. 17/2/11), *How to Die in Oregon* (HBO, tx. 23/1/11), *Four Corners: My Own Choice* (ABC, tx. 16/9/13), and *How to Die: Simon's Choice* (BBC2, tx. 10/2/16). Analysis of these programmes and their reception in the press is coupled with interviews with some of the documentarists involved in their production as I consider how these programmes and those involved in their production deal with questions of care, and the ways in which medical ethics and television documentary ethics intertwine in the making of these programmes.

Part II of *Television/Death*, 'Dramas of grief, bereavement and the television afterlife', offers three sets of case studies to explore the ways in which television drama depicts life after death, for the dead and for those that survive them. The first chapter in this section, 'A good death? Death and the afterlife in US television fiction', turns our attention towards the representation of death, dying and the afterlife in North American television drama and dramedies. In this chapter, I counter the view of television as a vacuous distraction from 'real world' issues, and instead consider the ways in which 'viewing for pleasure' might simultaneously be seen as 'viewing to make sense of life *and death*'. This work thus joins the writing of Charlton D. McIlwain (2005), Gary Laderman (2005), Laura E. Tanner (2006), Tina Weber (2011), Joanne Clark Dilman (2014) and others in exploring the hyper-presence of death as a topic on US television, the dead as both object and character, and the afterlife as both place and concept. The first part of this chapter provides an introduction to this subject, exploring the critical discourse around the hyper-presence of death on US TV and the idea of television as a 'post-mortem showcase'. It looks at the perceived 'pornography of death' on American television and at questions of excess and spectacle attached to the dead and dying body that I began to examine in my previous book, *Spectacular Television: Exploring Televisual Pleasure* (2016). It notes the prevalence of the 'absence/presence' paradox in the critical reception of US television (that death is seen as simultaneously absent from our lives in the contemporary moment and very present on our screens), or what has also been called the 'death denial thesis', and examines the problems in this discourse that seeks to understand/explain television's death-obsession. This section of the chapter then finishes with a brief critical exploration of the programme which has been widely credited as initiating a turn towards death on television: *Six Feet Under* (HBO, 2001–2005).

While the opening of Chapter 3 looks particularly at the emergence or hyper-presence of the dead body on our small screens, its second part considers the comedic programming in which the souls of the dead appear, exploring a recent cycle of televisual afterlives, in programmes such as *The Good Place* (NBC, 2016–2020), *Forever* (Amazon Studios, 2018), *Miracle Workers* (TBS, 2019–) and *Upload* (Amazon Studios, 2020–). This chapter considers these comedic series as 'postsecular' television, discussing the multiplicity of religious and secular sources for the afterlives created in this programming. This section examines the particularities of the afterlives created: these are deeply American visions of life after death which reveal much about the socio-historical context in which they were made. The analysis also considers these as afterlives of the digital future and explores the way in which these programmes speak to how our understandings of life, death and the concept of the soul are shifting right now. Ultimately, the chapter comes back to the idea of 'working through', to think about how we have learned to live with death through television entertainment about the afterlife.

In Chapter 4, 'Dramas of grief: Television and mourning', I begin with the realisation that the experience of grief is currently everywhere as a narrative focus in US television. The long-form serial dramas at the centre of this analysis include *The Leftovers* (HBO, 2014–2017), *This is Us* (NBC, 2016–2022), *Sorry for Your Loss* (Facebook Watch, 2018–2019), *Kidding* (Showtime, 2018–2020) and *Dead to Me* (Netflix, 2019–). In my critical engagement with this programming, I consider the narrative forms of grief and mourning, and, as mentioned above, discuss the fact that their long duration, seriality and narrative complexity allows for a verisimilitudinous representation of the experience of bereavement. The temporal volatility of these programmes – their oscillation backwards and forwards in time – shows us how grief is a constantly comparative state, where the 'before' and 'after' are held together in heart-breaking conjunction with one another. I turn in this chapter to Ien Ang's concept of 'emotional realism' (1989: 46), to describe the ways in which these dramas seek to connect with their audiences' experiences of grief, and in closing the chapter think about why we might want to watch others grieve. I argue that the answers to this might be found in how this television challenges outmoded conceptions of grief as a linear journey (cf. Kübler-Ross, 1969), and how communities of grief form around and in relation to television. Writing this chapter during an international pandemic sharpened my focus on the ways in which the television viewer might be addressed as a collective group that grieves. Of course, this has always been the case, but the visibility of grief was, I argue, heightened during the last three years.

Chapter 5, 'Haunted houses, haunted landscapes: Grief and trauma in the television ghost story', turns to a spatial analysis of dramas of haunting on UK and US television, drawing on Maria del Pilar Blanco's argument that to 'ghost-watch implies a vigilant perception of the landscapes depicted within it' (2012: 1) and that ghosts are always 'embedded in the story about a place' (ibid.: 8). This chapter acknowledges that the dead are spatially located, both bodily and spectrally, and our relationship to them must be worked out partly through an exploration of their setting. The ghost drama has a place in this study because ghosts are, of course, always the result of a death, the spectral remnants left behind by the death of a (usually human) body. This chapter sits alongside the previous one, with its focus on the televisual depiction of grief and mourning, and picks up from that chapter an interest in the structure of grief narratives on television. Like the previous chapter, it looks at how television uses serial narrative form to attempt to represent the experience of death and grief for characters with some emotional realism. In the case of the television ghost story, characters' experiences of death are most often traumatised experiences and through the course of the narrative they must explore a particular place – specifically a haunted house or a haunted landscape, what Hudson refers to as 'trauma landscapes' (2017: 20) – in order to work through that trauma, and to understand how and why that place holds the meaning and significance that it does. The chapter looks at two recent cycles of TV ghost stories: short serial ghost stories produced for British television over the last ten years (including *Marchlands* (ITV1, 2011), *The Secret of Crickley Hall* (BBC1, 2012) *Lightfields* (ITV1, 2013), *Remember Me* (BBC1, 2014), and *The Living and the Dead* (BBC1, 2016)) and longer, complex serial ghost dramas made for post-broadcast television in the US more latterly (for example *The Haunting of Hill House* (Netflix, 2018) and *Archive 81* (Netflix, 2022)). The chapter considers how grief and death-related trauma structures the television ghost story, building on my previous work on the Gothic in television (2016).

In the final section of *Television/Death*, I move towards an analysis of the concept of 'posthumous television', as outlined above. This section shifts away from a consideration of how death, dying and bereavement are depicted on television and instead focuses on where and how the dead (or the dead of the future) are captured on or incorporated into television programmes or held within/liberated from the television archive. Chapter 6, entitled 'Entering the mausoleum: Posthumous television', goes back to my interview with Vivien Whiteley-Toyn to think about the emotional experience of returning to posthumous television. This leads into an engagement with the critical literature on the recording of (potentially posthumous) images and/or sounds, via the work of André Bazin (1960) Roland Barthes (1981), Jeremy Tambling (2001), Jonathan Sterne (2003), Laura Mulvey (2006) and others, and, as discussed above, my argument that specificities of television's relationship with the posthumous have largely been overlooked. As I showed at the outset of this introduction, television captures life before death (including the moment of death) constantly. Television companies either broadcast television live or 'as live', simultaneously recording this live feed so it can be replayed almost instantaneously and incorporated into the programme at hand (think of replay moments within sports broadcasting or talent shows, for example) or shown at a later date, or they pre-record programming to be broadcast or streamed in the future. They therefore build up a vast archive of potentially posthumous sounds and images. Furthermore, the facts of television watching mean that viewers are now more able than ever to record, pause, rewind, replay and retrieve television for themselves. Television therefore has become the medium through which we have the greatest ability to play around with what Mulvey describes as 'embalmed time' (2006: 56).

Chapter 6 subsequently sets out to consider whether the television archive can be seen as a kind of mausoleum if the medium is understood as potentially posthumous. This analogy is a common, tempting and evocative one, implying that the dead lie waiting to be disinterred in the TV archive, re-broadcast, edited into new programming, re-circulated or re-screened in other contexts. However, unlike the mausoleum, which remains sealed save for the admission of fresh corpses, the television archive is an active facility, and the dead are constantly brought in and out of its environs. The first part of the chapter will consider, then, how television marks the death of the famous, both its own stars (and the television rituals that surround their death) and the role that television programming plays in the structuring of collective bereavement and mourning for the nation. It will reflect on television's own structures of memorialisation, as well as how TV is recycled by viewers online as a form of commemoration; the sharing of pictures and listings, clips, GIFs, interviews and bloopers mimic the way in which television itself deals with death as a prompt for the recycling of posthumous sounds and images. The chapter will then turn to look at a specific example of a dead television celebrity brought almost compulsively out of the archive, over and over again: the DJ, television presenter and serial sex offender Jimmy Savile. The analysis of Savile's posthumous reappearances on television will consider how the returning dead might not only delight but haunt the television viewer – and the television broadcaster.

In the final chapter of *Television/Death*, 'Ghost town: Posthumous television in the city', I offer an account of an archive-based project, *Ghost Town: Civic Television and the Haunting of Coventry*, that I have been running in Coventry, the UK city where I live and work, for the last five years. I consider in this chapter some of the methods and approaches that can be applied by archivists, historians, curators and others to open up the posthumous television archive and its holdings, beyond their inclusion in new television programming, and explore why this group of people would want or need to do so. As explained above, Chapter 6 discusses television programming made out of the broadcast archive, and analyses television's recycling of its own posthumous images, thinking about the potential affective power of encounters with the posthumous archive via television. Chapter 7, on the other hand, considers how else we might encounter posthumous television, shifting our focus from (inter)nationally significant posthumous television, edited into new programmes and packages and streamed and broadcast to a wide general public, to the local, the regional, and to thinking about the importance of posthumous programming in relation to a specific place and time. This shift in focus raises a set of attendant questions which this chapter will explore. How and why should we take historical (posthumous) television out of archives and universities and into the public realm? What happens when people encounter posthumous television in public spaces, and what is the role of the television historian in these encounters? How should we make sense of what people say at, about, and to, screenings of posthumous programmes? And what is the civic value of the television archive; why does posthumous television history matter to people of a particular city, a particular place?

As will have become apparent from the description of the chapters above, this study employs a mixture of methods to analyse the relationship between television and death. In order to consider such a complex object of study, I have become something of a methodological 'magpie'; my understanding of what television is, what it can be, and what it has meant to people has, across all of my work, been developed by approaching it from lots of different directions. This is in line with my earlier argument that there is 'a need for a multi-methodological approach to television historiography in order to produce a more rounded, holistic version of television history' (2007: 8), drawing on Ann Gray's proposal that we 'conceptualise historical research methodologies as a kind of contingent mosaic, in which television historians draw together different strands of the production/text/viewer triumvirate according to the particular needs of the project' (ibid.). In this book, each of these strands comes to the fore as and when they are needed.

Firstly, the analysis of television programming is at the heart of this study. As will be apparent from the above chapter descriptions, this is not just the analysis of the representation of death, dying, grief and bereavement, and various forms of imagined afterlife experiences on television, but also the analysis of programmes made out of the posthumous television archive.

I also reflect in this book on moments where my television viewing for pleasure and my viewing as a historian and theorist of television have intersected and diverged. This has necessitated moving from the analysis of programmes I watch regularly outside of my academic studies (as discussed in Part II of this book) to tracking down programmes in the television archive that haven't been seen since they were last broadcast, sometimes many years ago. I therefore both engage in the analysis of contemporary, popular television that 'everyone' is watching and the analysis of historic television that must be 'resurrected' from the media archive. Taking programmes out of the archive for close viewing and analysis means, of course, that they are not watched in the same contexts they were initially made to be seen in; they become 'orphan' texts that have been wrenched out of their broadcast flow and made to stand alone. I have therefore had to employ other methods in order to understand how and why these programmes were made and viewed.

One of the ways I have understood how and why television programmes were made has been to undertake interviews with those involved in their production. For this book, I have interviewed documentarists and their subjects, giving voice to some of those who chose to make programmes about death and dying. Including these voices in Chapters 1, 2 and 6 of this book has both contextualised my own analysis with some more concrete ideas about the intent behind the programmes, and also challenged me to think differently about dying experiences on TV – and their posthumous afterlives. The interviews, all long-form, semi-structured interviews with individuals, tease out a story of the production of death documentaries, attending to the practical and ethical considerations in programme making about death and dying while also exploring the affective experiences of being involved in this work, sometimes many years after it has taken place. Being able to look back with people involved in television documentary productions has brought new insights to the fore which I explore at length in this book.

I have also always been interested in how others have watched and received the programmes I am analysing (see Wheatley, 2016). In *Television/Death*, I have frequently engaged with reviews of the television at hand in order to track the conversations that circulate around this programming, from reflections in both the broadsheet and tabloid press on the ethics of showing requested death on television to journalistic 'think pieces' on the prevalence of certain death-related dramatic narratives and sub-genres. To understand the discursive contexts that surround this programming and its reception, I have also engaged with the wider literature on the cultural history of death, dying and bereavement and situated an analysis of television within a broader 'death studies' context. Understanding the nature of death and dying in its socio-historic context enables us to see why some forms of programming get made in the places and times in which they're made.

Finally, as will have become evident from my description of Chapter 7 above, I have also employed experimental methods to enable me to talk directly to people about the significance and impact of viewing posthumous television. While I expand on these methods at the start of Chapter 7, they largely involved observing people watching TV in public settings, and also gathering their feedback afterwards through a variety of methods (including conversation, more structured interviews and written responses). As with the interviews described above, these encounters have allowed me to figure out more about the meaningfulness of television for those who engage with it, particularly in its 'posthumous' forms. This was often an emotional experience and I observed and felt people's joy, sadness and anger, even, in these televisual encounters. I hope I have captured the spirit of these viewings, as well as what people said during or after them, in this book.

One of the reviewers of this book at draft stage asked why there wasn't more of 'me' in it, more reflection on my personal relationship with death. I guess for me it is there implicitly throughout this study, as it has been throughout my life as a researcher of television, but perhaps it is worth pausing to surface this story some more. A preoccupation with death (and specifically death on television) has run like a thread throughout my previous work: it is there in the morbid preoccupations of my study of *Gothic Television* (2006) as much as it is present in my analysis of the corpse on TV in *Spectacular Television: Exploring Televisual Pleasure* (2016), and this interest obviously pulls forward into this work. I suppose I would argue that the reasons for this are plain: we are all, in one way or another, moving towards death and the deaths of those we love, and living in the knowledge of this, facing up to this fact, allows us to better make sense of our lives. As I will argue below, the fact of our shared mortality is one of the things that binds us together as human beings (as well as television viewers). I wonder whether my awareness of this fact really stems back to my life as an undergraduate student when I worked in nursing homes to support my studies, sitting with the dying and dealing with the bodies of the dead at the relatively young ages of 19 and 20. This was an unusual series of encounters with death for a young person and I have since become fascinated with the question of how else we might 'get to know death' beyond this kind of immediate encounter with the dead and dying. As an adult, death entered my own life, and the lives of the people I love, in other, more immediate, and personal ways. I see now that death and grief can leave you floundering, leave you feeling alone, precisely at the time when you would most benefit from feeling part of a wider community. We may turn to television in the lead up to, and aftermath of, a death, seeking some comfort, or some answers, or to simply seeking to understand what lies ahead. This gives us a sense of the immediacy, urgency even, of the need to talk about death, to face it, and to accept it as part of everyone's lived experience. I hope, then, that this book will enable us to better understand the role that television tries to play in this process.

As will have become plain during the course of this introduction, this exploration of death, dying and bereavement on television, and of television's posthumous potential, is also in some ways a celebration of the historical and ongoing power and cultural importance of television. It conceptualises TV as a medium which continues to inform, educate and entertain its viewers from both within and outside of public service broadcasting systems. It explains why we need intelligent, thought provoking, honest, funny, illuminating, emotionally realist representations of death-related experiences on TV, in our homes and on our most intimate of screens. Finally, it makes a case for the ongoing opening up of television archives, whether that be for future viewers to access significant programming made about death, dying and bereavement in the past, or in order to reach 'beyond the grave' in some way, enabling us to be posthumously entertained by the dead, deal with their passing, or to return to their 'lost' histories via the TV archive.

There will inevitably be gaps in the histories contained within this book, and absences which some readers will find unfathomable. For instance, there has been no attention paid here to non-human death on television, even though animals regularly die on our screens across a variety of genres from natural history programming to annual coverage of the British horse race, the Grand National. How television programming deals with species death and the threat of extinction at the end of the Anthropocene is also a topic for an entirely separate book. There are further histories of the representation of specific causes of human death that are yet to be written,[10] a story to tell about the representation of death, dying and bereavement on children's television, and much more to say about the myriad ways we might engage with posthumous, archival programming. However, I hope what is here is a start and a provocation to think about television's relationship with death in new ways.

Part I
Death and Dying on Television

1

Everyday death: The early history of death on British television

As the introduction of this monograph has shown, the presence of death on television problematises Philippe Ariès assertion that death receded from the public realm in the latter part of the twentieth century (1994: 85). On the contrary, as the first section of this book will demonstrate, television programme makers around the world and throughout the medium's history have frequently worked hard to bring death, dying and bereavement into this realm via television, striving to counter Vivian Sobchack's claim that 'we do not see death on the screen, nor understand its visible momentum or contours . . . It lies over the threshold of visibility and representation' (1984: 287). While death may continue to lie beyond this threshold, this has not stopped programme makers from exploring the topics of death, dying and bereavement in a variety of generic and historical contexts, working to make sense of this most inevitable of human experiences for the television viewer (as well as with, and for, the subjects and participants in their programmes). Despite a lack of prior critical, historical work on television's engagement with these subjects, archival research reveals that this topic has had a place in UK television schedules since the late 1950s. Critical reconstruction and analysis of this history reveals that a range of programming from religious broadcasts and schools programming, to daytime television, one-off documentaries, the output of the BBC's Community Programme Unit, episodes of critically significant ongoing documentary series, and death-focused documentary series all explored how we face the end of life, and death, grief and bereavement. In this chapter, I will construct a history of post-war British public service television as a cultural forum in which critical debates about the end of life took place, countering the proposal that the subject of death and dying is largely a concern of contemporary television (Aaron, 2014: 157). The chapter concentrates mainly on mid- to late twentieth-century television, but it also ends with a brief look at two more contemporary documentaries about death and dying. The chapter thus fills in an absent history in British television scholarship, and in the study of death, dying and bereavement on screen more broadly, though not exhaustively (there is still more of this history to be told). Returning to his argument about the disappearance of death from the public realm in 2000, Philippe Ariès conceded that television programming had somewhat countered the absence of death in the public realm: 'Shown the door by society, death is coming back in through the window' (Ariès, 2000: 11). It is to the presence of death in this 'window' in the latter half of the twentieth century that we now turn.

The room afforded in this chapter to the exploration of death on British television in the last fifty years of the twentieth century is limited, and it is therefore important to acknowledge some of the death-related programming that I haven't found the space to discuss here. Firstly, there are some fascinating programmes not covered here relating to the 'science of death'[1] and to the medical, ethical and religious questions raised by subjects such as organ donation and 'brain death'[2], cryogenics[3] and abortion.[4] Further ethical questions were raised in this period by programmes exploring the topic of assisted dying (discussed in the following chapter) and the enormous number of documentaries and current affairs programmes on the death penalty which are not explored here.[5] There is also a specific history to be written about the coverage of AIDS-related death, dying and bereavement on television in the late 1980s and early 1990s that I have not been able to cover here.[6] There has also not been enough space in this chapter to explore the fascinating history of programmes about life after death, a topic that has been present on UK television since the mid-1950s.[7] Finally, I do not discuss here what my colleague Andy Medhurst referred to in conversation as the 'very dead', that is, television investigation of historical autopsies and the excavation of long-dead human remains.[8] It is also important to note that the history that follows is very BBC-centric. This is for two key reasons. Firstly, the large majority of programmes made about death, dying and bereavement during this period were made by the BBC. While there are notable exceptions discussed here, I see this as in keeping with the Corporation's public service broadcasting commitments to contribute to a lively public sphere, as I shall explain below. The second reason is a less satisfactory one and has to do with the relative lack of research resources for the historian of commercial television in the UK. As I have noted elsewhere (Wheatley, 2007: 9), this lack has led to a lopsided history of British television in the twentieth century, and this chapter on UK television's death programming is no exception. I am grateful that the BBC's investment in making their television archive increasingly more accessible and searchable has enabled the production of the rich history that follows, but my research is poorer for the lack of similar resources for ITV and Channel 4 programming. This is, then, the beginning of this history, rather than its end point, and I look forward to reading future analyses of the absent programming indicated above.

In an analysis of television interviews with the late writer and public intellectual Christopher Hitchens, towards the end of his life,[9] Michael Brennan explores the '[zeitgeist] and recent cultural tendency towards a public dying that is both highly visible and accessible' (2018: 100), arguing that

> Hitchens' public dying is significant ... because it threatens to force discussion of issues surrounding death and dying (of, for example, what constitutes a 'good death', the possibility of life after death, the experience of facing terminal illness, among others) back into the public sphere, where they become the focus for debate ... (ibid.)

Brennan is particularly interested in the way in which Hitchens's narrative about dying, in these interviews and elsewhere, underscored a humanist approach towards death, replacing the religious contextualisation of death and an anticipation of 'death bed conversion' to Christianity with the Enlightenment principles of reason and science. He relates this public dying to the genre of autopathography, published accounts of illness, bereavement or dying which either document 'the experiences of bereavement and of caring for an intimate other ... or [recount] the personal experiences of illness by individuals who are themselves facing a terminal condition' (ibid.: 105). Through the autopathography, Brennan argues, the dying become 'informal death educators' (ibid.: 109), and thus 'auto/pathographies and the media through which they circulate are an increasingly important means by which people learn what the experience of serious illness and dying are like' (ibid.: 125). Brennan is, I think, absolutely correct in his assessment of the value of the Hitchens interviews; he also draws on the work of Tony Walter (2009) on the public death of the reality star Jade Goody in his analysis of the importance of the celebrity autopathography. However, what is not acknowledged in this work is that the autopathography has a much longer history on British television which is largely unconnected to the history of the television celebrity. While these examples certainly raise the profile of the autopathographic narrative, the programmes discussed in this chapter might be seen as autopathographies of a more ordinary, everyday, and therefore more inherently televisual, variety in the late twentieth century. The programmes discussed below are full of the stories of people who were not known to the viewing public beyond their participation in a television programme about their experience of dying or bereavement; this perhaps leads us closer to an understanding that death and dying is something we will all experience, that it is an inevitable aspect of life in our own communities, homes and families.

In some senses then, the autopathographies of ordinary people (often recorded in their own homes and community spaces) bring death back into the home at precisely the moment, in the late twentieth century, when it had been thought to have been made absent from that space. Douglas J. Davies's history of death notes what was perceived to have been lost in the shift away from the practice of dying at home:

> To die at home had long been an ideal in many societies and, until the middle of the twentieth century, most people did so . . . To die at home ensured that death was a local and relatively ordinary event, one integrated within the family and neighbourhood community . . . Having the body in the house enabled family members to see the dead, talk to them and generally reflect on life. Neighbours and friends, too, could call and share sympathies as they talked about the deceased and reminisced about the past, all as part of the changing times that a death brings about. (2005: 70)

These practices, thought to have been (largely) lost in the late twentieth century, decentring the home and family and community in the experience of dying and death, are in some ways reflected in the autopathographic television programming discussed below. Television *re-domesticates* death: it brings it back into the home and creates space for its participants to share their stories, albeit with a much wider (national) community. As discussed in the introduction of this book, there is something fundamental about television, particularly in the late twentieth century, that speaks to Gerald Millerson's proposition that '[w]atching a television programme, we feel not so much that we are being taken into the world, as that the world is being brought to us' (1972: 201–2). Millerson is quoted at the beginning of Stephen Heath and Gillian Skirrow's seminal article on television and *World in Action* (Granada for ITV, 1963–1998), in which they also define what they see as being fundamental about television, implicitly drawing a line between community and communication:

> Direct, and direct for me. Television is the institution of an *occupation*: it occupies the viewer as subject in a permanent arena of 'communicationality'... Little matter in this respect what is communicated, the crux is the creation and maintenance of the communicating situation and the realisation of the viewer as a subject in that situation. The subject of television is a citizen in a world of communication; he or she is called – and occupied – there, for that world. Immediacy, intimacy and mass communication: television here and now, for me personally, for me as the unity of everyone. (1977: 56)

What is central to this history, then, is the sense that it is full of people telling their own stories of death to a group of viewers with whom they share a sense of unity, of community. Analysis of the death-focused programme thus brings us back to a consideration of the collective nature of television viewing, particularly in the latter part of the twentieth century. Television also takes on its 'bardic' function in this respect, to quote John Fiske and John Hartley (1978); it creates a multivocal space for the exploration of death, which is surely one of the central concerns of society. Television is presented through these programmes as an essential part of a public sphere in which death is not hidden out of view but conversely is brought to light, a cultural forum (to use Newcomb and Hirsch's term (1983)) in which the facts and feelings of death experiences may be worked through, in and for the public. As Newcomb and Hirsch propose, '[Television] often focuses on our most prevalent concerns, our deepest dilemmas. Our most traditional views, those that are repressive and reactionary as well as those that are subversive and emancipatory, are upheld, examined, maintained and transformed [by television]' (ibid.: 47–8). The analysis of the programming that follows will show how this was the case in relation to the early history of death on television.

Finally, before we turn to the programmes at hand, a word on ethics. The question of ethical programme-making practice is explored more fully in the next chapter through its analysis of the impact of making documentaries about assisted dying on the participants in these documentaries, their friends and family, the audience, and also the documentarists themselves. However, it is important to note here that programme making about death and dying brings critical ethical questions to the fore about the relationship between programme maker and subject, particularly concerning the power dynamics in this relationship, and relating to questions of consent and doing representational harm to the subject and their loved ones. In the most negative sense, this relationship might be seen as an exploitative one: 'The use of people for our advantage [in this case, to make a television programme about death experiences] is an ethically questionable undertaking: in its extreme it is exploitation in the literal sense' (Pryluck, 2005: 200). Pryluck's exploration of documentary ethics rests here on the idea of an unequal power relationship in which (for our purposes) the dying or bereaved person is the subject of (and under) the programme maker's control. Brian Winston nuances this point about ethics, consent and the power dynamics of documentary filmmaking when he proposes that the 'participant does not agree to allow the film maker to document his or her life [or death] but rather joins the film maker to document situations of the film maker's creation' (2005: 189–90). The idea that the documentary subject 'joins' the filmmaker in a process suggests a somewhat more collaborative endeavour, a productive relationship which is also examined in Vivian Sobchack's exploration of the ethics of documentary filmmaking about death: 'Here there is complicity between the filmmaker and the dying subject who has "invited" the former to watch and unblinkingly record the subject's death (which the filmmaker cannot prevent)' (1984: 297). The ethical questions raised by this programming then rest on whether we see a subject under the control of a programme maker, or a participant who is actively collaborative and complicit in the programme-making endeavour. These questions will be explored below, and they are certainly interesting questions in relation to the presence of death as a key subject for the BBC's Community Programme Unit, as this chapter will explain.

A similar ethical shift is also represented by the work of Susan Sontag, in the movement between her understanding of photographs of human suffering as fostering a chronic voyeuristic relation to the world in her 1977 work *On Photography* (xvi) to her reconsideration of an 'ethics of seeing' in her 2003 book *Regarding the Pain of Others* in which she refocused on the concept of 'bearing witness'. The idea of 'bearing witness' to the pain of others is absolutely central to the editorial impulse behind television's early death-related programming, for as John Ellis has argued, television must be fundamentally understood as a medium of witness (1999: 9). This also relates to what Brian Winston identifies as the 'shared rhetoric of a public right to know' (2000: 128), a rhetoric which is shared by filmed documentary in the Griersonian tradition and 'civic journalism' (or public service broadcasting). This shifts the question of media ethics away from thinking about whether a particular programme maker acted ethically in the production of a particular programme and towards a consideration of the ethical relationship between the viewer and the programme (and the participants represented within it). In calling for attention to the 'ethical relationship between reader and text as one of friendship, alliance or community' (2010, 2), Lisa Downing and Libby Saxton return us, implicitly, to the fact that these programmes seek to establish 'community' relationships, that they seek to articulate experiences of death, dying and bereavement within and on behalf of the (television) community, and that the viewer thus approaches this programming from a position of alliance. Similarly, Michele Aaron proposes that film, and perhaps implicitly and by extension, television, can 'connect us, ethically, to the vulnerability of others' (2020: 83). We are implored to watch these programmes not with the chronic, voyeuristic detachment Sontag saw in relation to the photographs of suffering in the 1970s, but with a sense of emotional attachment that comes from viewing as part of a community, 'where the one who looks and the one who is seen become the sum greater than the parts; that is where gazes meet' (Ledbetter, 2012: 4). This ethical, collective viewing position, relating to what Ledbetter describes as the 'ethical integrity of voyeurism' (ibid.: 3), seems particularly endemic to a medium which is identified by collective viewing and by witness. These programmes, broadcast across the daily schedule at all times of day and night, and in nearly all genres of factual television, build a picture of British public service broadcasting as a cultural forum in which experiences of death, dying and bereavement are communicated to and for the wider viewing community.

Everyday autopathographies: facing death

Roland Barthes, writing in 1981, proposed that 'Death must be somewhere in society; if it is no longer (or less intensely) in religion, it must be elsewhere' (1981: 92). Following Barthes's logic, my first proposal is that death was most certainly on television in the latter part of the twentieth century, and, indeed, that the early history of death on UK television is bound up with televisual responses to the increased secularisation of British society (see Brown, 2012) and an institutional desire on the part of the BBC to find space for moral, ethical, philosophical and religious debate in its programming. This programming illuminates some of the debates about the purpose of religious broadcasting on the BBC and elsewhere and can be seen as characteristic of some of its key forms. I therefore want to briefly situate the religious programming which fairly frequently took the matter of death as its subject within the wider history of this branch of UK broadcasting.

Discussing contemporary religious broadcasting in 2011, Catriona Noonan argued that 'universal themes of identity, morality and mortality' (2011: 727) dominated its programmes. I propose at the start of this chapter that these themes were also present in the 1960s, 1970s and 1980s when the subject of death emerged on British television.

As Rachel Viney's work has shown us, the BBC began broadcasting religious services in 1946, and by 1955 it was televising a monthly worship service, alongside the developing religious broadcasting of the 'other' channel (and particularly ITV's programme *About Religion* (ATV, 1956–1966)) (1999: 3). To accompany the broadcast of religious services, the BBC and ITV also began to produce new forms of religious programming, including debate shows, magazine programming, and talk shows with a participatory audience (Noonan, 2013: 198). Catriona Noonan's histories of British religious broadcasting also note that during the period in question, the BBC, in particular, shifted from aligning itself with the Christian faith in the early days of broadcasting to a much more pluralist approach by the mid-1970s:

> In the early days of broadcasting the church and the BBC shared many of the same ambitions for religious programming. The BBC was keen to seek the assurance and support of the church, and so programmes proselytising the Christian faith were often the norm as both groups worked together. Eventually, when competition entered the market, broadcasters became more aware of the increasingly secular demands of audiences and they focused on delivering output which could appeal to a wider spectrum of beliefs. (2011)

Viney (1999: 7), Noonan (2011: 730) and Brown (2012: 372–3) track this change in their work, and Noonan proposes that shifts in the Christian faith, the arrival in the UK of significant numbers of Muslims, Sikhs and Hindus, and the increasing secularisation of British society prompted a widening of the belief systems represented in religious programming between the mid-1950s and the late 1970s: 'A more complicated religious picture was emerging and debates continued publicly over where society was moving in terms of its religious identity and future. It was within this evolving social context that religious broadcasting negotiated its role' (2013: 199). One of the most telling testaments to this shift can be found in the Central Religious Advisory Committee (CRAC)'s submission to the Annan Committee on the future of broadcasting in 1975. The CRAC had been set up twenty years before to oversee and advise on the development of religious programming, meeting twice a year with the broadcasters and members chosen by the BBC and ITV.[10] Their evidence to the Annan Committee laid out the following:

> In the 1960s, the stated aims of religious broadcasting were to:
> - reflect the worship, thought and action of those Churches that represent the mainstream of the Christian tradition in this country;
> - bring before listeners and viewers what is most significant in the relationship between the Christian faith and the modern world; and
> - seek to reach those on the fringe of the organised life of the churches, or quite outside of it.
>
> In the 1970s CRAC recommended to the Annan Committee that these aims be amended. Religious broadcasting should seek to:
> - reflect the worship, thought and actions of the principle religious traditions represented in Britain, recognising that those traditions are mainly, if not exclusively, Christian;
> - present to viewers and listeners those beliefs, ideas, issues and experiences in the contemporary world which are relevant to a religious interpretation or dimension of life; and
> - also to meet the religious interests, concerns and needs of those on the fringe of, or outside, the organised life of the churches. (Viney, 1999: 7)[11]

It is in the context of this shift that we must situate our first case study in this analysis of the early death programme on television: the religious panel show.

The panel show, a format which transferred easily from radio to television in the first decades of broadcasting, could be found across a variety of different televisual genres in the late 1950s and the 1960s on British television. From afternoon programming for women to children's television, to the late night schedule of 'serious' discussion of scientific, philosophical and psychological matters, assembling a panel of experts to debate and share opinion on the pressing matters of the day became a mainstay of British television in its first decades. It is therefore unsurprising that the topic of death was first present on television in the context of the panel discussion. This was primarily found in the religious programming of both channels, which frequently brought together key figures from (mainly) Christian faiths with other experts, including those we might see as 'public thinkers' (for example, Richard Hoggart, John Betjeman). Both of the BBC's long-running religious panel programmes, *Meeting Point* (1956–1968) on Sunday evenings and *Seeing and Believing* (1960–1976) on Sunday afternoons, turned their attention to the topic of death. For example, in July of 1960, *Meeting Point* scheduled an episode entitled 'Facing Death' (BBC, tx. 24/7/60) which brought together nurse and author Pamela Bright, Bishop Anthony Bloom (then Metropolitan bishop of the Russian Orthodox Church and a regular contributor to the BBC's religious programming) and an unnamed consultant psychiatrist, to discuss whether a person should be told when they are going to die.[12] *Seeing and Believing*, on the afternoon of 24 June, 1962, chaired a discussion between the Reverend Dr Austin Fulton (then Moderator of the General Assembly of the Presbyterian Church in Ireland), actors John Breslin and James Grout and chorus master and conductor John Alldin for the episode 'Death and the Purpose of Life'. Alongside other panel discussion programmes about how we should face death which were not made by the religious broadcasting unit, such as *Lifeline* (1957–1961), which focused on discussions of psychological matters[13] and *Perspective* (1961–1963), a wide-ranging panel programme produced in the afternoons by the BBC's Women's Programmes Unit,[14] death was brought onto television via the panel show as a topic of great public interest. Debating this topic with those who represented a variety of faiths, or no faith at all, was in keeping with a turn towards the CRAC's reformulated commitment by the mid-1970s to 'present to viewers and listeners those beliefs, ideas, issues and experiences in the contemporary world which are relevant to a religious interpretation or dimension of life' (Viney, 1999: 7).

While no copies of the earliest religious panel programmes on death exist for re-examination, we can turn to a later revisitation of this form, the late night panel programme *Choices* (BBC1, 1982–1987), made by the Religious Programming Department through much of the 1980s, to get a sense of how this genre of programming handled questions of death and dying by the middle of this decade. In August 1986, Rabbi Julia Neuberger, the second female rabbi in the UK and later author of a number of books on death and dying, chaired the panel discussion 'Facing Death'. This programme involved the Right Reverend Tony Bridge, then Dean of Guildford, an artist, author and contemporary of the writer Dylan Thomas who turned away from his earlier atheism to become an Anglican priest, the neurologist Dr Vicky Clement Jones, a campaigner for the rights of cancer patients and the founder of the British Association for Cancer United Patients, who was also in the later stages of dying from ovarian cancer herself, Dr Tom West, medical director of St Christopher's Hospice in London and a pioneer in palliative care, and Professor Ted Honderich, philosopher of consciousness and committed atheist. We can see very clearly in *Choices* a kind of microcosm of Newcomb and Hirsch's 'television as cultural forum' argument, where multiple, opposing perspectives on the subject of death are allowed to coexist in a programme whose form rests precisely on the idea of balance through the airing of diverging viewpoints.

Choices opens with a title sequence that visually expresses the multiplicity of voices and perspectives that will be heard in the programme: a split-screen image with 9 square 'tiles' in a grid brings together moving footage of diverse people engaging in everyday life practices, while a central 'tile' scrolls through stills of people of multiple ages, races and genders, giving an impression of a cultural forum made up of people from a variety of identities and life experiences. We also see a variety of religious practices reflected on screen, as well as images that don't relate in any direct way to organised religion at all; this short title sequence therefore expresses the multi-faith dimension of this religious broadcast, as well as the fact that space will be made within the programme for an exploration of humanist/atheist beliefs, and that the programme will explore a variety of life experiences. Following the title sequence, Neuberger's introduction expresses something of the 'uncertainty' of death and explains that after the end of the Second World War, a 'new generation developed which pushed death under the carpet . . . and death, although all round us, became a stranger'. She therefore situates this edition of the programme as part of the push back against death's receding from public life and establishes television as a forum for facing death. Neuberger introduces the panel and the studio audience, asserting that some of the audience have been invited to talk about their particular relationships to death (for example, the Chair of the Voluntary Euthanasia Society, a practicing Buddhist, people who are themselves dealing with terminal illness or who have had near-death experiences or lost a loved one). The studio set-up and audience constitution is therefore a bit like long-running, current BBC political panel show, *Question Time* (BBC1, 1979–) which, as Livingstone and Lunt have explored, sits among a range of programmes that seek to replicate a (more or less successful) version of a participatory public sphere (1994). The responses from the panel to Neuberger's prompts, and the subsequent contributions from the studio audience, explore what the facts of death bring to light about life, asking questions such as 'What is the meaning of life?', 'Have we lived good lives or valued our life experiences properly?', 'Does God exist?', 'What are the moral, psychological and ethical issues raised by an encounter with death?' and so on. This programme therefore uses death as a springboard to explore some big, philosophical questions, and the conveying of personal experience is given more space in the programme than professional, religious expertise.

While *Choices* doesn't seek consensus in its panellists and participating audience, it emphasises that television programming can make room to air a range of differing opinions on, and experiences of, death, without conflict or discord. The design of its studio setting suggests a space of neutrality, openness and exchange: the set is dressed in beige and cool blues, with its panellists sitting around a kidney shaped table facing into the diegetic studio audience who are metaphorically seated at the 'missing' side of the table. It therefore presents the democratising vision of the religious debate show. Less than a decade after this death-focused panel programme, Barrie Gunther and Rachel Viney published research that showed that while 74% of people thought that religious broadcasting should be for those who are unable to attend a service of worship, 49% of people saw this programming as being for those who needed comfort in some way, and 39% saw it as providing a service for those who needed guidance (1994). The guidance that such a programme provides is perhaps questionable: the multiplicity of voices and experiences heard in the programme suggest no single route through death and dying. However, perhaps the 'comfort' that is provided here is the comfort to be found in being part of a community, in sharing sometimes difficult experiences with those who appear on television. Outside of the context of religious broadcasting, this comfort is also provided in our next case study: the autopathographic documentary.

As explained in the introduction to this chapter, television has been a key location of the autopathography of 'ordinary' people since the 1960s. While Brennan (2018) and Walter (2009) point towards the importance of the celebrity autopathography on television in the 2000s, documentaries about death experiences have been a feature of British television from a much earlier point. Autopathographies more broadly are, as Brennan suggests, a 'key means by which people in contemporary Western societies learn about and make sense of [the experiences of dying, death and bereavement]' (2018: 102), and also, for their participants, offer an 'apparent sense of agency, control and symbolic mastery that comes from writing or telling in a situation of terminal decline otherwise characterized by the absence or loss of personal autonomy and control' (ibid.: 108). This aligns with Michele Aaron's discussion and enabling of filmmaking as a critical aspect of palliative care (2019, 2020).[15] The autopathography might therefore be seen as therapeutic for their makers, as well as essential viewing for their audience. This counters the suggestion made by John Horne that the dying individual 'is mostly screened for the benefit of the spectator' (2015: 129) and that we need 'the moral solace offered by the sacrificial spectacle of the dying individual: the promise that dying *can* be comprehended *and* made meaningful *and* contained within a framework' (ibid.: 129). We can look to the autopathographies made for British television in the 1960s, 1970s and 1980s to see that there were multiple benefits for subject *and* viewer in television documentaries which sought, very firmly, to give voice to the dying.

As we saw in the death-focused panel programme, this sub-genre gave considerable screen time to those who had *personal* experiences of death, whether through facing dying themselves, or through an experience of bereavement. However, more sustained and intimate portraits of the experience of death and dying were found elsewhere in the television schedule. For example, the long-running current affairs documentary series *Man Alive* (BBC2, 1965–1981) provided space for multi-perspectival accounts of dying, employing the series' characteristic observational style in episodes at the beginning and end of its run to offer the dying a voice on British television. The 1966 episode 'Living with Death' (tx. 30/11/66) took cameras to the pioneering hospice, the Hostel of God, in Clapham, London, to allow people living in the hospice to tell their own stories about what it was like to live with the knowledge that they were dying. While *The Observer* newspaper described this episode as potentially 'monstrously intrusive', it also conceded that 'all the patients in the programme volunteered to appear' (Anon., 1966).[16] Later, in the final run of the series, *Man Alive* returned to the autopathography with the episode 'Fighting for Time' (tx. 22/1/81), a three-part documentary by filmmaker Angela Holdsworth that focused on the experiences of three 'ordinary' people – Ken Thomas, Tim Martys and Jean Cameron – living with the knowledge of their impending death and tracking their attempts to bring a variety of dying wishes to fruition. Unlike the earlier episode, 'Fighting for Time' was shot largely in the homes of the three subjects and was conversational in tone: they and their loved ones are interviewed in these domestic spaces, chatting about their impending deaths, or that of their partners, while performing such mundane tasks as cooking and planting flowers. It therefore speaks to what James Chapman describes as the influence of Direct Cinema on British television documentary of this period and the particular suitability of the observational mode to television: the 'intimacy of television made the "human" element [in the observational documentary] more immediate [given that] television allows a sense of closeness to the subject that is different from cinema' (2015: 198).

At the centre of the episode, for example, Tim Martys's wife Polly is seen in her kitchen assembling sandwiches. The accompanying voiceover explains

> All through [Tim's fundraising] campaign he's had the backing of his two sons and his wife, Polly, who's a civil servant and earns the money that now supports the family. It's been a very difficult twelve months for her, but she manages to put on a brave front most of the time

as the scene cuts between shots of her hands slicing bread and a slow zoom into her face as she concentrates on her task, emphasising, simultaneously, the everydayness of her task and the sense of emotional fatigue she is facing. Following this brief scene of Polly's everyday life, she is interviewed with the camera facing her directly. A voice off screen asks, 'At your worst moments how do you feel about things?' to which she smiles and replies: 'At my worst moments, desperate'. While the interview itself is direct and intimate in its style, taking place in Polly's home and covering the topic of her husband's impending death, the shots of everyday life that precede it emphasise the ordinariness of this couple's experience and depict relatable space and activity (the kitchen, the assembling of lunch), attempting to draw a connection between the subject and the viewer.

Perhaps one of the most poignant and interesting examples of the autopathography of ordinary people on television was the 1975 documentary *Remember All the Good Things* (BBC1 North West region, tx. 12/11/74), a programme directed by Alan Murgatroyd and co-produced by Murgatroyd and Ray Colley for the BBC's North West region. *Remember All the Good Things* was subsequently screened for the whole of the nation on 30 March 1975, as part of BBC2's *Network* series of observational and investigational documentaries from around the regions. The documentary followed the artist Tony Whiteley (a friend and colleague of Murgatroyd's from Manchester Polytechnic, where they both taught) through the final stages of his life as he was dying from lung cancer, simultaneously documenting the experience of his wife, Vivien, as she prepared for life alone with their children: Joseph, aged three, and baby Thomas, who was four months old. Described by *The Observer* newspaper as a 'deeply emotional documentary' (Anon., 1976: 30), the film is made in an observational style, following Tony and Vivien through their everyday lives, while also interweaving direct and candid interviews to camera with both of them (together and separately), talking about their experiences of this moment, their hopes for the future of the family, and so on. Vivien remembers the filming of the documentary during a period of difficulty in their lives as 'good fun', and that Joseph, her eldest son, had been excited about the arrival of the crew and all their equipment. She also remembers the crew as kind and caring towards her and Tony, one day bringing roses with them, sent by one of their wives from her garden, and treating the pair of them as collaborators on the film.[17] The film was a significant creative outlet for them and something that enabled them to assert some agency at a point in Tony's illness when they might otherwise have felt quite powerless. This tallies with Michael Brennan's description of the autopathography as offering 'an apparent sense of agency, control and symbolic mastery' (2018: 108) at a time when the subject-collaborator is feeling most vulnerable and powerless, as discussed above.

One of the key things to note about this autopathography is that while the family initially viewed the production of the film as an opening up of the topic of preparing for death (of which, more below) and as 'a distraction and something to do instead of just sit and die',[18] both the press coverage that framed it, and the programme itself, emphasise the documentary's position as a kind of memento mori for Tony's family of his life and work. Writing in the *Radio Times*, Ian Hamilton describes the fact that, in response to his declining health,

> [Tony] began painting again, and also to keep a diary, for his children ... At the same time, he agreed – perhaps partly from the same wish to leave his children with some living memory – to make *Remember All the Good Things* (1975: 13).

At the start of the documentary, speaking over a montage of close-ups of the children, the family dog, the mundane details of their home, Tony describes this impulse, initially looking down at the diary lying open in his lap:

> Well, this diary, this was done originally for the children, Vivien afterwards, because it's very difficult because you want to know what your father was, what kind of a man he was. If you could have a piece of his writing, written for you when you were a little baby, I think that would help a lot. I started writing about the last weeks of whatever it's going to be, so that they'll know their dad, they'll know what their dad thought.

The configuration of the documentary itself as part of this process of memorialisation, interlinked with the diary writing, is particularly interesting, given that it was made, in 1975, in an era which preceded home video

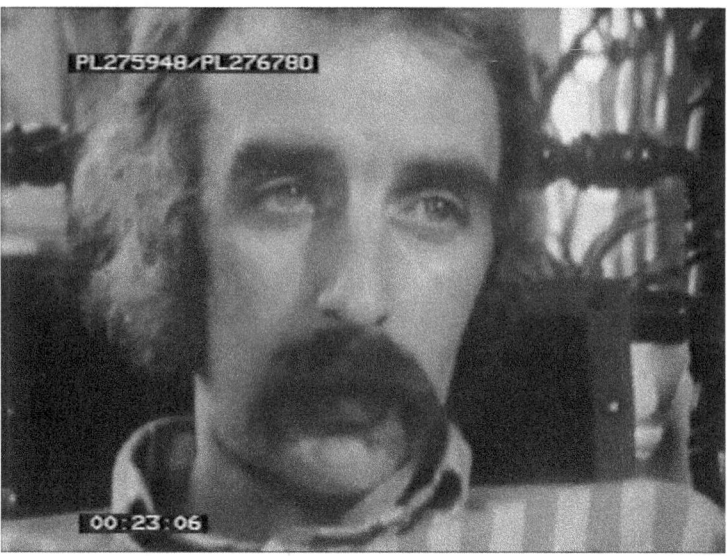

Figure 1.1 Tony Whiteley, close up, *Remember All The Good Things* (BBC1 North West region tx. 12/11/74).

equipment. The BBC did not supply the Whiteleys with a finished copy of the film, nor did the family have the means to watch a copy, initially.[19] One may presume, then, that in describing the film as a memento mori at the time of its production and broadcast, the Whiteleys were relying on the fact that the documentary would sit within the BBC's archive until such time as their children wished to access and view their father in *Remember All the Good Things*, for its broadcast happened four months after Tony's death when the children would still be too young to understand what they were watching, and then repeated for national broadcast another four months after that.[20]

In the *Radio Times*, Vivien Whiteley described the experience of her encounter with this memento mori on the documentary's first broadcast, four months after her husband's death: 'Her own response (though she had been rather dreading its appearance) was straightforwardly one of relief – "it was so good to see him again"' (Hamilton, 1975: 14). She later recalled that the BBC had covered the cost of her social worker coming to watch the broadcast with her, giving her the opportunity to talk through her feelings about the documentary; she reiterated that it had been good to see Tony 'not right at the end . . . but talking and in charge of himself and happy about doing [the documentary], and having things to say'.[21] Perhaps these feelings of relief and familiarity about being given access to the 'old Tony' in the family home were partly facilitated by the programme's emphasis on an aesthetics of intimacy through which this extraordinary moment in the couple's life together was captured in great detail. This brings to mind Emma Wilson's description of Annie Leibovitz's photographs of her partner Susan Sontag's dying which, according to Wilson, capture

> moments of being that will be recalled and rearranged after death. Through their indexicality, the images give the impression of recording a loved gesture, an intimate, or public, or extreme experience. Yet the charge, the affect, of the images changes over time. They record past moments offering pristine imprints yet also provide a future repository, a resource for pursued love. (2012: 3–4)

What demarcates an aesthetics of intimacy in this televisual documentary is firstly the use of the close-up: the documentary opens with a tight close-up on Tony's face (see Figure 1.1) and continues to feature close shots of his and Vivien's faces throughout. This emphasises this couple's experience of dying and grief as intimate, a very personal experience, with the face acting as the key signifier for this fact. Faces are not only seen via the close-ups shot by Murgatroyd's camera, but also through a montage of family photographs; the photographic montage acts at the beginning of the documentary to suggest the relatability of this family's story (their family photographs look remarkably like 'ours') and also denote the making of programme, like the family photograph, as an act of everyday memorialisation. As Amy Holdsworth has noted in her work on the BBC series *Who Do You Think You Are?* (2004–), 'The family album is perhaps a practice of photographical collection and exhibition that many of us recognise, and it attaches an image narrative to our personal memories' (2011: 71). This montage of photographs also constitutes what Michael Renov calls the 'work of mourning' on film and video, being 'composed of a combination of words (via first-person voiceover or interview-based testimony) and images (relics of pastness, evocations of memory) whose meaning depends upon their overall arrangement via editing' (2004: 125). The image narrative of personal memories offered through the photographic montage is therefore both familiar to the wider audience as a form of memorialisation, and intimately specific to this particular family. The observational documentary's emphasis on the quotidian detail of everyday life, and of 'capturing' ordinary conversation, also constructs what we might understand as an aesthetic of intimacy: for example, Vivien's account of receiving Tony's diagnosis given in the living room of their home in the North West of England is full of coincidental detail as she recalls feeding her eldest son toffees to keep him quiet while they digested the news. Vivien is also shown later in the documentary discussing her husband's impending death, and how she will cope with it, all heard in voiceover as she pushes the baby's pram along the cobbled road of her home town; this coupling of the most ordinary activities and spaces of everyday life with intimate conversations about the experience of death once again emphasises an aesthetic of intimacy for this autopathography and reminds us that death occurs precisely in the midst of life.

The reception of *Remember All the Good Things* suggests that the programme was ultimately successful in its attempts to tell a relatable story to the television audience:

> When the film appeared locally [in the North West] Vivien received several letters from the recently bereaved, praising her for the way she and Tony had handled their predicament, and wishing they themselves had done the same. These ... surprised her – she had gloomily expected the motives behind the film to be misunderstood. (Hamilton, 1975: 14)

In total, Vivien received around twenty letters from viewers which she described as 'mostly from youngish people who felt that it was important for them to have '[a] discussion about whether they would want to know [about a terminal diagnosis]'.[22] She heard from people who had faced bereavement themselves, but also young people who expressed sentiments of empathy, saying 'Well if this happens to us, if and when, we'll do exactly the same'.[23] This gave Vivien the sense that the purpose of their documentary and its intimate style had 'landed' with precisely the community of viewers it had been imagined for.

The same article, accompanying the programme's second broadcast, also outlines that Vivien found purpose in making the documentary, beyond producing a memento mori for her own family:

> [She] now feels that the whole project has real value as a contribution to the continuing 'Should Doctors Tell?' debate ... The television film, the viewers' letters to her, even this *Radio Times* story have encouraged her to view her widowhood, and all that led up to it, as an example, a model of how best to face such things. To some, such a responsibility might well have been intolerable. For her, it has been a way of salvaging sense and instruction from her loss. (Hamilton, 1975: 14)

Vivien later emphasised that this was their *key* reason for taking part in the documentary, and that telling their story would show ordinary television viewers that being informed about terminal diagnosis was the right thing to do: she argued that this gave them a 'positive purpose' towards the end of Tony's life. Vivien's reflections on this in later life are also reflections about class and the address to 'ordinary people' through television:

> I think ordinary people probably agreed with [the right to know] much more, especially working-class people, that you should be told, rather than the middle-class people who kept things under wraps . . . Maybe it wasn't our place to say stuff like that . . . you know, whether we wanted to know if we were dying or not . . . [But] we were trying to break that taboo, I suppose.[24]

This informal death education, located by Brennan (2018) as the key purpose of the celebrity autopathography, is made all the more poignant, all the more impactful, through a documentary that highlights the very *ordinariness* of the family, and the dying man and bereaved woman, at its heart. Vivien Whiteley, through the letters she received from viewers, was able to experience and understand the direct connection she had made to her community via television. Following its first broadcast, a TV reviewer in the *Liverpool Echo* called for a follow-up documentary to be made 'showing how Tony's wife Vivien is coping with her new role as a young, widowed mother', and stating '[s]he could surely give some help and advice to many other families who are facing, or must face in the future, a similar problem' (Ariel, 1974: 2). This very documentary was indeed commissioned and made as *Vivien Whiteley: On Her Own* (broadcast in the North West on 24 October 1975, and then on BBC2 nationwide on 15 April 1976), largely produced in the same observational style as *Remember All The Good Things* and giving Vivien space to describe and discuss her life without Tony. While the second documentary opens with an intertitle that expresses that this is Vivien's continuing autopathography – 'Suddenly you are alone, instead of being one of two people. It's hard at first, and just when you think you are going along alright, its brought home every time, you're on your own, you're on your own' – over the sound of her giving the children a bath, the following scene gives us the testimony of an unnamed Professor of Community Care from Sheffield University who is brought in to comment on Vivien's experiences throughout the documentary: 'The widow, delightful as she may be, also symbolises death, bereavement and the ending of life'. This diverges from the straight observational style of Murgatroyd's first documentary about the Whiteleys somewhat; however, the professor's remarks are clearly included to further emphasise the relatability of Vivien's personal experience to the experience of others in the wider viewing community. They therefore underscore the wider role of the autopathography on television to provide 'unofficial' death education and to convey something of the affective experience of death, dying and bereavement.

This fascinating example of the television autopathography is by no means a 'one-off' for UK broadcasting. The following month, on 24 May, the BBC's *Horizon* series broadcast Michael Roemer's 1976 PBS documentary, *Dying* (tx. 29/4/76), a few weeks after its initial broadcast in the US. Roemer's autopathography follows three people living with and dying from cancer over a two-year period. Made with a grant from the National Endowment for the Arts, this work is sometimes treated as 'not television' in the critical literature on death on film (Malkowski, 2017). However, David Dempsey's review of this programme for the *New York Times* precisely acknowledges its televisuality when he argues that 'Television . . . becomes a medium for dying' (1976: 1) via Roemer's documentary, and later states that television plays a role in the 'high technology dying of our age . . . it becomes a new kind of life-support machine – one that gives the patient – if not restored health, at least an outlet for what remains of his [sic] humanity. It's a way of publicly saying goodbye' (ibid.: 29). The television-ness of this documentary is particularly demarcated by its focus on the domestic and the everyday. As Jennifer Malkowski notes, Roemer was keen to point out that this was not a handbook on how to die, that we cannot *learn* to die on television, but rather that *Dying* places emphasis on the various ways which one might die, and therefore that a multiplicity of dying experiences on TV must be represented (2017: 85).

Like the *Man Alive* episode discussed above, *Dying* is a triptych of end-of-life stories, and while a number of critics have concentrated on the third of the three, which focuses on the death of Reverend Bryant and which for many demonstrated what a 'good death' might look like (the Reverend dies surrounded by his family and is mourned by his community), the middle story of *Dying*, which focuses on Bill and his wife Harriet, and their kids, as Bill is dying of cancer, is perhaps the most interesting in relation to a reading of *Dying* as a television-specific or television-appropriate autopathography. The story of Bill's illness and his terminal decline is presented as taking place within the midst of everyday life, as a family saga. The structure of this sequence of the programme shuttles between scenes of everyday domesticity – Bill and Harriet playing with their kids at the lake, the children bickering about laying the table for dinner and getting homework finished,

Figure 1.2 Bill and Harriet looking bored, *Dying* (PBS, tx. 29/4/76).

the performance of mundane tasks like mowing the lawn and watering the plants – and scenes of Bill's treatment at the hospital. These latter scenes are presented in the context of Harriet's sniping at Bill (and at his doctors) about the length of time it is taking him to die, and about how that impacts on her and the children, and also on scenes of mundanity – Bill and Harriet are frequently shot looking bored and fed up, side-by-side in their silence.

For Malkowski (2017), Bill's death serves as a representation of the 'bad death' – it is miserable, drawn out, and stressful in comparison to the other deaths represented in the film. However, it is also possible to view this as a jarringly truthful representation of death in the midst of everyday life – meals still have to be prepared and eaten, homework still needs to be completed – even while the process of dying and the negotiation of its aftermath takes place. By extension, it is perhaps precisely the kind of representation of dying that television invites or evokes. With its focus on the intimate details of living, and its attempt to present the extended duration of dying, it presents death *televisually*, trying to give its viewers a sense of where death, dying and grief might fit into quotidian experience. Harriet is unguarded about her (difficult) feelings, which is a mode of self-presentation that is perhaps more at home on television than on film. Television provides the mouthpiece for all the awful, anxious, bored, stressed, irritable things she is feeling. And we imagine ourselves in her position. This story of dying draws precisely on television's emphasis on intimacy and empathy: Bill's is not a 'good' death but it is also not a 'bad' death either. It is an ordinary death in the midst of life.

Perhaps the inclusion of Roemer's documentary for PBS in the US in a chapter on the early history of dying on UK television might seem a little odd. However, the remediation of death documentaries from around the world made up a significant aspect of British television's cultural forum on death in the latter part of the twentieth century. The long-running series *Europa* (BBC2, 1966–1974), which brought together news, documentary and current affairs programming from around Europe, broadcast at least six episodes on the subject of death,[25] and the similar, later series *Europeans* (BBC2, 1989–1990) also featured the episode 'On Death' (tx. 17/8/89). Dutch documentary 'Parting', produced by Ton Koole and Kalahari Film Productions for the Humanist Society and following the last days of the doctor and humanist counsellor Aleida Hartstra, was also broadcast as part of the BBC1 *Everyman* (BBC1, 1977–2000) series in the UK on 20 January 1990. We therefore see that the subject of death, while very present on UK television during this period, was also circulating transnationally, in a much broader televisual field.

While much of the autopathographic programming discussed above was found in 'serious documentary' slots on evening television in the UK, this was not its only location. The six-part series *Living with Dying* (BBC1, 1990), presented by news reporter Martyn Lewis, was broadcast on BBC1 on Wednesday afternoons in a slot most usually reserved for consumer affairs and adult educational/advice programming. The programme was introduced in the *Radio Times* as dealing with 'dying, death and bereavement', promising that '[s]pending just a little time in preparation for our death can be really helpful to those left behind. The programme explains how to go about making a will, and goes on to explore how living, accepting life has an end, can be far from morbid.'[26] The series, in many ways, prepared its viewers as consumers of end-of-life services: practical advice was offered on, for example, the importance of wills for LGBT+ people or how to get the best experience out of working with a funeral director, but it also gave voice to individuals' death experiences, from a focus on those benefiting from the burgeoning hospice movement to a montage of women all discussing their experiences of losing a loved one in the third episode. Death, dying and bereavement in this context, in this most ordinary of genres and most mundane of scheduling slots (the mid-afternoon lull), was thus firmly situated as part of everyday life.

This emphasis on death occurring in the midst of everyday life, noted as an identifying characteristic of all the televisual autopathographies discussed above, was also a feature of the death-focused documentaries produced by the BBC's Community Programme Unit. As Jo Henderson's work has shown, the Community Programme Unit (CPU) was set up with the direct purpose to give voice (and editorial control) to 'ordinary' people on television; Henderson defines the ordinary in this case 'as in the everyday; . . . as in the common; and . . . as in the shared' (2019: 25). Also known as 'access television', the programmes of the CPU were designed to use video technology as Raymond Williams had imagined it, offering 'a more democratic culture in which people had chances to discuss issues, formulate ideas and creatively envision their lives' (Spigel, 1992: xiii). Henderson's history of the CPU documents how it 'sought to give voice to groups of people under represented by the BBC . . . [introducing] difficult subjects to the broadcast agenda' (2019: 27). While other histories of the CPU have focused on the often contentious voices it allowed to be heard in connection with the history of race relations in the UK (Oakley and Lee-Wright, 2016; Hendy, 2018), the idea that the Unit opened up 'difficult subjects' on air can also be related to the representation of death, dying and bereavement. For this history of the autopathography on television, the *Video Diaries* (BBC, 1990–1996) series, in which 'ordinary people' were given the 'opportunity to make extended or feature length documentaries about themselves in conjunction with a dedicated producer editor . . . [offering] unprecedented levels of participation in all stages of production [including filming and editing the documentary]' (ibid.: 170), is particularly significant. For example, the first season episode, 'Just for the Record' (tx. 26/5/90), made by David Francis with producer Jeremy Gibson,

> [S]tarted with the intention of representing everyday life in a close-knit rural Welsh community [but while] making the film, [Francis's] grandmother died unexpectedly, and the film became a self-reflexive social documentary on the process and rituals of bereavement and community. (ibid.: 173)

In the second season, the episode 'Surviving Memories' (tx. 1/6/91), produced by Tony Steyger, documented feminist activist and photographer Jo Spence's coming to terms with a terminal diagnosis while exploring her difficult relationship with her brother. However, perhaps the most poignant autopathography in the series was fourth season episode 'Time for Tom' (tx. 11/9/96), which captured the final months of Tom Kettlety's life as seen through the eyes of his mum, Christine. Diagnosed as suffering from Tay Sachs disease and given only a few years to live under constant care, 'Time for Tom' documents the gruelling impact of Tom's day-to-day care on his entire family (including sisters Ruth and Hannah, and his dad, Rob), as well as how his parents, siblings and respite carers deal with his inevitable death. Addressing the viewer directly at the start of the film, Christine offers her rationale for working with producer Emma Read on the episode:

> It may surprise you that I have chosen to share the last moments of Tom's life with you. I desperately wanted to have a lasting record of Tom. With this video diary, I hope to introduce him to as many people as possible because in his short life he would not have had the chance to meet you.

Interestingly, Christine switches here from expressing her desire to capture a memento mori for herself (and presumably her wider family) to situating Tom as part of a wider community of television viewers (and therefore registering his life, and death, as significant in some way to that community). The subsequent account of Tom's extraordinary life (and his death) is interwoven with the story of the Kettletys' very ordinary everyday life – footage of Tom's care is entwined with school assemblies, caravan holidays, the other children being silly and making a mess with yogurt and stickers. The title, 'Time for Tom', is referred to via a kind of 'ordinary lyricism' throughout the documentary in which shots of clocks and diaries emphasise both the scheduling of Tom's complex care routine and the passing of time that marks his family's experience of his decline, death and their subsequent bereavement. Ultimately, the whole of the programme acts as a kind of conversation between Chris, Rob and the television audience: they talk through the process of their child's death with each other, but also *for us* (and sometimes even directly *with* us, via a direct address to camera). This series of conversations, a kind of 'working through' of Tom's death, perhaps expresses what Kilborn and Izod have called the 'explicit therapeutic function' of *Video Diaries* (1997: 83). They also afford the Kettletys a sense of control (over the production of the documentary, the telling of their story) at a difficult time in their lives, and the ability to make meaning from Tom's death is therefore significant for them. This tallies with Giles Oakley's suggestion that '[f]or the diarists [in this series] there was something beautifully liberating about being able to record the most intimate aspects of life [and, presumably, death], knowing they retained power of decision over whether or not to broadcast, right up to transmission' (Oakley and Lee-Wright, 2016: 225). The autopathography in *Video Diaries* thus empowered the documentary subject at a key moment in their experience of death and grief.

Following these individual episodes of *Video Diaries*, in 1997 the CPU (under the direction of series producer Bob Long) made seven ten-minute shorts called *Before I Die* (BBC2), which were broadcast before the news and current affairs programme *Newsnight* (BBC2, 1980–) at 10.15 pm on a Thursday evening. The series featured a string of first-person accounts of dying, from the story of two teenagers with spinal muscular atrophy, to the musings of journalist Oscar Moore, who was dying from an HIV infection, to a range of adults dying of various forms of cancer and exploring topics such as euthanasia and the impact of their deaths on their families. In the first episode of the series, 'What About the Children?' (tx. 30/1/97), mother of four Sheila Chapman offers a snapshot of her life after discovering she is dying from secondary bone cancers, having lived with a breast cancer diagnosis for nine years. The opening shot of this episode, self-shot on video camera, is a stark close-up of Sheila's face as she explains the facts of her life and diagnosis; following this, a shot out of her kitchen window of the washing blowing in the breeze in her garden signals the lyrical, but decidedly ordinary, existentialism which characterised the output of the CPU in the 1990s, a moment of contemplation (like the shots of clocks in 'Time for Tom') in the middle of a busy life. As with the other autopathographies discussed above, shots of Sheila going about her everyday life – cooking, watching television, tidying up, working on her allotment, shopping – are coupled with her voiceover as she worries 'What are the children going to do? How's John [her husband] going to cope?'. Most revealingly though, the episode closes on a scene in which Sheila screens some footage of her talking direct to camera on the TV in her living room, in order to confront her two youngest children with her worries about dying. At the start of the scene, we see Sheila settling down in front of the TV, with her twelve-year-old daughter at her feet, while in voiceover she says:

> Somehow, I hadn't been able to confront my death with John and the kids, but I had been talking, on my own, to the camcorder the BBC gave me. One day, I thought I should show them what I feel by using the tapes I had made. I didn't expect them to understand everything, but it was a start.

Following this, shots of Sheila and the children watching the television are coupled with the lined image of her face, shot from the diegetic television screen, as she cries and anxiously worries about how her children will cope when she's gone. The three figures in the room are silent – there is no further discussion of the impact of watching this footage together as the episode comes to an end – but the suggestion from the scene is that taking part in the process of documentary making has been therapeutic for Sheila, part of her palliative care, and will form the basis of an ongoing discussion about death in her family, as well as, ultimately, playing a role in the children coming to terms with their bereavement.

Making sense, working through: grief, bereavement and the business of the funeral

> 'The one unbearable dimension of possible human experience is not the experience of one's own death, which no one has, but the experience of the death of another' (Jacques Lacan, 1977: 37).

While the subject of grief and bereavement will be dealt with in greater detail in the second part of this book, it is clear that this early period of death-related broadcasting in the UK speaks to Kenneth J. Doka's description of grief as a 'continuum of reactions, very personal pathways that encompass the range of reactions individuals have to loss' (2018: 37). This analysis therefore acts as a precursor to the book's later, more in-depth analysis of the fictional representation of grief and bereavement on television. Doka's work, as explored in Chapter 4, emphasises the multiplicity of experiences of grief (against the fairly rigid road map of 'inevitable' stages of grief set out by Elizabeth Kübler-Ross (1969) and others). It therefore contextualises the drive on British television in the latter part of the twentieth century to provide access to a variety of narratives of people's experiences of grief. Contra to Fulton and Owen's analysis of American television in the same period, which proposed that '[w]hile prime time television features death and violence relentlessly, particularly among the young, it portrays grief and the ruptured lives that death can leave in its wake only superficially' (1987–1988: 383), this chapter will close by briefly looking at the complex ways grief was portrayed in British television documentary in this period.

The documentary programming that examined grief, bereavement and mourning in this period generally sought to do one of two things: either (as has already been explored above in relation to autopathographic programmes such as *Vivien Whiteley: On Her Own*, *Video Diaries: Time for Tom*, and *Before I Die*) attempt to convey the feelings and emotional experiences of grief and bereavement, or, alternatively, expose the customs and rituals of mourning via an anthropological approach to the death industry. The former aim speaks to what John Ellis describes as the documentary's ability to 'cut through the complexities of issues to *show us what it feels like* to be an individual experiencing them directly' (2012: 98, my emphasis). As I will argue in the following chapter, this attempt to work through the emotional experience of death, dying and bereavement *with* the documentary subject and *for* the television viewer might be related to Holdsworth and Lury's argument that television 'in certain instances (and perhaps particularly in relation to the programmes produced by a public service institution such as the BBC) is a "caring technology"' (2016: 190). We see this care for the bereaved and those experiencing grief across a range of genres, moments in the schedule, and channels on British television in the late twentieth century, from the documentaries discussed above to a series of talk show episodes that focused on the subject of bereavement. The afternoon talk show *Esther* (BBC2, 1996–2002), for example, featured multiple episodes where a live studio audience discussed their experiences of losing loved ones. This included an episode about infant death fronted by Anne Diamond, a television presenter who had herself experienced the death of her own baby through sudden infant death syndrome (tx. 2/3/98), to a wider episode on bereavement presented by Jill Dando which interwove the stories of famous invited bereaved participants with the testimonies of the studio audience (tx. 9/12/97).[27] It was not only the BBC that used the talk show format to explore grief, however: an episode of the medical current affairs-discussion programme *Where There's Life* (Yorkshire/ITV, 1981–1989) in 1981 opened with presenter Dr Robert Buckman explaining:

> I'd like to discuss something that is actually extremely difficult to talk about and it's a thing that people don't usually like talking about and something that's never really discussed on television and that is grief. The problem is that I, like many doctors, really feel very embarrassed dealing with grief, partly because of lack of training and partly because of fear of what me might, errr, precipitate when we deal with grief, but maybe we could all be a little less embarrassed and a little less frightened if we could learn more about our patients' experiences.

Following this opening, Buckman chairs an exploration of the studio audience's experience of the emotions associated with grief, from a young woman called Melanie who talks about developing depression through bereavement, to the testimony of an older woman, Rosemary, who lost her daughter in her twenties to cancer. Sitting around and among them, the audience act as a diegetic representation of the viewers watching at home (what Jane Shattuc calls the 'inscribed viewers . . . [that] embody the immediate "you" to whom the host refers' (1997: 5)), the raked seating in the studio a microcosm of television's function as a forum for the exploration of the emotional experience of grief and bereavement. As the studio audience join in the discussion, sharing difficult and harrowing personal experiences (the death of a child in a road traffic accident, a breakdown and a suicide attempt associated with bereavements), we see the programme employing what Mimi White refers to as television's 'therapeutic strategies' (1992: 8), as person after person talks through their experiences of grief. While for White, the therapeutic mode of television, and the talking through of problems on screen, was related strongly to the growth of consumer culture in the US, and particularly, though not exclusively, to the development of women's genres on TV, we can clearly see that on British television in the same period the therapeutic mode was associated with the medium's public service imperatives, certainly in its attempts to explore death, dying and bereavement with and for its viewers.

Programming that focused on people's experiences of bereavement was not always separated out from what is identified above as an exposé of the customs and rituals of mourning via an almost anthropological approach to the death industry, however. Two documentaries, made for the BBC in the late 1960s/early 1970s, sought to bring these two things together, intertwining explorations of people's stories of grief at the death of a loved one with commentary on what the programme makers saw as the increased mechanisation/industrialisation of death. The first of these, *Death Today* (BBC1, tx. 13/6/69), was produced in the North West of England by the documentarist Don Haworth. Haworth, a former print journalist who had been working as a producer on the *Tonight* (BBC, 1957–1965) and *Panorama* (BBC1, 1953–) programmes during the 1960s, and later became known for a series of programmes about the Bolton steeplejack Fred Dibnah, opens his film with a stark shot of two women in overalls arranging flowers.

To the sound only of the creaking and clanking of the operation of machinery, the camera pulls back from the women as the title 'Death

Figure 1.3 The factory-like funeral home, *Death Today* (BBC1, tx. 13/6/69).

Today' appears on screen, revealing that they are standing at the bottom of a factory-like 'funeral home', with coffins clanking up a conveyer belt in the foreground. This single shot announces the intention of this documentary to explore a marked shift in funeral and mourning practices in the late twentieth century, a shift which the documentary goes on to identify as a product of the Industrial Revolution. Like the later documentary *In the Midst of Life* (BBC1, tx. 1/10/74), which also features a coffin 'assembly line' scene, this emphasis on the mechanisation/depersonalisation of funeral practices is further expressed later in the documentary through very 'matter of fact' footage of the business of cremation, showing in detail the operation of the cremator, the lighting of the furnace, cremains being dragged out and treated (screws removed with a magnet, bone and ash swept up and ground down) in an extended, dialogue-less montage in which we are asked simply to observe the facts and practices of cremation. While sequences such as these focus our attention on the mechanical processes associated with the handling of the dead, offering what Caughie has called the 'documentary gaze' (2000: 111) on the business of the funeral, dispassionately and without sentiment, Haworth's documentary also uses sound montages to introduce the human experience of bereavement into his account. For example, an extended sequence of the progress of a coffin from town to grave – shots of a hearse driving through town streets (both of the car itself and from the perspective of its driver as people lower their hats as the hearse drives by), and of cemetery workers preparing and lowering the coffin into a grave – is accompanied by a montage of unidentified voices. These voices are heard in voiceover, taking the place of the 'voice of God' narration that has punctuated the documentary to this point and mixed with diegetic, dialogue-less sound of the coffin's movement towards the grave:

> *Man 1*: After my wife died, she had been saving quite a little of my wages for when I was retired, and unfortunately we had no time together, you know, at retirement. She died in a terrible state, really, and it really give me a great shock.
> *Man 2*: You've got to be realistic about it, because life's got to go on, and the quicker you face up to a grief, the quicker you get over it. In every family, someone has to be bereaved, and in my case, I'm glad I was the one who was left.
> *Woman 1*: I had that awful feeling – blindly hanging on. It's an odd mixture of numbness and tearing apart. You are half-numb but ticking. Far away. And yet this something or other was making you try to keep as near to normal as possible in a completely abnormal situation.
> ...
> *Man 3*: Well people get older, their personalities change, and you see the person you've been fond of, who's been a very pillar of your youth, turn into a selfish old person, mean and malicious and it happens to us all, and you know it's going to happen to you. Far better to die suddenly, before your faculties go, than drag on and on.
> ...
> *Woman 2*: At the time of the death you're in a strangely euphoric state. I felt a terrific life force in me when my husband died, though I did have the wit to say to a friend of mine of bleak times coming. A vast emptiness.
> ...
> *Woman 3*: There's no way round grief. You have to go through it and come out the other side. I think you need a year, you somehow need to see all four seasons come and go, before your private grief begins to grow less. Of course, you have to put a face on it long before that because even your dearest friends get bored, really, with your grief and they just want you to become your normal self again.

The montage of voices in this burial sequence is quoted at length here as it captures the multiplicity of experiences of grief and bereavement that are represented in *Death Today*. While the visual elements of this sequence present the facts of burial dispassionately – the hearse cuts through bustling streets where life 'goes on' regardless, the grave site is prepared with no ceremony or fuss – the voices heard here speak of the complexities of, and variations in, the emotional experience of bereavement. The fact that these voices are 'unidentified' – not assigned to an identifiable person, other than perhaps through the markers of class, race, gender and regional background in the tones of these voices – makes the point that they are 'just like us', the viewing public, that the people speaking are thus part of 'our' community. Their insertion into the programme as a replacement for the received pronunciation, in the rest of the documentary, of narrator Derek Hart, an authoritative voice well known from the current affairs programme *Tonight* (BBC/BBC1, 1957–1965), serves the purpose of democratising death at this point in the programme. These are the voices of 'ordinary folk', reflecting on their lived experience of death; to refer back to the start of this chapter, this is television explicitly operating its 'bardic' function (Fiske and Hartley, 1978), creating a multivocal space for the exploration of death.

In Angela Pope's documentary *In the Midst of Life*, produced five years after *Death Today*, we see once again a use of voiceover to signify access to the 'inner thoughts' of those experiencing grief, as well as to comment elegiacally on the shift in death practices and ritual in the modern day. At the heart of this film, over shots of a (staged) funeral service, a young woman describes her experience of attending a funeral, presumably of someone she loved:

> We got to the crematorium but we had to wait for about ten minutes because there was another body in there being disposed on. I remember, my eyes were fixed on that chimney and I couldn't take my eyes off it, it was terrible, and then all of a sudden 'Puff!' and the smoke went up in the air and I thought 'Oh well, we can go now'. So we drove up, and um, inside it was this sort of unpolished wood, no fripperies. I felt that I would also have rather a sort of Gothic Victorian church with all the ornateness, because at least it would give it some character and this was nothing. It was all specially built, just for disposing of bodies. I felt well, you know, here we are, we're the living, and this man probably thinks he's here to comfort us, but how can he do that when he sees [us] for such a short time? And it just struck me that the vicar was sort of like, you know, a foreman on a destruction line, if you like. Well, I felt he was the keeper at the gate of death.

While we might presume that the young woman seen on screen walking into the crematorium is the person we can also hear speaking (unlike the sequence above from *Death Today*), the non-diegetic dialogue in voiceover here gives us, once again, the impression that we are accessing her innermost thoughts about the experience of bereavement. Further, the presentation of the funeral as a kind of mechanised 'destruction line' in this dialogue offers, again, a sense that death in the late twentieth century is changing, and that the emotional experience of death will change with it. This narrative is also at the heart of the 1987 documentary series by the poet Tony Harrison, *In Loving Memory* (BBC2). Part death travelogue, in which Harrison visits Naples and Paris to examine centuries-old death traditions, this series of poem-films is also an elegy to the passing funereal customs of old England, especially in the penultimate episode 'The Muffled Bells' (tx. 30/2/87). This episode couples the story of the death of local miller Stanley Hall, in Breamore, Hampshire, with documenting the passing of certain aspects of rural life (dying trades and crafts, shifts in the landscape and in property ownership, and so on). As Tony Harrison wanders around the graveyard at Breamore, he opines:

> Craftsman, wheelwright, blacksmith, undertaker, who also turned a skilled hand to the plough, gathered in harvests, grateful to their maker, are in decline ... Now that the village's last miller's dead, the craft of milling flour has also died. Flour from Breamore fields went into bread has been replaced by pre-sliced Mother's Pride.

Harrison continues, over shots of the village, and accompanied by mournful violins:

> The new commuters eye the empty mill, sequestered vales. A teeming motorway. But in spite of creeping yuppies, Breamore's still the sort of churchyard known to Thomas Gray, though the curfew's been tolled for the old ways and the mill and manor a developer's desires.

In Harrison's poem-film, grief is expressed not for the death of the man at the centre of the episode necessarily, but for the loss of a way of life. The death of Stanley Hall, the miller, is treated as signifying a broader sense of impermanence, speaking to Elisabeth Bronfen's argument that:

> Dying, burial and commemoration are always also public matters. As cultural anthropology has shown, death in that it removes a social

> being from society, is conceived as a wound to the community at large and a threatening signal of its own impermanence. (2009: 77)

This brings us back to the point that we started with at the beginning of this chapter. As we have seen, television programming in the late twentieth century has worked hard to process the facts and experiences of death for its viewers, even offering commentary, as this last trio of documentaries does, on the cultural and historical shifts in commemoration practices and experiences of bereavement in this period. As discussed above, John Horne's argument that we need the 'moral solace' offered by the sacrificial spectacle of the dying individual (or, we might add, the sound of the bereaved working through their experience of grief on screen *for us*) to bring us the 'promise that dying *can* be comprehended *and* made meaningful' (2015: 128) is what contextualises the readings of the programmes discussed in this chapter. These programmes work through and worry at death, dying and bereavement in a public cultural forum at precisely the moment when others were announcing the receding of death from public life.

Television autopathographies today

The account of death-focused programming set out in this chapter captures a particular moment in British television history: the era of television as a two-, three- and four-channel public service system, during which the viewer was addressed as a citizen, a member of a viewing *community* for whom death had to be worked out or worked through. But what happens to the autopathography in the twenty-first century and in an era of multi-channel television, streaming platforms and post-broadcast television? As the next chapter will show in relation to programming about the topic of assisted dying, the autopathography does still exist. Whether through public service broadcast television, or on commercial networks, or on streaming platforms such as Netflix, television continues to make sense of death for its viewers by creating platforms for those who are dying to tell their stories. The form and style of these documentaries may change, but their fundamental *raison d'être* remains the same. We continue to need television to insert death and dying into our public and private lives. In 2014, for example, the UK commercial broadcaster Channel Four commissioned the four-part Love Productions series *My Last Summer* to tell the story (over two years) of five 'ordinary' members of the public who were at various stages of dying. Marrying the autopathography with the reality show, these five people were brought together at a rural retreat, sometimes with friends and family joining them too, to 'come to terms with' their dying by building connections with each other and sharing the emotional and physical difficulties of facing death. The voiceover at the start of the series sets out the programme's approach, as well as introducing the participants and the palliative care experts Nigel Dodds and Ann Munro (who are palliative care nurse and psychotherapist respectively, but also diegetic interviewers throughout the series), asking:

> How can you possibly prepare for the end of your life? ... Neither the Health Service, friends, or even family can truly understand how to help someone die. So now five terminally ill people who have never met ... are going to prepare for death together, so that they can finally speak freely about dying, help their partners plan for life without them, and make the most of the time they have left with their children. What can dying teach us about life? And what can we learn about how they choose to end it? You're about to meet five extraordinary people ... determined to make a better death than any of us can imagine.

This introduction sets up the programme (as many other reality programmes have been) as a kind of 'unique social/psychological experiment': this is confirmed later, as palliative psychologist Ann Munro says 'None of us actually knows what it's like to face our own death. By bringing these five people together we're providing a unique way for them to share their experiences as they approach their own deaths'. While Munro refers explicitly here to the participants' sharing with each other, their sharing with the television audience is also implicit. Viewers are drawn into this narrative of intimate sharing through the use of frequent confessional interviews and speech direct to camera; for example, one of the participants, Lou, addresses a therapeutic 'conversation' with her absent partner straight into a self-operated camera, drawing the viewer into this mode of direct communication via programme making. The programme therefore works hard to make us *feel* alongside the participants as they go through their fraught journeys towards death. This emphasis on affect is seen, for example, in the fact that episodes often end with melodramatic montage sequences, as in the end of Episode 2 where Junior, who is the closest to death of all the participants, says he wants to marry his girlfriend Sonia and the episode is played out to a montage soundtracked by Peter Gabriel's version of 'The Book of Love', an emotive piece of popular music about being in love and wishing to marry. The casting of the programme, with participants representing a 'cross-section' of society, diverse in terms of race, class, age and sexuality, also surely invites the television viewer to recognise themselves in these stories, to experience both a sense of connection with the people on screen and the affective charge of knowing that the dying subject 'could be me'.

As the series continues the connections that are built between the participants, and, implicitly, between them and the viewers, means that the final episode, in which the participants begin to experience deteriorating health and die, one by one, is emotionally raw and difficult to watch. One of the final scenes in *My Last Summer* focuses on a visit Lou makes to see fellow participant Andy in hospital, shortly before his death. Andy has lost the ability to speak easily at this point in the narrative, and Lou's breathing and movement have both become more laboured and difficult due to the motor neurone disease which is slowly killing her. As they sit together for a final time, Ludovico Einaudi's mournful 'White Night' plays extra-diegetically over the shot, a tight close-up showing Lou leaning forward, head bowed, one hand resting against Andy's chest and another grasping his own hand.

This image speaks of the connection that has grown between two participants in a reality-TV-style documentary series, but it also, implicitly,

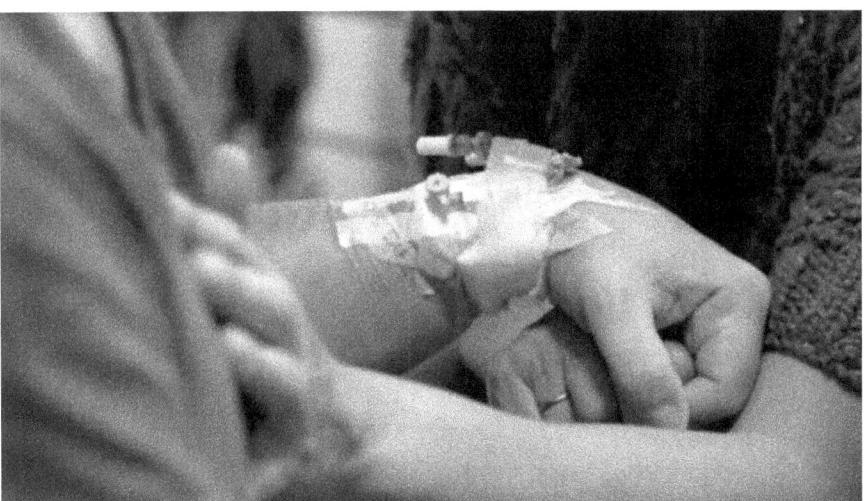

Figure 1.4 Lou comforts Andy, *My Last Summer* (Love Productions for Channel 4, 2014).

represents kinaesthetically and symbolically the connection between viewer and subject of the autopathography. The image of silent closeness brings to mind Heath and Skirrow's assertion that

> the subject of television is a citizen in a world of communication; he or she is called – and occupied – there, for that world. Immediacy, intimacy and mass communication: television here and now, for me personally, for me as the unity of everyone. (1977: 56).

We are held within that tender embrace, part of it.

As it did in the 1960s and 1970s, so does the television autopathography of the twenty-first century emphasise subject agency (enabling dying people to tell their own stories in a direct way) as both allowing the dying to 'take back control' of their lives and speak to the viewing public, becoming informal death educators. While *My Last Summer* achieves this through its intimate reality-TV-style form, the 2017 BBC2 documentary *A Time to Live* (tx. 17/5/17) is structured around twelve sets of talking heads in which the only voices heard are those of the programme maker Sue Bourne (off camera) and twelve people who are living with a terminal diagnosis. It's striking that in an interview to accompany the broadcast of the programme on BBC Radio Four's *Woman's Hour* (tx. 16/5/17), Bourne stated that this production decision was made because:

> I don't think we've listened to or heard the voices of people who are actually terminally ill, and we did a lot of pre-research and I talked to a lot of experts in palliative care and I said: 'I just want to speak to the people who are ill'. And they said: 'That's really good, because very often what happens is the person who's got the terminal diagnosis looks around at the grief that is going to be caused when they leave, when they die, and they start event managing to protect their families and their partners'. And they said: 'If you can just clear with clarity what's going on inside the heads of the dying person, that would be good'.

The suggestion here – that the dying have not previously been listened to or heard – is interesting in the context of the history which has been sketched out in this chapter. As we have seen, from at least the early 1960s onwards, British television has provided a regular platform for the dying to speak: for themselves, to their loved ones, to policy makers and to the wider viewing public. This raises something of a critical issue for me and for this book: if a programme maker such as Sue Bourne is unaware of this history, if it remains largely inaccessible to her (and other viewers) beyond its moment of broadcast or soon after, do the facts of television broadcasting mean that we constantly lose or forget these important articulations of the experience of dying. Are people – their stories, their voices, their faces, their lives – lost in the posthumous television archive until a historian or an archivist or a programme maker 'resurrects' them, brings them back to light and back to life? Surely, this is both a shame and a waste of these vital articulations of the experience of dying which might, were they to have been recorded for another kind of medium or platform, have remained more accessible and more readily revisitable? These are critical questions which this book will return to in its final section.

For now, though, we reflect on what we have learned about a previously under-explored genre of programming: the television autopathography. We have seen through the analysis in this chapter that television programme makers – from the producers of television panel and talk shows to the makers of television documentaries about death – have underlined the very ordinariness of dying experiences on television. Factual television in the UK depicts death and bereavement not as something exceptional and spectacular (as it might have been presented in contemporaneous television dramas) but as a ubiquitous part of life's experiences and as something that comes to us all. Techniques such as filming/interviewing subjects about death in the midst of quotidian settings and activities, and a shooting style which emphasises closeness to and intimacy with the subject, bring this fact to mind. Furthermore, narrative structures or moments of montage which express a multiplicity of experiences of death and allow multiple voices of the dying or the bereaved to be heard ensure that on UK television in the late twentieth and early twenty-first centuries there was no such thing as *death* on television, only *deaths*. Factual television's presentation of death and dying is a deeply personal one; its overall purpose is to try to capture the many ways we might face death – both our own deaths and those of the people we love – while accepting that what lies beyond death for those who die remains mysterious and out of our grasp (though as Part II of this book will show, television programming has also tried to imagine what this might be). The programming discussed in this chapter pictures us as part of a community made up of the dying and bereaved, not in order to terrify us about the closeness of death but to reassure us of the very ordinariness of death as a fact of life.

2

Signs of care: Assisted suicide on television

While the previous chapter explored death, dying and bereavement broadly in the late twentieth century on British television, we turn here to look at the television representation of a specific kind of death in more detail: assisted dying. As with the previous chapter, this analysis will be concerned with questions of representation (how is assisted dying depicted in television documentary) and also grapple with questions of intent: for whom is the assisted dying programme made? How does it work though the complex moral and ethical questions raised for those who seek, those who watch, and those who film an assisted death? Assisted death is chosen as a topic because it has a long and contentious televisual history. For many viewers, their only encounter with the ethical, philosophical and moral debates surrounding assisted dying, as well as its practicalities and processes, will have been via television. In the UK, an encounter with these issues and debates may have come via news coverage of the failed 2015 Assisted Dying Bill or the 2021 Private Members Bill in the House of Lords, or through the BBC1 drama *A Short Stay in Switzerland* (tx. 25/1/09), or while following the ongoing soap storylines of Jackson Walsh in *Emmerdale* (ITV Yorkshire, 1972–) in 2011, Hayley Cropper in *Coronation Street* (Granada for ITV, 1960–) in 2014, and Peggy Mitchell in *Eastenders* (BBC1, 1985–) in 2016 or even via the sitcom *Way to Go* (BBC3, 2013), with its homemade 'McFlurry of Death', made by the hapless owners of a makeshift assisted dying business. Just as Fran McInerney has argued that the topic of 'requested death' has been very present in films but not film studies (2014), and Leen Van Brussel has explored the way in which print media have treated the topic of assisted dying (2014), so we might see this chapter as bringing to critical light a subject which is already very present on television itself. I was first familiarised with the processes and debates surrounding assisted dying via a number of autopathographic documentaries made for the BBC in the UK and by other (mainly public service) broadcasters around the world in the 2010s: *The Suicide Tourist* (PBS, tx. 2/3/10); *Terry Pratchett: Choosing to Die* (BBC2, tx. 13/06/11); *Dignitas – la mort sur ordonnance* (RTS, tx. 17/2/11); *How to Die in Oregon* (HBO, tx. 23/1/11); *Four Corners: My Own Choice* (ABC, tx. 16/9/13); *How to Die: Simon's Choice* (BBC2, tx. 10/2/16). These documentaries, and the television programming on assisted dying that preceded them in the UK, are the focus of this chapter, both in its analysis of these programmes and in the chapter's discussion of the debates and discourses about care, death and dying that have surrounded their production and broadcast, drawing on interviews with some of their key programme makers in the UK. This is not an exhaustive trawl through the history of assisted dying representation on television, but rather a critical illumination of key programmes in this history. The chapter ultimately proposes that we see a number of caring relationships on, through, and in relation to these autopathographies of assisted death, beyond their revelation of the relationship between medical practitioner and patient – we see the programme makers' care for their subjects, the necessary self-care of the production team working on these programmes and, crucially, care for the television audience evidenced by the assisted dying documentary.

The research conducted for this book shows us the importance of television (particularly in a public service context, as in the UK and elsewhere) in working through and worrying at pressing social concerns of the day, as well as in raising awareness about broader moral, emotional and ethical issues around death and dying. While the previous chapter discussed the public service impetus of death-related programming at the end of the twentieth and beginning of the twenty-first centuries, the more contemporary documentaries which are the main focus of this chapter are evidence of television's *ongoing* role as a medium of care, as it explores these issues and provokes dialogue, debate, conversation and thought about all kinds of dying experiences. This shows that the attitude of care towards the television audience isn't lost in the era of post-broadcast television,[1] aligning with Holdsworth and Lury's position that 'television in certain instances . . . is a "caring technology"' (2016: 190). Whereas their focus is on the 'small pleasures' of television in its caring role (particularly pleasures produced for the very young and very old), I suggest that television's provision of information about, and exposure to, that which worries or upsets us can also be seen as providing care for a broad range of viewers. This linking of the public service ethos with the idea of care is acknowledged in what Holdsworth, Lury and Tweed call the 'often neglected terrain of the "public good" of public service television' (2020: 4). Of course, a counter argument might accuse such programmes of sensationalism and exploitation, or even propose that television works to make 'safe' or 'comfortable' difficult subjects. There is, then, an underlying worry in the discourse surrounding these programmes that exposing audiences to the practices and processes of assisted dying on television might precipitate an increase in those seeking or supporting this kind of death. This figures those 'at risk' of potentially being persuaded of the benefits of an assisted death by a television programme (both the very ill, those facing the pain and indignity of a terminal illness, and their friends and family) as 'vulnerable' viewers without the 'media savvy' to evaluate the coverage of this subject (Holdsworth, Lury and Tweed examine this kind of underestimation of the television viewer in the introduction to their recent collection on care on/in/around the media (ibid.: 9–10)). In this chapter, I trace these anxieties about the vulnerability of audiences, alongside an exploration of care for the documentary subject, viewer and programme maker throughout the history of television broadcasting.

A suitable case for television? The history of assisted dying on British television

Before moving on to discuss the contemporary television documentaries at the heart of this chapter, it is worth pausing to look at the history of the treatment of assisted dying on TV; this contextualises the analysis that follows and carries over the discussion of twentieth-century television as death-focused cultural forum from the previous chapter. While the analysis in the rest of the chapter looks at programming from all over the world, we focus here specifically on the introduction of this topic in UK television as a case study, as well as those programmes which were made elsewhere but available to UK viewers in this period. Unsurprisingly, given the findings of the archival research in Chapter 1, in the UK we can trace the topic of assisted dying through the history of the panel show, as a subject of the ongoing serious documentary series such as *Man Alive* and *Everyman*, as a contentious issue explored by both sides of the euthanasia debate in programmes made by the BBC's Community Programme Unit, in a variety of programme forms which seek to examine the legal processes behind various bids to decriminalise assisted death, and in autopathographies of a single person seeking an assisted death, the direct precursor to the documentaries at the heart of this study. This BBC-centric history figures public service broadcasting as a system which sought to care for its viewers by providing 'balanced' explorations of the topic of assisted dying. It is a history of programming which acknowledges the legal, medical and moral complexities of the subject, and in which care for the viewer is both expressed as compassion for those seeking an assisted death as a way out of pain and indignity and as care for those who might be made vulnerable by a change in the legal status of euthanasia.

The first extended discussion of assisted dying on UK television was on the psychologically focused panel programme, *Lifeline*. The episode, 'The Right to Die' (BBC, tx. 16/4/59), was broadcast late on a Thursday evening in April 1959, and featured a debate between an unnamed consultant psychiatrist, C. K. MacDonald (chairman of the Euthanasia Society), the liberal Protestant minister the Reverend Leslie Weatherhead, and the Right Reverend G. P. Dwyer, then Roman Catholic Bishop of Leeds. The BBC billed this as a discussion of the following in the *Radio Times*:

> If you were suffering from a fatal, incurable, and painful illness, should you be allowed to ask a doctor to kill you by some painless method in order to shorten your sufferings? As the law stands, any person who deliberately ends his own life is guilty of suicide and any person who helps him, no matter how mercifully, is guilty of murder.

It is striking that while *Lifeline* was not a part of the BBC's religious broadcasting output, the topic of assisted dying is still treated as a matter of religious debate in this programme. Initially described in the *Radio Times* as a 'series of programmes dealing with the psychological and moral problems of our time', *Lifeline* rarely featured members of the clergy in its discussion of wide-ranging topics such as homosexuality, psychopathy, the psychological impact of plastic surgery and the efficacy of corporal punishment, but this episode on assisted dying did. We should not assume, however, that this led to a wholly anti-assisted dying stance in the programme, although the Rt Rev. Dwyer represented the Catholic church's absolute rejection of euthanasia in his contribution, stating that legalising assisted death would be the 'most retrograde step possible' (Anon., 1959).[2] On the other hand, however, the inclusion of Rev. Leslie Weatherhead on the panel is a particularly interesting one. Weatherhead was becoming an outspoken supporter of assisted dying, who wrote in his 1965 book, *The Christian Agnostic*,

> I sincerely believe that those who come after us will wonder why on earth we kept a human being alive against his own will, when all the dignity, beauty and meaning of life had vanished . . . I, for one, would

> be willing to give a patient the Holy Communion and stay with him while a doctor, whose responsibility I should thus share, allowed him to lay down his useless body and pass in dignity and peace into the next phase of being. (1965: 187)

During the programme, Weatherhead stated that he was '100 per cent with the Euthanasia Society' (Anon., 1959), aligning himself with the views of his fellow panellist C. K. MacDonald and therefore providing something of a counterbalance to Dwyer's absolute rejection of euthanasia on moral and theological grounds. The unnamed doctor on the panel, who was himself suffering from an incurable disease, said that he had often contemplated suicide as an end to his own suffering but that he had resisted this on the grounds of his faith. According to the National Catholic Welfare Conference News Service which reported on this episode to colleagues back in the United States, the debate was concluded by a consultant psychiatrist who stated that doctors must continue to fight against illness and pain 'to the last extremity' and that 'the doctor who didn't recognise that the preservation of life was his highest goal was on a slippery slope' (ibid.). Underlying this reporting there is an anxiety about what bringing this topic onto television might achieve for its audience, a fear of 'normalising' assisted death by situating debate about it in the home (via television), as well as an assertion that the anti-euthanasia stance represented by the Catholic church must be validated by its treatment by the BBC. Ultimately, it seems that this late-1950s panel show was uncontroversial in its conclusion that assisted dying was a worrying and undesirable practice (at least according to this partisan reporting on the programme), but nevertheless *Lifeline* allowed important voices of dissent on this topic to be heard on television in the 1950s.

In the following decades, long-running current affairs series returned to the topic again and again. *Man Alive* featured two episodes on assisted dying, 'The Mercy Killers' (BBC2, tx. 29/6/66) and 'The Right Time to Die' (BBC2, tx 1/3/72), both of which focused on the decisions faced by doctors during end-of-life/critical illness care. 'The Right Time to Die' was reshown again six months after its initial broadcast, following an unprecedented audience response, and some of these audience members were interviewed by Jeremy James for an addition to the original episode. This further confirms that television was operating as a cultural forum for death-related topics in the late twentieth century, as explored in the previous chapter, and that the broadcaster's care for its viewers might be demonstrated by providing opportunities for them to explore their thoughts, feelings and beliefs on this topic. The *Everyman* episode 'The Last Right' (BBC1, tx. 30/12/79) intermingled scenes from Brian Clark's 1978 play *Whose Life is it Anyway?*, an adaptation of his earlier ITV television play from 1972,[3] which explored a paralysed sculptor's struggle to convince hospital staff that he should have the right to choose to die, with real-world stories from those facing end-of-life decisions. *Everyman* also returned to this subject much later in 'The Trial of Dr Death' (BBC1, tx. 23/11/97), which followed the trial of controversial doctor Jack Kevorkian who had helped more than fifty people to commit suicide in the United States, defended by his lawyer Geoffrey Fieger. Finally, *Panorama* also tackled this subject in the documentary 'Whose Death is it Anyway?' (BBC1, tx. 6/3/95), which examined the concept of 'living wills' and whether doctors should respect the wishes of the seriously ill who want to die. In these documentaries, an exploration of the topic of end-of-life care was interwoven with a concern with the BBC's care for their viewers in handling a 'difficult' subject with sensitivity and balance.

As with the death-focused programming discussed in the previous chapter, the BBC's Community Programme Unit also offered an important space for opinion on both sides of the euthanasia debate to be heard, in keeping with its aim to 'give voice to groups of people under-represented by the BBC ... [introducing] difficult subjects to the broadcast agenda' (Henderson, 2019: 27). Arguably, then, an ethos of care underpinned the establishment of the CPU, in that giving 'voice to the voiceless' might be seen precisely as an act of care for viewer and programme-making participant alike. In the 1970s, the CPU's first series, *Open Door* (BBC2, 1974–1983), had a remit to produce single-issue programmes made by special interest groups that had applied to take considerable editorial control of an edition of the programme (with oversight from BBC producers).[4] In its first year, a film entitled 'The Good Death' made by the Voluntary Euthanasia Society (BBC2, tx. 20/5/74) made up half of an *Open Door* episode[5] and promoted the society's cause; later, in the following decade, the series *Split Screen* (BBC2, 1986–1989) allowed the Voluntary Euthanasia Society back onto television in a series which was designed to air two opposing (and often controversial) points of view. The episode, 'People Should Have the Right to Choose to Die' (BBC2, tx. 7/7/86), featured two films made by the VES and Dr Colin Currie, an Edinburgh-based consultant geriatrician, and was described in Laurie Taylor's introduction to the programme as an alternative to people firing opinion back and forth at each other across a studio in the panel programme. While Dr Currie's film is an impassioned plea from a charismatic doctor for the rights of older people to independent living and compassionate hospice care, the VES film assembles a series of personal testimonies from high-profile supporters of assisted dying (Ludovic Kennedy, the Reverend Lord Soper), 'ordinary people' wishing for an assisted death, and Dr Pieter Admiraal, a doctor from the Netherlands who had become one of the world's leading experts on physician-assisted suicide. As with the panel programme discussed above, the appearance of balance in the treatment of this subject was paramount in the BBC's intent; it proposed two alternate versions of end-of-life care, and, by extension, demonstrated both the VES's and Dr Currie's care for the television viewer who might be vulnerable to pressure from either opposing side of the debate. The CPU's final exploration of the topic of assisted dying was in the series *Counterblast* (BBC2, 1997–2001) which once again gave a single contributor the opportunity to voice their opinion on a controversial subject. 'Journey to Death' (BBC2, tx. 6/5/98) concluded *Counterblast*'s second series with a film made by Professor Ilora Finlay, a hospice medical director and specialist in palliative care vehemently opposed to assisted dying who proposed that the fear of death is what leads people to believe that an assisted death is their only option, and that patients' distress can be at least partially alleviated by addressing their fears directly. We can see, then, that across the thirty-two-year period that the CPU was in operation at the BBC, it allowed both sides of the euthanasia debate to be explored on British television.

While the innovations in television documentary brought about by the Community Programme Unit enabled impassioned contributors to 'tell their own stories' about assisted dying (or the reasons for their opposition to it), shifting the topic away from the standard panel/discussion programme towards an 'access TV' format, the BBC also played with the presentation of studio-based debate in the 1970s in the stand-alone programme *A Suitable Case for Killing* (BBC2, tx. 8/2/75). Producer Tam Fry created a ninety-minute drama/studio discussion programme that explored the story of Dr Geertruida Postma, the Dutch doctor whose 'mercy killing' of her own mother, Margina Grevelink, led to her being tried for the crime of committing euthanasia in 1973; this case became a focal point for those wishing to legalise euthanasia in the Netherlands. This stand-alone programme was part verbatim re-enactment of Dr Postma's trial based on the translated court transcripts (for the first half-hour of the programme) and part studio-based discussion (with an assembled group of campaigners,[6] medical practitioners,[7] clergy,[8] lawyers[9] and people who themselves faced the problems of dealing with seriously ill relatives[10] who were positioned as a live audience for the trial in the first part of the programme).

Figure 2.1 Studio trial set-up, *A Suitable Case for Killing* (BBC2, tx. 8/2/75).

Opening with some direct testimony from Dr Postma herself who explained her own experience of giving a lethal injection to her seriously incapacitated mother, this unusual programme format enabled a lengthy exploration of the emotional impact of administering the lethal injection for Dr Postma, as a daughter and a GP. This was presented through the filmed interview and Gwen Watford's performance as Dr Postma in the trial re-enactment. The programme also considered the moral, ethical and legal implications of Dr Postma's lenient and suspended sentence in both the summing-up of the judge (Geoffrey Chater) in the dramatised trial and in the hour-long studio discussion,[11] and what a change in the law would do to the future of geriatric and hospice care in the UK. The Brechtian device of situating the panellists as a diegetic audience for the dramatic re-enactment, who could be seen taking notes and later responding to the performance in the studio, sought to encourage the viewer at home to view the dramatised section of the programme with some detachment, to remain active and questioning audience members invited to 'weigh up' the evidence before them (just as the actors in the court scene and the studio-based audience-participants had done). This programme thus demonstrated a public service ethos in its approach to the topic of assisted death on television, with the BBC emphasising care, balance and impartiality throughout.

None of the above could be considered straightforward autopathographies, but the autopathography of the assisted death does not simply begin with the more contemporary documentaries at the heart of this chapter. On 20 October 1994, the Dutch public service channel Ikon broadcast *Dood op Verzoek/Death on Request*, the autopathography of Cees van Wendel de Joode, his wife, Antoinette, and their doctor, Dr Wilfred van Oijen, as Cees sought, and received, an assisted death due to the rapid deterioration of his physical and mental health because of motor neurone disease. Produced by Maarten Nederhost, this intimate documentary caused huge controversy in the Netherlands and beyond as the very first programme to show an assisted death on screen, despite the fact that this practice was still only barely allowable by law in the Netherlands (see Sutcliffe, 1995; Sharkey, 1995). The documentary, which focuses on the last couple of months of Cees's life, as well as his death, took great care to explore the medical and legal processes that accompanied assisted death in this particular national context. It both explored the emotional impact on Dr van Oijen of his involvement in multiple assisted deaths, as well as Cees's and Antoinette's experience of Cees's illness, and the manner of his dying. After its initial airing by Ikon, the documentary went on to be sold for broadcast in twenty-seven other countries, reaching a total of thirteen million viewers worldwide (Henley, 1995). In the UK, Stephen Lambert at the BBC bought *Dood op Verzoek/Death on Request*, and with some reframing (an English voiceover, some adjustment of its music to suit 'British sensibilities'), presented it as a high-profile episode of the first series of *Modern Times* (BBC2, 1995–2015), broadcast on Wednesday 15 March 1995, at 9 pm on BBC2.

Of all the programmes discussed in this book, this documentary caused the most controversy on its broadcast (in practically every country it was screened in). In the UK, even before it had been shown, the anti-euthanasia group ALERT campaigned against its broadcast; Maggie O'Kane in *The Guardian* reported that anti-euthanasia organisations had begun referring to *Death on Request* as a 'snuff film' (1995) in the run-up to the broadcast, and a letter was sent to *The Times* (see Twycross et al., 1995) condemning the BBC for showing the film. The MP for Broxbourne, Marion Roe, one of the signatories of this letter, also tabled an early-day motion criticising the BBC for showing the film, signed by 106 MPs who had all yet to see it, and Roe spoke in Parliament, chastising the BBC for 'failing to give a "complete and balanced" account of euthanasia in the Netherlands' (Roe, 1995). In response to both the letter in *The Times*, and to Roe's early-day motion, the pro-assisted dying campaigner Ludovic Kennedy complained in a letter to the same newspaper that both 'not only deplored the BBC's screening of the [documentary] . . . before they had even seen it, but made scaremongering comments on what to expect if voluntary euthanasia was ever permitted here' (Kennedy, 1995). The Voluntary Euthanasia Society, of which Kennedy was Vice President, also subsequently took out adverts in *The Times* and *The Guardian* the day after the broadcast to recruit new members. The handling of the documentary and concomitant criticism of Dutch law in the UK

Parliament also prompted an angry response from the Dutch ambassador, Jan-Herman Van Roijen, who wrote to all 106 signatories of Roe's early-day motion to correct their misunderstandings of the law in the Netherlands (Beesley, 1995). Meanwhile, various Christian faith groups also took great exception to the broadcast. The Vatican had pronounced the film a 'horrifying spectacle' (Henley, 1995) when it had been shown in Italy, and in the UK the Catholic Media Office stated that it was 'wrong to have that kind of public accessibility' to the matter of assisted dying, while the Venerable George Austin, Archdeacon of York, called the documentary 'voyeuristic' and the BBC 'sick' for broadcasting it (Brooks, 1995). After watching the broadcast, Peter H. Millard, Professor of Geriatric Medicine, wrote to the *British Medical Journal* with severe misgivings about the screening of the programme in the UK, stating: 'Have no doubt. This is propaganda. The BBC's aim is clear' (Millard, 1995: 746). This claim of 'propaganda', or the failure to offer 'balance', which was one of Roe's key criticisms, is particularly interesting in the context of the wider history acknowledged in the opening of this chapter. As we have seen, the BBC made programmes that worked hard to offer balance on the subject of assisted dying within their own bounds, as well as an even balance of programming that took a particular position for and against euthanasia.

While politicians and clergy made pronouncements against the showing of *Death on Request* before its broadcast, more thoughtful responses came from reviewers and journalists who picked up on the pressing questions about what Peter Barnard in the *Radio Times* described as the issue of 'what should and should not be televised' (1995). Bryan Appleyard in *The Independent* found the documentary 'well-made and moving', but then stated:

> But something is obviously wrong. What is wrong is that we are watching and that means that, through each stage of these harrowing proceedings, a camera crew was looking and listening, checking the light and sound levels even as the poison was flooding through van Wendel's veins ... And when Mr. van Wendel lay on his bed for the last time, did he not wonder about the propriety of this, about the strangeness of the fact that his life was ending under the gaze of a BBC [sic] camera. (1995)

Appleyard questioned the presence of death more broadly on television in this review, proposing that the medium 'is primarily about entertainment and seriousness can easily become faked, ghoulish' (ibid.). His argument, then, was that television gives a false impression of the experience of death on screen ('It is a more effective liar than any other medium precisely because it seems so like the truth') and that it covers up our culpability for that death taking place before us:

> Watching *Death on Request* or an execution on television is not the same as being there. So much is left out – the smells, the touch, the atmosphere, the eye contacts, our own participation. All these contribute to the occasion, implicating us in the proceedings whether we like it or not. (ibid.)

The series editor of *Modern Times*, Stephen Lambert, challenged Appleyard's reading of the programme by firstly stating that Cees and Antoinette had both elected to take part in the programme, and that the documentary had been made to contribute to the debate on euthanasia (indeed, the broadcast was directly followed in the UK by an edition of *The Late Show* (BBC2, 1989–1995) which was, in essence, a return to the panel discussion format with all the 'usual suspects' present from both sides of the debate).[12] He also, interestingly, emphasised a caring relationship and an intimacy that had been built between the documentary's subjects and its crew, stating that Antoinette had only remembered that the crew were there 'because she heard sobbing in the corridor' which was 'the cameraman giving vent to his feelings' (Lambert, 1995). This sense of the film as a tender, empathic and intimate documentary was also expressed in other broadsheet reviews. Allison Pearson in *The Independent* claimed it was 'edited for contemplation rather than for shock' (1995), John Naughton in *The Observer* reported watching in 'awed silence, for it brought one face to face with death in a manner almost unknown on television' (1995) and Ian Mayes in *The Guardian* described the programme in the following terms:

> [A] remarkable achievement, holding the viewer in an almost unbearable intimacy with what, probably for most of us, is an almost unthinkable situation. It did this in a way in which no other medium could, and without provoking feelings of indecent intrusion or voyeurism, providing a sense not of watching but engagement ... Its strength, rather than its weakness, was its concentration on one case with little contextual reference to the broader debate. It settled for saying this is the reality at the heart of it all. (1995)

The suggestion here that television had produced an engagement, an implied ethical or caring relationship created in the nexus between subject,

Figure 2.2 Cees's death, *Dood op Verzoek/Death on Request* (Ikon, tx. 20/10/94).

programme maker and viewer at home, which 'no other medium could' is interesting and pertinent to the analysis that follows. This aligns with my own reading of this programme's impact, from the mournful and contemplative montage which establishes a domestic closeness between the viewer and both doctor and patient in the opening moments of this documentary, to the filming of Cees's death which emphasises a tender closeness between the bodies on screen: Cees's dying and dead body, the bodies of Antoinette and Dr Oijen as they cling to each other for comfort, the off-screen body of one of the camera operators,[13] squeezed in down the side of Cees's bed, and the body of the viewer watching at home.

This moment of intimate televisual kinaesthesia[14] draws all of these bodies together: as Dr Oijen asks Antoinette 'Does this seem wrong now?', huddling close together at Cees's bedside, she replies 'No. I'd imagined it differently, but this has been beautiful', possibly speaking for the viewer experiencing this most intimate of moments, as well as for herself. The domestic setting of *Death on Request* thus brought assisted death from one home into another, creating the intimate engagements noted above and explored in relation to the contemporary documentaries at the heart of this chapter below.

Caring through and in television production: contemporary autopathographies of assisted dying

In Vivian Sobchack's seminal 1984 essay on the representation of death in the documentary film, she explores the filming of both violent and natural death. Of the latter, she argues that the 'humane stare' of the documentarist's camera may 'settle, rather than fix itself [on the dying subject] . . . inscribing the intimacy and respect and sympathy it feels with those who die in its vision' (1984: 297). As the adjectives in the latter part of this quotation suggest, she defines the relationship between filmmaker and subject in the filming of natural death as an implicitly caring one and explores the ethical positions of those filming it. Bill Nichols qualifies Sobchack's classification of the humane gaze of the documentarist's camera on the subject dying a 'natural death' by arguing that it only 'occurs in cases where death cannot be prevented by intervention' (1991: 86). Obviously, there are some shifts to make from Sobchack's and Nichols's discussions when considering the television documentary about assisted dying. These are not unpreventable deaths (though the inevitable 'natural' deaths of the subjects are closer at hand than most), and the filming of these deaths and the subjects moving towards them focuses on 'intimacy and respect and sympathy', as we have seen already in the above example of *Dood op Verzoek/Death on Request*, but is implicitly different from the filming of natural death as outlined by Nichols and Sobchack. Implications of complicity with the act of assisted dying have to be carefully worked through by the programme maker, and the act of consent taking is subsequently repeatedly highlighted within autopathographies of assisted deaths. This is also, of course, not film, but television, a medium which potentially intensifies the intimacies of the death documentary by bringing them up close to the viewer in a domestic reception context: via television, it is possible to stumble upon the intimate image of someone taking their life as part of an evening's regular television viewing, which perhaps underlies some of the anxieties about broadcasting this subject that were explored above. This already intimate sub-genre of documentary filmmaking thus shifts into an increased sense of intimacy through the implicitly close relationship between the viewer and the text that is inscribed into television programming.

There is a growing field of critical literature that examines film and television as sites for the exploration of ethics and ethical looking relations. As Downing and Saxton argue, 'While there is no established body of theory that might be described as "ethical gaze theory", the idea that ethics is an optics through which we habitually view and conceptualise is a persuasive one' (2010: 2) (see also Watson and Arp (2011) and Aaron (2007)). Downing and Saxton thus draw on Michele Aaron's suggestion that 'looking in cinema is never innocent or neutral but always complicit and thus ethically implicated' (ibid.: 4). This is an argument that will be familiar to anyone who has studied documentary and, particularly, Bill Nichols's work on the filmmaker's ethical or moral point of view. When looking at the assisted dying documentary, Nichols's delineation of axiographics, 'an attempt to explore the implantation of values in the configuration of space, in the construction of a gaze, and in the relation of the observer to the observed' (1991: 78), is particularly significant. When the topic of a documentary is the planned death of its central subject, understanding the ethical questions surrounding consent is critical, and the programme maker must construct an axiographics of compassionate, caring neutrality that reflects the position of the medical caregivers who act in relation to the subject. Therefore, the first 'sign of care' which takes place off camera with the production team and then, repeatedly, on camera with the medical team in every one of the autopathographies of assisted death is the taking of consent. The 2011 Swiss documentary *Dignitas: la mort sur ordonnance* begins with a shot outside the Dignitas facility in Zurich where a voice can be heard asking whether something will taste bitter. We are therefore aware straightaway that this documentary begins *in medias res*, or rather, at the end of the process of seeking an assisted death, though for a brief moment we are held outside that scene. As an edit then takes us inside the facility where a woman lies on a bed, next to an older woman who is kneeling beside her, holding a drink, the first woman jokily says, 'Ask me if I want to die', to which the second answers, 'Yes, of course'. There then follows a stream of questions that check the woman's identity and her desire to take her own life (she is the French theorist, translator and author Michèle Causse). These are all presented in the same static medium shot, the camera lingering on this careful round of consent taking. This moment, perhaps shocking in its procedural everydayness in the taking of consent for such an extraordinary action, is discussed here not because it is unusual but because it is typical and indicative of any number of pivotal scenes in the assisted dying documentary. *Dignitas: la mort sur ordonnance* thus begins with this act of consent taking, positioning the camera in a neutral, intimate, but not intrusive, position. While Causse's jollity makes this scene tonally unusual in some ways, the camera's steady taking in of this exchange of consent demonstrates its centrality in this sub-genre of documentary programme making.

The self-conscious opening of *Dignitas: la mort sur ordonnance* also speaks to the fact that a number of theorists, including Calvin Pryluck (2005) and Andrew Belsey (1992), have noted the congruence of media and medical ethics around the taking of consent. While what is depicted on screen is the taking of medical consent, there is an implicit story being told here about the subject's consent to being part of a documentary. When Sir Terry Pratchett asks, at the beginning of the BBC documentary *Terry Pratchett: Choosing to Die*, 'How do you guarantee sincere consent [in an assisted death] and what happens to those that get left behind?', he might equally be discussing the consent of the documentary subject, as well as that of those requesting an assisted death. In the UK context, the programme makers interviewed for this research who had made documentaries on this subject talked about the importance of the BBC's Producer Guidelines, and how crucial they were in ensuring that contributors were treated honestly, with respect and with care, particularly around the taking of informed consent, and in relation to their care for the subjects' families following the production and broadcast of their documentaries and the death of their loved ones. Charlie Russell, director of *Terry Pratchett: Choosing to Die*, argued that in all documentaries the taking of consent is careful and considered, but that they were more mindful about consent taking in this context.[15] Rowan Deacon, director of *How to Die: Simon's Choice*, also discussed how the process of consent taking began with extended conversations with the BBC's legal team and their head of editorial policy, before the production team even approached their subjects.[16] It is subsequently clear that these processes are then reflected in scenes of extended consent taking in the documentaries themselves and that these scenes can be understood as signs of care within the programme.

There are many ways in which care for the documentary subjects is in evidence in these programmes, but this chapter focuses on two themes to explore the concept of care in more detail: first, the idea of the giving of a voice to the dying subject as a form of care and, secondly, the care of the subject's family in the documentaries and after their production, and care in and through their bereavement. In relation to this first theme, we can see the production of the assisted dying documentary as part of the palliative care of the dying subject, in which they (and their family and friends) work through their thoughts and feelings about their approaching death and the process of assisted dying on camera. These documentaries are made in the unusual situation in which their participants are acutely aware of the 'timetable' of their death, and their direct address to camera in a 'confessional' mode allows them to explore their feelings about this. For example, in *How to Die: Simon's Choice*, Simon Binner discusses the progressive worsening of his health – he has motor neurone disease – in a series of interviews and self-filmed voxpops throughout the documentary. He talks about the emotional impact of falling over while playing with his dog, and later interviews speak of his worsening mood as he struggles to cope with his loss of independence. Simon's wife, Debbie, also works through her feelings about the choices Simon is making about his death on camera; when discussing the earlier death of her daughter from cancer, and the palliative care that led up to her death, she speaks directly to the camera, while sitting in her car:

> Losing a child, there's nothing worse than that but there was something … more natural? I don't know. In that … there was still hope with my daughter, right up to the end … and I guess there's a bit of anger in me that, you know, why can't Simon just do that? You know, your life closes in when you get ill, I think, but we still really enjoyed watching telly together, or eating together, and it's those little things that become so … So, maybe, there's a bit of me that thinks, 'Oh, why can't you, you know, do that?'

This language, the sense of grief and uncertainty that it conveys, suggests that Debbie is actively working through her thoughts and feelings about Simon's death on camera. Naomi Richards (2013), Michele Aaron (2019, 2020) and Emma Wilson have all explored the idea of filmmaking as offering a kind of palliation, with Wilson seeing it as 'a space of working out, of anticipatory engagement with mortality, with our own death and the deaths of others, and with the consuming emotions that attach to loss' (2012: 13). It is important to acknowledge, therefore, that while assisted dying often stands in opposition to palliative care in the debates that surround it, as we have seen in the numerous panel and campaigning programmes discussed in the opening of this chapter, palliation actually begins at an earlier point for the subject of the assisted dying documentary, and programme making becomes a key aspect of this.

Allowing the subject to speak and giving voice to their lived experiences of approaching an assisted death is particularly highlighted in the autopathography of assisted dying. Sequences of Cees van Wendel de Joode struggling to talk and type punctuate *Death on Request*, and in *How to Die: Simon's Choice* the loss of Simon Binner's voice to the motor neurone disease that is killing him becomes a major thematic component of the documentary. The documentary begins with the sound of Simon's voiceover footage of his funeral (or what we will come to understand as his voice, performed by the voiceover actor Simon Nock, who reads Simon's words from a letter to his wife, Debbie). This immediately draws our attention to the documentary's ability to allow Simon to speak, even beyond the time of his death. During the early parts of the documentary we see him frustratedly struggle to talk and then to communicate with his family using an electronic talker, and later we see him involved in the selection of the actor who will provide his voiceover throughout the documentary; these moments, and the sequences when we see the voiceover artist reading Simon's words in a darkened recording studio, consciously draw our attention to the way in which being involved in the documentary gives a voice to the dying subject who is going through the process of losing theirs, first through ill-health and then through death. Indeed, we see this right at the end of Simon's life, where he uses his iPhone to play a message to his family at the moment of his death. As his friends and family gather round his bedside, Simon is seen playing a sound file on his phone, resting it on his stomach and smiling at those around him as they listen:

> Hi, Debbie. It's Simon here. I've loved you very, very much, Debbie. I haven't deserved you, or Hannah or Zoe. Such loving and caring young ladies and I've been such a grumpy Gruffalo for much of the time . . . The one blessing of a slow decline is that we've had time to speak about things over ten long months, not like losing me in a car smash. We've really said everything that needs to be said.

His words in this moment speak of being able to say all there is to be said, of he and Debbie having been given the opportunity to work through their feelings for each other and what was happening to Simon via a series of conversations. In this sequence in the documentary, the use of the voiceover artist to speak Simon's words was added in post-production; on the sound clip Simon played on his phone in Zurich, his daughters read the letter but because the sound quality was poor, and to give an added coherence to the use of the voiceover, it was dubbed over later. This is a poignant moment that highlights what John Ellis means when he says that 'documentary characters speak knowing that they will be heard and act knowing that they will be seen', concluding that 'documentary material should therefore be seen as a series of attempted communications' (2012: 103). Here, the programme becomes inextricably linked with Simon's own attempts to both speak in his moment of dying and beyond his death, and to mark his passing through letters and recordings, a kind of public memento mori or what Naomi Richards calls 'a prophylactic against death' (2013: 196). When the recording comes to

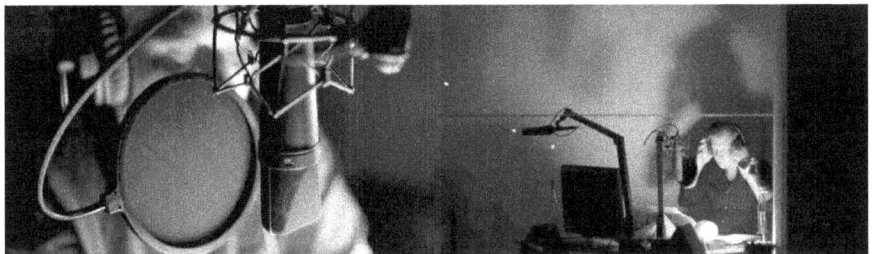

Figure 2.3 Simon Nock, end of the voiceover, *How to Die: Simon's Choice* (BBC2, tx. 10/2/16).

an end, and the voiceover artist stops speaking, Simon releases the medication which will kill him and the screen cuts to black to register his dying. Following this, the documentary cuts to the darkened studio where Simon Nock, the voiceover artist, removes his headphones and leaves the booth he has been working in.

In this place, the static pause on an empty room draws attention to the importance of speaking and being heard in the documentary: for Simon, participating in the programme has clearly given him a voice at a crucial moment in his life and death. Many of these conversations would, of course, have taken place without a camera crew present, but through the documentary Simon and Debbie must talk through thought processes, disagreements and feelings for the camera, increasing communication between them and capturing each stage of this process for posterity. Rowan Deacon, the programme's director, discussed watching this scene in the post-edit screening with Debbie and remembered Debbie's friend who attended the screening with her, asking whether she was sure that she wanted to show this intensely private moment, to which Debbie replied that this moment 'wasn't just for me it was for the cameras as well . . . he was always public, you know'.

In interview, Deacon explicitly discussed the giving of a voice to her subject when talking about the casting of Simon Binner and his desire to take part in the programme:

> Rowan Deacon [RD]: Simon was up for it straight away. Simon was the kind of person – he'd been on telly before, a dating show in the '90s – he was just one of those people who was an exhibitionist, but in the nicest possible way . . . So immediately he thought, this was wonderful that there was this documentary crew that wanted to document his story. He also had only just been diagnosed with the worst thing you could imagine being diagnosed with, and . . .

> Simon's reasoning, as I later understood it ... [was] that he felt somehow it dignified a really undignified [situation] ... He felt it documented and ... stopped him from kind of shrinking. He wasn't the kind of person who would shrink into the corner and be the quiet person, that was what he feared, because losing his voice; it was the worst diagnosis for a man who was so exuberant and outgoing and I think it kind of filled a hole that having his body and his voice took away [made], if that makes sense ...
>
> Helen Wheatley [HW]: I guess there's lots of reasons why people might get involved from being a kind of a naturally brilliant exhibitionist person, to maybe being in a campaigning position – 'this is important and people should know about this'. And/or also a sense of creating some sort of memorial for themselves. Did you get a sense of any of those reasons for participating in Simon's case?
>
> RD: Probably the memorial, probably the legacy ... He definitely didn't do it for campaigning reasons, I think. I don't think he thought this film will change the law. I think he thought ...
>
> HW: It was a lot more personal than that ...
>
> RD: Yeah, I think he thought, the process of having my story documented is going to help me, I'm going through hell ... And I think he thought this is a good thing. This is a positive thing ... So I think it was a ... almost like a psychological decision for him.
>
> HW: Taking hold of the situation ...
>
> RD: Taking control, yeah maybe it was about that.

Similarly, when discussing one of the participants in *Terry Pratchett: Choosing to Die*, Charlie Russell stated,

> When it finally got very close to the day that [Peter Smedley] would kill himself, I just said, 'Should we be there? Do you want us to come along?' and Peter, I think, had been thinking about it for a while, he just implicitly got it and wanted his death to mean something.

For Russell and his subject then, making this death public, bringing it to light and giving the dying subject a voice, was also extremely important, but for different reasons. These documentaries allow their subjects to very consciously speak 'beyond the grave', either in an emotional register that enables them to speak directly to their family via television (as in *Simon's Choice*) or by giving a voice to their position on the perceived injustices of the current policies on assisted dying and therefore addressing policy makers and voters, as Peter does, even if obliquely, in *Terry Pratchett: Choosing to Die*. Again, both of these positions simultaneously relate to Michael Brennan's argument that the autopathography offers 'an apparent sense of agency, control and symbolic mastery' (2018: 108) to the dying subject, as discussed in the previous chapter.

As suggested above, these documentaries demonstrate an axiographics of intimacy in the conveyance of a caring or humane gaze on the dying subject and their friends and family. This demonstrates Bill Nichols's identification of an 'emphasis on the continuing proximity of camera and subject despite the encroachment of death and the direct acknowledgement of a human relationship between filmmaker and subject through dialogue and commentary' through the humane gaze (1991: 86). This intimacy is manifest in a number of ways in these television documentaries, and not only through footage shot specifically for the programme: for example, montages of home movie footage, that 'death-denying technology' par excellence according to Sandra M. Gilbert (2006: 219–20), reveal intimate moments which capture life and death, posthumously. *How to Die: Simon's Choice* ends with home movie footage of Simon dancing joyfully around his kitchen with his dog, for example. This interpolation of these found images, sometimes also supplied via montage sequences of family photographs as in poignant moments in *The Suicide Tourist*, creates a sense of intimacy in these documentaries, making the audience privy to private moments recorded for posterity in a variety of different contexts that bring the posthumous subject back to life.[17] There is also an image repertoire of shots that seek to affectively convey moments of intimacy, whether that be through close-ups of pained and/or

Figure 2.4 Holding hands, *Terry Pratchett: Choosing to Die* (BBC2, tx. 13/06/11).

crying faces speaking directly to camera, or, particularly poignantly, shots of hands clasped, stroking or letting go in moments that convey a deep sense of grief or loss.[18]

As discussed in the introduction, we see this in *Terry Pratchett: Choosing to Die*, as Peter Smedley says, 'My wife is very good at putting me to sleep by just stroking my hand'. In this moment we focus on a close-up of a tender, habitual, familiar act, just after Peter has taken the draft that will kill him. The image of hands entwined are the emblem of care here and in other documentaries, such as the PBS documentary *The Suicide Tourist* from 2010, and the shots that convey this to the audience at these poignant moments seek to represent a sense of care. Sometimes, care for the viewer and the subject is also conveyed by the removal of the intimate image, as in the cut to black at the end of Simon Binner's life, or in the removal of the camera (but not the sound recording equipment) to outside the house at the end of the documentary subject's life in HBO's *How to Die in Oregon*. However, more often, care for viewer and subject is expressed in images and moments of extreme intimacy in the assisted dying documentary.

What was most striking in the interviews I undertook with Rowan Deacon and Charlie Russell were the stories the documentarists told about their experience of caring both for their subjects and for themselves during the programme-making process. There is a brief moment that indicated this in *How to Die: Simon's Choice* where, unusually for this documentary, Rowan Deacon's voice is heard asking Simon from off camera 'Are you scared?' at his final 'going-away' party. This follows a failed suicide attempt at home, and an unexpected acceleration of the time frame of Simon's death. We hear in this moment both her concern for Simon, and also an element of personal fear and trepidation (we wonder if she is also scared, upset or worried?). This brings to mind the work of David Hesmondhalgh and Sarah Baker (2008) and Laura Grindstaff on the production of the reality talent show and the talk show, respectively, and the latter's proposal that television producers 'find themselves performing emotional labour while simultaneously struggling to distance themselves from its emotional effects, to make it just another aspect of the job' (2002: 133). This emotional work, and the self-care needed to cope with it, is also expressed in Bill Nicholls's acknowledgement that 'witnessing the act of dying ... places an acute emotional and ethical strain on the documentary filmmaker' (1991: 83). We see, during the course of these documentaries, programme makers caring for the dying and the bereaved, ceremonially marking deaths and helping to produce a lasting record of lives and manifesting a general sense of care and compassion in the process of producing of a documentary. For example, I was carefully told by both programme makers about the post-production care of the remaining friends and families of the documentary subjects, and, specifically, the emotional labour of the post-edit screening for the bereaved which both documentarists found difficult in different ways.

Both programme makers I interviewed talked about the production process as emotionally gruelling for them and their team from the very outset of conducting initial interviews. Rowan Deacon talked about the importance of sharing and debriefing on this work with a small team, and about its emotional impact:

> HW: How do you prepare for the initial work? You must have had lots of quite gruelling conversations.
> RD: Yeah, they were, they were actually ... So [these] were gruelling and they were long meetings and you often felt quite responsible for them having handed over all this information. And it was good that it was me and Lizzie [Kempton, associate producer], because we did a lot of talking about it afterwards, I think talking about it afterwards helped ... It would have been harder on our own. I honestly think that.

Similarly, Charlie Russell discussed the fact that on their documentary, this early interviewing had been done by a junior assistant producer, Rosy Marshall. Russell talked about the ways in which she was supported in this work:

> Charlie Russell [CR]: Rosy ... probably spent about six months talking to people on the phone and pretty much crying every day and Craig would support her in the office, and I would ring her up and keep talking it through and keep trying to help her. And she, because she'd done that first phone call, she then went to meet people and she shot little reccy tapes with people and just went very slowly. And surprisingly a huge number of people were ... up for filming if they were in that situation [of planning an assisted death], but you never knew really if they were.
> HW: You said that during this process of meeting people and setting up interviews, you had to support Rosy through doing that. Can you tell me a little more about in what ways you did this and what sort of support she needed?
> CR: The way that I work and a way a lot of people work in documentaries is not big teams, and that's sort of why we like it, and I think it's quite good to have someone who isn't me, be the first point of call

> and it will often be a woman, because they're more empathetic, if we're going to generalise, you know just good with people essentially. And Rosy was all that and very driven and determined and knew what it would entail and wanted to do it. And it was sort of just important for me to be on the end of a phone, or we met in London a couple of times, we went down to meet Terry, and just sort of talking it through, and I'm sort of being the counsellor to her and she's being the counsellor to them. In the same way that therapists you know have their own therapists. You're just trying to give an outlet so they can just talk it through.

There are obviously some revealing statements here about the emotional labour of documentary production, and the ways in which this labour is gendered, in particular. While Russell's account is still a story about collaboration and being part of a 'caring team', the initial gruelling work of lengthy interviews with the dying and the grieving is assigned to a young woman on the basis of her age and gender (as well as her particular interpersonal skills).

Both programme makers drew attention to the need to care for themselves and their production team throughout all stages of this process, not just in the early research process. For example, they were also very eloquent on the 'emotional' fallout at the end of production:

> RD: I think we finished the edit . . . and in the edit as well we were like got to make the story work, and you know, we've got to make this good, [this] became the distancing thing. And then we had a cut of the film and finally . . . there's a scene at the end where Simon does his little funny dancing with his dog Ralph and I sat in bed watching, because I had to check through before we sent it finally to the BBC, and I just wept. And I just wept and wept and wept, and it was the first time that I had . . . I think because the film was done . . . I mean the grief, because Simon was amazing, and we were in his life for a short time but quite an intense time.

Charlie Russell also talked at length about how therapy (for him) had been built into the programme-making process, after a previous experience of doing this following *Looking for Dad* (2008), his earlier BBC2 documentary about his father's death.

Finally, as well as caring for the production team during the process of filming and taking care of the dying subject as they work through their feelings about their approaching death, a clear duty of care for the bereaved is in evidence in all of these documentaries and was spoken about at length by their programme makers. We see those involved in the production of the documentary taking care of grieving friends and families on screen. This is particularly notable in *Terry Pratchett: Choosing to Die*, where the presence on camera of Pratchett and his assistant Rob Wilkins during Peter Smedley's death, and the implicit presence off screen of Charlie Russell behind the camera, pushes us to think about their relationship to Peter's widow, Christine, in this moment. Discussing the filming of this moment, Russell again points to the caring work of those making the film:

> CR: I was just very conscious of trying to maintain myself as physically small as possible when it was happening so that his last memories weren't a camera in his face and her memories of her husband dying wasn't us getting in there and getting the shot . . . I think they wanted us there and I think Christine wanted some friendly Brits who she knew and . . . You know, once he died, we put all the equipment down and left the room and when the time was right, I think Rob, Terry's assistant, got out a bottle of brandy and we all had a drink and toasted him with Christine and just gave Christine hugs essentially. And just, well, just really it was amazing they let us be there but also by that point we all knew her . . . Everyone was in tears . . . They were just an extraordinary couple so you just couldn't help but be in love with them and be desperately sad for what was happening.

It is striking that as in our first example of the autopathographic narrative of assisted dying, *Death on Request*, the programme maker recounts here both the need to be present but also to recede into the background of the room in which their subject is dying, to be 'physically small', and also to acknowledge the production of this documentary as an *emotional experience*.

As has already been explored, the assisted dying documentary also acts as a memento mori of a life and a death for the bereaved. In *How to Die: Simon's Choice*, Debbie is interviewed just before the closing scenes of the documentary, in a scene in which she acknowledges that she can remember very little of her trip to Zurich for Simon's death. Here we become aware of the potential power of the television programme to capture this moment for the person wracked and muddled by grief. Rowan Deacon spoke of her ongoing caring relationship with Debbie and the rest of Simon's family, both during the process of editing the film, as discussed above, but also following the broadcast:

> RD: We were very fond of Simon, but I can't pretend to be grieving in the way that his friends and family have lost him, but . . . I felt at one

stage before Debbie had seen the film, I think an element of guilt. I thought, because I think I knew then that the film was a strong film, and I think there was part of me of course that was pleased we'd made a strong film but that I'd stolen something from Debbie. I felt that her husband's death had allowed me to make a strong film and that was something ... I had to talk that through a lot, there was a kind of guilt, and I think that was why I was so anxious that she like it and the film was a positive thing. And that's ongoing. Debbie is still connected with us and that feeling of whether she wants to forget about the film or remember it ... you know, it doesn't just stop because the production has stopped.

Caring for the viewer: the persistence of television as cultural forum

Ultimately, the caring work of the assisted dying documentary is evidence of the persistence of television as a medium that seeks to work through life – and death – for its viewers, and, therefore, of the continuing relevance of Newcomb and Hirsch's idea of television as cultural forum (1983). The 'bringing to light' of this form of death might be seen as an act of care for the viewer themselves, or what Brian Winston calls 'the rhetoric of the public right to know' (2000: 128). Just as Jostein Gripsrud (2004), Milly Buonnano (2008), Graeme Turner (2009) and Helen Piper (2016) all argue that ideas of cultural responsibility and public service remain critical for broadcasters and viewers in the era of 'post-broadcast' television, so these documentaries might be seen as concrete examples of this. The rhetoric of 'working through' death has been applied to the presentation of death in almost all forms of art and culture but seems particularly apt when applied to television which literally brings the sight of death back into our homes. The structures of television, and particularly the interstitial material that surrounds each documentary, emphasises the act of care for the viewer in relation to assisted dying and the illnesses that lead people towards it. For example, we are directed to expect upset by the voiceover announcement that precedes *How to Die: Simon's Choice*, which dubs it 'an emotional documentary ... with scenes some viewers may find upsetting'. At the end of the broadcast, we are offered the opportunity to take part in an Open University debate about assisted dying (a bit like *The Late Show* debate that followed *Death on Request*) and are also directed towards the BBC's Action Line and information about motor neurone disease and bereavement. Rowan Deacon argued that following the broadcast of her documentary there was 'a sort of national conversation [about assisted dying] grounded in lived experiences' which took place across the press and social media, and which she saw as evidence of the continuing 'power of television' to have a public impact.

But what do we do about the fact that these programmes are accessible outside of their broadcast flow in the post-broadcast moment, or that we might not necessarily encounter these documentaries in their initial broadcast context and surrounded by the interstitial mechanics of care? It is possible to access all the documentaries discussed in the second half of this chapter either online, via YouTube or Vimeo or the educational streaming platform Box of Broadcasts, or on commercially available DVD. Milly Buonnano, drawing on Horace Newcomb's work, conceptualises a 'shift in the symbolic meaning and the central function of the television medium [in the post-broadcast era]: from forum to library' (2008: 70) and we see this reflected in the Australian ABC documentary *Four Corners: My Own Choice* where the subject and his mother discuss how important watching television documentaries via YouTube had been in relation to his decision to seek an assisted death. While what we see here is evidence of Newcomb's 'library' in the ways in which this mother and son view programmes online, the documentaries viewed by them on YouTube are not made for that platform or library but rather are the remnants, the afterlife, of public service broadcast television as cultural forum. The assisted dying documentary thus transcends its national relevance via its online circulation but continues to perform a 'civic' or emotional duty online. It was clear that the programme makers I spoke to who had made films about assisted dying felt both a duty of care to their subjects and a duty to the public 'right to know', and that they were aware that both of these things continued beyond the initial point of broadcast. This discourse of necessity, the establishment and nurturing of a series of caring relationships around the broadcast text, is clearly in evidence. Whether informally, via the online circulation of documentaries, or as part of a more formal programme of education and training about death and bereavement, television's capacity to convey care for and understanding of those facing an assisted death continues and should not be underestimated.

Parts of this chapter were first published in Helen Wheatley (2020b) 'Signs of care: Assisted suicide on television', in Amy Holdsworth, Karen Lury and Hannah Tweed (eds) Discourses of Care: Media Practices and Cultures, New York and London: Bloomsbury, pp. 21–37.

Part II

Dramas of Grief, Bereavement and the Television Afterlife

3

A good death? Death and the afterlife in US television fiction

While the first part of this book explored the coverage of death in historic and contemporary documentaries made (mainly) by public service broadcasters in the UK and elsewhere, we also see televisual explorations of death, dying and life beyond death in a range of fictional programmes. This part of *Television/Death* examines the ways in which contemporary television drama, much of it made for commercial television channels and streaming services in the United States, takes its audience through the experience of dying and out the other side, whether to a fictional encounter with the afterlife, or to explore the impact of death and dying on those that are left behind. Death as a topic for television drama, comedy, and particularly the hybrid form known as 'dramedy', has become increasingly prevalent since the turn of the millennium. Contra to bell hooks's suggestion in the mid-1990s that 'Dying that makes audiences contemplative, sad, mindful of the transitory nature of human life has little appeal [in American popular culture]' (1994: 91), the series discussed in this chapter and the next can exactly be considered as contemplative about death, dying and what follows, even while they are also funny and/or entertaining. This counters the view of television as a vacuous distraction from the 'real' world, and instead considers the ways in which 'viewing for pleasure' might simultaneously be seen as 'viewing to make sense of life *and death*'.

The first part of this chapter, 'Death and the dead in American television', provides an introduction to this subject, exploring the critical discourse around the hyper-presence of death on US TV and the idea of television as a 'post-mortem showcase'. It looks at the perceived 'pornography of death' on American television and questions of excess and spectacle attached to the dead and dying body that I began to examine in my previous book, *Spectacular Television: Exploring Televisual Pleasure* (2016), and does so specifically in relation to the programme which has been widely seen as initiating a turn towards death on television: *Six Feet Under* (HBO, 2001–2005).

Moving away from the body to the souls of the dead, the latter part of this chapter considers the comedic programming in which they appear. Here I explore a recent cycle of televisual afterlives, in programmes such as *The Good Place* (NBC, 2016–2020), *Forever* (Amazon Studios, 2018), *Miracle Workers* (TBS, 2019–) and *Upload* (Amazon Studios, 2020–) and consider the multiplicity of religious and secular sources for the afterlives created in this programming. I also examine the particularities of the afterlives created: these are deeply American visions of life after death which reveal much about the socio-historical context in which they were made. The analysis also considers these as afterlives of the digital future and explores the way in which these programmes speak to how our understandings of life, death and the concept of the soul are shifting right now. Ultimately, the chapter comes back to the idea of 'working through', to think about how we have learned to live with death through television entertainment about the afterlife. This paves the way for the analysis of dramas of grief and bereavement which follows in the next two chapters, linking what Tanner describes as our 'cultural fascination with the dead' with 'our collective need to recuperate the lost body even in the process of giving voice to loss' (2006: 215–6).

Death and the dead in American television

A small girl pushes through a thronging crowd to see her father who has been brought before the king. While the expectant crowds around her call for his execution, her sister, standing near the king and his party, smiles at her father, knowing, as the viewer watching does, that a deal has been struck and her father will confess to treason and be banished and not killed. Following her father's confession, the king speaks, the camera cutting between the two sisters, the crowds, the king and the accused man. He says he rejects calls for clemency from his mother and fiancée (the girl's sister) and orders her father's beheading. Swiftly, as an acquaintance of her father shields her eyes, pleading with her not to look, the girl's father is beheaded. Her sister faints, horrified at having witnessed this unexpected death.

The above is a description of the final scene of 'Baelor' (S1, E9), the penultimate episode of the first season of *Game of Thrones* (HBO, 2011–2019). This scene has been noted as the first of several brutal and unexpected deaths in this series, where lead characters are killed in shocking

Figure 3.1 Ned Stark's daughters witness his death, 'Baelor' (S1, E9), *Game of Thrones* (HBO, 2011–2019).

ways (here it is Ned Stark, played by Sean Bean, one of the narrative centres and arguably the 'hero' of this first season). It is also a scene which implicitly dramatises a number of assumptions about the role of death on television.

The two sisters, Arya (Maisie Williams) and Sansa (Sophie Turner), might be seen as the imagined, vulnerable (child) audience of television's depictions of death, in need of protection from the sight of death and the dying, and traumatised when that protection is not provided.[1] The baying crowds and bloodthirsty king (Jack Gleeson), on the other hand, represent an imagined (largely adult) television viewer, hungry for the spectacle of a violent death. The unexpected nature of this death, surprising both characters within the diegesis and the audience at home, has been seen as having 'changed television', leading to what journalist Emily VanDerWerff described as subsequent television seasons that were 'drowning in cheap, sloppily executed deaths' (2016). While VanDerWerff attributes the 'Ned Stark effect' of death on TV ratings as the cause of this, arguing that a death 'raises [a] show's dramatic stakes [and] automatically creates lots of conversation' (ibid.), other cultural commentators have taken a less cynical view, seeing the increasing presence of death on television as a barometer for a wider interest in death in the United States in the twenty-first century (McIlwain, 2005). Roger Luckhurst charts this as a steady growth from the 1960s of a '"pathological public sphere" that organises conceptions of community around the spectacular display of injured, ruined or dead bodies' (2017: 105). While feminist scholars have previously drawn attention to the way in which '[d]ead women litter the cultural landscapes of the 2000s' (Dilman, 2014: 1), there seems to have been a much broader turn towards the dead in US television culture, with corpses of all genders piling up on screen.

As explored in the introduction of this book, death permeates television, appearing across all genres and platforms of programming. It has become something of a critical commonplace to note the hyper-presence of death across the whole of American television, from news to drama and beyond (for example, Fulton and Owen, 1987–1988; McIlwain, 2005: 50). Some critics have argued that this has led to death becoming so omnipresent on our television screens that it somehow fails to register, fails to make an impact anymore. Schiappa, Gregg and Hewes (2010: 462–3) discuss this position, as does Kristen A. Murray:

> People living in contemporary American society encounter media about death so frequently, and often fleetingly, that the experience may become unremarkable. Stories, images and information about death form the core of most news programmes and a significant number of entertainment programmes. (Murray, 2016: 53)

Many will be familiar with the eye-watering statistics produced by a number of historical and contemporary studies of television's death representation. In 1971 the American Academy of Pediatrics reported that 'by the time a child in America is 14 he or she can be expected to have seen on average the deaths on television of 18,000 people' (Deacy, 2012: 6). In the late 1980s, the National Institute of Mental Health similarly noted that 'By the age of 16 . . . the typical American has witnessed some 18,000 homicides on television' (Kearl, 1989: 383). By the early 1990s the film critic David Thomson reported in *Film Comment* that the 'American 18 year old has seen 20,000 acts of killing in movies and on TV . . . We have witnessed a lot of killings . . . I wouldn't doubt 100,000 . . . [but] I have seen two dead bodies [in real life]' (1994: 13). In the mid-2000s, the Parents Television Council in the United States was reporting that the corpse count had 'more than double[d]' from 2004 to 2005 (reported in Foltyn, 2009: 47), prompting Jacque Lynn Foltyn to note that 'Macabre images of dead bodies in morgues are propagating like locusts across media land' (ibid.). More recently, a smaller, but perhaps more rigorous, study of the number of deaths in the US 'sweeps week'[2] noted a tripling of deaths between the 2015 and 2016 seasons (VanDerWerff, 2016).[3] While the methodologies used for calculating some of these figures remain unclear, the sheer scale of the numbers here serves the rhetorical purpose of producing fear about the ways in which television might render the young, and in fact anyone, unwitting witnesses to multiple deaths (and particularly murders) on a grand scale, signalling a 'piling up' of bodies on American television that stretches across five decades.

This ever-increasing hyper-presence of death on television is explained by many as a result of what has been called the absence/presence paradox or the 'death denial' thesis: that an absence of death and dying in American homes, a lack of familiarity with the processes of dying which have been moved out of sight into hospitals and hospices, or what McIlwain refers to as 'an ecology of denial and fear' (2005: 9), has permeated American culture in the twentieth and twenty-first centuries (cf. Fulton and Owen, 1987–8; Kelly, 2003; Tanner, 2006; Aaron, 2014). Jennifer Malkowski's work sums up this position:

> The United States presents the most extreme case of the opposing social conditions that typified the twentieth century culture of death denial. While removing dying bodies from public space and repressing the taboo topic of death in public discourse, mid-century US culture nurtured a simultaneous obsession with its fictional media representation. (2017: 8–9)

This is a persuasive argument in many ways: there has definitely been a shift in the sites of death and dying out of the home during the period in question, and certainly death has been very present on our screens, both large and small. However, one wonders for how long cultural critics will be able to claim death's absence from American life when such a multiplicity of deaths and dying experiences are found across our viewing, reading and listening material. Bethan Michael-Fox does a good job of refuting the death denial thesis in her study of death and the dead in late postmodern culture, which I quote here at length:

> [S]ome authors position the current preponderance of death on screen as an example of death's denial, like Gorer[4] seeing it as a form of disturbing and distracting pornography that has emerged as a consequence of, and alongside, the denial of death as a 'natural process' in the twentieth century. However, others pay close attention to the diversity of death and the dead in . . . screen culture. They examine the presence of death and the dead in day-to-day life in the twenty-first century and argue that rather than being denied, they are all around us. (2019: 78)

Following the lead of theorists such as Jonathan Dollimore who also refuted the death denial thesis ('in philosophical and literary terms there has never been a denial of death' (Dollimore, 2001: 126)), Michael-Fox argues that rather than being simultaneously absent and present, death in the twentieth century is just simply very present, a point of cultural fascination, obsession even, rather than a denied or missing object or experience.

This death-obsession is nowhere more evident than on television. Ariella Azoulay refers to US television as a 'postmortem showcase' (2001: 4), a term which encourages us to move beyond simply counting the numbers of deaths and the dead on screen to consider the aesthetic qualities of the presentation of the dead on TV. Following the anthropologist Geoffrey Gorer's lead (1955), both Foltyn (2009: 48) and Dilman (2014: 20) have discussed what they see as the 'pornography' of death on television. Making a comparison between 'old TV' and new, Foltyn argues that the representation of the corpse has fundamentally shifted in contemporary US television towards increasing verisimilitude and a kind of gross display:

> I knew Quincy's[5] corpses were not real. Today's fictive corpses are imbued with verisimilitude, designed to appear real in ways that I have no doubt would have shocked Gorer were he living today. The new pornography of death ... dazzles the audience with grisly corpses, flashy forensic technology and exotic causes of death that are far removed from their experience. (2009: 48)

The televisual fascination with the human body, both living and dead, was examined in the final chapter of my previous book, *Spectacular Television: Exploring Televisual Pleasure* (2016). In this study, I explored 'the intense fascination with bodies on television, seeing the presentation of increasingly intimate spaces of the human body across television genres as a product of scopophilia, literally the "love of looking" on screen' (ibid.: 154). Drawing attention to the idea of television as a medium of spectacle, I proposed that

> [Just] as we pull away from some of the intimate spectacles of the human body on screen, so are we drawn towards them; in this sense they are properly spectacular, threatening to overwhelm us just as they hold us fixed in an intense gaze at the screen (ibid.)

A good deal of the work on death in contemporary US television drama has considered the presentation of the corpse, and the push and pull towards and away from it I describe above. For example, this 'push and pull' is also noted in Weber's work on television corpses as a simultaneous 'fascination and disgust' (2011: xi), and is in line with what Jacobsen proposes as a new fifth phase or age to add to Philippe Ariès's *Western Attitudes Toward Death from the Middle Ages to the Present* (1994) described as the age of 'Spectacular death ... a death that has for all practical intents and purposes been transformed into a spectacle' (2016: 10).

As Foltyn's work suggests above, forensic drama has been particularly pivotal in marking this shift towards a 'pornographic' presentation of death on television, or the spectacularisation of the dead human body, and the attendant critical literature has paid particular attention to this. Robert Hampson argues that in the forensic drama 'the human body is staged as spectacle through incidents of violent death, the disposal of bodies, [and] the processes of decomposition, dismemberment and autopsy' (2017: 227). Foltyn refers to this programming as 'corpse porn' which 'transforms the dead body in theatrical ways, designed to disturb and titillate' and describes the fictional forensic lab as somewhere that 'invites our eyes to linger, presenting death as an enticing sight' (2009: 49). Elke Weissman's work on the US series *CSI: Crime Scene Investigation* (CBS, 2000–2015) has similarly described the presentation of the corpse as 'pornographic' and/or 'carnographic',[6] 'horror-like', and explores the simultaneous attraction and repulsion of the abject body in this drama:

> Crawling with maggots, melting away in decomposition, discoloured and mutilated – the bodies in *Crime Scene Investigation* are clearly meant to disgust. They disrupt the narrative flow with their abject qualities, but by doing so also provide particular pleasures to the viewer. (2007)

Weissmann's evocation of the abject, and the dead body as object of attraction and revulsion, is also reflected in Tina Weber's monograph on the corpse in US television, which notes the 'objectification' and 'violation' of corpses as key trends in their fictional presentation (2011: 75). Forensic drama has, then, become one of the key sites of body horror in the 'postmortem showcase' (Azoulay, 2001: 4) of US television.

Arguably, the verisimilitudinous representation of the dead body which might be seen as a characteristic of televisual body horror has also been at the heart of what has been seen as the new era of 'quality TV'. Denison and Jancovich note this when they argue that the presentation of gore on television was one of the strategies used to distinguish television programming from the mainstream, to mark it out as 'special' or 'different'. Drawing on John Caldwell's delineation of 'televisuality' (1995), which called for a reconsideration of television's visual qualities and an analysis of those elements of television style which drew attention to themselves in the mid-1990s, Denison and Jancovich argue that Caldwell's work 'offers a possible explanation for the supposed shift from the televisual dissipation of horror to the current plague of gory excess' (2007), leading towards a surfacing of the taboo and the presentation of the previously unacceptable on screen (body horror). The presentation of death as subject, and the dead as both object and character, might thus be understood as a marker of distinction on TV along these lines. This was certainly the case in the marketing and reception of the first case study in this chapter: *Six Feet Under*. Kim Akass and Janet McCabe have argued that *Six Feet Under* was

> [Proof] of [HBO's] antipathy to the mainstream approach. 'This show is unlike anything that has ever been on network television' [Chris] Albrecht[7] declares ... Not having to appease advertisers and network executives [on a subscription channel] allows for creative integrity ... contentious subject matter and edgy scripts which include levels of sex and nudity, violence and profanity rarely, if at all, seen on US TV. Such criteria are intrinsic to the HBO brand identity and key to its appeal. (2005: 7)

While Akass and McCabe don't explicitly list the handling of death as a taboo subject and the dead as a confronting image in their list of contentiousness or 'edginess' here, this is implied in their characterisation of what HBO was 'doing differently' at the start of the twenty-first century.

Over sixty-three episodes, *Six Feet Under* tells the story of the Fisher family's funeral home and their fight to maintain independence from a large commercial funeral corporation that threatens, at various points in the narrative, to aggressively take their business over. It is also a meditation on how the Fishers deal with death and grief (both their own and that of their customers), and how key characters (particularly Nate (Peter Krause), David (Michael C. Hall), and Claire Fisher (Lauren Ambrose), and their mother, Ruth (Frances Conroy)), learn to live with, or face up to, death. Indeed, the show begins with the death of the family patriarch, Nathaniel Snr (Richard Jenkins), and the reverberations of this death are felt across all five seasons. It also, as the following analysis will reveal, marked a sea change in how American television imagined the afterlife.

The series has been understood as resonating particularly with a shift in the presence of death more widely in American culture: for example, Rob Turnock invokes the absence/presence paradox in his summing-up of the timeliness and significance of *Six Feet Under*:

> Within modern society [a] secularised, institutionalised and economically rationalised approach to death and dying turns death into a taboo subject ... If grief is hidden from public view, then media

> representations of bereavement take on a new importance . . . *Six Feet Under* emerges as progressive precisely because it breaks the taboo of death and the silence surrounding bereavement, as it places dying, the dead body and intense sorrow at the heart of its drama. (2005: 49)

On the other hand, refuting the position that *Six Feet Under* brought death to light as an otherwise unspoken subject in American culture, Mandy Merck states that we should see the series' focus on death as part of a *continuing* obsession with this topic, arguing that 'The claim that mortality has replaced sex as America's most censored subject is itself geriatric' (2005: 59). However, the series has also been seen as resonant in relation to the presence of death in American society in a more specific historic context: Akass and McCabe argue that the fact that *Six Feet Under* premiered only months before the terrorist attacks of 9/11 meant that the series 'was well positioned to respond to the haunting elegaicness of a nation in mourning' (2005: 11). Indeed, by the fifth season of the show, the sister (Amy Spanger) of a dead amputee soldier (Billy Lush) who had killed himself at the beginning of the episode 'Static' (S5, E11) confirms this resonance:

> We are living in, like, the unluckiest time ever . . . I mean I grew up thinking I was born in the time of the internet, you know, and the fall of Communism, and the Gap. Turns out my time is like when there's 9/11, a bunch of wars, and the end of everything.

Whether one subscribes to the absence/presence paradox in understanding the topicality of *Six Feet Under*, or whether one examines the ways in which it connects with particular societal shifts in our relationship to death and dying prompted by catastrophic events such as 9/11, it is clear that the show 'looked death square in the face, scrutinising every mole and crevice' (Chilton, 2021), dramatising experiences of death for the viewer in new ways. It was also absolutely evident to me when I began writing this book that I would need to re-engage with *Six Feet Under*, given how central it had been to our engagement with death via television, and to our feelings about death, dying and what might lie beyond it. To test the impact of *Six Feet Under*'s directness about death and dying on its viewers, Schiappa et al. conducted an audience study among college students and concluded that 'exposure to approximately ten hours of *Six Feet Under* appears to have led participants to experience a mild increase in their general fears of death . . . [but] prompted less fear about what happens to the body after death' (2010: 471). This latter finding is particularly interesting: while the student viewers in this study felt slightly more frightened about death in general after watching *Six Feet Under*, it seems that their new familiarity with the 'processing' of corpses as represented in this series had 'demystified' the materiality of death in some way. It is to the corpses of *Six Feet Under* that we now turn.

In *Six Feet Under* the corpse is variously the (sometimes spectacular) object of a fascinated gaze, often prompting us to wonder how the visual effects team achieved such impressive levels of grotesque verisimilitude in its presentation, or the object of our appalled imaginings (the most horribly disfigured corpses, such as that of the baker who is killed cleaning an industrial dough mixer in the Season 1 episode 'The Foot' (S1E3), are never seen on screen), or, frequently, a character able to speak beyond death to the Fisher family as they inhabit various spaces in their funeral home, from the mortician's gurney to its ceremonial lounges. The dead in this latter role act like the chorus of a Greek tragedy and have more to say about the hidden internal lives of the Fisher family than they do their own lives or deaths; I will return to this aspect of the series below. For now, though, we concentrate on what Laura E. Tanner explains as *Six Feet Under*'s acknowledgement of 'the immediacy of the dead body through graphic depictions of embalming procedures and camera angles that locate the viewer in uncomfortable proximity to the dead body' (2006: 220), or what David Lavery describes as its 'infatuation' with the 'unashamedly grotesque' corpse (2005: 24–5).

The presentation of the corpse, as suggested above, was one of the key indicators of 'quality' (or 'televisuality', in Caldwell's terms (1995)) in this series, not just in the sense that HBO 'dared' to show the material facts of death. Considerable, and conspicuous, money was spent on producing realistic corpses for the series, including, for example, the body of a woman, for the Season 1 episode 'Crossroads' (S1E8), whose head had been caved in by hitting a road sign when she had jubilantly travelled through Las Vegas with her torso thrust through the sunroof of her limousine, celebrating the finalising of her divorce.

When her body is brought into the industrial funeral home run by the Fishers' rival, Kroehner International, the Fishers' star mortician, Rico (Freddy Rodriguez), is lured into doing some moonlighting for Kroehner on the grounds that it will test, and showcase, his professional abilities. After he has contemplated the abject spectacle of her stoved-in face (see Figure 3.2) and completed his restoration, he exclaims to his wife, Vanessa (Justina Machado), that 'Her head was like a watermelon that got hit by a sledgehammer. Come on, a case like that doesn't come along every day',

Figure 3.2 Stoved-in head, 'Crossroads' (S1E8), *Six Feet Under* (HBO, 2001–2005).

to which she agrees 'She really is your Sistine Chapel'. While the commentary here is directly on Rico's abilities as a mortician, it is also indirectly about the success of the show's visual effects and particularly the work of the MastersFX makeup effects studio on the series (arguably the divorcée is *their* Sistine Chapel in its 'before' state). Executive Producer Alan Poul has argued that the work of MastersFX 'is a huge element of the show because if these bodies or injuries don't look one hundred percent real we wouldn't be giving viewers the you-are-there sense' (Anon., 2004). Describing the production of prosthetic corpses for *Six Feet Under*, which are used sparing because they 'cost roughly the same as a moderately priced car', Todd Masters, CEO of the studio, argues that 'A body's creation represents equal parts technology and artistry . . . drawing, sculpting, performing, painting. Everything you can do in a creative environment' (ibid.).

Throughout the series, corpses frequently stretched what could be shown on screen in terms of good taste and 'decency': gruesome deaths, such as the man whose body is cut in half by a malfunctioning lift in 'Untitled' (S4, E12) or the woman who has her face impaled on a fireplace when shoved off a chair by her disgruntled husband in 'A Coat of White Primer' (S5, E1) certainly manifest the body horror of *Six Feet Under*. Ultimately though, one of the hardest corpses for the viewer to observe is that of Nate Fisher himself, who dies towards the end of the show's final season. At the start of the episode 'All Alone' (S5, E10), which takes place a short time after Nate's death, his brother David, a seasoned undertaker, goes to a morgue to pick up Nate's corpse in advance of his funeral. As a morgue operative unzips Nate's body bag, both David and the viewer are confronted with the sight of Nate's body after organ donation, a stark image of the material facts of death.[8] His eye sockets are shown packed with cotton wool, and his torso is bisected by rough stitching. David expresses his own shock – he was not aware that Nate had signed up for organ donation – while we also experience our own surprise/horror at seeing a replica of a regular cast member presented as a corpse; arguably the waxy pallor and brutal incisions present on Nate's body both repel us from the image on screen and draw us towards it in a kind of sickened fascination.[9] That this is Nate has particular resonance: from the start, *Six Feet Under* has tracked Nate's coming to terms with death, both with the death of his father at the beginning of the series and the inevitability of his own demise. Nate has done this, partly, through confrontation with a series of corpses across all five seasons of the show. When he first sits behind the wheel of the hearse that his sister drives, after the difficult experience of identifying his father's body, we understand this as a symbolic action indicating that Nate is on a journey towards the acceptance of death's role in life which will include getting up close and personal with the dead. On the first full day of his new job as an undertaker in the second episode of *Six Feet Under*, 'The Will' (S1, E2), Nate is immediately confronted with the hard, bodily facts of death: he accidentally reveals the erect penis of the corpse he picks up from the morgue, and then has to deal with the sound of the body's post-mortem moan in the back of the hearse, and the smell of the excrement that the body ejects on his drive back to the funeral home. Later, in the following episode, Nate's fear of death is brought to the fore when he is confronted with the most abject of bodies: as he drops (off screen) the jumbled and putrefying body parts of the chopped-up baker who died in the industrial mixer (mentioned above), we see Nate fall to his knees in the horrific knowledge that he is holding an unidentifiable body part, and then subsequently vomit into a nearby sink. However, this is an immersion in the materiality of death that will ultimately lead him towards the acceptance of death's place in life.

Towards the end of the first season, Nate has a conversation with his girlfriend, Brenda (Rachel Griffiths), that expresses his fears about death, following scenes in which Brenda pretended she was dying and shopping for her own funeral to enable Nate to witness how other undertakers work:

Brenda: You counsel people about death every day, Nate, when death is what you're most afraid of. What's wrong with this picture?
Nate: Well of course I'm afraid of it! What sane person isn't?
Brenda: I'm not.
Nate: Yeah, well I said what sane person. You spooked me, Bren.
Brenda: What, the idea of me dying?
Nate: Well yes
Brenda: I will die someday. We die, Nate. We all die.

We continue to see Nate's aversion to death and the dead throughout the series, as well as seeing his attitude evolve. This evolution is most poignantly revealed in the fourth season of *Six Feet Under*: by the time the police find his wife Lisa's (Lili Taylor) body, which is in a state of advanced decomposition and has been partly eaten by fish, Nate is able to handle the natural burial she wanted, alone. He drives her body to a secluded spot, a look of peace on his face as his wife's remains lie behind him in his hearse, and digs throughout the night, ultimately lowering her corpse into the grave with him and undertaking the grisly task of tipping it out of its plastic body bag. Nate performs this latter action in an understandably disturbed state, quickly pulling himself out of Lisa's grave, sobbing, and by the time the dawn breaks we see him complete the task of filling in the grave and howling in emotional distress at his loss. Nevertheless, though, the fact that he faces this confrontation with the most unimaginable body horror, and with the mangled corpse of someone he loves, with bravery and alone is significant. Here he is not driven away by abjection, but confronts it head on.

While Nate's encounters with the many corpses of *Six Feet Under* bring him closer to an acceptance of the inevitability of death, his meetings with the 'living' dead are also important. Nate's encounters with his father after his death enable Nathaniel Snr to confront Nate about his fears of dying, fears which become sharpened when Nate discovers that he has an arteriovenous malformation, a potentially fatal brain condition which could cause him to have a seizure or stroke at any time. For example, in the first episode of the series, as Nate identifies his father's corpse, the 'living' dead Nathaniel goads his son from his afterlife position, saying 'You've been running away from this your whole life'. Here, the 'this' is not only death as the mainstay of the family business, but also refers more broadly to Nate's fears about his own mortality. While his sister Claire's interactions with her dead father are more about how she is dealing with her grief, and his brother David comes to terms with his sexuality through conversations with the dead, Nate's conversations with his dead father punctuate the show as a series of existential crises as he faces the fact that he may soon die. In *Six Feet Under*, then, the afterlife is permeable, and the dead present in the midst of life. Alan Ball describes the reappearance of the dead in the series as 'a literary device to articulate what's going on in the living characters' minds' (Magid, 2002), and television scholar David Lavery sees it as an element of the show's 'magic realism' (2005: 29). The dead can mingle with the living, commenting on their struggles and accessing their inner fears. They are very present in the everyday life of the Fishers, and thus the afterlife is largely imagined in this series as co-present with the living world, and not a separate place, save from one scene in the third season episode 'I'm Sorry, I'm Lost' (S3, E13). In this episode, Claire walks through the graveyard with her dead father and passes through a bead curtain into a sunny park with a carnival atmosphere, brightly lit and shot in soft focus. Here she meets her ex-boyfriend Gabriel Dimas (Eric Balfour), now dead, who talks to Claire about how much better his life is in this paradisical afterlife world. While this is not an image of what Greg Garrett calls the 'fluffy cloud heaven' (2015: 7) of many Christian imaginings of the afterlife, the depiction of the afterlife as a harmonious, multi-racial but separate space from the world of the living feels recognisable within the image repertoire of paradise, an Elysium Fields separate to, but in the middle of, Los Angeles. This therefore can be seen as a significant, if brief, moment in the series' attempts to bring its characters closer to an acceptance of death's place in life, as if to reassure that there will be something, or *somewhere*, beyond death.

The persistence of the soul: television afterlives

The above scene in *Six Feet Under* might be seen as a short precursor to what was to become a remarkable cycle of narratives imagining afterlife worlds in the next two decades on American television. Here I focus on these programmes, or on what we might see as 'post-death television'; it shifts our attention, therefore, from the body of the dead to their souls. Greg Garrett, describing the prevalence of narratives of the afterlife more broadly in Western literature and culture, proposes that

> Whether one explains the passage of the soul through the prism of religion or logic, death is an irrevocable boundary. On one side we find the living; on the other, passing on either to nothingness or another form of existence. (ibid.: 30)

How we imagine this 'other side' depends, of course, on a whole variety of things: clearly it depends on our religious beliefs (or lack of them), our national identities and the kind of education we have had, but it also depends on the afterlife stories we have seen or heard, how an afterlife or afterlives have been imagined for us. Afterlife stories seek to reassure but also act as cautionary narratives, and they help us make sense of the world; they seek to 'assure us that the universe has ultimate meaning and order, even if we may not perceive it around us in our everyday lives' (ibid.: 192). I draw, in the latter part of this chapter, on a wide range of critical literature that considers the creation of fictional afterlives across art, film and literature and other cultural forms and media. Turning the scrutiny that has been focused on previous creative visions of the afterlife towards television, I seek to understand why the afterlife has become such a prevalent narrative space in US TV, and what afterlife narratives might have to say about the concerns of the day, for as Alice Bennett argues:

> In secular, western cultures today, with belief in some form of an afterlife by no means standard, literary engagement with life after death has entered a new and abundant phase . . . Fictional engagement with the afterlife has historically combined elements from different religions and folk traditions, as well as addressing the immediate cultural and social concerns of the living. Afterlives accumulate new details depending on present concerns and their form and function changes with the times. (2012: 1)

Whereas Bennett argues that film and literature present the most prevalent popular imaginings of the afterlife (ibid.: 16), if she had been writing in 2023, she would surely have included television in her study.

I am also interested in why the afterlife has become such a popular setting for US television in particular. As the analysis in this chapter will reveal, the afterlives imagined in the last five years in programmes such as *The Good Place*, *Forever*, *Miracle Workers* and *Upload* can be seen as quintessentially American. In his study of the digital afterlives of the twenty-first century, Kevin O'Neill charts what he sees as the evolution of the American death narrative, which, he argues, is plotted around four key themes:

> [Optimism] about the fate of the dead; a belief that the boundary between life and death is permeable and easily crossed, going both ways; a do-it-yourself sense of entitlement in describing/designing the afterlife; and a willingness to enlist technologies, old and new,

to represent and enable the new death narrative and to furnish the afterlife. (2016: 192–3)

All of the characteristics of the American afterlife mapped out by O'Neill here can be seen in the programmes at hand. There have been a large number of afterlife dramas on US television in the last two decades, not just those programmes on which this chapter focuses, and these have increased exponentially in number in the last five years. In 2020, the journalist Steve Greene noted of this burgeoning genre of programming that 'Judging by the uptick in the number of shows and movies set in whatever place of existence awaits us when we die, the afterlife is a place of infinite possibility' (2020). For the sake of clarity and a manageable corpus, I focus here specifically on the afterlife shows where characters enter another afterlife world, rather than concentrating on the many shows where the dead return to the 'living world' in some way. These other shows include what Lyons refers to as 'supernatural deed-oriented procedurals' (2018: 112) such as *Dead Like Me* (Showtime, 2003–2004), *Tru Calling* (Fox/SyFy, 2003–2005), *Pushing Daisies* (ABC, 2007–2009), and *Reaper* (The CW, 2007–2009), and the 'mind dependent world' (Deacy, 2012: 67) of *Russian Doll* (Netflix, 2019–). This chapter also doesn't include analysis of shows in which characters don't realise they're dead (as in the dénouement of *Lost* (ABC, 2004–2010), described by Garrett (2015)) or look at the narratives of resurrection and the returning dead discussed by Bethan Michael-Fox (2019) and James Hodkinson (2020). Nor, indeed, do I discuss here any of the ghost or zombie series which can also be viewed as forming part of the wider post-death canon (in the case of ghosts, these come in the next chapter). I am more interested here in the imagined post-death worlds of recent televisual afterlives, and what they tell us about the preoccupations of contemporary American society. Generically, the programmes at the heart of this chapter are all what we might see as 'dark' dramedies, and, as Kirsten A. Murray notes, dark comedy emerges from 'significant shifts in people's relationship to, and understanding of, death in contemporary American society' (2016: 41). While Murray doesn't focus specifically on afterlife comedies/dramedies, her work astutely calls up the role of dark humour in facing death and loss when she concludes that 'dark humour is not an instantaneous, superficial response [to death], but an ongoing, provocative endeavour – an attempt to articulate the impact of grief and ascribe meaning to loss' (ibid.: 55). These are, therefore, often very funny programmes which have a lot to say about the very serious topic of death and dying.

If we are now turning away from the body, and towards the soul, and looking at how afterlife television treats the body and soul as two separate entities, we first need to understand what the soul is. In his analysis of the afterlife in film, theologian Christopher Deacy offers us a useful working definition of the soul: 'in Platonic terms, the soul has tended to be seen as the essence of the person, with the body seen merely as a vehicle for the soul in its manifold incarnations' (2012: 40). Deacy goes on to propose that the 'immortality of the soul is . . . intrinsic to the way in which the afterlife is formulated for many thinkers throughout Christian history' (ibid.: 43). Belief in the afterlife, whether a religious belief or not, rests on a belief in the soul: in 1997, a Gallup/Nathan Cummings Foundation/Fetzer Institute Study found that '[most] Americans believe they will exist in some form after death' and that their expectation was that

> [The] experience will be positive; they will be on a journey of some kind; they will experience spiritual growth; and the quality of existence will depend on things done in one's life and one's spiritual state at the time of death. (McIlwain, 2005: 12)

This raises the question of religious belief at the outset of this analysis of television's afterlives, and the extent to which afterlife narratives might be seen as evidence of the ongoing relevance of Christian, or at least religious, thinking in American television, even in the context of the increasing secularisation of society. It is to this question that we now turn.

* * *

A woman wakes up to find herself sitting on a sofa in a smart, corporate-looking office. On the wall in front of her in large letters are the words 'Welcome! Everything's fine'. She is soon joined by a well-groomed man in a peacock-patterned bowtie who ushers her into his office to explain that she is dead, her life on earth has ended, and she is now in the next phase of her existence in the universe. Having had the manner of her death explained to her, she asks 'So who was right? About all of this?', gesturing around her at her afterlife surroundings. The man sitting opposite her explains 'Let's see – Hindus are a little bit right, Muslims a little bit, Jews, Christians, Buddhists, every religion guessed about 5%, except Doug Forcett . . . a stoner kid who lived in Calgary during the 1970s. One night he got really high on mushrooms and . . . Doug just launched into this long monologue where he got like 92% correct'.

In the opening of *The Good Place*, described above, this exchange between newly dead Eleanor (Kristen Bell) and Michael (Ted Danson), 'architect' of what we believe in the first season to be the titular 'Good Place', sets out the basis of the show's imagined afterlife: that it will be drawn from a variety of religious treatises on the destination for souls after death, as well as, or in fact more so, from more secular imaginings of what happens to us after we die. This bit of dialogue might be seen as a neat encapsulation of the ways in which contemporary afterlife narratives on television work: that they reflect the multiplicity of religious doctrines and practices at play in the US today, while holding on to a number of competing or complementary secular worldviews, rendering these programmes good examples of what we might see as 'postsecular television'. In their introduction to the postsecular in cultural theory and analysis, James Hodkinson and Silke Horstkotte propose that 'once stable conceptual distinctions between "religion" and "secularity" are becoming blurred' in the contemporary moment, leading to the deconstruction of 'long-held assumptions about the connection between modernity and secularity' (2020: 318). Drawing on the work of Kristina Stoeckl, Massimo Rosati and Robert Holton, who define a postsecular society as one in which 'religion remains collectively meaningful without being opposed to secularity, because society itself is plural and Christianity has lost its monopoly on the Western imagination' (2012: 2), Hodkinson and Horstkotte argue that 'religious pluralism leads to new and diverse understandings of the secular' (2020: 319). For them, the 'postsecular turns into a methodological lens through which an open-ended engagement with the intersections of religion and secularity can begin' (ibid.: 320).

This turn towards the postsecular prompts us to consider how religious and secular conceptions of the afterlife intermingle, in television fictions and beyond, for as Greg Garrett has acknowledged,

> Cultural and narrative understandings can ... help shape our ideas about these future [post-death] places or states of being; our perceptions of sacred as well as secular matters are always being informed by secular texts as well as holy ones ... Our modern, Western concepts of the afterlife have been largely shaped by such things as medieval images of heaven and hell and the *Divine Comedy* of Dante. Art, literature, and other forms of culture represent visually and dramatically the sacred abstractions that we otherwise know only through the stories of our faith traditions. Sometimes our cultural imaginings reinforce the impressions we receive through our faith; sometimes they call them into question. They can encourage us to believe; they can cause us to doubt. But always these imaginings are part of our process of creating meaning. (2015: 5)

For example, Garrett sees the obsession with angels in contemporary America as stemming as much from the imaginative work of theologians, artists and writers as it does from the books of the Bible (ibid.: 69). Garrett's point here concurs with what Bennett calls the 'contested ownership' of the afterlife 'between, loosely, mass culture and the theologians' (2012: 9), and affirms Deacy's entreaties that theology and film studies must come together in the analysis of the afterlife on screen, and that 'eschatology cannot simply be seen as the preserve of theologians alone' (2012: 14). While some journalists understood the turn towards afterlife narratives on American television at the start of the twenty-first century as a shift, particularly post 9/11, towards a greater 'religiosity' and 'conservatism' (see Stanley (2003), for example), others have argued that this programming wasn't finding all of its answers, or its sources for answers, in Christianity or in any other religion. As Hal Hinson acknowledges

> The message seems to be that it's possible to create shows dealing with religious subjects without wrapping them up in miracle-of-the-week platitudes and that metaphysical issues can be addressed artistically in an arena of exploration and discussion rather than one of moral absolutes. (2004)

While the series at the heart of this study do not create what Garrett has called 'fluffy cloud heaven' (2015: 7) or a 'fire and brimstone' hell, proffering afterlife worlds which are immediately recognisable from previous visualisations of the Christian afterlife, this does not mean that the depiction of the afterlives on offer in these series is wholly secular either. Series creator of *The Good Place*, Michael Schur, has referred to the series as 'agnostic' (McFarland, 2017), and also argues that he made it very clear when pitching the series to NBC that 'it was not a religious show', qualifying this by saying that 'In this omniscient point-value version [of the afterlife], there's no benefit or harm to any kind of ethnicity, gender, age, whatever' (Egner, 2017). Schur later claimed that he stopped doing research on conceptualisations of the afterlife in world religions because he 'realized [his series is] about versions of ethical behaviour, not religious salvation . . . The show isn't taking a side, the people who are in it are from every country and religion' (Burton, 2018). For Schur, it appears, the fact that *The Good Place* isn't monotheistic and the fact that it focuses on ethical, rather than pious, behaviour to guarantee a spot in 'the good place' is what makes this show 'not religious'. However, if we think of *The Good Place* as postsecular television, we can see that it both constructs a secular/humanist vision of the afterlife and also borrows quite liberally from a variety of religious stories and doctrines, whether that's the fact that the series has a 'good' and 'bad' place in the first place, in line with Christian ideas of heaven and hell, or that the 'architect' Michael is named after St Michael the archangel, judger of souls (Egner, 2020), or, indeed, that there is a recourse to Buddhist conceptions of death and rebirth in its final episode, 'Whenever You're Ready' (S4, E13). This makes sense if we look at James Hodkinson's description of the postsecular in the television dramas about resurrection that he examines:

> Postsecularity . . . describes not so much the wholesale return of religious experiences that had vanished from the world as it does a return to focus on hitherto less visible religious ideas within contemporary cultural production and criticism, often in complex and ambiguous forms (2020: 399).

The messy, complex and ambiguous incorporation of religious ideas of postdeath experience into the secular visions of the afterlives under examination here are, therefore, what renders them 'postsecular'. These programmes draw on multiple sources to construct their visions of the afterlife in order to make sense of death and dying for characters in the diegesis, and for the television audience.

Afterlife programmes might also be seen as a site in which belief can be debated and explored. The futuristic afterlife series *Upload* follows the arrival of Nathan (Robbie Amell) into 'Lake View', an expensive, designer, digital afterlife paid for by his rich girlfriend (Allegra Edwards) after he dies in an autonomous vehicle crash. Nathan is guided in this afterlife by Nora (Andy Allo), his 'angel' (a term used to describe the service administrator designated to take care of each post-death avatar/consciousness in Lake View). Nora is still alive, but she and Nathan become close through their interactions during the first season, gradually falling in love as they become embroiled in each other's lives. When Nora's father, Dave (Chris Williams), a widower, visits the digital afterlife in the episode 'Bring Your Dad to Work Day' (S1, E7) (Nora is attempting to persuade him to upload to Lake View in the event of his death, taking advantage of her employee 'perks'), Nathan and Dave wander through the Lake View hotel, having a debate about the religious beliefs that are preventing Dave from taking advantage of this offer:

> Dave: You see, Nathan, when you died your soul went to real Heaven, so whatever simulation I'm talking to now has no soul. It's an abomination.

> Nathan: OK. Or, there is no soul and there never was and in a sense both of our consciousnesses are simulations, mine on a silicone computer, and yours on a computer made of meat, your brain.
> Dave: But there is a soul.
> Nathan: OK, so you expect to be playing a harp on a cloud or something?
> Dave: If I told you I *knew* my wife was waiting for me, and the only thing I've been thinking about ever since she left me was to hold her in my arms again, what could you say to me to get to upload [into Lake View]?
> Nathan: Nothing. So, you believe in it all literally?
> Dave: I believe I was happiest when we were all together, and the only way for us to be together again, including Nora, is after we're all dead.

Here, belief in the Christian afterlife is set against a subscription to the digital afterlife created in the series, and the merits/possibility of both are debated by characters with opposing belief systems in the series. Arguably then, this postsecular television dramedy doesn't either wholly subscribe to a monotheistic religious vision of what happens after death, nor does it abandon the idea of a belief in this. Other programmes in this cycle are even more ambivalent about a faith-based afterlife (see, for example, June's (Maya Rudolph) rant in church following the death of her husband in the second episode of *Forever*, in which she shouts 'There's no God! There's no plan! This is all bullshit!'), and programme creators have been keen to point out the secularity of their vision of the afterlife (as with the case of Schur/*The Good Place*, discussed above). Nevertheless, we cannot help but read these afterlives as at least influenced or inflected by a long history of religious conceptions of heaven, hell, purgatory and so on.

'Uplifting views. Healthy pursuits. Timeless Americana'

Setting aside the question of the extent to which these series offer a vision of the afterlife which is drawn, in some large or small way, from religious teachings or theological imaginings, if these are secular – or, more properly, postsecular – visions of life after death, what kind of secular society do they represent or reflect? If, as Alice Bennett argues, 'Afterlives accumulate new details depending on present concerns and their form and function changes with the times' (2012: 1), what are the present-day concerns which are immediately present in, and recur across, this programming? Firstly, we can think about these dramedies as offering a particularly American vision of the afterlife, in which the afterlife is modelled on recognisably American spaces and places. As has already been acknowledged in this chapter, these programmes conform closely to what Kevin O'Neill describes as 'a uniquely American confidence in reaching the afterlife, an equal confidence in being in touch with that realm, and a boldness in reshaping the afterlife in one's own image' (2016: 14). In *The Good Place, Forever* and *Upload*, emphasis is placed on the fact that the design of each of these afterlife worlds has been 'perfected' to reflect an idealised American suburbia (in the first two) and the 'timeless Americana' of the grand Victorian hotels of North America in the latter. When Michael welcomes a new cohort to the 'Good Place' (in 'Everything is Fine' – S1, E1), he reassures them during a slick, corporate-sounding presentation that the afterlife is a series of 'perfectly calibrated' suburban neighbourhoods and that 'In each one, every blade of grass, every ladybug, every detail has been precisely designed and calibrated for its residents'. This promise of suburban 'perfection' as a specifically American fantasy, the architectural embodiment of the 'American Dream', is, of course, the promise of affluence and plenitude, and a visualisation of the idea that America itself is a kind of 'promised land' where all is possible. *The Good Place*'s design team worked to produce a vision of the afterlife as a space of specifically American luxury:

> [Production designer Dan] Bishop, who previously worked on *Mad Men*, was tasked with creating a heaven in the style of Disneyland and The Grove, an outdoor shopping centre in Los Angeles . . . The show [also] makes clever use of the lavish grounds of the Huntington Library and Botanical Gardens in San Marino, California. (Munro, 2018)

Ultimately though, we learn that this perfected, 'perfectly calibrated' 'Good Place' is in fact the 'Bad Place', designed by Michael (not saintly architect, but demon in disguise) to place the characters at the centre of the narrative in a perpetual Sartre-style hell in which they will torture each other. This takes the 'shine' off this image of perfect Americana and draws our attention to its artifice and the horror of its uniformity. Indeed, even once the characters do get to the *real* Good Place in Season 4, we find it once again to be a similarly Los Angelean-luxe image of heaven which brings to mind a kind of ennui (its inhabitants are bored to death by their everlasting life). Heaven, then, is perhaps *too* perfect in its representation of affluent America.

In *Forever*, the first afterlife narrative from Amazon Studios, the central characters June and Oscar (Fred Armisen) similarly find themselves in a 'perfect' American suburban afterlife. While Oscar clearly enjoys the uniformity of their mid-century modern home and surroundings, the carefully manicured lawns of their affluent suburban neighbourhood that they cannot leave, and the endless crosswords and games of shuffleboard with the neighbours, June quite quickly appears bored and stifled by them. While we know that she was already feeling this of their relationship before death (as I will explain below), the design of the 'perfected' American suburbia June finds herself in underlines and exacerbates these feelings. As with *The Good Place*, images of American 'perfection' are ambivalent; suburban surroundings represent affluence and comfort, but also vacuousness and boredom. When June and Oscar's rebellious neighbour Kase (Catherine Keener) moves in next door, June begins to understand Kase's discomfort with her place in the afterlife through the fact that she repeatedly tries to set a classic mid-century modern sideboard on fire outside her house. Each time she performs this act of mutiny against the affluent suburban aesthetic, the sideboard simply reappears intact in her house again. In this series, then, post-death America is depicted as a place which is both comfortingly and horrifically familiar; the experiences of these characters in the afterlife extend the struggles that they faced in life itself.

In *Upload's* first episode, Nathan's arrival in the digital afterlife is narrated by Nora who repeats some standard marketing speak about this particular vision of the American afterlife as Nathan is regaining (digital) consciousness on arrival in Lake View:

> Nora: Welcome to Lake View by Horizon, the only digital afterlife environment modelled on the grand Victorian hotels of the United States and Canada. Hope it's not too Ralph Lauren for you.
> Nathan: I mean it was never really my thing, but it's kind of cool.
> Nora: Yeah. Uplifting views, healthy pursuits, timeless Americana.
> Nathan: Are there slaves?
> Nora: What? Are you serious? One, this is just a design scheme and two, that's not even the right period. Lake View is open to all races, religions, genders, absolutely anybody.

There is a lot to unpick here – both the association of classic, American, luxury leisure spaces with yet another televisual vision of the afterlife,[10] as well as Nathan's clumsy reminder that the affluence and opportunity afforded by the 'American Dream' has always been contingent on a series of privileges. While Nora reassures that Lake View is an inclusive place, open to 'all races, religions, genders', Nathan's gaffe about America's violently racist past brings us up short partly because it is a reminder that this is a vision of the afterlife which is still clearly built on existing privilege (in this case, class/wealth privilege rather than racial identity). Here, then, as in *The Good Place* and *Forever*, the very American-ness of the afterlife is what marks it out as ambivalent rather than paradisical, even while its neighbourhoods are presented as 'perfected'. When Nathan wanders around the grounds of Lake View later in this episode, this image of perfection is also undercut by (a) the constant intrusion of digital concierges trying sell him things; (b) the awareness that everything, even the leaves on the trees, carries the Horizon trademark; and (c) that the elegant landscapes that surround him glitch and shudder as they struggle for bandwidth. Here perfect, 'timeless,' Americana is repeatedly spoiled by the cold hard facts of twenty-first century American (digital) capitalism, a fact which is further emphasised at the beginning of the second season with the introduction of the 'Ludds', an anti-capitalist, anti-tech sect living a communal, forest-based life that vehemently rejects all that Lake View represents.

In post-death television, the American afterlife is also frequently imagined as a world of drudgery and boredom. While *Upload* envisions the digital afterlife as a leisure-focused society serviced by row upon row of digital service operatives at desks back in the real world, *Dead Like Me*, *The Good Place*, *Miracle Workers* and other dramedies present the afterlife, wholly or in part, as a stultifying workplace, an office or factory where souls are dealt with by those caught up in the business of 'processing' souls.[11] The image of heaven or hell as an administrative hub of one kind or other might speak to Garrett's proposal that in the contemporary afterlife narrative, angels and demons have been 'domesticated' and 'brought down to earth', having moved beyond their role as 'awe-inspiring' supernatural beings (2015: 59) to become something more like the servants of bureaucracy. To turn to a 'supernatural deed-oriented procedural' (Lyons, 2018: 112) for a moment, *Dead Like Me* is based on the premise that following their deaths, some people become 'reapers', tasked with the job of herding the souls of others into a more heavenly-looking afterlife. The series follows George (Ellen Muth) as she learns to become a reaper under the tutelage of Rube (Mandy Patinkin), swapping the dead-end office job she had just started in life for the banality of more filing, self-assessment forms, data entry, and following instructions passed to her daily on Post-It notes in death. Describing this drudgery, Daisy (Laura Harris), one of the other reapers, moans 'The magic of creation? That turns out to be a 9–5 grind with lots of paperwork. It's so, it's so every day!' When George points out that lots of people die and move on to the next plane of existence, whatever that may be, and that there's 'nothing every day about where they're going', Daisy says 'How do you know that that's true? Maybe we just keep moving from one filing job to the next. Oh my God! We're all temps!'. Here, Daisy's existential crisis figures life *and* death as a state of endless drudgery, the afterlife narrative offering a critique of capitalist America and its concomitant tedium.

The dramatic spaces of *Dead Like Me* – the grubby diner, and especially the badly lit, open-plan office complete with glitchy, old-fashioned computers that the reapers do their annual review on – are also returned to in *The Good Place*, particularly when we see the administrative offices of the afterlife in the third and fourth seasons. In the episode 'Janet(s)' (S3, E9), for example, Michael and his anthropomorphised digital assistant Janet (D'Arcy Carden) visit The Accountant (Stephen Merchant) and the large open-plan office where the value of people's souls is calculated.

Here Merchant plays The Accountant as an excruciatingly perky Bristolian, holding an 'Existence's Best Boss' mug, and cracking terrible accountancy jokes. By his side is a completely dead-pan Janet (also D'Arcy Carden), whose monotone delivery of lines speaks of the horror of an eternity spent crunching the figures that decide the fate of the dead. When The Accountant agrees to give them a tour of the office, we cut to a wide-angle shot of the room, where desks, desk dividers and old-fashioned green screen CRT monitors stretch as far as the eye can see, along with the drably dressed office workers that sit at them (see Figure 3.3). Matt (Brad Morris), one of

Figure 3.3 The Accountant's office, 'Janet(s)' (S3, E9), *The Good Place* (NBC, 2016–2020).

The Accountant's workers, peers over his office divider and says, 'I'm still waiting on a response to the request I filed for immediate suicide', and The Accountant grins, saying 'Request denied! I love Matty – he's hilarious'. Here the bureaucracy of the afterlife is nightmarish, and once again life post-death is imagined as a horrible copy of corporate America. While *The Good Place* imagines the afterlife here as a form of white collar hell, the 'heaven' of the first season of *Miracle Workers* is depicted as a somewhat dysfunctional factory run by a disaffected God (Steve Buscemi). In this rickety, under-funded factory, Craig (Daniel Radcliffe), a low-level angel responsible for handling all of humanity's prayers, and Eliza (Geraldine Viswanathan), a recent transfer from the Department of Dirt, attempt to save humanity from their petulant boss's nihilistic whims. As Charles Bramesco noted in his review of *The Good Place*, *Forever*, and *Miracle Workers*, 'In each case the series generate comedy by offering a banal solution to the grand mystery of what happens after we shuffle off this mortal coil', concluding that heaven is 'devastatingly similar to a place on earth' (2020).

While *Dead Like Me*, *The Good Place* and *Miracle Workers* imagine the afterlife as a place of corporate drudgery, *Forever* expresses most clearly the idea that, to quote Jean-Paul Sartre, 'hell is other people' (1945). Although June and Oscar experience other people in their suburban afterlife neighbourhood as hellish, the series is particularly eloquent in representing the boredom of their long-term relationship (both in life and post-death) and the fact that June is finding being in this relationship unbearable. The opening episode, 'Together Forever', begins with a four-and-a-half-minute-long dialogue-less montage of the story of June and Oscar's relationship, from first meeting to the present day. In this sequence we see the transition of repeated actions (such as Oscar catching and cooking a trout for June at their lake house) from novelty, to comfortable familiarity, to the despair experienced by June as she is presented with a fish for one last time. The sequence closes with a zoom into June's face which captures her ennui. The fact that this montage is accompanied by an instrumental version of Miles Davis's 'It Never Entered My Mind' is also telling; the lyrics of this song, were they present, encapsulate the bittersweet feelings associated with the end of a relationship, and it thus forewarns of the trouble to come. When June arrives on the street in their suburban afterlife in Episode 3, immediately following her own death in the previous episode, her panic at the fact that there is no structure to their new after-death life together other than simply living each day side-by-side also expresses this:

> June: What are we supposed to be doing?
> Oscar: I don't know.
> June: Does anybody know?
> Oscar: Not really. No one sits you down and gives you an information packet. I mean that would have been cool. I love packets.
> June: I kind of feel like I got tossed in at the deep end here. Can we sit down for a second? [They sit on the kerb]. So this is it? We just keep going? I mean how long does this go on for? I mean what's the point of all this?
> Oscar: Well, what was the point of the thing before this?
> June: Oh, God. Oh, boy. Oh, man. Is this really happening? Am I hallucinating?

On the one hand, June's panic relates to the fact that death has failed to bring clarity to the meaning of life. June (perhaps like anyone who chooses to engage with the imagined afterlives of television, film, literature, and so on) had hoped for an answer to life's big questions, having passed from the known world of the living and into the previously unknown world of the dead. However, her panic also relates to her dawning realisation that she is stuck with Oscar forever. At the end of this episode, as Oscar serves her his traditional Trout Almondine in their new afterlife home, the sound of his chatter about the fish is slowly drowned out by Miles Davis's mournful trumpet, reprising the music of the opening montage of the series as the camera zooms into June's face, again subtly registering the fact that she is trapped in the relationship, this time *really* forever. When Kase's arrival in the fourth episode shakes up the monotony of their lives together, and June's curiosity about her new neighbour forces her to break into and explore her house, she exasperatedly exclaims 'We do the same five things every day and at least this was a new thing!' to which Oscar responds that 'Breaking and entering can't be the new thing! I like the five things we do.' Following Kase's lead, June burns Oscar's favourite chair at the end of Episode 4, knowing that it will simply reappear again the following day, and when she exclaims at the end of 'Another Place' (E5) 'I feel trapped. I mean we are actually trapped here!', Oscar tries to reassure her that 'It's safe here, it's nice. Look at this house!' With Kase's persuasion, June travels to the other side of the afterlife to a Gothic hotel on a cliff, known as Ocean View, where a group of people experience life after death in a more hedonistic way. Here she momentarily escapes the drudgery of her life for something more challenging and exciting, but when Oscar catches up with her, she begins to feel the pull between what is new and exciting and the comfort of love and familiarity that Oscar represents.

We will return to an analysis of the conclusion of *Forever* in the conclusion of this chapter, but it is clear to see that in this version of the afterlife, being stuck in a relationship becomes a kind of hell. We also see this explored in *Upload*, where Nathan feels both trapped by the girlfriend who is paying for his continued digital existence, and by the staff and residents of Lake View with whom he is forced to share eternity. Furthermore, in *The Good Place*, Michael's initial plot to torture Eleanor, Chidi (William Jackson Harper), Tahani (Jameela Jamil) and Jason (Manny Jacinto) is precisely based on the extent to which they might drive each other mad,[12] though as the philosopher (and series consultant) Todd May argues in the *New York Times* 'What the demon Michael . . . discovers is that, contrary to Jean-Paul Sartre's dictum . . . hell is not always other people. He learns, in fact, that other people may be necessary for one's own moral redemption' (2020). This conclusion is also shared by Joel Mayward, reviewing the final episode in *Christianity Today*: '*The Good Place* proposed that heaven is other people; the loving friendships of the "soul squad" were genuinely salvific for the entirety of humanity' (2020). Here, then, we see that the televisual afterlife explores the connections that we share with other people, connections which might be severed, or indeed strengthened, by death.

In its dramatisation of the current concerns of American society, the afterlife drama also explores how our place in society, and our experience of death and dying, might be being transformed by the technologies of the digital future. This theme calls back to a long-standing relationship between the development of new media technologies and popular and critical emphasis on their resurrectory qualities (cf. Bazin, 1960; Davies, 2005; Fuss, 2013; O'Neill, 2016; Penfold-Mounce, 2018; Michael-Fox, 2019). As Jeffrey Sconce has documented, tales of 'haunted media', and the imagined connections that new technologies produce between the living and the dead, have spanned the advent of telegraphy and the wireless to contemporary developments in 'cyberspace' and virtual reality. Writing in 2000, Sconce closed his historical analysis of haunted media technologies by wondering

> [Whether] cybertechnologies [will] truly prove to be the first in a series of innovations to reconfigure reality and redefine human subjectivity or whether, instead, our current visions of media disembodiment are simply the last round of fantastic folklores generated by the modern world's most uncanny innovation: electronic media. (2000: 209)

In 2023, we feel perhaps closer to the answer to Sconce's musings, though the idea of media disembodiment and continuing digital life beyond death is still, of course, something of a fantasy. A number of scholars have explored the idea of the digital afterlife (cf. O'Neill, 2016; Steinhart, 2017), considering the ways in which digital technologies might enable a consciousness to live on beyond death. Kevin O'Neill provocatively opens his book on the internet afterlife by asking

> Are we living at the end phase in history in which human beings actually died? Are we at the dawning of a new world in which the dead will live among us in digital form, and when they – and we – and the entire universe will morph into one enormous simulation? Will the virtual absorb the real? Will time and space come to mean nothing? (2016: x)

He then goes on to track the digital dead across a variety of sites, including 'virtual cemeteries, YouTube memorials, Facebook legacy pages and group memorial pages, services that promise to post tweets after one died and other services designed to send postmortem emails' (ibid.: 5). While O'Neill provides a contemporary cultural history of the digital afterlife, Steinhart details the new philosophies of the 'digitalists' who are 'developing new ways to think about life after death' and arguing for 'computational theories of resurrection and reincarnation' (2017: 256). He goes on to explain that digitalists propose 'that bodies are machines running souls like computers run programs' and that they therefore 'affirm the possibility of resurrection: if you are uploaded, then your organic body in our universe is resurrected as a software body in some software universe' (ibid.: 268). Reading the work of O'Neill and Steinhart, it is clear to see where the thinking behind programmes such as *Upload* or the digital afterlife episode of UK/US TV series *Black Mirror* (Channel 4, 2011–2014; Netflix, 2016–2019) 'Be Right Back' (S2, E1)[13] come from; their writing sets out the discursive context for these television dramatisations of digital life after death.

As has already been suggested in this chapter, Amazon Studio's *Upload* manages to present the digital afterlife as simultaneously utopian and dystopian. Ben Allen's review of the series points out its ambivalent attitude towards the digital future (and the particular ironies of this vision of the afterlife being produced by/for Amazon):

> [Greg] Daniels [*Upload*'s creator] is clearly paranoid about the impact technology is having on us right now and its capacity to become more and more intrusive over time. The central joke is that we're going to be slaves to giant tech companies even beyond the grave, which is ironic, seeing as it's Amazon, the third largest in the world, that has stumped up the money for him to bring his vision to life (2020)

The series opens on an advert for Lake View, where a voiceover asks, 'What is the reward for a life well lived and an upload well planned for?' over shots of happy, rich-looking, white people enjoying leisure pursuits (kayaking, golfing, hiking, and so on) in picturesque surroundings.

The voiceover goes on to answer its own question: 'The most perfect natural beauty that man can design. The best days of your life could be after it's over. You did well. You deserve Lake View by Horizon' (see Figure 3.4). As the camera pulls away from a final shot of the Lake View hotel, overlaid with Horizon's logo, we discover that this ad is running on repeat on a digital screen behind the heads of people on a packed train, and soon understand that this is an aspirational digital afterlife beyond the financial reach of many, if not all, of the people travelling on overcrowded public transport. *Upload* explores both the promise of (digital) life after death as a fact of the American near-future as well as exposing the societal inequalities that make citizens' experience of death very different depending on their financial status. We know, for example, that Nathan only has access to Lake View because his rich girlfriend pays for it; Nathan's family are shown in the first episode of Season 1 discussing the kind of afterlife they would be able to afford in comparison, and indeed later in the first season we learn that Nathan's death was probably not accidental, given the threat posed to the big afterlife corporations by the more affordable digital afterlife he and his business partner were developing. In 'The Sex Suit' (S1, E4), Nora gives Nathan a tour of the

Figure 3.4 The afterlife advertised, 'Welcome to Upload' (S1, E1), *Upload* (Amazon Studios, 2020–).

'2Gigs' accommodation, a place in Lake View where people who have paid for a budget afterlife are stuck with no view, and nothing to do, some with no clothing or with missing body parts, even. When Nathan wails 'Horizon should just give anybody a penis, or clothing, or an entire book!', Nora responds, 'Well they want people to pay for upgrades. It's called capitalism.' This is also where Nathan ends up when he ends his relationship later in the season, opting for 'freedom' and digital impoverishment at the same time. While the vision of this 'perfected' post-death world might initially seem like an attractive fantasy of plenitude and abundance to Nathan, he soon learns that this comes at a price and that Lake View is far from perfect. Katherine VanArendonk argues that *Upload* is exceptionally grim fantasy of life after death and that its comedy is just 'window dressing': '*Upload* does quite a bit of tap-dancing to disguise how bleak everything is' (2020). She proposes that 'The best way to approach *Upload* is not as a funny story about the afterlife. It's best as a show that asks what would happen if [Amazon CEO] Jeff Bezos could add "heaven" to the services offered by Amazon Prime' (ibid.) It is clear, then, that there is a dark humour drawn from the self-referentiality of the televisual afterlives imagined for Amazon and Netflix; these are dramas produced by digital media giants about a future in which we must pay for our digital survival beyond death (*Upload*), or, as in *The Good Place*, in which the afterlife can be constantly altered, enhanced or rebooted to torture its inhabitants (as in the beginning of Season 2 of the show), in a way that suggests that life beyond death is now 'virtual', and remotely controlled by a never-quite-revealed authority or corporation. In relation to this constant tweaking and rebooting, *The Good Place*'s handling of narrative time is exceptionally complex, conforming to what Bennett describes as the complicated handling of infinite time in the contemporary afterlife narrative where 'time is reversed, looped, annexed or ballooned' (2012: 71) and in which 'endings can be added to infinitely [and] every ending is provisional' (ibid.: 198). In *The Good Place*, this handling of infinite time is arguably a product of the imagined future/afterlife as implicitly digital in its design/execution. This is, therefore, deeply self-referential television which both encourages its audience to think about life, death and the meaning of existence, and also challenges us to consider the nature of digital storytelling and the role of digital media in the world.

So where has this analysis of the televisual afterlife taken us in our critical journey towards understanding the ways in which television has tried to make sense of death and dying? Firstly, it has brought us back to the idea that confronting death through television prepares us in some way for our own deaths or the deaths of those we love. The programmes discussed here have enabled us to think about what it might mean to die, or what might come after that most unknowable of experiences, even while they have also entertained us. They have all, in some way, contributed to the human search for the meaning of existence, and tried to answer questions which continue to remain out of our grasp, and have enabled us to think about how life, and death, might be changing right now. These are big claims to make for a clutch of American television dramedies, but this chapter has shown that they are claims with good basis. They are also claims that have been made by others. McIlwain argues that 'television programming about death and dying ... can benefit individuals and our society as a whole in terms of how we view death, as well as how we respond to its occurrence' (2005: 27); Bethan Michael-Fox concurs, proposing that 'television operates as a space through which people experience and engage with complex social understandings [of death]' (2019: 9).

If these afterlife narratives attempt to demystify death and dying for their viewers by imagining a continuing life beyond death, they are also perhaps even more concerned with the question of what it means to live a good life. Drawing on the work of the early Christian scholar Origen, Christopher Deacy suggests that we see cinematic afterlives as 'a spiritual, moral and rehabilitative training ground where we have the capacity to evolve and change' (2012: 152). This description also works well to summarise *The Good Place*'s exploration of ethical living. As discussed above, the series strives to replace a monotheistic belief in a particular kind of pious (or impious) behaviour leading to a particular kind of afterlife with a greater focus on questions of morality and ethics; the characters in *The Good Place* learn, in death, how to live good lives, and, by extension, they teach us this too (cf. McFarland, 2017; Egner, 2020). Throughout the four seasons of the show, Eleanor, in particular, learns to live in a better way (by way of becoming Chidi's 'ethical guinea pig'), caring for her fellow human beings and becoming less selfish and more community minded in the process. This is also true of Nathan in *Upload*, and in the way that June and Oscar learn to be better partners to each other by the end of *Forever*. Whereas Maxine Shen argued that 'Television has found a new way to get viewers to appreciate their lives: make shows about dead people' (2004), we might suggest that television has also found ways to encourage viewers to live better lives (as well as appreciating the lives that they have).

In the Season 2 episode of *The Good Place* 'Existential Crisis' (S2, E4), Chidi finds that he has to teach the demon Michael about the end of human life in order for him to understand ethics, explaining that 'life has an end, and, therefore, our actions have meaning'. Michael, who has previously never contemplated this as an immortal being, is asked to imagine his own death for the first time, which sends him into a spiral of despair. He asks, 'How does anyone do anything when you understand the fleeting nature of existence?' and later declares that 'Parties are mere distractions from the relentlessness of entropy. We're all just corpses who haven't yet begun to decay!' As a result of Michael's existential crisis, we also see flashbacks to Eleanor's past confrontations with death (specifically the death of her dog as a child) and a 'freak out' at the realisation of the permanence of death in a local hardware store. These experiences, though, ultimately enable Eleanor to counsel Michael:

> Eleanor: You're learning what it's like to be human. All humans are aware of death, so we're all a little bit sad, all the time. That's the deal.
> Michael: Sounds like a crappy deal.
> Eleanor: Well yeah, it is. But we don't get offered any other ones. And if you try and ignore your sadness, it just ends up leaking out of you anyway. I've been there. Everybody's been there. So don't fight it.

The episode ends with Chidi suggesting that they all read *Death* by Todd May (2009). This is significant as May, a consultant philosopher on the series, offers in this book a treatise on how we might live as creatures who die, and who know we are going to die. Indeed, May appears as himself in the final episode in this series ('Whenever You're Ready', S4, E13), taking part in one of Chidi's classes in the real 'Good Place' and arguing that 'Mortality offers meaning to the events of our lives'. Ultimately, this is the key point that is made by *The Good Place*: that we must live well knowing that life is finite and that the fact of death, and the knowledge that we will someday die, should guide us to lead better lives.

While the afterlives imagined in these dramedies suggest that life after death takes place in a tangible, knowable, mappable, world, many of these shows go on to undercut this, particularly in their final episodes. As discussed above, *Upload* holds on to the possibility that there is a non-digital life after death, like that imagined in the Bible, for example, but this form of afterlife still remains uncertain or unknown in the series. At the end of *Forever*, June and Oscar decide to strike out on their own beyond the known afterlife neighbourhoods of Riverside and Oceanside; even though they have been told repeatedly that there is nothing beyond these neighbourhoods by the mysterious Traveller (Peter Weller), they walk hand-in-hand into the sea and across the ocean floor, arriving at the other side to look in wonder around them. In this final shot of the series, all the viewer gets to see is June and Oscar's excitement as they walk towards and past the camera, just before the closing credits start to roll. Their ultimate destination remains a mystery, then, unknown and undepicted, perhaps even a product of their own belief. Similarly, at the end of *The Good Place*, successive characters decide to leave the titular 'Good Place' through an archway in the woods, which leads to what they are told is the end of their afterlives. Each character deciding to walk through this archway articulates this decision as accepting a final ending, a true death, perhaps, although what actually happens to them in this moment also remains a mystery. When Eleanor walks through the archway, the last to make this journey, we don't see her disappear; rather the camera tilts up as golden sparkles scatter into the treetops above. We can read this, I think, as a release of human energy, of the soul, maybe, into nature (Eleanor and Chidi have discussed Buddhist belief in such a thing earlier in the episode), or we can see this as the series' recourse to the mystery of death: the true final destination of the soul must ultimately remain unknown. While Spencer Kornhaber in *The Atlantic* worried that this ending's depiction of voluntary death promoted suicide to potentially vulnerable viewers (2020), Emily VanDerWerff praised the finale's 'gentle acceptance of death' (VanDerWerff, Wilkinson and Matthews: 2020). While we do not know what happens to Jason, Chidi, Eleanor and other inhabitants of the Good Place once they walk through the archway and towards death, the journey is only taken once each character is at peace with their decision.

This recourse to the unknown somewhat challenges the argument constructed in the first part of this book that engaging with death on screen helps us work through our feelings about our own inevitable deaths. In his book on the philosophy of death, Todd May argues that

> [The] salient fact about death is that it is for each of us *my own death*. We can hear all about the death of others, go to funerals, even see someone die. These are weighty matters. However, they do not replace the singularity of one's own death ... One's own death cannot be understood by coming to terms with someone else's death. (2009: 9)

May's thoughts here – that death cannot be managed or understood through engagement with the deaths of others – would explain why each of the series discussed above reinserts some mystery into their representation of the afterlife in the end. Death remains fundamentally unknowable and unshowable. This narrative 'return to the mystery of death' also problematises the idea that watching deaths on television, whether real or actual, will tell us anything about our own deaths. However, what the first three chapters of this book have shown is that we will continue our search for knowledge and understanding about death, and that television has an important part to play in this search.

4

Dramas of grief: Television and mourning

If, as argued in the previous chapter of this book, death and the dead have become much more present in recent television drama and comedy, we might be forgiven for asking whether television, like film, can be seen as depicting the 'sensational heat of relentless dying... with no time to mourn' (hooks, 1994: 10). This, according to bell hooks, characterises the way in which media in general, and Hollywood film in particular, depicts death: at a fast pace, with a focus on the material, but not the emotional, consequences of it. Laura E. Tanner makes a similar case when she argues that 'images of the dead in contemporary American mass culture often direct our attention to death by engaging in representational processes that obscure the embodied dynamics of loss in the very process of depicting the lost body' (2006: 211); Schultz and Huet's work also acknowledges the absence of normal grief reactions in Hollywood film, replaced by a focus on sensation and spectacle (2001: 137). Spectacular death on screen might therefore be seen as leaving us with a body, flayed, dismembered, bleeding and decomposing, but with no sense of how or by whom that body (or the person who once inhabited it) might be mourned.

However, alongside this 'television of attractions' in which the corpse is rendered the spectacular object of a simultaneously fascinated and appalled gaze, an alternate strand of programming has developed which precisely focuses on this absence: the television of grief. At some point in 2019, I realised that nearly all of the contemporary US serial dramas I had been watching for pleasure over recent years focused on a central character or characters going through the emotional processes of grief and mourning. From the complex family dramas *This is Us* (NBC, 2016–2022) and *Big Little Lies* (HBO, 2017–2019), to shows such as *The Leftovers* (HBO, 2014–2017), *Kidding* (Showtime, 2018–2020), *Sorry for Your Loss* (Facebook Watch, 2018–2019) and *Dead to Me* (Netflix, 2019–) which more explicitly announced themselves as explorations of bereavement and loss, grief seemed to be suddenly everywhere on television. This trend was also noted in a number of reflective pieces of journalism on recent television drama: in 2015, Sarah Hughes had argued that 'Sometimes, sitting on the sofa on a dark autumn evening, it's hard to escape the feeling that the most popular theme on television right now is bereavement' (2015). More recently, Madison Feller noted that there was 'something unexpected at the centre of every Good Thing I had watched . . . women grappling with grief and loss in messy, difficult, wildly divergent ways, just like real people' (2019). This was precisely not the spectacular death explored at the beginning of the previous chapter of this book and by Weber (2011), Dilman (2014) and others, but rather dramas that were more interested in exploring what was experienced after a death, rather than the death itself. The deaths (or disappearances) at the centre of these dramas typically took place either before the beginning of the drama or were not revealed until some way into their temporally complex narratives. Deaths and the bodies of the dead were, therefore, precisely *not* at the centre of these narratives which explored the aftershocks of this delayed or absent event and object. Their turn towards grief coincided precisely with what George E. Dickinson describes as a 'new trend in the twenty first century . . . trying to bring the topic [of bereavement] "out of the closet" and into the room' (2018: 14). For Dickinson, this 'grief trend' can be seen in the advent of 'death cafes',[1] organised gatherings of people talking about death and grief-related issues, but also in the presence of grief in the media, which has rendered the subject even more visible.

As with the previous chapter, the HBO series *Six Feet Under* (2001–2005) can be seen as something of an urr-text for this cycle of grief-focused dramas. While it was noted in Chapter 3 that *Six Feet Under* became the turning point for the representation of the corpse on contemporary US television, remembered for its spectacular 'deaths of the week' and for its depiction of life after death, the series more thoroughly explored the impact of the death of Nathaniel Fisher, Sr (Richard Jenkins) in the 'Pilot' episode on each family member at the centre of the drama, across all five of its seasons. The series was co-conceived by creator Alan Ball, partly in relation to his own experience of grief as a teenager following the death of his father and sister, and plots how the grief and mourning of its central characters continues and transforms throughout its narrative (Miller, 2016). In 2021, Saul Austerlitz revisited *Six Feet Under* on its twentieth anniversary, and reflected on the fact that the power and quality of the series' handling of grief had only increased in the intervening years, and particularly in the context of watching it during a global pandemic:

> The pandemic and its disruptions are finally beginning to recede in the United States, but the vast scale of collective loss the country endured – and in some areas continues to endure – is hard to fathom. Dying and grieving and losing and surviving are all experiences that we as a culture, as a people, as humanity, are grappling with in such an unrelenting way right now. [Lead writer Kate] Robin said 'It feels like that aspect of the show, while always relevant, has become even more universally so.' We have been shaken by the presence of death, but life still beckons to us, asking us to find a way to carry on. (2021)

Six Feet Under thus managed to marry the spectacle of death with a more meditative approach to the representation of grief, despite the fact that many television critics have seen these two things as antithetical. As Elias has argued:

> On-screen deaths are usually written in for shock value or for shameless ratings grabs during sweeps weeks ... in these shows, death is spectacle. Rarely do shows attempt to explore the largely uncharted emotional territory of what happens after a character dies, the grief. Grief is an ancillary emotion generally found lurking in the background of ghost stories. (2018)

Contemporary dramas of grief and bereavement absolutely strive to challenge Elias's argument here; they explore the complexity of grief, its multifaceted nature, its long duration and its seriality, as I shall explain in more detail below. The multiple strands of long-form serial narrative also allow for an examination of grief from multiple points of view, with multiple characters reacting in a variety of ways to the same death. This turn in contemporary US television therefore shows us that television can be understood as a medium of mourning *par excellence*. In viewing contemporary television as a cultural forum for working through or worrying at the *impacts* of death, or depicting death and the rituals that surround its mourning as an ongoing part of life, we see a refusal to let it recede from the everyday. Bronfen reminds us that 'dying, burial and commemoration are always also public matters ... [Death], in that it removes a social being from society, is conceived as a wound to the community at large and a threatening signal of its own impermanence' (2009: 77). These dramas allow us to see the results of death, not on the body of the dead individual, but on those who grieve and mourn.

The narrative forms of grief and mourning

As suggested above, the contemporary multi-part drama series at the heart of this chapter are particularly well able to depict the processes of grief for three specific reasons. Their long duration, serial form, and their playfulness with narrative time (what Mittell would call their 'narrative complexity' (2006)) all allow for a verisimilitudinous depiction of the experience of grief in contrast to what hooks defined as American cinema's portrayal of the 'sensational heat of relentless dying ... with no time to mourn' (1994: 10). Aaron's proposal that that 'dull ache of mourning' is 'rarely seen' on screen (2014: 1) cannot be upheld if we are to look at contemporary US television drama; by contrast, that dull ache is everywhere. There is, arguably, something inherently *televisual* about these three identifying characteristics of narrative form which transcends the platform for which the drama is made; television's extended duration, temporal volatility and constant returns, enabling a depiction of grief as an ongoing process, are seen in programmes produced for broadcast TV (for example, *This is Us* for NBC), streaming services (for example, *Dead to Me* for Netflix) and social media platforms (for example, *Sorry for Your Loss* for Facebook Watch). In their seriality and their extended length, they are most definitely television and not film. Thus, each of these examples explores grief and mourning in a quintessentially televisual way. Contemporary US serial drama depicts mourning in narratives which expand and oscillate (seemingly) endlessly, allowing for the exploration of the multifaceted dimensions of grief.

This argument, which will be explored through a discussion of indicative examples below, is similar to one made by Stacey Abbott in relation to the representation of love, fear and mourning in television horror (2016). Abbott proposes that

> [The] seriality of television ... provides a unique opportunity for TV Horror to both confront the audience with these fears and to slowly unpack the emotional response to death and loss by extending the narrative beyond death to its effects upon family, friends and the community. (ibid.: 171)

While the working through of bereavement in genres of the supernatural is explored in detail in the following chapter of this book, here it is Abbott's comments on this 'slow unpacking' of grief and mourning that I wish to explore. One of the most striking examples of this is seen in the NBC series *This is Us*, which follows the story of the Pearson family across 106 episodes and six seasons. We are not in fact aware that Jack Pearson (Milo Ventimiglia), the father of the family and one of the central characters in the narrative, has died at the beginning of the series, with an episode structure that skips constantly between the past and the present (documenting the lives of this family back and forth). However, from the very beginning of the series we see the repercussions of that death for his three children, Kevin (Justin Hartley), Kate (Chrissy Metz) and Randall (Sterling K. Brown), as they respectively suffer with depression and alcoholism, feelings of misery and chronic obesity, and crippling stress and anxiety, all of which are directly tied to grief in the narrative. Throughout the episodes that follow, this grief grows ever-more complex (these three are joined by multiple other characters experiencing other forms of grief and loss, and the siblings' own story arcs are complicated by multiple experiences of grief). *This is Us* therefore shows us that there is a longevity and a seriality to grief: bereavements will keep on coming, and continue to be felt over and over again, throughout our lives. The series also emphasises that our experiences of grief make us who we are.

To focus in on television's playfulness with temporality for a moment, and the structuring of long-form serial narratives around flashbacks and flashforwards, programmes such as *This is Us* depict grief as a constantly comparative state in which we contemplate life before, and life after, a loss. For the Pearson family, the constant flashbacks to the children's early and teenage years initially establish the stakes of what and who is lost and mourned in the scenes in the present: each of these different time frames features prominently in each episode. Later, however, as the series progresses, these flashbacks enable both characters and viewers to question the version of the past, and the remembered figure of Jack, that has formed for each of the characters, and to see how individual responses to grief in the series develop. The past becomes a complex site of contested histories and contradictory family stories. We also see the importance of the comparative 'before and after grief' moments at the beginning of *Sorry for Your Loss*, a detailed study of a young widow and her extended family coming to terms with the unexpected death of her husband. Following a pre-title sequence where the central grieving character, Leigh Shaw (Elizabeth Olsen), describes her pain at a bereavement support group, we see Leigh being woken up by her mother (Janet McTeer) and experiencing the misery of another morning without her husband, Matt (Mamoudou Athie).

As she whispers into her mattress 'I don't want to be awake' and her mother explains that no one does, a shot of Leigh in black, gazing into the distance, is intercut with a flashback scene of Leigh trying to wake Matt up for a trip to see her mother, the sound of Leigh's whispers ('Get up, get up,

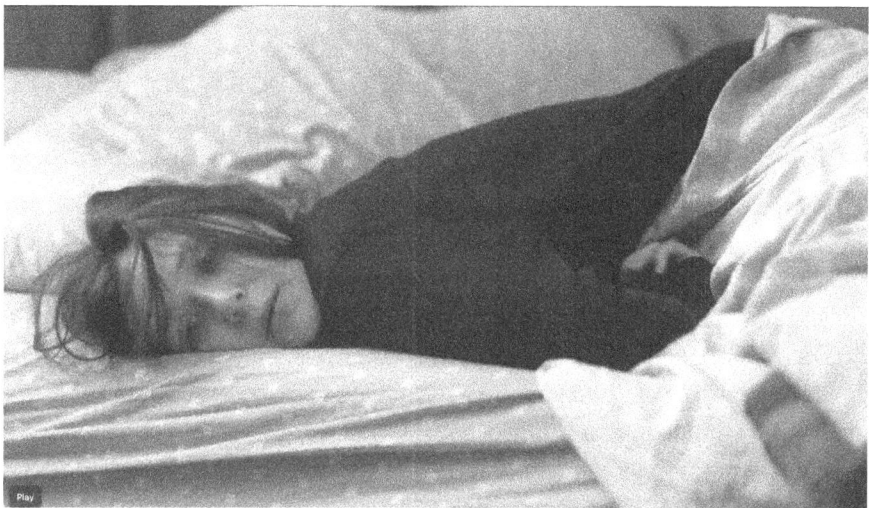

Figure 4.1 Leigh weighed down by grief, 'One Fun Thing' (S1, E1) *Sorry for Your Loss* (Facebook Watch, 2018–2019).

get up') bleeding between the present and the past bedrooms. Here the black clothes and the cool greys and blues of Leigh's room in the present are swapped for a white t-shirt and the warm, sunny tones of her marital bedroom; her loneliness is replaced by the close companionship of Leigh and Matt's gentle teasing. Again and again in the early part of this series, we see what Leigh has lost through the flashback sequences, which mark out tonal differences between then and now. At the beginning of Episode 2 she enters their old apartment to start packing up and the flashback to how she saw the same space for the first time is marked by a shift in colour palette, from greyness to warm yellow light. While this 'before and after grief' structure is later challenged by Leigh's discovery of the 'real Matt' rather than her idealised version of him, and the revelation of his struggles with depression, we understand the volatile temporality of the programme's narrative structure as emphasising grief as a constantly comparative experience.

Emotional realism and the experience of grief, on and off screen

So does recent television drama challenge the view that television is capable of only superficially depicting grief, seen here in Fulton and Owen's analysis from the late 1980s?

> Death's presence in the media is simultaneously everywhere and nowhere; it is at once illusively fantastical and frighteningly real ... While prime time television features death and violence relentlessly, particularly among the young, it portrays grief and the ruptured lives that death can leave in its wake only superficially. (1987–8: 370–83)

It is my contention that recent dramas both make grief more frequently present on screen and seek to do so in ways that aim for a sometimes difficult and painful form of emotional realism, striving to reach beyond the superficial. I make reference here to Ien Ang's work on the US soap opera *Dallas* (CBS, 1978–1991) and her outlining of the ways in which female viewers related to its 'tragic structure of feeling', defining, as a result, the 'emotional realism' of popular melodrama on television (1989: 46). Ang recognised that the women she spoke to about their pleasures in viewing this series on the grounds of its 'realism' and relatability to their own lives recognised not the similarity of its setting or the social context in which the drama took place, but rather 'a subjective experience of the world ... [in which] emotions form the point of impact for a recognition of a certain type of structure of feeling' (ibid.: 45). As we have seen already in relation to the dramas under discussion in this chapter, the 'messily' realistic nature of the way in which grief is handled is stressed time and again in reviews and previews of the series at hand in order to place emphasis on the series' emotional realism (Feller, 2019). Liz Feldman, creator of *Dead to Me*, argues that in her exploration of the grief of her central characters, Jen Harding (Christina Applegate) and Judy Hale (Linda Cardellini), the 'facts are made up but the feelings are real' (2019). This emotional realism is partly achieved through the sense that grief is depicted 'warts and all' in these series, showing characters airing 'difficult' emotions not normally expressed in television drama; it is also seen in the ways in which characters are shown experiencing the extremities of emotion associated with grief while undertaking mundane, everyday tasks, siting grief in the midst of life. If we take *Dead to Me* as our central example here, we see both of these elements of emotional realism at play from its very outset.

Dead to Me tracks the friendship that is formed between Jen and Judy following the death of Jen's husband in a hit-and-run accident (from early on in the first season both the viewers and Judy know that she was secretly responsible for this death). Throughout the series, we see Jen strive to come to terms with her loss through therapy, exercise, random hook-ups, Marie Kondo-style house clearance and a variety of other methods, but her grief remains fairly constant, expressed largely as a kind of wailing anger and resentment. Jen and Judy meet at a bereavement therapy group; despite a fake 'dead husband' cover story, Judy is, in fact, grieving for the loss of her relationship, multiple miscarriages, and possibly also the man that died as a result of her driving (Jen's husband). Much humour is subsequently found as the two women face their loss(es) differently: Judy maintains a (falsely) positive disposition in the face of Jen's howling grief and rage, bringing to mind Kristen A. Murray's suggestion that 'dark humour entreats people to engage, at least momentarily, with the experience of loss' and that humour 'is an ongoing, provocative endeavour – an attempt to articulate the impact of grief and ascribe meaning to loss' (2016: 55). To give an example of how Jen's grieving rage surfaces in the first season, the series opens with her neighbour, Karen (Suzy Nakamura), bringing over a 'Mexican lasagne' to Jen's house: this is at once a seemingly pleasant, neighbourly exchange and a chance for Jen to 'let out' her violent and angry feelings about her husband's death while maintaining a thin veneer of niceness and respectability. After handing over the lasagne, Karen simpers 'Jeff and I are here for you if you ever wanna talk', to which Jen replies with a terse 'Thanks'. Karen continues: 'I just can't imagine what you're going through', and Jen's response, with a thin smile across her face and in a studiedly measured tone, is 'Well, it's like if Jeff got hit by a car and died suddenly and violently. Like that'. The brutality of this response causes Karen to gulp, audibly, as Jen swiftly shuts the door in her face. Here we see grief rupturing Jen's everyday existence, an occurrence which continues to be shown throughout this episode and beyond. Even in the title sequence which directly follows this scene, a poignant irony is built in the contrast between stock shots of sunny Laguna Beach, Judy Garland on the soundtrack singing 'Get Happy',[2] and Jen crying quietly in her car as the music continues. This expresses the incongruous feelings of grief in the midst of life, and her inability to 'get happy' despite her surroundings and the people she interacts with. As the episode continues, we see Jen's grief continue to erupt in the most mundane of moments: for example, after putting her youngest son to bed we see shots of her crying heavily into her pillow as she sits on the toilet with her trousers around her ankles, pausing momentarily to grab some toilet roll and wipe her vagina. The episodic form of this and other dramas like it therefore allows for a representation of grief as repeatedly returning to interrupt/disrupt the everyday, from scene to scene and episode to episode.

The episodic nature of grief, and the emotional realism of a depiction of grief as a disruption of the everyday, is also eloquently expressed in *Kidding*, in which Jeff Pickles (Jim Carrey), the ever-sunny, almost child-like star of a puppet-based programme for children's television, grieves for the loss of his son, Phil (Cole Allen) who was killed suddenly in a car accident. Throughout the series, Jeff experiences moments of violent rage and howling sadness that jarringly disrupt his seemingly anodyne appearance. We have a glimpse of this in the opening episode of *Kidding* where Jeff Pickles stands outside the house next door to his ex-wife's house as new potential neighbours are shown round. As he tries without success to reconnect with his son, Will (Cole Allen), Phil's surviving twin brother, who calls his father a 'pussy' and cruelly comments on the end of his marriage, Jeff's gaze shifts to a house-shaped mailbox on the front lawn. In the following shot the mailbox is shown smashed to pieces on the ground, but we do not see how this happens; the inference here is that despite his pleasant, even tone and his patience with his son's attempts to hurt him, Jeff's grief transforms into a blistering rage in this elided moment. While these suppressed feelings continue to be alluded to throughout the first season of *Kidding*, it is not until the end of Episode 7, 'Kintsugi', where we really see Jeff's hold on his grief dissipate. After the end of a failed relationship, Jeff pays off his ex-lover's debts, and his accountant comments to him on the phone that 'She's lucky to have a friend like you. We all are.' Sitting in his father's office, Jeff puts down the phone and is suddenly overwhelmed by the awfulness of his grief and loneliness. As a horror film-style soundtrack of discordant synthesised music replaces the diegetic sounds of Jeff's breakdown, we see his body bent backwards, mouth open, in the classic pose of what French neurologist Jean-Martin Charcot described as the 'arch of hysteria' (see Boddice, 2019).

He screams, smashing up the office in a violent rage, spinning in the centre of the space with a lamp held aloft and a terrible grimace on his face, until the final act of smashing an LCD TV screen showing his own face visualises the complete breakdown of the grieving self that Jeff has held so carefully in check (see Figure 4.2). In this moment, golden light emits out of cracks in the on-screen shot of Jeff as Mr Pickles, the image referring to the Japanese kintsugi pottery of the episode's title, a ceramic art in which broken items are fixed with visible seams of gold to make them whole and beautiful once more. Here the shot of the cracked and golden Jeff symbolises that at last we have seen *all* of him, in all his brokenness and fragility; indeed, this is a turning point where Jeff finds himself more able to 'let his grief out' and subsequently finds a renewed personal strength. Here the violent disruption of everyday life by Jeff's grief is productive even while it is painful. In these dramas of bereavement, grief becomes both the horror beneath our everyday lives, always threatening to resurface as it does for Jeff Pickles in *Kidding*,

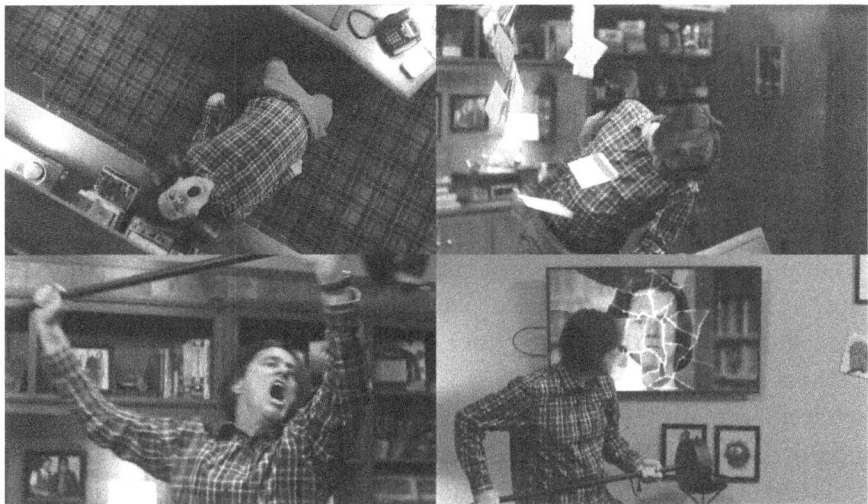

Figure 4.2 Jeff's trauma, 'Kintsugi' (S1, E7) *Kidding* (Showtime, 2018–2020).

and also the thing that we have to learn to live with. In the 'Meet Mr Pickles' film on the DVD of Season 1 of *Kidding*, Jim Carrey says of Jeff:

> I think he's an example of someone who's going to suffer a terrible, terrible loss and at the end of it all he's going to be better and he's going to be deeper and there won't be anybody out there after all this that he can't reach.

We can therefore see Jeff's breakdown, and his acceptance of his grief, as a moment of rebirth.

Watching others grieve: new ways of thinking about grief

Why have these images of grief and bereavement flooded our television screens in the last decade? Why would we wish to watch others grieve? Is it for the same reasons that Michele Aaron says we watch others die, to inure and harden ourselves against its potential threat?

> In crude terms, others suffer instead of us: the more we watch the death of others, the more we master it and are reassured of our own survival . . . The more violent and graphic the representation of murder, the more clearly the Western subject seeks to avoid the subject of

> death ... We become inured to the place of death in our lives, hardened to it, precisely through the *graphic* visualisations of death and dying. (2014: 4, original emphasis)

Perhaps by 'subjecting' ourselves to scenes of grief and mourning, rather than graphic death, we fail to escape the inevitability of death and its consequences but rather seek to harden ourselves against the psychological and emotional danger that grieving poses? From the earliest studies of mourning onwards, consideration has been given to 'good' and 'bad' grief, and the psychological damage that can be done by those grieving 'badly'. As Kenneth J. Doka acknowledges, 'Freud's 1917 paper "Mourning and Melancholia" while not actually the first paper offered on grief, is oft considered the beginning of the current psychological and scientific study of grief' (2018: 30). In it, Freud explores productive and functional grieving through the processes of mourning versus the unproductive and dysfunctional experiences of bereavement which develop into melancholia. Freud understood the latter as manifesting in the following symptoms:

> [P]rofoundly painful dejection, cessation of interest in the outside world, loss of the capacity to love, inhibition of all activity and a lowering of the self-regarding feelings to a degree that finds utterance in self-reproaches and self-revilings, and culminates in a delusional expectation of punishment. (1957: 244)

What was at the heart of the difference between mourning and melancholia for Freud was a kind of mindful letting go of the deceased through mourning and a reinvestment in other relationships instead. I will come back to this idea in the following chapter, as well as exploring the works that have challenged it via the 'continuing bonds' paradigm (Worden, 2009; Doka, 2018; Paxton, 2018), below.

Following Freud, a large body of work has been built that examines the processes of grief, attempting to chart its shape and form, account for its 'stages', perhaps even to map out an expected 'narrative structure' for grief. This has particularly been seen in influential work by Swiss-American psychiatrist Elisabeth Kübler-Ross in her 1969 book *On Death and Dying* which mapped out five stages of grief (denial, anger, bargaining, depression, and acceptance) in her terminally ill patients, and which was later expanded through a collaboration with David Kessler to include any form of personal loss, such as the death of a loved one, the loss of a job or income, the end of a relationship, and so on (Kübler-Ross and Kessler, 2014). Kübler-Ross's work was highly influential, perhaps because of its promise of a reassuringly predictable and linear pattern for the complex and difficult experience of grief. However, this promise has, more recently, been challenged by works that refuse the simplicity of the Kübler-Ross model. In more recent psychological and sociological works on grief, this state of being is no longer viewed as a series of stages to be worked on and through, but rather characterised as having a more messy and complicated structure. Kenneth J. Doka argues:

> We no longer view grief as a series of universal stages – rather we now see a continuum of reactions, very personal pathways that encompass the range of reactions individuals have to loss – from resilience to more complicated forms of grief. We recognise the variety of losses that can engender grief – not just a death. We realise how factors such as culture or gender can influence the process of grieving. We understand that grief is not about detachment but rather that we retain continuing bonds with people we loved. Finally, we acknowledge that individuals not only cope with grief but that grief offers opportunities for significant growths. (2018: 37)

Recent theories of grief therefore recognise the shape of grief as individuated and non-linear, perhaps cyclical and episodic, and, often, continuous, a series of oscillations between feelings and experiences that do not come to a complete end (Thompson, 2017: 138). In these new theories of grief, we learn to live with grief, rather than actively shrug it off or move through and away from it. It makes sense, then, that a verisimilitudinous representation of grief in serial dramas for television presents the experience of it and the emotions attached to it as complex and ongoing. These programmes also often remind us that grief is an individual experience, not a one-size-fits-all pattern, as illustrated by the analysis of *Dead to Me* above. When sitting together on the beach towards the end of the first episode of the first season of the programme, Jen says to Judy 'Thank you . . . for not being repulsed by my version of grief'; grief here is individually experienced, which is why Jen finds grief therapy so problematic, a fact I will return to later in this chapter. Further into Season 1, Jen expresses her incredulity about the building of makeshift roadside shrines at the site of road traffic accidents ('It's such a weird thing that people do, putting all that shit here'); here, and in many other places, the series acknowledges that there is not one single way to grieve.

The television drama that demonstrates the conflict between forms of grief and individuated experiences of grieving most dramatically is the

HBO series *The Leftovers*. This supernatural drama series begins three years after a global event called the 'Sudden Departure', during which 140 million people, 2% of the world's population, suddenly and simultaneously disappeared. The series explores, across three seasons, the impact of these disappearances on individuals, families, and other societal groups, with characters differentiated from one another by the ways in which they grieve. Characters find themselves isolated from their communities by their grief, as well as finding solace in points of connection and recognition in how others cope with loss.[3] Organised religion struggles to make sense to anyone in the face of such widespread loss; Matt Jamison (Christopher Ecclestone), the local reverend in the town of Mapleton in which the first season is set, loses his church and his congregation as a result. However, *The Leftovers* also depicts the formation of religious cults that offer markedly different collective responses to grief, most notably the followers of a healer, The Holy Wayne, and the Guilty Remnant, a group of white-clothed, chain-smoking nihilists who reject sentimental forms of grief and mourning. As Tom Perrotta, writer of both the source novel and script of *The Leftovers*, proposes

> In the [series], grief is a complex phenomenon, experienced by people in very different ways – some cope through ritual, others try to deny it and still others use it as fuel for social and personal transformation. The big question is, can we get back to the life we had [before grief] or do we have to find some new way to live? (Hughes, 2015)

The conflict at the heart of the series – conflict about *how* people grieve – becomes bitter and violent. In the first season, members of the Guilty Remnant are killed for their belief that the bereft should never forget or move on from their grief, never get comfortable with it. The cult in turn breaks into the houses of townsfolk, firstly to steal photographs of missing loved ones and later to situate models of them back in these homes, causing pain and anger and, ultimately, causing the people of Mapleton to turn on the cult's properties, burning them to the ground. In this heinous action, the cult utilises the products of the commodification of bereavement which we see throughout the series. These models are first seen in the third episode, 'Two Boats and a Helicopter' (S1, E3), in which Matt's housekeeper (Olga Sasnovska) watches a television advert for them, marketed as Loved Ones Bereavement Figures, which we hear described on the ad as Matt stumbles disconsolately around the supermarket:

> They're gone but so much of them is still here. You've tried to move on, tried to live a normal life, but you haven't let go because you haven't known how. Loved Ones Bereavement Figures allow you to say that goodbye. With as little as a single photograph, Loved Ones can create a tangible likeness of your departed, a bereavement figure for burial or cremation allowing you and your family to finally feel whole again.

The figures, which bear an uncanny resemblance to the departed, become one of the cathectic points for the narrative's explorations of the individuation of grief. They are meant to act as a physical stand-in for the disappeared, designed to be buried or cremated in a ceremony of 'good mourning' that allows the bereaved to move on. Of course, turning grief and bereavement into an industry requires the general public to be grieving in the same or similar ways, and to demonstrate similar needs. However, the complicated ways in which these models are treated in the series, from love and reverence to absolute revulsion, shows that this is not the case.

Matt's sister, Nora (Carrie Coon), one of the central characters in *The Leftovers* and who lost her husband and two children, works for the Department of Sudden Departure, for whom she interviews potential beneficiaries for their Departure Benefits. She initially encounters a Loved Ones Bereavement Figure at a bereavement industry conference, when she attends an orgiastic party held in the hotel room of the Loved Ones rep (in the episode 'Guest' (S1, E5). We see in this episode, as elsewhere, that the Sudden Departure causes all kinds of people in society to act recklessly/hedonistically, having altered characters' perceptions about risk and the future. The rep (Billy Magnussen) delivers his sales pitch for the models to Nora, offering the promise of the reassurance of a tangible object to mourn, before drunkenly coming on to her. Nora responds by incredulously asking 'People pay forty thousand dollars for this?' and then mounting and kissing the lifelike dummy passionately. At this point she rejects its uncanny nature (it is clearly 'played' by Magnussen as well) and here playfully uses the dummy as a further outlet for the recklessness that is being explored in this episode. Earlier in the episode, Nora had paid a prostitute to shoot her in the stomach with a gun loaded with blanks, as she struggled with feelings of disconnection from the world through her grief; not only had she lost her family, but she had also lost herself, lost connection with her own feelings. However, the next time Nora comes face to face with a Loved Ones Bereavement Figure is when she enters her own kitchen on the morning that the Guilty Remnant have placed the models in the homes of the townspeople (in 'The Prodigal Son Returns Home' (S1, E10)).

Figure 4.3 Loved Ones: the reassembled dead, 'The Prodigal Son Returns Home' (S1, E10) *The Leftovers* (HBO 2014–2017).

As she sees her husband and children, seated around her kitchen table (see Figure 4.3), Nora experiences a moment of absolute horror and torment, her face contorted into a silent scream of pain as she sinks to the floor. Here the encounter with the lifelike facsimiles of her lost family causes her to realise that despite her attempts to have healed and 'moved on' (via various mourning processes, through a new relationship with Kevin (Justin Theroux), the town's Chief of Police, and even through a healing blessing from the Holy Wayne (Paterson Joseph)), she is thrust back into a state of melancholia and struggles to let them go. When we return to Nora's house later in the episode, we find her sitting calmly, holding the hands of each of her 'children' and her gaze takes us into a close-up of each of the dummies' faces. We then witness her writing a letter to her lover which we first understand as a suicide note, and then read as an emotional goodbye, over shots of her putting the 'children' to bed with a sheet stretched over them as if they were corpses. She then leaves the house to deliver the letter to Kevin:

> You're strong, you're still here. But I can't be, not any more. I tried to get better, Kevin, I didn't want to feel this way so I tried to take a short cut but it led me right back home and do you know what I found when I got there? I found them, Kevin, right where I left them. Right where they left me. It took me three years to accept the truth but now I know there's no going back, no fixing it. I'm beyond repair. Maybe we're all beyond repair?

Nora's emotional internal monologue via the writing of the letter speaks of her struggle to move on and 'get over' her bereavement; the Loved Ones Bereavement Figures remind her of the difficulty/impossibility of letting go. However, in the closing scene of this episode, where she discovers an abandoned baby on Kevin's front porch, Nora finds a new purpose and a 'replacement' for the family that she lost. Ultimately, the fracturing of this small town in the first season, and its repercussions throughout the rest of the series, the relationships decimated by the experience of loss, stands as signifier for the complexity of grief and people's individual experiences of it.

As with the other series discussed here, *The Leftovers* frequently makes use of flashbacks, and the penultimate episode of the first season, 'The Garveys at their Best' (S1, E9), is entirely structured around a flashback to the events leading up to the Sudden Departure and the advent of worldwide grief. We see exactly what is at stake in the loss for the Garvey family in particular, including the loss of Kevin's wife's (Amy Brenneman) unborn foetus at the end of the episode. This flashback therefore shows us the moment of trauma and the origins of grief, but flashbacks in these programmes can also be potentially traumatic in and of themselves, experienced by characters experiencing trauma (as in Judy's brief and inadvertent flashbacks to the moment she hit Jen's husband with her car, in *Dead to Me*, or in Jeff's repeated momentary flashbacks to the road traffic accident that killed his son, Phil, in *Kidding*). While we will explore the connection between grief, trauma and the flashback/complex narrative time in more depth in the next chapter, for now we acknowledge that however it functions in each of these dramas, the comparative time of the serial narrative is most frequently experienced as painful, showing grief as a constantly comparative state where individual characters (and through them, the audience) *feel* the comparison of life before and life after death.

Further to the flashback/flashforward structure, we also see the comparison of moments in time through the use of screen media in these series, in line with Sandra M. Gilbert's proposal that the home movie is a 'death denying' technology (2006: 219); a number of these dramas feature the smart phone or laptop as the site of home mourning, where re-encounters with the dead via digital video storage allow the past to come flooding back. Perhaps unsurprisingly for a television series made to screen on Facebook, *Sorry for Your Loss* demonstrates the complex role that social media plays in the processes of grief and mourning. In this series, Facebook is both a source of discomfort when people with whom Leigh has a fairly superficial relationship intrude on her rituals of mourning (see the episode 'I Want a Party' (S1, E6)), and also provides Leigh and Matt's brother, Danny (Jovan Adepo), with some solace when home video stored on the platform allows them to re-encounter Matt, bringing the past back into the present (see the end of the episode 'I Hate Chess' (S1, E7)). This confirms Margaret Gibson's argument that 'Facebook, while not specifically associated with death and community, is nevertheless increasingly a site where the dead remain virtually present and where expressions of grief and condolence are made by friends, families, and other social ties' (2011: 22). *Sorry for Your Loss* dramatises the role that the platform plays in Leigh's grief, as well as depicting Matt's phone as a repository of memory and both a container of the identity of her lost husband and a storage facility for their lost relationship. At the beginning of Season 2, Leigh indicates her desire to move on from her grief for Matt (via building a new kind of relationship with Danny), by putting Matt's phone away and abandoning this digital archive, initially at least. Ultimately, though, these series use home media of various kinds to nod towards what Paxton and others have called the 'continuing bonds paradigm' (2018: 3), whereby an ongoing relationship is maintained with the dead, even when those who mourn go on to form new relationships and ostensibly 'move on' with their lives.

Sorry for Your Loss's streaming on Facebook Watch means that it has both dramatised the role that social media can play in the processes of grief and also become framed by the communities that form around the experience of grief on the platform. It is very plain to see how viewers relate the experiences of Leigh and her family to their own experiences of death and loss, as responses to the series constantly emphasise this. This communal experience of grief, whereby individuals who have experienced death and loss in their lives are brought together through communal activity to compare or relate to the experiences of others, is not only seen in *Sorry for Your Loss*. Whether in *Dead to Me*'s grief therapy groups or *The Leftovers*' cult activities or characters who bond and form new relationships precisely because they have both experienced loss, we see the formation of grieving *communities* in these dramas. These communities potentially represent diegetically a larger community of those who grieve that are implicitly addressed by these serial dramas. As vividly illustrated by the reception of *Sorry for Your Loss* on Facebook, the television viewer frequently feels themselves to be part of a wider community of grief that is given an outlet in the dramas of grieving under discussion in this chapter: we will all experience death and loss in our lifetimes and therefore the depiction of a variety of experiences of grief on television take on greater resonance and importance in relation to this. In their analysis of the ethics of film and film viewing, Lisa Downing and Libby Saxton examine the relationship between cinema and what they call 'distant suffering', arguing via Luc Boltansky's work (1993) that 'watching suffering from a distance can act as a spur to ethical thought and action' and that images 'imparting knowledge of suffering confer on us an obligation to do something about it' (2010: 65). They explore in this context the ways in which we might experience death on screen, highlighting the link between their analysis and the ideas set out in Sontag's *Regarding the Pain of Others* (2003), and detailing the need for reflective thought and action following a filmic encounter with death. If we transpose these ideas onto the experience of encountering the suffering of grief on television, we might similarly ask where our witnessing of the distant suffering of grief takes us, and what action it inspires. Do we learn to accept, understand and tolerate the experiences of our own griefs and those of others via watching television drama? Do we become attuned to the lonely experiences of grief and how we might, paradoxically, become united with others through these (shared) experiences? The viewer experiencing the distant suffering of others' grief might be theoretically figured as also lonely and grieving themselves, as well as forming part of a communal experience of grief through viewing.

This positioning is significant if it is accompanied by what Walter sees as the potential for connection in grief: 'the sharing of loneliness may not be a cure for individualism [in grief] but it can be very effective first aid' (1994: 35). While characters in these dramas are always depicted as lonely in their grief, they search for and often find connection and solidarity during the course of the narrative. There is, however, a deep and ironic scepticism about grief therapy in many of the dramas under discussion. Seale describes the thinking behind the 'medico-psychiatric discourse ... of bereavement counselling and support groups' as 'a late modern ritual for repairing damaged security, allowing mourners to reconstruct narratives of self-identity so that they can imagine themselves to be contained within the secure bonds of a caring community' (1998: 8). While the dramas discussed in this chapter depict the rituals of mourning, or what we might see as 'grief work' (Gross, 2015: 5), grief therapies often fail and are depicted as problematic, manipulative and shallow. *Dead to Me* offers the most sustained version of this narrative: its central characters meet at a grief therapy group, and the series initially seems to both buy into the idea of therapeutic culture and the self as something to be worked over and on and uses grief therapy sessions as a useful narrative device for externalising emotion, manifesting conflict and extrapolating plot. However, grief therapy, as a practice and as an industry, is soon derided in the series, by Jen in particular. For example, in 'I've Gotta Get Away' (S1, E5), Jen and Judy attend a 'grief retreat' in Palm Springs. Jen, having recently discovered her husband's infidelity, attends the retreat armed with a huge amount of scepticism and with the intention of hooking up with one of the other bereaved attendees. Group therapy sessions at the retreat are figured as uncomfortable and inauthentic: while attendees intone 'I am not broken' during Judy's 'Baby Death' session in an almost hypnotised manner, a slow zoom into Judy's face reveals that she, in fact, *is* broken. As Jen leaves the 'Big Question' session drunk and in the company of her bereaved love interest in Palm Springs, she drawls

> Pastor Wayne has a way of saying things without saying anything... He just goes on and on about how you can have your feelings but I just think he wants you to stay sad, like wallow in it all. It's good for his business. I actually was in his grief group and I didn't get anything out of it.

Ultimately, while the grief group is seen as shallow and inauthentic in the solace that it provides, Jen and Judy both find shared experience and camaraderie in their relationship with each other. Indeed, the end of the first season sees the two women bonding over the murder of Judy's manipulative and dishonest ex-husband. These dramas thus ultimately conclude that grief is something we learn to live with, rather than recover from, in keeping with Leeat Granek's rejection of the medicalisation of grief (2017: 267), and that solidarity might be found in the sharing of these experiences outside of a medical context. By extension, we might understand the viewer as a lonely and grieving subject who similarly seeks or receives solace via the vicarious, hypersocial connection offered by identification with the grieving protagonist and the representation of shared experience on TV.

Does the assumption that the viewer is a figure who also grieves need ultimately to be understood in the context of situating these programmes within a wider 'era of mournfulness', and in doing so must we see and know the viewer as an already grieving subject who is addressed by highly resonant images of bereavement? Michele Aaron has argued that the contemporary obsession with death in film has to be understood as culturally, critically and historically located, in relation to 'the urgencies surrounding the world's economic crises, continuing and emerging conflicts, depleting resources and aging populations' (2014: 12). Even before the global pandemic we faced as I wrote this book, we had begun to face the possibilities of mass death and human extinction brought about by climate change, and in the time of Covid, these feelings have only been sharpened. George E. Dickinson argues that from the end of the Second World War on, 'The threat of "megadeath" became a constant reminder of the fragility of life and the uncertainty of existence' (2018: 11), prompting what Dickinson describes as a 'resurrection of death' (ibid.) in the public consciousness. If we increase that threat of 'megadeath' to one of extinction, it is perhaps understandable that these programmes might be viewed as being made in an era of wider mournfulness. By the second series of *Sorry For Your Loss*, and particularly by Episode 5 of this season, '17 Unheard Messages', we understand Matt's experience of depression and melancholia in relation to the threat of species extinction (he tells a story to his therapist about the loss of the last African white rhino, linking it to his own feelings of despair). As with *Dead to Me*, everyone in this series is depicted as experiencing some form of grief. As a species, as a society, these television dramas represent us as overwhelmed by (potential) death and grief. This is also eloquently expressed on numerous occasions in *Kidding*: when Jeff's sister (Catherine Keener) asks his father (Frank Langella) 'How much longer do you think we have?', referring to Jeff's deteriorating mental health, Jeff's father, Sebastian, replies 'As a species?'. Later, in the final episode of Season 1, Jeff's breakdown at a nationally televised Christmas tree lighting ceremony sees him relating his personal grief to the death of the planet caused by hormones in our milk and plastic in our oceans. *Kidding* is therefore haunted by the existential dread of the end of the Anthropocene. Watching these programmes in the context of the pandemic, especially a programme like *The Leftovers* where grief and mourning is globally experienced, feels particularly poignant. While Sarah Hughes argues that this series was initially inspired by the events of 9/11, she says that it 'continues to examine bereavement on a grand scale' (2015). As discussed in the previous chapter, Charlton D. McIlwain has argued that

> Individual and collective contemplation of death provides an impetus for collective identity, despite the varieties of otherness we encounter . . . That death is a topic of public discourse engaged in by members of a given community is . . . the most significant element of building and sustaining community itself. (2005: 8)

The dramas and dramedies of grief that are explored in this chapter are evidence of the fact that the television viewer forms a community not just around the contemplation of death, but specifically around the experience of grief and bereavement. The emotional realism of these depictions of grief, and the messy and complicated narratives of those coming to terms with loss, invite us in to share in the pain explored in these fictions.

5

Haunted houses, haunted landscapes: Grief and trauma in the television ghost story

A girl runs through a wood, her knitted green cardigan and yellow sun dress blurring into the foliage around her. Then she disappears. A grey-green moor, cloudy, frames the house that an old man is preparing to leave. A young woman gazes out of her window into a garden where a revolting figure leers at her from the trunk of a tree. A woman walks through swaying grass in the sunshine, her face hidden from view in the haze of distant memory, her connection to the old man, and the fire that this image is cross-cut with, uncertain. A house stands quiet in the darkness, shrouded in fog. Shaky footage shows a panicking young woman running through endless corridors.

The above haunted houses and landscapes – all snapshots from the opening moments of the dramas discussed in this chapter – call to the viewer to understand them, to decipher their meanings and significance. As viewers, we wish to know these places: where is the wood and why is the girl running? Why does the moor seem so mournful and what has it got to do with the old man's story? Where is this garden and where did the leering man come from? What secrets does this house contain? Setting is thus one of the central enigmas in the television ghost story. Maria del Pilar Blanco has argued that to look for ghosts in a text is always to study place: in this endeavour we seek to understand how each haunted landscape is 'distinct from one another – and to vigilantly account . . . for the spatiotemporal coordinates that merge to produce a site of haunting' (2012: 1). Del Pilar Blanco, writing about North American literature, proposes that to 'ghost-watch implies a vigilant perception of the landscapes depicted within it' (ibid.: 1) and suggests that ghosts are always 'embedded in the story about a place' (ibid.: 8). The dead are thus located in a place, both bodily and spectrally, and our relationship to them must be worked out by, and worked through, an exploration of their setting.

What place does an analysis of the contemporary TV ghost story have in this study of television and death? Ghosts are, of course, the result of a death, the spectral remnants left behind by the death of a (usually human) body; in the ghost narrative, the soul left behind by this death is frequently a tortured one and those left to mourn that death are often traumatised by it (or by a spectral encounter with the dead). As Tom Gunning argues of ghosts across modern media, they 'carry, even if repressed, a warning of mortality and limitations, of the inevitable horizon of death' (2013: 232). This chapter sits alongside the previous one, with its focus on the televisual depiction of grief and mourning, and picks up from that chapter an interest in the structure of grief narratives on television. Like the previous chapter, it looks at how television uses serial narrative form to attempt to represent the experience of death and grief for characters with some emotional realism. In the case of the television ghost story, characters' experiences of death are most often traumatised experiences and through the course of the narrative they must explore a particular place – specifically a haunted house or a haunted landscape, what Hudson refers to as 'trauma landscapes' (2017: 20) – in order to work through that trauma, and to understand how and why that place holds the meaning and significance that it does.

Characters in ghost dramas either search a landscape for some understanding of how and why a death took place, or of how they can learn to live with their feelings about that death. They explore haunted houses to attempt to deal with the reverberations of a death or deaths, to make sense of half-remembered sounds and images and to piece together traumatised memories into a comprehensible narrative. While the literature on the representation of trauma has often made a case for either the difficulty/impossibility of trauma representation or the need to represent trauma through experimental or avant-garde cinematic or televisual forms (an idea explored at greater length below), this chapter proposes that the television ghost drama is ideally suited to the representation of trauma, given that its serial form allows for the kinds of temporal volatility, and complex past–present relations, necessary to represent traumatised memory and experience. Characters' processes of working through their traumatised relationship to a death or deaths are complex and messy and therefore the serial narrative works well to represent that complexity. The chapter looks at two recent cycles of TV ghost stories: short serial ghost stories produced for British television over the last decade or so (including *Marchlands* (ITV1, 2011), *The Secret of Crickley Hall* (BBC1, 2012), *Lightfields* (ITV1, 2013), *Remember Me* (BBC1, 2014), and *The Living and the Dead* (BBC1, 2016)) and longer, complex serial ghost dramas made for post-broadcast television in the US more latterly (for example, *The Haunting of Hill House* (Netflix, 2018) and *Archive 81* (Netflix, 2022)). These can all be seen as 'ghost melodramas', using Michael Walker's description of narratives in which a ghost seeks justice or bears testament to loss, rather than those ghosts which seek revenge in the more classic horror text (2017: 11–12). Indeed, the notion of melodrama is particularly pertinent here, given that location and setting has been considered as playing 'a part as important as characters in carrying meaning' (Mercer and Shingler, 2004: 53) in the melodrama.

If the relationship between trauma and memory is at the heart of the television ghost story, and subsequently at the heart of this chapter, then arguably the television ghost story builds on what has been seen as the burgeoning of trauma across the arts and culture, but especially in narratives of haunting. This is described by Jeffrey Andrew Weinstock as a 'recent preoccupation' with trauma in spectral discourse (2004: 5) and by Roger Luckhurst (with reference to the equation of ghosts with trauma) as so present as to be 'almost a cliché' (2008: 93). Alan Gibbs, in his critical account of 'trauma studies' and the representation of trauma in American culture, has cautioned against the over-reading of trauma across cultural forms and sites: 'As the trauma paradigm was more widely disseminated through American culture during the late twentieth century, so a tendency developed to read everything through its increasingly monolithic and programmatic critical prism' (2014: 1–2). Gibbs is particularly critical of the work of Cathy Caruth, whose foundational analysis of the representation of trauma has been so widely cited across the field of 'cultural trauma studies'. When Caruth argued that 'to be traumatized is precisely to be possessed by an image or event' (1995a: 4–5) she drew attention to what she saw as the interconnectedness of trauma as a clinical condition and trauma as a subject of (audio) visual media representation. While Caruth's analysis of trauma fictions proposed that media representation of trauma necessitated the development of experimental artistic and literary forms to properly represent the disconcerting experiences of this condition, Gibbs and others have challenged Caruth's position, critiquing the imposition of 'formulae that have in turn produced a narrow approved trauma aesthetic' (2014: 17), and a 'moral injunction against straightforward or realistic representation of trauma' (ibid.: 26). Gibbs, and also Luckhurst, push back against Caruth's suggestion that trauma can only be presented via 'the most indirect and experimental aesthetic forms possible' (ibid.) or through 'a specific Modernist aesthetic and a narrow canon of films' (Luckhurst, 2008: 178) and in doing so open up a critical space for the analysis of trauma as it is represented in popular television drama, as in those programmes at the heart of this analysis. Although the ghost dramas discussed in this chapter can be described as narratively complex, with a spatiotemporal volatility that drags both viewer and protagonist constantly back and forth in narrative space and time, they are also popular mainstream/primetime television dramas that reach narrative conclusions and, to a greater or lesser extent, trauma resolutions. This chapter will subsequently propose that the serial form of the television ghost drama is particularly well suited to the representation of traumatised memory.

Exploring haunted landscapes: the British television ghost story

In the ghost dramas made for British television in the last decade or so, landscape is key to the past–present relations which are so central to the depiction of a haunting. In the ghost story, different time frames coincide within the same place; a glance out of a window, through a door, into a wood or over a lake might take us back or forward in time, enabling the living and the dead to coexist within the same space. As Maria del Pilar Blanco notes, haunted landscapes are frequently marked by an 'increasing awareness of simultaneous landscapes and simultaneous others living within unseen, diverse spaces' (2012: 7). Martyn Hudson's idea of sedimentation in the ghost text is also useful here. Hudson reads the ghost as a figure of 'congealed social memory', and employs a landscape metaphor to describe this, considering the 'mentalities of both the living and the dead as strata deposited by history and culture' and proposing that 'There is no index or inventory to this sedimentation and the only way to understand it is, to use Freud's archaeology metaphor, to excavate it as one would a ruined and blasted city' (2017: xvii–xviii). Hudson subsequently describes haunted landscapes as 'historically sedimented and stratified by the multiple memory of the dead' (ibid.: 17), and argues that '[t]he co-existing landscape of the living and the dead is one within which both contestation or collaboration can take place' (ibid.: 128).

There are numerous examples we could turn to in the dramas at hand to illustrate these points about ghosts and landscape: for example, the haunted house narratives of the *Secret of Crickley Hall*, *Marchlands* and *Lightfields* all shift constantly back and forward in time around the occupants of a single house within a specific landscape in two or three time frames, and in each case the haunting becomes apparent in the narrative when characters, sounds and objects from each time frame break out of their temporal boundaries. All of these dramas demonstrate Martyn Hudson's point that haunted houses themselves are sedimented landscapes, 'containers for the congealed histories and trauma of the past, or of their inhabitants' (2017: 77). Barry Curtis concurs in his evocation of an archaeological metaphor: 'All explorations of the haunted house invoke a kind of archaeology, the uncovering of an occluded narrative' (2008: 33). However, the sedimented landscape in which the strata of different, coexisting time periods are written onto fields and woodland is most clearly seen in the 2016 BBC drama series, *The Living and the Dead*.

The Living and the Dead follows the story of Nathan Appleby (Colin Morgan), a psychologist who inherits a house on the edges of an isolated village in Somerset. Nathan, and his second wife Charlotte (Charlotte Spencer), whom he married following the death of his son, move to this house to farm its land and lead its community. However, they are soon troubled by strange occurrences which are subsequently revealed as hauntings from Shepzoy's past and its future. The woodland, farmland, moorland and the bodies of water that surround Shepzoy play an important role in the series; Matt Gray, Director of Photography on *The Living and the Dead*, describes the landscape as an 'ever-present character' in the drama,[1] and the location filming (in Gloucestershire, which stands in for rural Somerset here) is critical in the unravelling story about the haunting of Nathan Appleby. For example, in Episode 2 of the drama, Charlie (Isaac Andrews), a young boy from the local village, is haunted by the ghosts of five workhouse orphans who suffocated years earlier in an accident in the tin mine owned by Nathan Appleby's grandfather. Following a scene in which Charlie assists in the reopening of the mine during survey work for a forthcoming railway, he is haunted by the ghost children who lure him into the woods late at night, as Nathan hunts for him and is also haunted by the sounds of the orphans playing. In this moment, the landscape of *The Living and the Dead* is clearly marked by traumas of the past associated with the dead; this dense woodland is not only the site where Charlie is haunted by the dead orphans, but it is also troubled by the ghost of a woman (Gina Bramhill) murdered by a spurned lover and the multiple spectres of villagers massacred during the English civil war. The woods are also inhabited by ghosts from the future, from beyond Nathan's own death: in the aforementioned scene, before Nathan locates Charlie playing among the ghosts of the dead orphans, he sees and hears traces of a car careening towards him (bright headlights, screeching tyres), despite the fact that the main narrative of this drama is set in 1894. In the previous episode, he looks up through the trees of the graveyard at the edge of the wood to see an aeroplane trail in the sky above, and with increasing frequency he follows the 'ghost' of a woman (who, we later discover, is Lara (Chloe Pirrie), one of his descendants) carrying an iPad through Shepzoy House and its surrounding landscape. When Nathan locates Charlie in the scene discussed above, he initially hears the ghost orphans as he approaches, and landscape (here the woods) is marked as aurally haunted (in the ghost drama, particular landscapes are frequently associated with recurring sounds: laughter, phrases, songs, and so on). As Charlie looks back, a point of view shot shows the ghostly orphans, dressed to appear as if they have literally risen out of the earth, and therefore marked as figures of and from this landscape. Landscape, then, is figured in the ghost drama as a series of 'shadow sites', to use Robert Macfarlane's phrase (2012: 48); it constantly reveals the geographical connections between past, present and future, illustrates the coexistent 'congealed' histories of the families who live within it, and resurfaces their dead. As Nathan searches through the wood, he searches not only through space, but also through time, in order to investigate a series of hauntings.

Even outside of the haunting, the landscape of Shepzoy is fraught with trauma and anxiety: the villagers worry about the impact of the industrial revolution on the land (the coming of the railway, the mechanisation of farm labour) and are deeply superstitious about the 'cursing' of land during harvest time. It is therefore a troubled landscape from the outset. There is something quite specific about the positioning of the English rural landscape as an elegiac marker of loss and decline, an image perhaps first identified in W. G. Hoskins's seminal *The Making of the English Landscape* (1954), for as Roger Luckhurst's work has reminded us, we move away from the 'wooliness' of the 'spectral turn' in cultural criticism by considering the ghost in its specific locale (2002). In his writing on the 'eeriness' of the English countryside (2015), Robert Macfarlane 'considers the unsettling allure that accrues around [it] and the paradox that what is, on the one hand, traditionally conceptualised as a pastoral idyll, equally operates as a magnet for the "eerie"' (Armitt, 2017: 291). In British horror cinema, the eerie English rural landscape becomes 'a residuum of old beliefs that have survived the modernization and urbanization of British society' according to Peter Hutchings (2004: 36), and there are traces of this in the television ghost story, including in *The Living and the Dead* which is punctuated by the village folk performing rituals in and for the land, living in fear of cursed harvests and the threat of modernity on their lives and locality.

There is, then, something specifically unsettling about the English landscape that has to do with the disruption of nostalgia for the country's pastoral, pre-industrial heritage (as noted in my book *Gothic Television* (2006), and in Peter Hutchings's writing about the uncanny British landscape (2004)). To quote Hutchings, this landscape is 'suffused with a sense of profound and sometimes apocalyptic anxiety; it is also a landscape of a comprehensible dispossession and vacancy' (29). The writer of *The Living and the Dead*, Ashley Pharoah, captures the unease of this landscape in an article for the series' press pack:

> Point a camera at a field of wheat on an English summer's day. What do you see? A blue sky over yellow crop. A soft breeze moving the wheat like an inland sea. The murmur of a bee. It's pretty. It's comforting, nostalgic. But let's leave the camera running. Keep our attention fixed on that same landscape. Perhaps a cloud slides across the sun, slowly darkening the yellow. Or a stronger gust of wind makes the branches in the trees grind. A crow caws. Now the English landscape can feel unsettling, a place that's drenched in history that includes war and death and unhappiness. Eerie, that's the word. And that was the starting place for *The Living and the Dead,* to see the skull beneath the skin of the English pastoral. (BBC, 2016)

Referring elsewhere to his series as 'Thomas Hardy with ghosts',[2] Pharoah suggests here that the ghost story portrays the 'underside' of the English pastoral (see Figure 5.1); he borrows from Macfarlane's essay on the eeriness of the English countryside (2015) the phrase the 'skull beneath the skin of the English pastoral' to describe *The Living and the Dead*, and specifically the way in which its narrative space is imbued with death. All of the UK TV ghost dramas discussed in this chapter thus depict recognisably English rural space as troubled by death, whether that be coastal landscape (in *Lightfields* and *Remember Me*), woodland (in *Marchlands* and *The Living and the Dead*), agricultural land (*Lightfields* and *The Living and the Dead*) or moorland.

To look at the latter in more detail, the moor is a particularly resonant space in another key ghost serial from this cycle of dramas: *Remember Me*. This drama, set in the towns and moorland of West Yorkshire and the coastal areas of North Yorkshire, follows the story of Tom (Michael Palin), a pensioner who is desperate to leave his home and is dogged by the ghost of his Indian nanny, Isha (Mayuri Boonham), who was drowned at sea after being

Figure 5.1 The pastoral eerie in *The Living and The Dead* (BBC1, 2016).

sent back to India once Tom and his family had arrived back in England from their colonial home. Hannah (Jodie Comer), a teenage care worker from the retirement home Tom is moved to, and Rob (Mark Addy), a detective investigating the death of Tom's social worker (Rebekah Staton), work together to get to the bottom of the mysterious events surrounding this old man, while dealing with their own stories of grief and loss; Hannah's family has been shattered by the death of her father, while Rob has been isolated by his divorce and the emigration of his daughter. Of all of these dramas, *Remember Me* most clearly positions the exploration of a haunting as a narrative of detection and the working-out of a series of death-related enigmas, an important aspect of the ghost drama according to Michael Walker (2017: 20). The series was shot in and around the Colne Valley in sites such as Pole Moor, Marsden and Slaithewaite, a location often used to convey a kind of wild desolation in films and programmes set in Yorkshire such as *The League of Gentlemen* (BBC2, 1999–2002), *In The Flesh* (BBC3, 2013–2014) and *A Monster Calls* (J. A. Bayona, 2016). This is a deeply melancholic landscape, to draw on Jacky Bowring's proposal that 'landscape holds within it the natural habitat for melancholy, as the locus of places of contemplation, memory, death [and] sadness' (2016: 4). In *Remember Me*, the moor consistently hangs over Tom, Hannah and Rob, even when they are depicted in domestic space or on public transport: it is constantly visible in the background of almost every shot as a reminder of the grief and loss that haunts all three of them. Gwyneth Hughes, the writer of *Remember Me*, reflected on the resonance of the moorland setting in an interview for the *Huddersfield Examiner*:

> I live in Yorkshire, so naturally I tend to want to set my stories here. But particularly for *Remember Me*, the big skies and deserted landscapes seemed very suitable . . . It is also great to get [actors] who really understand the landscape and the way of life here, so that the film stands a chance of being really true to itself and can offer a real sense of place. (Atkinson, 2014)

This sense of place taps into a long representational history of moorland as '"ill-omened", "sombrous", "dreary"', according to William Atkins: 'It [is] a place of unreachable loneliness, the stage for sacrifice, exile and the outplay of grievance' (2014: xvii). Martyn Hudson also describes moorland as a lacuna: a space and landscape 'in which the ordinary world is suspended' (2017: 6), while Lucie Armitt argues that in Britain in the late twentieth and early twenty-first centuries, 'our cultural awareness of moorland is almost entirely overwritten by a real life "ghost story"' (2017: 292). Here she refers to the moor as the site associated with Ian Brady and Myra Hindley, the duo commonly known as the 'Moors Murderers', and Saddleworth Moor in particular, where their victims were buried, as 'a landscape beyond humanity' (2017: 292). While Mark Fryers's work has analysed the liminal coastal setting in *Remember Me* as a place of 'death and terror' (2015), the deployment of dark grey skies and misty moorland as a constant reminder of hidden pasts and unprocessed grief is perhaps even more pervasive in the series. Director of Photography Tony Miller uses what I believe to be a graduated neutral density filter to give the moor a very dark and brooding look in the series. His cinematography seems to directly reference other representations of the moor, particularly Fay Godwin's photography of the Yorkshire landscape, collected in her book *Land* (1985), which is described by William Atkins as 'death everywhere' (2014: 153), full of black clouds, seas of grass and moorlands wreathed in mist.[3]

It is clear, then, that the traumatic deaths of the ghost story are explored through landscape in these contemporary British dramas. *Remember Me*'s writer, Gwyneth Hughes, has said that 'All ghost stories have to emerge from a sense of loss and loneliness, I think, and all these characters have lost something very precious' (Atkinson, 2014). While she is discussing her serial in particular, she could in fact be talking about all of the dramas at hand. All three key themes examined in relation to the contemporary

UK ghost serial – grief and mourning, trauma, and the search for truth and reconciliation – relate to how death is dealt with or worked through in the ghost drama. In relation to grief, many of the narratives at the heart of this study centre on a character or characters who must come to terms with a loss. As such, the British television ghost narrative is often about learning to grieve 'successfully', to not allow grief to overwhelm or prevent someone from 'moving on' in their lives. As discussed in the previous chapter, in Freudian terms this means to move away from melancholia to mourning through a process of 'reality testing' whereby the mourner comes to accept that the object of their loss is really gone. Freud argued that the 'opposition [to this acceptance] can be so intense that a turning away from reality takes place and a clinging to the object [lost person] through the medium of hallucinatory wishful psychosis' (1957: 244); it is not difficult to understand why an encounter with a ghost or ghosts might be seen as a manifestation of Freud's melancholic psychosis. As Tom Gunning notes of the Freudian approach to grief,

> [S]urviving the dead depends on our ability to slowly and purposefully forget them, to let them leave our world. But this work of mourning involves as well a task of remembrance, the conscious process that differentiates mourning from the disease of melancholia. (2013: 235–6)

As suggested above, grief, mourning and melancholia are marked on the specific landscapes of each drama in this study. In *Marchlands*, for example, the death of Alice (Millie Archer), the little girl in the green cardigan mentioned in the introduction of this chapter, sends her mother, Ruth (Jodie Whittaker), compulsively back into the wood in 1967, both psychically and physically, as she struggles to come to terms with her loss. We see this in the dream sequence that opens this series, where Ruth dreams Alice back into existence in the wood to explore the place where she died, but it is also illustrated in a moment from Episode 4 of *Marchlands* where Ruth stands in Alice's bedroom, regarding a painting of woodland on the wall. This painting links the parents at the centre of the haunting in all three time periods in this haunted house drama, and Nisha Parekh (Shelley Conn) revealing this painting in the 2010 section of the narrative while decorating a nursery becomes a catalyst for the return of Alice's ghost – and Ruth's reconnection with it. Ruth's connection to this woodland landscape here (in 1968) is a sensory one: first, she gazes into the picture, as if scouring it for her lost daughter; then she presses her hands and her face onto the landscape, as if trying to feel for her absent body.

Figure 5.2 Ruth in Alice's bedroom (E4), *Marchlands* (ITV1, 2011).

As she pushes herself onto the picture, imagined sounds of Alice calling to her bleed from the wood, until an edit takes us, and then Ruth, into the wood itself. Here her grief and melancholy relating to the search for the child whose traumatic loss she must come to terms with by the end of the narrative is both aurally and kinaesthetically expressed within a specific landscape (the woodland surrounding the house, Marchlands). When her husband (Jamie Thomas King) later suggests to Ruth that they move away and start afresh, she says 'She's here in the house, in the woods. I can't leave her Paul'. In *Marchlands*, then, landscape encompasses, stands in for, and represents the lost body, and only through these constant repetitions and returns to the landscape can the characters at the centre of the drama come to terms with their grief. As Stacey Abbott also notes of this serial

> The refusal to believe in the ghost is presented as tantamount to the denial of the loss in the first place. As a result, the house is haunted by unresolved grief and the echoes of the initial trauma that fractures the family in 1967 also threatens the two families involved in 1987 and 2010. (2016: 162)

Here we see an articulation of the way in which place becomes imbued with grief and trauma in the television ghost story.

Similarly, grief for a lost child haunts Eve (Suranne Jones) in *The Secret of Crickley Hall* and Nathan's grief for his dead son is at the centre of *The Living and the Dead*. His shift from being a rational 'man of science' at the start of Episode 1 to a tormented figure who is plagued by grief and a growing belief in the spectres that haunt him is partly linked to his descent *into* the landscape. The further he is immersed into the land (the lake, the woods, literally into the hills via his descent into an abandoned mineshaft), the more immersed he becomes in a melancholic sense of grief. His inability to sleep, and subsequent struggle to discern which sounds and images around him are real or not, and his loss of interest in his wife (he says to Charlotte 'I can't recall what I liked about you' as he purposefully drives her away to be alone with his grief, and his ghosts), all mark him out as a classic Freudian melancholic. This melancholia has an impact for the community that surrounds him: the community 'pays the price' for Nathan's melancholia when he refuses to let the local priest exorcise his son's ghost and the other ghosts drive the rest of the villagers away. From the end of Episode 4 of *The Living and the Dead*, where the harvest rots and a heavy fog descends on the village, Shepzoy is rendered a deeply 'melancholic landscape' (Bowring, 2016: 4); it begins to reflect Nathan's mental state, and his feelings of deep grief (see Figure 5.1 again). There is a melancholic beauty in this and other ghost dramas; again, Bowring's work is useful here, and her argument that 'the paradox of a beauty founded in sorrow, a love of loss, of longing, is melancholy's gift to aesthetics' (2016: 18). This is, in many ways, spectacular, beautiful television (see Wheatley, 2016), though the images of landscape and the haunted houses at the centre of these dramas are also deeply, symbolically related to the depiction of grief and melancholy, rather than being 'simply' beautiful or spectacular.

We might also understand Nathan as a traumatised figure, and the connections between trauma and haunting are well documented (del Pilar Blanco and Peeren, 2013; Weinstock, 2004), for as Michael Walker argues, 'The presence of a ghost necessarily signals the existence of a past trauma… usually bereavement, but occasionally other types of psychological trauma involving loss' (2017: 31). Landscapes in these ghost narratives bear the marks of trauma; they are indeed what Martyn Hudson refers to as 'trauma landscapes' (2017: 20). In *Lightfields*, a series of characters struggle to recover from the burning of a barn (and the subsequent death of the girl trapped inside it), and this traumatic event is repeated over and over again in the narrative, via flashbacks from various characters' points of view. In 1975, Vivien (Lucy Cohu), a character with a troubled mental health history, struggles to recover the memory of what happened to her in 1944, and flashes of the fire burning in the field continually traumatise her: as she says in Episode 4 of the drama, 'I set fire to the barn . . . I can feel it – it's at the root of all my trauma'. As will be explored below, flashbacks and recovered memory are the markers of trauma representation in the television ghost story, but the remains of the burnt-out barn stand as a marker on the landscape of this past trauma, even when it is not seen in flames via flashback. Trauma is thus ever present in this landscape. In *Remember Me*, interwoven traumas (the death of Hannah's father, the loss of Rob's family through divorce and emigration, and the tragic circumstances surrounding the death of Tom's nanny, and then his wife) must be 'worked through' in order to reach some form of narrative resolution: for Hannah and Rob this resolution comes via a journey over the moors and to the sea as they talk through, or set aside, their traumas, whereas for Tom, resolution to his trauma comes via a descent *into* the landscape as his body slips into the depths of a mill pool with Isha's ghost at the end of the serial.

A particular marker of trauma on the landscape in many of these ghost stories comes through the compulsive return to particular spaces. Ruth's constant return to the woods in *Marchlands* has already been discussed above, but we also see her future employer, Mark (Elliot Cowan), running the same path through the landscape, over and over again, in 2010, and Amy (Sydney Wade), the daughter of the family in 1987, is also seen retracing Alice's steps through the woods and towards the pond. These compulsive repetitions of actions within a specific landscape are a kinaesthetic expression of trauma, for as Huppert et al. have shown, there is a direct link between compulsive behaviours and recovery from trauma (2005). We also see characters in *Lightfields* travel up and down the same road in a compulsive manner expressive of traumatised experience, and in *Remember Me* characters are compulsively drawn back to the beach where Isha's corpse first appears. Hannah repeatedly dreams herself into this space, and says 'I can't stop thinking about it, dreaming about it. I can't stop and I don't know why'. Following the work of Zoë Shacklock (2017), I would argue that the serial television narrative is eminently capable of making this kinaesthetic trauma clear to us through its embodied repetitions and returns. This directly contradicts Michael Walker's argument that the television ghost story lacks 'the development and dramatic possibilities of a feature film' (2017: 383). Rather, the serial narrative returns us repeatedly to the sites of trauma and loss, across the course of its narrative, and expresses something of the extended processes of grief and mourning for its characters through its complex landscapes.

Sometimes in the ghost drama, the appearance of a ghost or ghosts is prompted not just by a personal sense of grief or trauma but by a need to right past wrongs, to bring injustice to light or to bring about a process of truth and reconciliation. Barry Curtis has argued that

> 'Haunted' fictions often seek to restore to attention something – such as injustice, neglect, murder or slavery – that is absent from the record. In this respect [ghost narratives] are often on the side of the overlooked and demand that understanding and reparations are their due. (2008: 24)

As Michael Walker has explored in detail, the narrative of *The Secret of Crickley Hall* revolves around the bringing to light of past abuse done to the children in the hall at the hand of the sadistic Augustus Cribben (Douglas Henshall), but this is also a narrative about understanding a hidden landscape (in this case the underground river which drowned both Cribben and some of his victims). In *Marchlands*, the association between Alice's death and the infidelity of her grandfather (who was seeing his mistress when he should have been watching her) is the neglect that must be uncovered, but this is achieved by the completion of the repeated (partial) flashback of Alice running through the woods. In *The Living and the Dead*, Nathan must come to terms with the 'neglect' of his son (who drowned when he was not paying him enough attention, distracted by his work), as well as uncovering the injustices suffered by the boys in the mine, the murdered girl in the wood, and the wise woman drowned in the mill pool as a witch. As with many of these ghost narratives, the landscape itself is ascribed a form of subjectivity, almost as if it has borne witness to these past wrongs, been scarred by the associated trauma, and thus looks on at, or precipitates, the haunting. At the end of *The Living and the Dead*, the cause of the death of Nathan's descendant, Lara, who drove off the road when confronted by Nathan's ghost while trying to discover why the ghost of Gabriel (Arthur Bateman), Nathan's son, was haunting her, is revealed when her car, and presumably her body, is pulled out of the East Marsh at the edge of the Applebys' land. As the historically anachronistic vehicle is hauled out of the marsh, the Applebys' maid, Gwen (Kerrie Hays), says 'Maybe this is what's been troubling the land?', implying that the landscape itself has been troubled, haunted in some way. Following this scene, in which Nathan sees Lara and Gabriel walk away hand-in-hand (and thus accepts their passing, shifting away from his melancholic position), we cut to a new landscape montage labelled 'Summer, 1895'. Here we return to the sunny, pastoral imagery of Episode 1 – swaying grass, blue skies, golden fields and green trees – and thus the land is once again (momentarily) resolved, at peace.[4] To conclude this analysis of the UK ghost drama then, del Pilar Blanco is correct when she proposes that ghost stories are always 'embedded in the story about a place' (2012: 8). In the contemporary UK television ghost serial, landscape is vital in constructing a story about death, grief and mourning. In some cases, we see a strong connection between the landscape and the physical remains of death (described by Hudson as a result of 'the human obsession with the remnants of the dead' (2017: xiv)); bodies are found *within* landscapes, and they thus become *part of the land* in a very tangible sense. In other narratives, landscapes take on the shape of the sadness, guilt, horror and despair that we feel in the face of death. A grey cloud in a wide open sky, a burning tree on the brow of a hill, the swelling of an underground water course, the dank wetness at the centre of a wood all do affective work in the ghost narrative's working through of death, grief and trauma. This is not to read landscape as symbolic in a straightforward sense, building a 'land as metaphor' argument, but rather that the interconnectedness of body, landscape and emotion in the television ghost story produces a series of meaningful places which convey mood and theme, and develop our understanding of character's experiences.

Trauma, temporality and the haunted houses of post-broadcast television

While the serials discussed in the first half of this chapter can be seen as a continuation of the British Gothic television I explored in my previous monograph (Wheatley, 2006), the television ghost story has also, more recently, found a home on post-broadcast television, in programming made in the US for an international streaming market. Netflix in particular has developed its own brand of television horror (broadly), and, specifically, produced a set of complex television ghost serials, including *The Haunting of Hill House* and *Archive 81*, the two dramas at the heart of this analysis. The latter part of this chapter considers this new cycle of ghost dramas and thinks about how it continues and extends the focus on death-related trauma in the television ghost stories discussed above. While thematically we see continuities between the dramas discussed in the front end of this chapter, and those discussed here, Matt Hills has noted that Netflix's 'genre TV productions' may represent 'an entirely new phase in television horror' (2021: 125). Derek Johnston's analysis of the adaptability of the television ghost story to new contexts and platforms concurs with Hills's suggestion that post-broadcast television offers a new, or redeveloped, iteration of this genre: 'As television has developed, the ghost story has also presented regular opportunities to experiment with form, with technology, and with narrative' (2017: 379). Johnston goes on to suggest that the new television ghost story is more visually rich, even more capable of producing a dense, complex *mise-en-scène* in which the ghost can (momentarily) appear:

> As the image quality of television has improved, then the possibilities for 'hidden' images has increased . . . Ghost stories often make use of empty spaces on the screen as places where horror *may* emerge or *may* already be lurking, thereby inviting the audience who are familiar with these devices to pay close attention to the spaces *around* the lead characters, and adding a sense of presence to shots which do not apparently contain individuals at all. (ibid.)[5]

He acknowledges that the distribution strategies (whole serials launched at the same time) and viewing patterns (binge-watching) of contemporary television have led to formal shifts in the television ghost story that have an impact on the ways in which narrative unfurls: '[this seriality] allows for building a greater density of character, story, and backstory while retaining the finite nature of the classic ghost story' (2017: 384). Similarly, Hills proposes that 'binge-watching has . . . [intensified] audiences' emotional connection to texts, having the potential to render "the most affective of genres" even more potent' (2021: 130). He goes on to argue that the strength of feeling surrounding the home as a space of threat in television horror is increased by the facts of binge-watching: 'a more powerful sense of immersive belonging is created for TV audiences via bingeing . . . [it] facilitates a greater affective sense of the diegetic world as "home", making narrative threats within this world more resonant for bingeing fans' (ibid.: 131). The image of post-broadcast horror portrayed by Hills and Johnston, then, is of a serial text which creates a particularly intense relationship with its viewer, with a complex *mise-en-scène* that has the ability to frighten through the details that 'lurk' within the frame.

Seriality is, therefore, critical to the affective power of the Netflix ghost story. As I argued in the previous chapter of this book, and as Stacey Abbott's work has also suggested (2016: 171), serial form enables an emotionally realistic representation of grief, showing how grief unfurls and transforms, experientially, over time. This is true of representations of grief both in the television ghost story (as shown in the first part of this chapter, and in Abbott's analysis) and outside of it (as in the serial dramas discussed in Chapter 4). However, as well as an emotionally realistic representation of grief, the complex serial narrative is also well able to convey the complexities of traumatised experience. Adam Daniel has argued, in relation to the Netflix drama *The Haunting of Hill House*, that the narrative complexity of serial television enabled showrunner Mike Flanagan to 'play around with time' in its representation of traumatised lives (2020:142), and this 'messing with time' was also critical to David Lynch's attempts to construct a narrative around trauma in his original *Twin Peaks* (ABC, 1990–1991), according to Roger Luckhurst (2008: 199). Specifically, the long-form serial drama is particularly able to represent traumatised forms of memory, and the complexities of lost, restored and recovered memory which are at the heart of contemporary thinking about trauma as a diagnosis, as well as being central to the trauma text as a cultural form, as the analysis in this chapter will show.

Traumatised memory has been characterised in a number of ways. For Baer, it is excessively detailed:[6] 'Very much like a photograph, traumatic memory can be characterized by the excessive retention of details that cannot be integrated into a nontraumatic memory or comprehension of the past' (2013: 432). The other side of the excessively detailed memories described by Baer are the gaps and absences in traumatised memory, alongside these returning, or partially restored, ultra-vivid memories. This means that narratives representing trauma experiences are rarely, if ever, linear and straightforward in their handling of time. As Luckhurst notes '[Trauma] has a time signature that must fracture conventional causality' (2008: 9), drawing on Cathy Caruth's vision of trauma as 'a crisis of representation, of history, and truth, *and of narrative time*' (ibid.: 5, my emphasis). Luckhurst asserts that this marked disruption of linear temporality was particularly present in a cycle of trauma-related films made in the 1990s 'with plots presented backwards, in loops, or disarticulated into mosaics that only retrospectively cohere' (ibid.: 178). Arguably, we are now in the midst of a cycle of television ghost narratives that explore trauma in similar ways, using contemporary television's characteristic narrative complexity (Mittell, 2015) to fit the temporal volatility of the trauma narrative. In the Netflix ghost drama, as I will explain below, characters constantly experience flashbacks and flashforwards in narrative time; time is handled subjectively[7] and is organised around what we might understand as the excesses of 'traumatic time' (Laredo, 2020: 70). Central to this is the idea that traumatised memory is 'belated', that it is prone to unexpected 'flashbacks' or to the return of memories, triggered by an external stimulus or returning as if 'from nowhere', that invade the consciousness, flooding the subject with both *'the truth of an event,* and *the truth of its incomprehensibility'* (Caruth, 1995b: 153, original emphasis). As Gibbs explains, Caruth's reading rests on a Freudian understanding of belatedness in trauma:

> The idea that trauma is always characterised by a temporary or permanent latency period of amnesia, during which the source of the originating trauma is unavailable to the sufferer's memory, derives from the work of Freud, who introduced the concept of *Nachträglichkeit*, or belatedness, in *Project for a Scientific Psychology* (1895). According to Caruth's influential reading of Freud, after this period of forgetting, memories belatedly return. (2014: 10)

While Gibbs counsels against the overstatement of belatedness and restored memory as an aspect of trauma (he believes Caruth overemphasises this aspect of trauma in her work, without any basis in research), the return of memory, often at unexpected or unwanted moments, has certainly characterised the representation of trauma in audio-visual fictions, and, in particular, in the television ghost serial, as we saw in the analysis of the dramas above. Bliss Cua Lim argues that the ghost narrative in East Asian cinema invites us to think about time in 'disaccustomed terms' through its destabilisation of past, present and future (2009); the very same could be said of time in the Netflix-produced ghost drama.

The Haunting of Hill House, the first of the Netflix case studies in this chapter, is a ten-part adaptation from 2018, loosely based on Shirley Jackson's 1959 novel of the same name. Whereas Jackson's novel centred upon a disparate collection of people brought together to explore the mysteries of the eponymous house, Mike Flanagan's Netflix adaptation transposes the story of Hill House onto the experiences of a single family, the Crains, as they move into the house in the summer of 1992 so that Hugh (Timothy Hutton) and Olivia (Carla Gugino) can do up the house to sell. The narrative of the drama switches between this time period, in which we discover that the Crains and their children, Steven (Paxton Singleton), Shirley (Lulu Wilson), Theo (McKenna Grace), Luke (Julian Hilliard) and Nell (Violet McGraw) are increasingly haunted by the spectres of the house, leading to Olivia's death and Hugh fleeing from the house with the children, and the Crains in the present day as they struggle to come to terms with the trauma of their experiences in the house and Olivia's suicide. In the present day, we see the impact of these events on the adult Crain siblings: Nell (Victoria Pedretti), still haunted by her experiences in Hill House and struggling with her mental health following the death of her young husband (Jordane Christie), returns to the house to (apparently) commit suicide;

her twin brother, Luke (Oliver Jackson-Cohen) is a recovering addict who continues to be haunted by spectres from the house and is deeply troubled by his sister's death; Theo (Kate Siegel), now a child psychologist who is world-weary and isolated from other people, struggles with the 'gift' of being able to sense people's traumatic past experience when she touches them; Shirley (Elizabeth Reaser), a talented mortician and undertaker, deals with her own traumatised relationship with death by building a livelihood out of working with the dead and bereaved; and Steven (Michael Huisman), the family member who has least belief in, and connection with, the supernatural, makes a living out of writing true-life ghost stories (including the story of Hill House itself), thus creating conflict with his siblings which must be resolved by him confronting his past once more during the course of the narrative. As this brief synopsis shows, *The Haunting of Hill House* is shot through with death and its after-effects, and with the psychological impacts of subsequent hauntings. As such, a range of critical responses to the serial have reflected on the centrality of death-related trauma to its narrative. Jeanette A. Laredo has claimed that the serial has been hugely popular 'not for its jump scares or special effects, but for how it portrays the psychological trauma of the Crain family' (2020: 63). In her review of the series for *The Guardian* newspaper, Aida Edemariam argues that 'It's clear from the initial episode that the programme makers intend to plumb all the ways in which [Shirley] Jackson suggests a haunting can be just as much about trauma, about memory and the unquiet unconscious as about the paranormal' (2018). Each character in the series, then, goes on an emotional journey in relation to death-related trauma which the viewer must follow.

We see the working through of death, and of experiences of grief and bereavement right from the opening of the serial. For example, we are introduced to the adult Steven in 'Steven Sees a Ghost' (E1) when he is recording the story of a woman (Saidah Arrika Ekulona) who claims to have encountered the ghost of her dead husband. While Steven surprises the widow by being sceptical about the existence of actual spirits, he talks to her about the reason we might need/manifest imagined ghosts in relation to a death: 'A ghost can be a lot of things. A memory. A daydream. A secret. Grief, anger, guilt. But in my experience, most times they're just what we want to see . . . Most times a ghost is a wish'. Just as Steven's work brings him into contact with the bereaved and grieving, so does Shirley's. At the beginning of the following episode ('Open Casket'), Shirley talks to a little boy, Max (Trace Masters), about the trauma of seeing his grandmother ill and dying; his parents wish for him to see her in her open casket, a thought which terrifies the child, and Shirley tries to persuade and reassure him in her role as undertaker. Following this scene, we are shown a montage of Shirley's embalming process as she 'fixes' the body of the dead grandmother, attempting to eradicate the traces of death in advance of the viewing; as Laredo notes, she aims to '"fix" the trauma by returning the dead person to a time before they were dead . . . [but] can only make their condition more permanent or "fixed" [which] instead leads to a proliferation of trauma' (2020: 67). While Shirley is presented as a professional undertaker, talented at dealing with people in their 'hour of grief' and at doing the restorative work required for the open casket viewings of the dead which are popular in the US, we also understand this work as compulsive for her, driven by her own death-related trauma. The episode flashes back between her first experience of death as the kittens she cared for as a child die, and her stoic attempts to deal with her sister's death in the contemporary moment, including preparing her corpse for viewing and burial. When, back in the 1990s, one of the kittens dies, Shirley not only

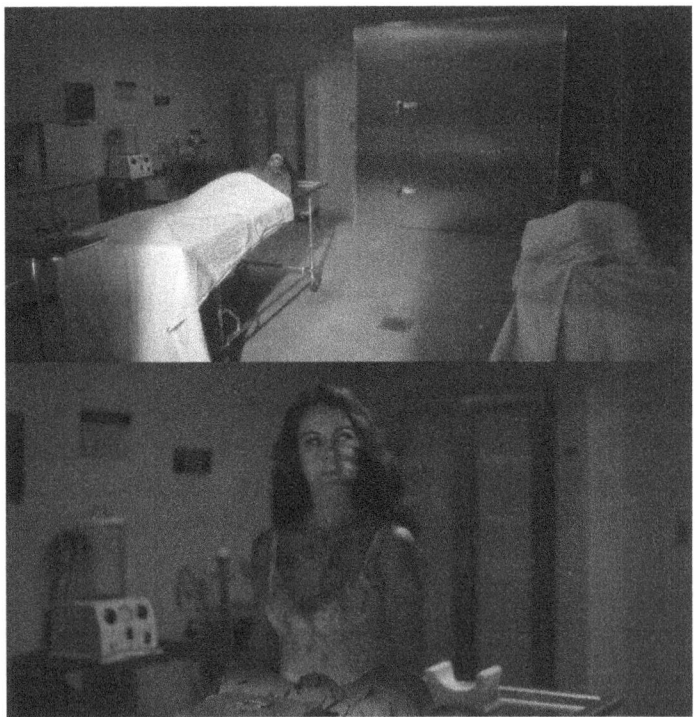

Figure 5.3 Nell and Olivia in the morgue, 'Open Casket' (E2), *The Haunting of Hill House* (Netflix, 2018).

learns about grief, but is also confronted with the abjection of the dead body for the first time; she initially believes that the kitten is coming back to life when its face moves but is then horrified by a beetle crawling out of the dead kitten's mouth. This image is cross-cut with Shirley staring at the gurney in her mortuary, as she discusses picking up her sister's body with her assistant. Later, her counselling of Max about seeing his grandmother's body is intercut with a flashback to her own reluctance to see her mother's dead body as a child, as she remembers the role of a kindly undertaker who escorted her to her mother's coffin. Shirley has thus built a career out of her own grief and trauma and is constantly returned to this trauma even though she works hard to set it aside. When she is embalming Nell, elbow-deep in her corpse, she is shown to be resilient in the face of death, fully able to confront the bodily realities of dying. However, once she has finished the work on Nell's body, she looks back into the room to see her dead mother on the gurney beside Nell, as her corpse sits up and is animated by dappled light. Olivia is the return of what Shirley has repressed (the trauma of death and confronting the abjection of the dead body) here; her ghostly image is a palimpsest of Shirley's death-related trauma.

Whereas Shirley struggles to repress her trauma in order to professionalise her relationship with death, Luke's relationship to the trauma of death is so extreme that when the narrative focuses on his experiences in the hours following Nell's death, we see his body kinaesthetically register his empathy with the corpse of his dead twin. At the start of the episode 'The Twin Thing' (E4), Luke wakes in the night as Nell dies, and he sees her appear in his dorm room in this moment. However, during the following day, as Luke travels the city trying to help his friend from rehab, his body grows colder and stiffer, and he becomes more and more corpse-like as the day goes on. When Shirley eventually tells him of Nell's (apparent) suicide towards the end of the episode, Luke instinctively touches the back of his neck (Nell died from hanging). Here, then, Luke's body is haunted by death; it involuntarily registers the death of his twin and thus he embodies the trauma of death.

As suggested above, *The Haunting of Hill House* is structured in a complex way whereby the viewer is constantly shuttled back and forth between different time periods. We often understand the narrative move from present to past as a form of flashback (although unusually these flashbacks can be multi-perspectival, and not taken from a single character's point of view, in keeping with a narrative focused on a traumatised *family* rather than a single individual). Flashbacks are significant in the history of both trauma diagnosis *and* trauma representation. As McNally (2004: 8), Luckhurst (2008: 177), Köhne et al. (2014: 6) and others have noted, there is a congruence between the development of the flashback as a filmic narrative technique and its cementing as a recognised symptom of post-traumatic stress disorder:

> In the earlier twentieth-century literature of trauma there is no mention of flashbacks, and according to McNally it is only after the emergence of the flashback as part of film culture that it becomes connected with trauma. The flashback is first constructed and then widely disseminated as a trauma symptom, after which its presence becomes finally self-fulfilling, as people experience their trauma as photographic reenactments. (Gibbs, 2014: 4)

These authors all suggest, therefore, that the flashback develops as a recognised symptom of trauma through the process of representing trauma audio-visually. Robson notes of the flashback in narratives of trauma in audio-visual media:

> The intrusion of the present on the past as a form of flashback is frequently used to examine repressed memories and traumatic pasts in film and television ... Such flashbacks imply the substantial impact of memory on the present – a memory that cannot be easily recalled, but one that lies dormant in the subconscious of the character. (2019: 4)

Similarly, Luckhurst's examination of trauma representation in narrative film and television views the flashback as an 'intrusive, anachronistic image that throws off the linear temporality of the story' (2008: 180). He goes on to propose that the flashback can 'only ever be explained belatedly, leaving the spectator in varying degrees of disorientation or suspense, depending on when or whether the flashback is reintegrated into the storyline', and describes the 'brutal splicing' of temporally disjointed images as 'cinema's rendition of the frozen moment of the traumatic impact: it flashes back insistently in the present because this image cannot yet or perhaps ever be narrativized as past' (ibid.). Flashbacks, therefore, work hard to represent the confusing qualities of traumatic memory, the belatedness at the heart of trauma memory for Caruth and others, and the compulsive/involuntary return of repressed or restored sounds and images.

Robson's work forensically dissects the representation of subjective memory in *The Haunting of Hill House* and shows how complicated and interwoven characters' memories are. Her excellent analysis of a single episode from the serial ('Two Storms' (E6)) opens with the claim that the serial's complicated narrative structure, with its continual flashbacks and flashforwards, 'draws the focus away from the haunted house itself, towards a complex examination of trauma' (2019: 1), although she goes on to discuss how that trauma is registered spatially and, particularly, in relation to the 'haunted house'. Similarly, Laredo notes that the past is repetitious in *The Haunting of Hill House*, becoming 'an event that "in effect, does not end"' (2020: 64). We see this complexity and repetition right from the beginning of the serial, particularly in the events that surround Nell's death. When we are first introduced to the young Nell in this episode, we see, in the culmination of the pre-credits sequence, the 'Bent-Neck Lady', the key figure that haunts Nell throughout her life, standing behind her as she sleeps. While we initially understand her to be one of the spectres of the house, a sinister, ghostly woman with her face hidden from view by her dark, straggly hair, by the end of the eponymous fifth episode, we know that the Bent-Neck Lady is in fact the adult Nell after her hanging (hence the 'bent neck'), a spectre from the future that foretells Nell's death and appears time and again to the young Nell and throughout her lifetime. Nell is thus haunted by her own body, from the future, and by her lack of control over it, and this haunting is shown in the compulsive repetition of certain actions by, and images of, that body. Somatic repetition, and Nell's lack of control of her own body, is, for example, demonstrated in the way that she dances around Hill House towards the end of the first episode, in the scenes that lead up to her death by hanging, as if she is being held by a spectre which is invisible to the viewer. Here, this dance represents the fact that Nell is stuck in an ever-repeating loop of grief and trauma, involuntarily revisiting her tragic, traumatic past as her body swoops and glides around the house towards its death.

It is important, then, that from the outset, the traumatised Nell is represented as 'stuck' in a series of repetitive bodily actions which will lead up to her re-enacting the place and nature of her mother's death. Nell not only repeatedly sees her own dead body from the outset of the drama, but towards the end of the serial, she and Luke (as children) also confront their mother about (potential) dreams that portend and map out the story of their future lives and 'deaths', and the traumas they will face, in 'The Screaming Meemies' (E9):

> Nell: What if I dream that you kill us? What if I dream that you send us away into the dark, and we get hurt?

Luke: Really hurt.

Nell: You send us away out into the dark, and my heart breaks right in half, and I can't feel anything happy for weeks and months and years until I can't stand it anymore and I have to die . . . You send us out there into the dark, and the dark gets us, a piece at a time, over years and years and years, until I'm on a silver table with my jaw wired shut, and Luke is dead and cold on the floor with a needle in his arm. And it was you that killed us because you sent us out there, in the night, in the dark.

While we know already that the young Nell is precisely describing the nature of her death as an adult, this scene also narratively pre-empts Luke's overdose (a near-death experience which he will ultimately survive in the final epiosde). We therefore see how temporally complex the narrative of the *Haunting of Hill House* is. Others have argued that the series operates as a classic haunted house narrative, in which the house is presented as a complex, confusing and traumatised space that must be 'worked out' in order to reach some sort of resolution in the narrative (locked doors opened, mysterious noises investigated, the spread of black mould explained, and so on) (Bernico, 2020; Keller, 2020; McCort, 2020). Robson has also shown that the complexities of narrative time are interwoven with the complexities of narrative space, exploring the way in which the very long takes in 'Two Storms' lead us from one haunted house (Shirley's funeral home) to another (Hill House itself), tracking characters that cross the boundaries of both space and time. There is little point in repeating these analyses of the serial here, which all do a good job of exploring how death-related trauma is presented spatially in *The Haunting of Hill House*, other than to note that what these authors set out as the characteristics of the serial – troubling domestic spaces that symbolically represent the lives of their inhabitants, characters that find themselves traversing space and time in their explorations of a house, a lack of spatial and temporal fixity that expresses traumatised experience – might more broadly be seen as characteristic of the Netflix ghost story. They are all returned to in relation to our final case study of this chapter: *Archive 81*.

Archive 81 plots the story of two young people in two different time frames – the present day and 1994 – as their stories of hauntings, grief and trauma intertwine. In the present day, Dan (Mamoudou Athie), a young, Black film and video enthusiast who works as an audio-visual conservator is employed by Virgil Davenport (Martin Donovan), the CEO of the shadowy company, LMG, to restore a collection of fire-damaged videotapes housed in a remote facility out in the Catskills in upstate New York. As Dan – isolated bar occasional patchy phone contact with his friend Mark (Matt McGorry) and the unexpected arrival of a couple of LMG employees – begins to restore the tapes, they reveal the story of Melody Pendras (Dina Shihabi), a young graduate student living and working in the Visser apartment building in New York City in order to research the stories of the lives of those caught up with a sinister, demonic cult operating out of the building. Dan uses the tapes and other found objects to try to piece together what happened to Melody following a fire at the Visser, but as his work continues it becomes apparent that their lives are far more entangled than he initially thought. Melody is an ex-patient of Dan's father, Dr Steven Turner (Charlie Hudson III), who died in a fire at the family home, alongside Dan's mother (Africa Miranda) and sister (Emily Turner), leaving Dan traumatised and prone to nightmares and flashbacks to the day of their death. With increasing frequency across the serial, Dan and Melody begin to 'haunt' each other, finding themselves anachronistically shifted back or forwards in time and space. Their lives are thus interwoven by trauma, the struggle to return lost memories, and the need to understand their own pasts. Both 'orphaned' in sinister and unexplained circumstances (or presumed to be so), they reach across the boundaries of space and time to help one another come to terms with multiple bereavements and loss.

As the short synopsis above suggests, this is not a ghost story in the traditional sense. Just as in *The Haunting of Hill House*, what initially appear to be ghosts in this serial might more correctly be understood as the projections or manifestations of the traumatised pasts of its central characters.[8] In relation to Tzvetan Todorov's delineation of the fantastic, marvellous and the uncanny (1975), ghost stories that accept the presence of the supernatural in everyday life (in which ghosts actually are confirmed to be the spectral return of the dead), and in which ghosts appear to multiple individuals who are not figured as having 'just imagined them', can be identified as belonging to the category of the marvellous (for Todorov, the supernatural accepted). Indeed, Stacey Abbott has argued that 'It may be challenging to sustain Todorov's hesitation [referring to the uncertainty of the fantastic] across multi-episode serial television because the more often we return to the narrative world, the more likely we are to accept the existence of the supernatural' (2016: 157). On the other hand, however, programming where a lack of clarity remains about whether a character is being *truly* haunted, or whether the apparent ghost is a psychic projection from their past, present or future, might better be understood as belonging to Todorov's category of the 'fantastic', in which uncertainty about the supernatural nature of a haunting remains intact. Murray Leeder reads Jack Clayton's *The Innocents* (1961) as a film that belongs to this category,[9] in which it never becomes clear whether the haunting of Miss Giddens (Deborah Kerr) is all in her (increasingly disturbed) mind. In *Archive 81*, Dan and Melody are both figured as unreliable narrators whose perception of the supernatural is put under question in relation to their complex mental health issues. Dan suffers from nightmares and hallucinations tied to the deaths of his family and is figured as having suffered some kind of mental breakdown following the end of a previous relationship, whereas Melody has experienced blackouts and various other psychic responses to childhood trauma (the mental health issues Dan's father was treating her for) and continues to be positioned in the narrative as a 'troubled' individual. The serial's creator, Rebecca Sonnenshine, complicates the reading of Dan and Melody as projecting their trauma:

> They have similar depths of hurt about what has happened to them. They use different ways of coping, but still have a deep connection when they talk about it. I don't think either one of these characters necessarily projects that trauma onto the world. They internalize [it] and are boiling inside. (Fishman, 2022)

Whether Dan and Melody project their trauma onto their surroundings or whether they internalise it and 'boil inside', their mental struggles mean that we hesitate when viewing the hauntings of *Archive 81*. This means that the 'ghosts' of this serial, while clearly attached to the trauma of loss and bereavement, cannot easily or simply be understood as the supernatural spirits of the returning dead: while Dan and Melody both encounter what they believe to be demonic figures or manifestations (Dan via the videotape he is restoring, Melody through the mysterious rituals of the Visser and its inhabitants), and they both indeed 'haunt' each other at various points in the narrative, their 'unreliability' and the subsequent uncertainty about the supernatural remains intact until the final dénouement of the drama.

The central enigma of *Archive 81* is established in the pre-credits sequence of 'Mystery Signals' (E1), with its suggestion that videotape will be a channel for communication beyond death in the serial, and therefore a conduit for the relay of trauma. The serial begins with the 'white noise'

Figure 5.4 Melody: 'Please find me!', 'Mystery Signals' (E1), *Archive 81* (Netflix, 2022).

so familiar from analogue media, which then becomes joined by the indistinct sounds of fear and panic. Here we witness, for the first time, the fact that Melody's trauma has been captured/trapped on videotape. Melody's face then appears, terrified, in close-up as she implores the watcher: 'Please find me! Please help!'

She thus appears to be trapped within an undisclosed location (which we later understand to be the Visser) but also trapped within the videotape itself. This sets video up, then, not so much as haunted media (as in Jeffrey Sconce's description of the potential for electronic media to be 'haunted', possessed by a spectral image (2000: 126), or Derek Johnston's delineation of television as inherently 'uncanny' (2015: 17)) as it is *traumatised media*. The tapes Dan is given to restore in the drama are physically traumatised (they are fire, water and mould damaged), but they also contain, once restored, the traces of Melody's trauma, both historic and as experienced in the present day. Across the serial, the dropouts and glitches of analogue recording media (tape) are therefore understood as the markers of traumatised experience, and as audio-visual metaphors for the vagaries of traumatised memory. Just as Dan will work to painstakingly remove the marks of physical trauma from these tapes to make them viewable once more, so his connection with Melody and his increasing tenderness towards her will expose her trauma and seek to heal her (emotional) wounds (and his own). When, in 'Spirit Receivers' (E4), Melody appears in Dan's workplace in the Catskills and interrupts him working on the restoration at his desk, Dan explains his work to her: 'Films, tapes, photographs. Things that have been damaged, lost, or forgotten. I bring them back.' There is, of course, a double-meaning to Dan's words here; in exploring her, and his own, traumatised memories, Dan is also working to restore the gaps and absences in the memories of incidents that they both struggle to recall. In the Catskills, in the present day, Melody panics, struggling to make sense of her memories: 'It's all jumbled up in my head!' As she panics, Dan's memory flashes back to his sister explaining the nature of ghosts to him in the mid-1990s: 'Don't be afraid. They're just lost and don't know where to go'. While Dan (incorrectly) understands Melody as a traditional ghost here (she screams at him 'I'm not fucking dead!!', seemingly causing a power surge/outage and her disappearance), he is still right that he must work through her trauma in order to bring about some sort of resolution for them both and 'find herself' again.

Dan's fascination with analogue media is established from the outset of the serial: he buys VHS tapes of unknown quality, content and origin from a street vendor at the beginning of 'Mystery Signals' (E1), and thus the tape is figured as an opaque and palimpsestuous memory object. Just as with human beings, we can see the outer surface of the tape easily, but have no idea of its inner workings, and what is contained inside, without further investigation. Throughout this and subsequent episodes, we see Dan tending to tapes, and therefore nurturing and caring for memory, putting it 'back together again'. When his current boss asks him to attend to Virgil's first tape of Melody's research at the Visser, Dan takes it home with him, tenderly extracting it from its (traumatised, fire damaged) casing and carefully cleaning/restoring it. As Dan eventually plays the tape, he rewinds and pauses it on Melody's face, thus doing exactly what she asked in the pre-credits sequence, trying to 'find her' and 'help her' even if he doesn't know it yet, given that she is both trapped inside the Visser (a building he immediately begins to research) and trapped inside these tapes. When the sinister Virgil says to him later in the episode '[Karen] says you were the best man around to bring back lost things, and she was right', he could be referring either to the restoration of the tapes or to the returning of Melody 'from the dead'. Virgil draws on Dan's own experience of trauma to draw him into this work:

> Creating this archive, putting this puzzle together, finding out what happened at the Visser would mean the world to everyone who lost someone in that fire ... And I know you have a special understanding of a situation like that ... it seems you've spent your life trying to bring lost things back to people.[10]

Dan's work, then, like Shirley and Steven's in *The Haunting of Hill House*, is seen as a by-product of his death-related trauma, as a compulsion to work through his own experiences of grief and bereavement. Although he initially rejects Virgil's offer, Dan cannot turn away from this project for this very reason. As he walks away from the LMG building following their initial meeting, the scene cuts to some image and sound fragments from Dan's memories (his dog, Dan when young walking through the woods, humming, a hand playing the piano, the clicking of a metronome, a crow cawing, emergency vehicles in the night, Dan's sister turning her head, young Dan watching his house burn). However, right in the middle of this montage is a shot of Melody in the Visser. This sequence thus already intertwines Dan's fragmentary, traumatised memories of the deaths of his family with the footage that captures and gives him access to Melody. Neither Dan nor the viewer understands yet that their stories of trauma and loss are indeed intertwined, and we don't fully grasp the wider significance of each of the images above. However, we do have a sense from this sequence that this impressionistic montage of images represents Dan's traumatised, fragmentary memory in some way. While the sequence begins with him walking along the street (and we thus read it as a series of memories sparked by the conversation with Virgil), confusingly it ends with him waking up in bed in his apartment at night. This is the first of many sequences in which Dan's memories intrude into the narrative and, as a result, elide narrative space and time: he starts remembering in one place and time, and finishes in another. Dan's panic as he wakes suggests that he too is confused by this elision; the loss of narrative time, the confusion over whether this montage is a memory, a dream, or a hallucination or some kind of haunting is thus experienced by the (traumatised) protagonist and the viewer at the same time. We might argue, then, that Dan's viewing of the Visser tapes is what sparks off these traumatised flashbacks. This makes sense if, as Joshua Hirsch has argued, we understand film viewing as being able to 'trigger' a traumatised response:

> Trauma ... is not a thing, like a letter, that can be delivered ... There is no such thing as a traumatic image per se. But an image of atrocity may carry a traumatic potential, which ... may be repeatedly realized in a variety of experiences of vicarious trauma ... [Film] viewing can [therefore] lead to symptoms of posttraumatic stress (2004: 15–17)

Dan's experience of death-related trauma in his own life thus becomes intertwined with his endeavours to understand what happened to Melody, both in her childhood and at the Visser. He wakes up from the memory sequence/nightmare and immediately returns to Melody's tape, recognising his own dog in a photograph in her bedroom. This sequence thus eloquently describes not only the interconnectedness of Dan's and Melody's trauma, but the potential for the recorded sounds and images to reinvoke memories of that. These memory sequences thus also act like Caruth's description of the traumatic nightmare as 'undistorted by repression or unconscious wish', which, 'as Freud suggests . . . occupies a space to which willed access is denied' (1995b: 152). Whether in a waking daydream or a nightmare, Dan's memory montages involuntarily fling him back into his traumatised past.

Like *The Haunting of Hill House*, then, *Archive 81* is characterised by a temporal *and* spatial volatility. As Roxana Hadadi notes of the serial, 'Time is as unreliable as people's identities, and as in flux as their understanding of their own motivations' (2022). The lines between Dan's life and work as a conservator in the present day and Melody's struggles to uncover the secrets of the Visser in 1994 thus become increasingly blurred. As well as the gaps and elisions in time that they both experience, the spaces they find themselves in are also presented as troubling and 'unreliable' in the series: both Dan in the mid-century modern house he is living and working in in the Catskills, and Melody in the Visser in New York, search their new homes for answers to questions about their uncertain pasts. Both buildings are full of locked rooms, hidden floors, and corridors which open out in the 'wrong' place. They therefore act as potent spatial metaphors for traumatised experience: just as there are 'inaccessible' parts in their memories of their own traumatic experiences, so are there locked and unreachable rooms where they live, or confusing configurations of space which mean that they frequently, and accidentally, pass into each other's homes or are thwarted in their attempts at exploring and understanding the sinister pasts of the places where they live. For example, when Dan's father appears to him as a 'ghost' or some kind of psychic projection in the house in the Catskills (in 'Wellspring', E2), Dan follows him around the house, but then turns a corner and finds himself in the corridor of the Visser where he sees Melody. Both the Visser and the house in the Catskills also have ceremonial basement spaces which are uncovered by Dan and Melody's explorations, and, like the house navigated by the Crains in *The Haunting of Hill House*, both contain locked rooms and spaces and objects which are covered by a creeping black mould. In 'Wellspring' (E2), when Melody interviews Beatriz Reyes (Sol Miranda), a Visser resident who reads tarot cards and holds seances, Reyes reads Melody's cards and tells her what she sees: 'Grief. Pain.

You've suffered as a child. There's something hidden. Something that has guide you to this place [sic]. Not the light. Someone. That's why you're here.' This underscores the fact that, as with the classic female Gothic narrative (see Wheatley, 2006), Melody must explore the Visser in order to understand and deal with her own traumatised experience (her abandonment by her mother, her relationship with the Visser cult). Both homes are, as Hudson explains of the classic haunted house, 'places which are themselves containers for the congealed histories and trauma of the past' (2017: 77). The slippage between the two homes therefore spatially represents what Luckhurst calls the 'transmissibility' of trauma (2008: 3), that is, the sense that historical trauma (the trauma of death, endangerment and abuse in the past) can be passed between Dan and Melody.

At the end of *Archive 81*, Dan pieces together the narrative that unlocks the mystery of Melody's disappearance: rather than being killed in the Visser fire, Melody was transported to another dimension, the Otherworld, along with the sinister Samuel (Evan Jonigkeit), a Visser resident and the leader of its cult, when they attended a sacrificial ritual in the Visser basement. In order to rescue Melody from the Otherworld, Dan and his friend Mark re-enact the ritual with Melody's mother, Bobbi (Jacqueline Antaramian), in attendance. As Dan enters this space between death and life, reading the Otherworld as a strange sort of wish-fulfilling purgatory where his, and Melody's, memories are replayed, we are immediately confused when he finds himself not in an unfamiliar place but firstly back in the Catskills as time begins to slow, and then back in his childhood home, his family in attendance, as he sits down to eat with them. The house looks just as it did in his memories, except that it is filled with sparkling dust motes; these mark the space out as 'otherworldly' but are also suggestive of the audio-visual glitches that have characterised the memories captured on videotape in this drama. As Dan sits down to eat with his family, the scene shuttles between Dan as a little boy witnessing the fire that killed them and his uncanny experience as an adult, sitting at the table with his alive-again dead relatives. Dan asks, 'What about the fire?', to which his father responds that there was no fire; all is supposedly 'normal' and the traumatic experience removed from Dan's history. However, as the sound of the metronome in the background speeds up, Dan 'remembers' Melody (he has a limited time to rescue her), and we see shots of Melody from her own footage and elsewhere as the metronome clicks. Dan subsequently walks away from his own wish-fulfilling fantasy of his family alive and well, his trauma eradicated, to search for Melody, and immediately finds himself in the Visser. Once again, then, the boundaries between the dramatic spaces of *Archive 81* are dissolved, and space is defined by memory and consciousness, rather than geography. Back in the Visser, Dan is firstly transported to an endless-seeming corridor, and then, via the Visser common room, to the local church where he reunites with Melody. When he finds her, she says 'I thought you were a dream', to which he replies, 'Same'. While they have haunted each other throughout the serial, they have also become united in their bids to recover from the trauma of death and loss. Ultimately, while Dan manages to return Melody to her long-lost mother back in the present day, 'fixing' her trauma, he remains trapped in 1994. He thus becomes stuck in the very place that he had previously experienced via videotape and television screen, stored away as if trapped within the media memories he had spent his recent life investigating and restoring. This ending clearly sets *Archive 81* up for a second season in which Dan would be freed from this audio-visual Otherworld (a second season which sadly was never commissioned), but it also represents the impossibility of Dan escaping from his past. Even though he is trapped in Melody's New York City, found as a survivor of the Visser fire, his relationship with the past via (a) his own traumatised memories and (b) his relationship to analogue media and the memories that media has stored within it means that Dan cannot escape.

Martyn Hudson writes that 'the coexisting landscape of the living and the dead is one within which both contestation or collaboration can take place. The landscape [of the haunted narrative] is [therefore] the focus of mediation and communication' (2017: 128). In this chapter, we have seen the various ways in which narratives of haunting on UK and US television have worked through stories of grief and trauma via an exploration of place. Whether the moorland and woodland of the UK ghost mini-series, or the spatially and temporally confounding houses of the complex Netflix horror serial, the spaces of contemporary Gothic television resonate with the lasting emotional impacts of death. All of these serial narratives work hard to convey the lived experiences of those struggling to come to terms with bereavement or recover from death-related trauma. Their serial form allows for the slow revelation of the significance of memory-based sounds and images as they relate to these experiences; the meaning of shots and sequences glimpsed at the start of a ghost serial are often only fully understood, narratively and thematically, in the dénouement of the drama.

Archive 81 is particularly interesting in relation to this deferral of meaning and significance. Dan's memory montages have already been explored here, where remembered sounds and images from his family home take on increasing significance as the serial unfolds. However, we might also look at the fact that each of the serial's eight episodes begins with a piece of 'found footage' to understand the slow revelation of meaning and significance. While, as discussed above, the first episode opens with an extract from Melody's tapes, the following episodes start in the following ways:

- 'Wellspring' (E2) opens with static, followed by a test card and an advert for Wellspring, a company inviting the viewer to 'find your history, find yourself' via personal DNA testing.
- 'Terror in the Aisles' (E3) begins with a low-budget cable show from the Manhattan Community Channel called 'Terror in the Aisles with Peter and Elliot' which opens with a discussion of a schlocky horror film that morphs into a debate on the existence of true evil and the validity of faith-based stories about this.
- 'Spirit Receivers' (E4) starts with a glitchy, VHS advert from Christies, the auction house, for a sale entitled 'Spirit Receivers. Wall Estate', telling the story of Visser resident Eleanor Wall, whose artwork was seen as a conduit for the dead.
- 'Through the Looking Glass' (E5) opens on highly degraded found footage of a news and weather programme, reporting on the story of a man's death. As it progresses, this found footage 'breaks down' and the newsreader's voice becomes distorted and demonic as the tape stops.
- 'The Circle' (E6) begins with the opening of *The Circle*, a 1950s anthology drama episode made by a witness to the real-life snuff film discovered of the Visser cult's earlier ritual sacrifice. Following a lead-in countdown made to look exactly like archival television, the drama's on-screen narrator (Andrew Long) intones: 'Do you believe in a world other than our own?'
- 'The Ferryman' (E7) starts with the rights page of a scratchy 16mm library film from the Encyclopaedia Britannica organisation about Comet Kharon, 'named for the ferryman of Hades who carries souls of the dead across the River Styx'.
- 'What Lies Beneath' (E8), the final episode, opens with grainy, degraded, black-and-white footage from Visser resident Jess's (Ariana Neal) Fisher Price camera, including shots of Jess and Melody on swings in the park as they discuss the future (or rather Melody fails to do so).

On the one hand, these bits of mocked-up found footage serve as a teaser to the episode that follows; we soon learn that they hold the key to a forthcoming narrative development. However, they also provide an internal, self-referential commentary on the idea of 'haunted media' (Sconce, 2000) or rather on the ability for audio-visual, electronic recording to capture, and thus provide prolonged access to, the past and, by association, the dead. If, as Emma Wilson argues, 'lens based art' is a 'means of maintaining a sensory, amorous relation to the dead' (2012: 32), then these faux-archival extracts dramatise that relationship. This generically diverse collection of mocked-up found footage suggests that television, and the audio-visual archive more broadly, is a repository for afterlife images, that recorded sounds and images allow the dead to remain in circulation with the living, still part of their (media) landscape. This therefore draws us towards the final part of this book, and its examination of the ways in which television, and the television archive, is formed of posthumous images.

Part III

Posthumous Television

6

Entering the mausoleum: Posthumous television

Remember All the Good Things (BBC1, 1975), the documentary about the death of artist Tony Whiteley discussed in Chapter 1, was made with a particular afterlife in mind. As Tony himself acknowledged, one of the purposes of this film was for his children, too young at three years and six months old at the time of Tony's death to remember their dad in any detail from memory alone, to have a record of him and of this time in their life as a family. While, as explored in Chapter 1, the family initially had no recording of this broadcast, and then for many years had a bootlegged copy but no VCR on which to play it, the sheer fact of the recording's existence in the BBC's archive meant that Tony was, in theory, posthumously available to the Whiteleys through this television documentary. However, the technical barriers to accessing this recording of Tony after his death were not the only thing that made rewatching the programme difficult for the family. Eight years after the broadcast of *Remember All the Good Things*, Tony's widow Vivien was invited to appear on *Live from Two* (Granada for ITV, 1981–1982), an afternoon talk show presented by Shelley Rhode, which on 22 January 1982 focused on people's experiences of living with, and being bereaved by, cancer. Vivien agreed to be a member of the selected audience for this programme, to talk about her experiences as a young widow, but was totally unprepared for the production team to show an extract of *Remember All the Good Things* when Rhode came over to speak to her in the studio. This unexpected encounter with Tony eight years after his death via the television archive came as a terrible shock to Vivien:

> They played a clip from the film, and they hadn't told me they were going to do that ... They should have. But they didn't and the first thing was I just heard Tony's voice. It was a terrific shock. It was – and I almost welled up and I thought 'Oh, they'll be wanting me to cry! I won't be doing that!' ... So, I didn't look at it and I just heard his voice

and I let the clip go on and then they asked me questions about it: I can't remember what because it was a bit of shock. But, because of that, and because of my reaction to it, I never felt that I could watch it again because I didn't want to disturb the way I'd adapted and the way we'd been [as a family].[1]

For Vivien, in this moment, this unexpected encounter with Tony after his death via the television archive was jarring and upsetting; she never again brought herself to watch the film, even when it was technically possible to do so in the comfort of her own home. In some ways this is explained by Paul Sutton's exploration of the interconnectedness of film and television viewing and his own experience of bereavement: '[the] presence and absence that characterises the spectatorial experience, and that of being in love, is subject to precisely this sense of transience, the awareness that the loved object's presence, the film being viewed, will inevitably disappear, become absent' (2020: 59). Put simply, that sense of transience, and the fleeting return of a lost loved one, or even their voice, via television viewing, was simply too much, too painful and unsettling for Vivien.

Vivien also discussed with me the fact that she never sat down and watched the programme with the boys as planned ('It never seemed appropriate').[2] Tom, the younger of the two boys, chose to watch the film privately with his partner one summer, when his mother was away on holiday, whereas his brother chose to never watch the documentary, a decision which Vivien understood as relating to the difficulties he had experienced in dealing with his father's death as a child. Posthumous television for Tony Whiteley's sons brought their own relation to their father's death into sharp relief; they thus (understandably) chose to watch either with caution, having a posthumous encounter with their father via the television archive carefully, privately, and in a way that anticipated upset or difficulty, or not at all. Amy Holdsworth, in her *On Living With Television* (2021), explores what she describes as a 'life lived alongside television' and 'a knitting together of our on- and offscreen lives' (5). For Holdsworth this refers to her examination of the way in which our lives are inflected by the programmes we watch, but this sense of a life lived alongside television takes on a special meaning when we consider our lives as having been lived alongside the programmes we, and/or our loved ones, have appeared in. The posthumous nature of television, its ability to capture the dead while they are still living, takes on a particular resonance and significance for the Whiteleys in the case described above. While the appearance of the dead on television seeks to form what Bill Nichols describes as an 'empathetic bond across the barrier between the living and the dead' (1991: 86), we might equally see those continuing bonds as unsettling, upsetting or 'difficult' in some way, perhaps even haunting. As described in Chapter 1, the BBC undertook their duty of care towards Vivien Whiteley, attending to what Brian Winston calls 'an ethical consciousness . . . and a sensitivity to the impact of transmission and distribution [of documentaries]' (2000: 162) by enabling her social worker to be present while she watched the first broadcast of *Remember All the Good Things*, anticipating some level of 'upset' in the viewing of this documentary. However, the survival of this programme in the archive and its subsequent re-circulation via integration into a new television programme (*Live from Two*), and via recordings made outside of the archive, meant that this piece of posthumous television would continue to reverberate through the Whiteleys' lives in ways that the BBC's 'duty of care' towards Vivien as participant in, and viewer of, the programme didn't, and couldn't, cover.

The previous three chapters of this book have all explored the terrain of television dramas about life after death. They have dissected the ways in which narratives of continuing life beyond the grave abound in television fiction, for the dead or for those who continue to imagine, remember or manifest their existence in some way. In one sense, then, this book has shown television to be a 'posthumous medium' in relation to its obsession with the afterlives of the characters it creates. This diegetic posthumousness has been related at various points to a wider turn towards death and the afterlife in popular culture. However, as the above example demonstrates very clearly, television might also be seen as posthumous in an entirely different context, as one of the photographic arts capable of 'embalming time' (Mulvey, 2006: 56). In this sense, television is ontologically posthumous, always and forever capturing life before death and capable of bringing the dead back to life, though this aspect of television's identity as a medium is distinctly under-explored in comparison to that of photography and film, for example. In the final part of this book, television's posthumousness will be examined at length.

Conceptually, as Jeremy Tambling has noted, '[the] posthumous challenges a life-death distinction and the order in which that distinction is phrased; it throws chronology into disarray' (2001: 7). Tambling proposed the posthumous as 'a way of thinking about the pastness of the past, and about our own present' (ibid.: 8). For him, it was a new way of considering past–present relations in literature, though he also set out on his exploration of the posthumous by acknowledging that the 'posthumous present' is consistently enshrined within the photograph. Tambling argues that the 'photograph [thus] . . . haunts the present with the thought of its posthumous being, as a record of a past' (ibid.: 14). This chapter considers television as an extension of photography's ability to present the posthumous, looking at how television brings the dead back to life in a variety of different ways and contexts, and at what is specific about watching the dead on television, extending the already extensive work on this in relation to film. In some senses this is a return to the topic of the first two chapters of the book, which categorised how television documentary seeks to capture the end of life; this programme making can be seen as an anticipatory act that implicitly understands television's posthumous possibilities. However, arguably television's posthumousness extends beyond that programming which explicitly engages with death and dying experiences: this chapter will explain how.

Of course, Jeremy Tambling was not the first person to note photography's ability to capture life in the midst of death, or death in the presence of life. As Laura Mulvey explains, André Bazin's 'The ontology of the photographic image' (1960) essay and Roland Barthes's *Camera Lucida* (1981) can be found at the root of much critical thinking about the relationship between death, photography and the moving image. Mulvey argues that this thinking goes right back to Bazin's categorisation of art as 'the making of a likeness, as driven by the human desire to overcome death' (2006: 58). For Barthes, influenced by his mourning for his own mother, the presence of death was caught as the punctum in each photograph, expressed as the realisation that 'He [sic] is going to die' (1981: 96). As Barthes explains, 'Whether or not the subject is already dead, every photograph is this catastrophe' (ibid.). This is also described eloquently by Mulvey as that 'rather terrible thing that is there in every photograph: the return of the dead' (2006: 61). Susan Sontag concurs:

> Photography has kept company with death ever since cameras were invented, in 1839. Because an image produced with a camera is, literally, a trace of something brought before the lens, photographs had an advantage over any painting as a memento of the vanished past and the dear departed. (2002)

This sense that the photographic image is characterised as *inherently posthumous* thus permeates much critical thinking about photography as a medium: Sandra Gilbert refers to photography as a 'mortuary genre' (2006: 220), Eduardo Cadava discusses photography as a 'mode of bereavement'

(1997: 11), Douglas Davies argues that photography provides 'the possibility of direct representation of the dead' (2005: 100) and, as we have seen, Tambling positions photography as a 'record of death . . . a thanatography' (2001: 14).

A number of theorists, Mulvey included, take this characterisation of photography as a critical stepping stone towards an understanding of the relationship between death and film, arguing as Davies does that film and video made the photographed dead 'more dynamic' (2005: 103). This 'bringing to life' of the dead via film is recognised by Tambling (2001: 139), Fuss (2013: 29) and others. As we have seen, Emma Wilson's work on the filmed dead proposes that 'lens-based art' is a 'means of maintaining a sensory, amorous relation to the dead' (2012: 13). This critical narrative of film as a posthumous medium has run through the entirety of film history. For example, Ian Christie notes that the reporting on the very first film show by the Lumière brothers by a number of Parisienne newspapers focused on the same idea – that 'death will cease to be absolute . . . [and] it will be possible to see our nearest alive again long after they have gone' (1995: 111). Laura Mulvey, on the other hand, reflects that after 100 years of film history, it becomes all the more evident that film is capable of capturing and preserving the dead, given that so many of the people seen in the first years of cinema are now in fact deceased (2006: 17). Mulvey's discussion of cinema as a medium of memorialisation will be returned to below, but for now, her articulation of cinema's posthumous power sums up these critical approaches to the relationship between film and death:

> [The] presence of the past in the cinema is also the presence of the body resurrected and these images can trigger, if only by association, questions that still seem imponderable: the nature of time, the fragility of human life and the boundary between life and death. (ibid.: 53)

It is worth acknowledging here that while the narrative of cinema's position as a posthumous medium grows largely out of Barthes's and Bazin's attention to photography's ability to 'overcome' death, there is a concomitant history of the relationship between the development of sound recording technologies and the capturing of life before death that is relevant to our understanding of cinema (and television's) posthumous possibilities. Noting the congruence of the development of embalming practices and sound recording to capture and make accessible the 'voices of the dead', Jonathan Sterne's cultural history of sound has argued that 'If there was a defining figure in early accounts of sound recording, it was the possibility of preserving the voice beyond the death of the speaker' (2003: 287). While much of the work on film's posthumous possibilities focuses on the moving image, Sterne's work is a good reminder of the qualities and significance of posthumous sound.

What is striking about these shifts from the critical history of photography's relationship with death to the above explorations of film's ability to reanimate the dead is that they maintain a critical blind spot when it comes to television's posthumous possibilities. Even Michael Renov's delineation of death as a 'special calling of the camera arts' (2004: 122) fails to include a consideration of television. In all the above, television seems to be held outside of critical explorations of moving images as posthumous. This leads me to propose that we should reconsider this critical blind spot, and, to adapt Tambling's phrase, explore television's relation to the posthumous by also considering it's 'record of death' (Tambling 2001: 14); we should perhaps consider television as a form of 'thanatovision'. This extends work by Jacques Derrida and Bernard Stiegler on the television–death relation in which they argue that 'once [the televised image] has been captured, this image will be reproducible in our absence, because we know this *already* we are already haunted by this future, which brings our death. Our disappearance is already here' (2007: 117). There are a couple of critical issues to tease out of this proposal that open up the specifics of television posthumousness. Firstly, the idea of 'capture' is foregrounded by Derrida and Stiegler in a nod, I think, to the (potential) liveness of television. As I argued in the introduction to this book, television arguably 'captures' everyday life in greater detail, and with greater regularity, and with greater immanence, than cinema, so it stands to reason that it also more frequently captures the dead, if we are to understand television as a posthumous medium. Furthermore, the fact that Derrida and Stiegler acknowledge that the television image (and, presumably, sound too) will be 'reproducible in [their] absence' is a reminder that even live television is often recorded, and that television in fact produces a vast archive that is full of the 'captured dead'. The final part of *Television/Death* will explore this archive of the dead, and the ways in which the dead resurface via the television archive.

Jeffrey Sconce's book *Haunted Media: Electronic Presence from Telegraphy to Television* (2000) has also considered television's relation to the dead, but from a slightly different angle. Sconce writes about television as one of a number of *haunted media* in relation to its 'occult liveness' and a larger cultural mythology about the 'living' quality of media as haunted or possessed by the supernatural. This doesn't necessarily figure television as posthumous in a way analogous to Mulvey's exploration of film's relation to death, however. Rather, Sconce's history explores American culture's persistent association of new electronic media with paranormal or spiritual phenomena. By offering a historical analysis of the relation between communication technologies, discourses of modernity, and metaphysical preoccupations, Sconce demonstrates how accounts of the hauntings of 'electronic presence' have shifted over time. However, in the introduction of his book, Sconce makes a rather throwaway comment about television sometimes serving as a 'medium *of* the dead' (ibid.: 2, original emphasis), an idea which is not really explained in *Haunted Media* but which is picked up and explored at length in this chapter. Television is in many ways a medium of posthumous entertainment: the dead tell jokes on TV, they sing songs, act, appear in studio audiences, pass news cameras in the street and give expert opinion. They are simply present, as in life, in television's endless flow and in the television archive. Television's capacity to record and replay performances means that it is endlessly possible to rewatch the dead on TV. This is also acknowledged by Tina Weber who explains that 'We can watch actors, who died a long time ago, claiming their vivid presence amongst the living through the medium of moving pictures' (2011: 22). On television, as Ruth Penfold-Mounce's work has shown us, the dead are also there to endorse brands and sell us products and can be made to perform actions or in contexts that they never found themselves in in life. Penfold-Mounce's work considers what she calls 'the posthumous careers of the celebrity dead' (2018: 6), arguing that '[even] though the [dead] celebrities' physical bodies are gone, their image survives and is perpetuated in disconcertingly vivid and lifelike ways' (ibid.). She, like Denver D'Rozario (2016) and David Giles (2017), uses the Forbes Top Earning Dead Celebrities list as a springboard for discussing what we might think of as the reanimated dead on television: whether it's a body-morphed Marylin Monroe touting Chanel No. 5,[3] a CGI'd Audrey Hepburn selling us Galaxy chocolate,[4] or Fred Astaire dancing with a Dirt Devil vacuum cleaner in hand,[5] the dead are brought back to life on television by advertising companies in ways that may delight a set of nostalgic consumers or, alternatively, tumble 'down the slopes of the "uncanny valley"' (D'Rozario, 2016: 496). Perhaps the latter reaction relates to our fears that the dead have somehow been 'enslaved' for the purpose of selling products? A straightforward re-broadcast of a celebrity performance is one thing, potentially posthumously inspiring delight and nostalgia, but reanimating the body of a dead celebrity on television might produce the reaction noted by Denver D'Rozario to the CGI-d Audrey Hepburn in the example above, who was compared to a 'zombie' in the reception of this advert (2016: 497). As Bethan Michael-Fox suggests 'In visual media, the ways in which the dead might return are myriad and, at times, ethically fraught' (2019: 194).

There has been some attempt to think through the significance of the impermanence of television, in particular the 'live' qualities of the broadcast image, in relation to the posthumousness of the camera arts. John Ellis, for example, notes that photographic images 'strike us with their haunting sense of being the death-mask imprint of a moment that is already past (if on film) or is fleeting and almost ungraspable (if on television)' (1999: 10). While the latter might have been nearly true in an era of mainly live broadcast and no home recording technologies, television's more marked proclivity for the endless replaying of images, a constant recycling of moments within so many television genres, particularly in an era of digital image retrieval and manipulation, means that television is far more capable of repeatedly returning to such a 'death-mask imprint' than film, even, and far more readily does so. Indeed, it might seem too obvious a thing to state, but, as discussed in the introduction of this book, the ability to record, pause, rewind and replay television that is built into the technologies and platforms that most of us watch it on means that even if a moment on television is broadcast live, we are now able to revisit it again and again, as and when we wish to. If, as Tambling argues, the posthumous 'throws chronology into disarray' (2001: 7), then television's constant shifting back and forth in time, both within its programmes and in its mode of reception, is particularly well suited to the presentation of the posthumous image. Television captures life as it happens and then endlessly recycles that capture over and over again. It is, then, perhaps, the posthumous medium *par excellence*.

In this book, television's ability to capture the moment of death has been highlighted; think back to the examples discussed in the beginning of *Televsion/Death*'s introduction, or the documentaries examined in the first part of the book. Such moments bring our awareness to the medium's posthumous qualities, though we need not only look at moments of death on television to understand its ability to capture 'life before death' or 'death in life' in a Barthesian sense. Life and death, and posthumous sounds and images, are captured by television at all times and preserved in the archival record of historical TV. In the final part of this book, then, I consider a number of ways in which the dead are posthumously resurrected via the television archive. This chapter starts out by considering whether the television archive can be seen as a kind of mausoleum: this analogy is a common, tempting and evocative one, implying that the dead lie waiting to be disinterred in the TV archive, re-broadcast, edited into new programming, re-circulated or re-screened in other contexts. However, unlike the mausoleum, which remains sealed save for the admission of fresh corpses, the television archive is an active facility, and the dead are constantly brought in and out of its environs. The first part of the chapter will consider, then, how television marks the death of its own stars (and the television rituals that surround their death) as well as the role that television programming plays in the structuring of collective bereavement and mourning when figures of national and international significance die. It will reflect on television's own structures of memorialisation, as well as how TV is recycled by viewers online as a form of commemoration; the sharing of pictures and listings, clips, GIFs, interviews, and bloopers mimic the way in which television itself deals with death as a prompt for the recycling of posthumous sounds and images. The chapter will then turn to look at a specific example of a dead television celebrity brought almost compulsively out of the archive, again and again: the DJ, television presenter and serial sex offender Jimmy Savile. The analysis of Savile's posthumous reappearances on television will consider how the returning dead might haunt the television viewer – and the television broadcaster.

Television and memorialisation

In his 1967 essay exploring Valéry's and Proust's accounts of visits to the Louvre in Paris, Theodor Adorno famously explained the connection between the museum as a repository for works of art and the mausoleum:

> The German word, *'museal'* *['museumlike']*, has unpleasant overtones. It describes objects to which the observer no longer has a vital relationship and which are in the process of dying ... Museum and mausoleum are connected by more than phonetic association. Museums are like the family sepulchres of works of art. (2011: 110)

Such a spatial analogy between the museum and the mausoleum can be, and has been, extended to the moving image museum/archive as a place of interment for the dead: Amy Holdsworth discusses various attempts to exploit the holdings of the television archive as 'resurrections' (2011: 5) and explains that '[while] a few years ago there was a fevered interest in the "death" of television, its afterlife in the space of the archive is now at the centre of debate' (ibid.: 131). However, Holdsworth also notes that the 'romanticised image of the archive as dusty burial chamber' sits at odds with facilities like 'the modern storage, preservation and security systems of the National Media Museum archives' (ibid.: 134). Nevertheless, if we put aside the image of the dusty vaults full of the dead, is it still useful to see the television archive as a repository for the dead? To some extent, if we understand television as a posthumous medium, such analogies must be inevitable. For example, Mulvey, considering film's posthumousness via Chris Petit's video *Negative Space* (1999), argues that '[the] cinema is becoming increasingly about what is past. It becomes a mausoleum as much as a palace of dreams' (2006: 17). Emma Wilson, on the other hand, rejects the mausoleum analogy because she imagines 'cinema not as a mausoleum but as a wish-fulfilling, fevered, exotic space in which to live with the dead' (2012: 14). For Wilson, then, the moving image archive is too 'lively' a space to interact with the dead to be considered a mausoleum. Laura Mulvey (2006: 45–6) and Lynn Spigel (2010: 54–5) have both considered the film and television archives, respectively, as uncanny spaces; implicitly, the uncanniness of these archives for Mulvey and Spigel is found in the access that they provide to posthumous sounds and images. As we shall see in the discussion of the posthumous archive of Jimmy Savile's appearances on TV, encounters with the television archive can be difficult and can 'resurrect' problematic pasts and the reviled dead; the moving image archive can be, as Amit Pinchevski argues, 'the technological unconscious of . . . trauma theory' (2011: 258) whereby 'the past returns to puncture the present by means of a technological mediation' (ibid.: 259). On the other hand, the television archive can offer more benign access to the dead, particularly in relation to television's function as a medium of memorialisation. It is to this function that we now turn.

Amy Holdsworth has argued that television 'is marked by and generates our obsession with commemoration' (2011: 1). This drive to commemorate via television, to mark significant dates and anniversaries, is not always, but often, associated with death: television frequently becomes a site in which the dead are memorialised, mourned, and honoured, whether they are public figures, film stars, television performers or even characters from television programmes. Television therefore plays a significant part in forming what Margaret Gibson calls 'communities of mourning' (2011: 22): we have become very used to archive-based programming (or archive-based segments of news programming, for example) being deployed, sometimes at a moment's notice, when a public figure dies, an almost-instant form of television memorialisation. This form of programming is implicitly acknowledged by Laura Mulvey in her discussion of the deployment of archival images to memorialise dead film stars in *Death 24x a Second*, though there is a significant omission in Mulvey's analysis here:

> To see the star on the screen in the retrospectives that follow his or her death is also to see the cinema's uncertain relation to life and death. Just as the cinema animates its still frames, so it brings back to life, in perfect fossil form, anyone it has ever recorded, from great star to fleeting extra. (2006: 18)

What Mulvey doesn't explicitly acknowledge is that while the archives on which these retrospectives are based are indeed cinematic, capturing what she refers to as 'a memorial to those who personified [cinema's] modernity, its glamour, its triumph as both a popular form and an art form' (ibid.: 17), the medium for which such memorials are made is television. Television becomes *the* site for the filmic dead, whether that's via the 'In Memoriam' sections of an awards show, or in a retrospective, posthumous documentary or even in the (re)broadcast of their finest film performances. To use Mulvey's words here, it is television which brings the cinematic dead back 'in perfect fossil form'.

Joanne Garde-Hansen proposes that 'if it is through media that famous people come to be known then it is through media their deaths are mourned and memorialised' (2011: 32); television is perhaps *the* key site of this media mourning and memorialisation. In television studies, significant attention has been paid to the role that the medium played in mourning and memorialising the death of Diana, Princess of Wales, in 1997. Robert Turnock's book *Interpreting Diana: Television Audiences and the Death of a Princess* (2000) is based on the BFI's Audience Tracking Study which asked 'how [television audiences] responded to the news and the television coverage' (2000: 1) in the week of her death. He documents the fact that on the day of Diana's death '[normal] scheduling on the two main terrestrial channels, BBC1 and ITV, was abandoned and the day was given over to live and continuous news. BBC2 simulcast with BBC1 until 3 pm when it ran a revised schedule of programmes' (ibid.: 13). While Turnock doesn't focus on the use of posthumous archive footage in this programming (he focuses on the role of television as a 'comforter' and representer of the shared experience of grief instead (ibid.: 19)), he does explore the important role that television played in constructing communities of mourning in the aftermath of Diana's death. Therese Davis, on the other hand, acknowledges in her work on Diana as *the* face of the media age the 'incredible speed with which the world's media responded to news of Diana's death' and 'the way in which Western television networks and press produced elaborate photographic and televisual memorials to her within less than twenty four hours of her death' (2004: 80–1). These 'elaborate televisual memorials' precisely draw on television archives of posthumous sounds and images, constructing montages of the dead princess to honour and remember her. Jenny Kitzinger's work has shown, for example, that in the days following Diana's death 'Words . . . were less important than representations of the embodied Diana: moving, looking, gesturing, touching and being touched' (1999: 65). Kitzinger refers to Diana as a 'princess of the moving image' (ibid.) and documents precisely the kind of archive footage that was used for this memorialisation:

> Footage of the Princess interspersed commentary and news reports, and for several days compilations of scenes from her life rounded off lunchtime and evening news bulletins. We were repeatedly presented with Diana in her wedding dress, in fashionable evening gowns or in casual wear with her boys. We saw Diana garlanded with flowers on a visit abroad, Diana in landmine protection gear, or the blond and glowing princess, clothed entirely in white, embracing a sick black child . . . Diana was represented 'in memoriam' as having a glittering existence and great beauty, but also as a woman who suffered and a woman who cared. (ibid.: 66)

Kitzinger also discusses the ways in which this archive footage of Diana was manipulated for maximum memorial effect: 'Often these images were presented using cinematic conventions. Diana appeared in soft focus, the BBC framed scenes from her life with white lilies, shots were played in slow motion, there was seldom any synchronous sound' (ibid.). She argues that these 'conventions signal that this is not live coverage, suggesting flashbacks and dream sequences. They also carry a certain glamour, framing Diana in an angelic, "not of this world", light' (ibid.). Arguably, these conventions also signalled the posthumousness of the archival image (not 'Diana is alive and well and amongst us once more', but 'here the archive presents this voiceless angel from beyond the grave').

Diana's death was certainly an unprecedentedly televisual event which drew on the holdings of the TV archive, as the work discussed above has shown, and the television coverage of subsequent royal deaths proves that while Diana's 'star persona' was well suited to the kind of wall-to-wall archival memorialisations described above, others were perhaps less so. The announcement of her ex-father-in-law Prince Philip's death on Friday 9 April 2021, for example, saw slickly prepared archive-based montages inserted into the breaking news bulletins that interrupted the late morning daytime schedule. Cutting short *Paramedics on Scene* (BBC1, 2021), *This Morning* (ITV1, 1988–), and *Couples Come Dine With Me* (Channel 4, 2014–), and coming at the end of *Build a New Life in the Country* (Channel 5, 2005–), soundless VT packages of archive footage and stills of the Prince accompanied the announcement of this breaking news by news anchors across all the major UK channels. At 99 and in ill-health, the Prince's death had clearly been anticipated and prepared for with the requisite assemblages of news and documentary excerpts from the archive edited together and ready to go. If we look at ITV's coverage, for example, an interview with *Coronation Street* (ITV, 1960–) actor Alan Halsall on *This Morning* is cut short to switch over to the ITV 'Newsroom' and the newsreader Lucrezia Millarini breaking the news about Prince Phillip's death. As Millarini arrives on screen, she says 'Good afternoon. We are *breaking into programmes* to bring you an announcement from the royal household'. The language used is interesting here: 'breaking into programmes' suggests that this death has interrupted one bit of ordinary television (the daytime magazine show) talking about another (the soap opera) with news of this significant death. As previously discussed in this book's introduction, then, live television always carries with it the possibility of death. After Millarini reads a statement from Buckingham Palace on screen, a cut is made to a composite slide incorporating a black-and-white image of Windsor Castle and a colour image of the Prince, with his title and date of birth and death (1921–2021), as the national anthem plays over it. Following this, the statement is read again over a stills montage, before Millarini announces that

> The Duke of Edinburgh's role in the history of the United Kingdom is assured. In the next few hours we'll look back on his life and bring you reaction to his death as well as tributes to his contribution for many decades to the life of this country.

The news programme then switches to an archive-based montage of the Prince's life history, with accompanying voiceover by ITN's Royal Editor Chris Ship, once again demonstrating the posthumous possibilities of the television archive to revisit the dead. This mixture of archive, solemn commentary and guests' and reporters' reactions would characterise the rest of the day's broadcasting on ITV and the two main BBC channels, BBC1 and BBC2, which showed exactly the same news coverage. However, this led not to mass outpourings of public grief as it had done in the case of Diana, Princess of Wales, in 1997, but an unprecedented number of complaints to and about the BBC in particular. Writing for *The Guardian* newspaper, Jim Waterson reported that

> The BBC's wall-to-wall coverage of Prince Philip's death has become the most complained about moment in British television history, as viewers expressed their annoyance that shows such as *EastEnders* and *MasterChef* were replaced with royal tributes. At least 110,994 people have contacted the BBC to express their displeasure at the decision to turn most of the corporation's channels and radio stations over to rolling tributes to the Queen's husband. BBC One and BBC Two dedicated Friday (9 April) evening's programming to Philip, and their ratings fell as viewers switched off altogether, turned to streaming services or watched shows such as *Gogglebox* on Channel 4. (2021)

Here, the nature of complaint is precisely the interruption of the *ordinary television schedule* by endless rolling archive-based packages. The BBC was particularly singled out for complaint because it had set up a dedicated complaints procedure to deal with public reaction to their coverage of the Prince's death (which they took down two days later after becoming overwhelmed) (see Hancock, 2021), whereas Channel 4 was attacked on social media and in the right-wing press for not doing the same (see Davies, 2021). It is clear, then, that while the television archive of posthumous images is *capable* of providing access to the notable deceased, there may be a limit to how much we wish this to interrupt our regular viewing, in certain contexts.

One might have been forgiven for thinking that our relationship to television had changed to such an extent between the time of Princess Diana's death in 1997 and 2021 that the public reaction to the television coverage of Prince Philip's death, and the endless recycling of posthumous archive images of him, was evidence of a major shift in television viewing habits. However, as discussed in the introduction of this book, the death of Queen Elizabeth II, reigning monarch of the United Kingdom and widow of the prince, was an event which led to hour upon hour of posthumous archive-based programming being broadcast. While the extensive television coverage of the progress of the Queen's dead body from Balmoral in Scotland where she died, to its lying-in-state in Westminster Hall, to the day-long coverage of her funeral and the committal of her body at St George's Chapel at Windsor Castle later in the day is beyond the scope of this chapter, it is certainly true, as I have already shown, that sounds and images of the posthumous Queen were immediately brought out of the television archive as part of the broadcasting rituals surrounding her death. They were inserted into news programming about her death as soon as the announcement was made, edited into multiple archive-based documentaries about the life of the Queen and included in the programming that surrounded the coverage of her lying-in-state and funeral. Clips from the posthumous archive were also frequently shared on social media, assembled into widely shared listicles such as 'Six Times The Queen Made Us Laugh' (Anon., 2022) or posted directly on social media user's own feeds (see Breese, 2022 for an account of this). Bringing the Queen out of the television archive posthumously therefore became central to mourning on and off television screens.

It is not just the British Royal Family that television gives us access to after their death, though. The lives of television personalities are often also celebrated posthumously via the television archive. While some have 'unprecedentedly public' deaths (Walter, 2009), such as Jade Goody, Christopher Hitchens (see Brennan, 2018) and Dennis Potter (see Davis, 2004), which lead into an expected process of memorialisation via television, others die privately but are then repeatedly celebrated (and brought 'back to life') through deep-dives into the television archive, posthumously performing their 'greatest hits' or 'hidden/early archival treasures' on a loop. Such programmes seem characteristic of the non-linearity of television time, described by Amy Holdsworth as 'akin to a process of spiralling, looping or doubling – continually moving backward and forward' (2021: 9) and by Amy Villarejo as 'segmentation, repetition, seriality, frozen, paused, captured, looped, restored, lost, and found' (2014: 10). The posthumous archive is critical, then, to television's temporal volatility; it is the rich resource from which television's 'loopiness' is drawn. If we take the TV comedian, actress, musician, screenwriter, producer and director Victoria Wood as an example, who died of cancer on 20 April 2016, we can see just how memorialisation via the posthumous archive works. As someone who had a long and illustrious career on television, a true television star, Wood had already been celebrated several times over in retrospective archive-based shows before her death. For example, BBC1 had collaborated on the 2005 special *Victoria Wood: A BAFTA Tribute* (tx. 5/2/05) which incorporated clips of her work into an evening of celebration and contributions from her many colleagues;[6] in 2009, the BBC had commissioned *Victoria Wood: Seen on TV* (BBC2, tx. 21/12/09), billed in the *Radio Times* as featuring 'famous sketches, stand-up routines and songs from her repertoire, as well as interviews with celebrity fans and friends'; in 2010 she made *The South Bank Show Revisited: Victoria Wood* (ITV1, tx. 23/5/10), fifteen years after her first appearance on the show; and the ironically titled *Victoria Wood's Short Term Memories* (BBC2, tx. 9/6/12) compiled clips from her more recent television career. Following her sad, untimely death in 2016, the major UK broadcasters re-screened some of these earlier programmes,[7] took whole programmes back out of the archive,[8] held special 'tribute nights' where they showed repeats of her television programmes and previously unbroadcast live shows,[9] and also made the following memorial documentary clip shows, not just in the immediate aftermath of Wood's death in 2016, but almost annually in the years that followed:

- *Let's Do It: A Tribute To Victoria Wood* (ITV, tx. 15/5/16)
- *Our Friend Victoria* (BBC1, 2017) 6-part series
- *Funny Women: Victoria Wood* (Channel 5, tx. 29/12/17)
- *Victoria Wood: In Her Own Words* (Channel 5, tx. 20/12/20)
- *Victoria Wood: The Secret List* (BBC1, 2021) 2-part series

What is striking when you watch these documentaries in close succession is that they return again and again to the very same moments, the same fragments of television performance, the same gags and songs, the same bits of interviews, recycled and reframed in different ways, joined together by new interviews and bits of voiceover (often with the same set of friends and collaborators), but all endlessly familiar. There is perhaps a comfort in this; Wood continues to perform for us beyond her death, continues to delight in her very repetitiousness and familiarity. These posthumous clips also circulate beyond television: they were compiled, for example, as links in online news articles following her death (see Plunkett, 2016), shown as part of *Victoria Wood: A Tribute* at the BFI/*Radio Times* Festival of Television in 2017, and endlessly shared on social media by fans mourning her loss. As the television comedy historian Andy Medhurst commented:

> If 2016, this year of almost relentless celebrity deaths, has taught us anything, it's that YouTube has now become an invaluable mourning resource. The shock of Victoria Wood dying earlier this week sent me, as so many others, online in search of clips, sketches, songs, lines and gags from her incomparable, pioneering career, and then posting them on social media. Good comedy is always about togetherness,

> it offers comfort and balm in the shape of shared experience. Wood knew that more than most, which is why the collectively exchanged reminiscence of how she made us laugh is as fitting a tribute as any obituary. (2016)

Medhurst notes here the comfort of familiarity in much-loved and oft-repeated performance and the togetherness of sharing this in the face of grief, but we might add that the posthumous television performance, accessed via television's vast archive, provides the promise of some form of eternal 'liveliness', a comforting promise of life beyond death. As many of the tribute programmes noted, Victoria Wood may be gone but her television performances 'live on' via the television archive.

Haunted television: trauma and the spectre in the archive

There is, then, great comfort to be taken in the posthumous television archive. That our television entertainment is not limited to that provided by the living might be a truly wonderful thing. However, encounters with the dead through television's archival re-circulation aren't always so reassuring. They can, as mentioned at the start of this chapter, be unsettling, disturbing, *haunting*, even. As we have seen already, television is full of ghosts. They appear on screen in a wide variety of programming, from serial drama to situation comedy and children's television, often enabling a revisitation of traumatic histories and the revelation of injustice beyond death. As we saw in the previous chapter, and in my earlier work (Wheatley, 2006, 2012, 2020), the television ghost frequently brings about awareness and acceptance of past trauma, or avoidance of the repetition of the mistakes of the past. These are often classic Derridean spectres, with ethical and political potential to confront a traumatic history (Derrida, 1994).

Following Derrida, and as we saw in Chapter 5, the 'spectral turn' in cultural theory has become inextricably linked with trauma studies. To quote del Pilar Blanco and Peeren 'To be traumatised . . . is to be 'possessed by an image or event' located in the past. To be 'possessed' – gripped indefinitely by an anachronistic event – also describes the condition of being haunted' (2013: 11). Ghosts, then, 'are part of a symptomatogy of trauma as they become both the objects of and metaphors for a wounded historical experience' (ibid.: 12), according to del Pilar Blanco and Peeren. Television in the

UK has recently become a site of its own traumatic history, and to understand this, we must understand television as a medium which has become haunted by a spectral figure that epitomises the return of traumatic memory via the posthumous television archive. The latter part of this chapter explores the ideas that television itself can be 'haunting', that television companies and their archives might become haunted, and that the production of programming made from the posthumous archive can sometimes act as a form of exorcism, or at least a working through, of the traumas and hidden histories that the spectral figure represents.

We have already explored Emma Wilson's proposal that the moving image is a 'means of maintaining a sensory, amorous relation to the dead' (2012: 13) and that cinema (and perhaps, by extension, television) is 'not a mausoleum, but . . . a wish-fulfilling, fevered, exotic space in which to live with the dead' (ibid.: 14). But what happens when this sensory relation to the dead is disturbing, rather than comforting or reassuring? And what about when the dead, or the haunting figure, *keeps on returning* via televisual flow, not sought out as in Wilson's work or lovingly returned to in the home movie, a form of screening described by Sandra Gilbert as 'a party to which the dead have been invited' (2006: 210), keeping them '"alive and busy" – and seeming . . . still to be here among us' (ibid.: 219). What happens when these endless returns, and the sudden reappearance of the dead within the home, are the return of a predatory figure like the UK television personality and serial rapist, Jimmy Savile? If televisual flow, like the home movie, is a 'party to which the dead have been invited', or if it traps us in a 'sensory, amorous relationship' with the dead, like film, then surely television is truly haunted by the endlessly returning figure of Savile.

Jimmy Savile had a long career in British light entertainment television. He started out as a radio DJ (first on the pirate radio station, Radio Luxembourg, and then on the nascent BBC station, Radio 1) and then as a presenter of music television in the early 1960s. Savile was a fairly constant presence on British television from then on. He presented his long-running 'wish-granting' programme for children, *Jim'll Fix It* (BBC1), from 1975 to 1994, and following the end of its run, Savile made more sporadic appearances on television, as presenter, guest and documentary subject, including in the documentary *When Louis Met . . . Jimmy* (BBC1) in April 2000. Louis Theroux's documentary positioned Savile as a troubling but ultimately 'loveable' figure, and it raised and then dismissed rumours about Savile's sexual interest in children. It was subsequently revealed, however, following Savile's death in October 2011, that he was one of Britain's most prolific sex offenders and a serial rapist who used his position as a popular broadcaster and charity fundraiser to abuse and attack hundreds of women and children, including those he came into contact with while making programmes for the BBC and volunteering at Stoke Mandeville Hospital, Leeds General Infirmary, Broadmoor Secure Hospital and other hospitals, children's homes and facilities in England.

In 2012, alongside the horror of the discovery of Savile's crimes, a further scandal erupted when it was revealed that the BBC had pulled a report about this on their flagship news and current affairs programme, *Newsnight* (BBC2, 1980–) at the end of 2011 (Anon., 2012). For this move, the BBC was attacked for being cowardly (and possibly self-protecting). The BBC's most long-standing rival broadcaster, ITV, then 'broke' the story of Savile's crimes in their ITV1 documentary *Exposure: The Other Side of Jimmy Savile* in September of 2012. As Rowan Aust and Amy Holdsworth have shown, Savile has posed a particular problem for the BBC in that the discovery of his crimes 'presents a point where the history and memory *of* the BBC, popular history *on* the BBC and crisis *within* the BBC converge' (2017: 175). Savile's spectre troubles the BBC, an institution already endangered by a hostile Tory government threatening its funding structures (the television licence fee), and near-daily criticism in the Conservative press for excess and wastefulness, for being out of touch with people beyond the metropolitan elite, and for having a working culture which over-valorises (and overpays) its top 'talent'. The discovery of Savile's crimes (some of which took place on BBC property and during the day-to-day life of television production) truly haunted the BBC, *institutionally*, as I shall explore below; certainly, one of the Corporation's responses to this was to set about trying to eradicate the posthumous Savile from their archive of entertainment programming as Aust and Holdsworth have shown, though, as the authors acknowledge, 'despite efforts by the BBC to eradicate Savile from its televised (and online) archive . . . full removal [was] impossible' (ibid.: 171). In line with Dan Arav's proposal that television is a 'traumatic form' and that its flow is a conduit of televisual trauma (2016: 41), the constant posthumous reappearance of Savile's image and the story of his crimes presents him as a traumatising television spectre extraordinaire: not just traumatising to his victims and to the wider audience but to the institution itself. This reappearance, this series of returns, occurs occasionally through television reruns, but also through documentaries that seek to understand his crimes and how they remained undetected for so long, and, indirectly, via television dramas that produce characters in his image. Some of the programmes that draw upon the posthumous television archive will be examined in this chapter.

Why view Savile's posthumous image as spectral? The discourse of haunting relating to this figure has been circulating since the discovery of Savile's crimes in popular culture and via social media in the UK; this is not simply a critical construct applied after the fact, but rather a repetitive and tangible way of representing Savile observed across media. It is, to use Iwona Irwin-Zarecka's phrase, a 'framing' idea that guides our interpretation and understanding of the posthumous image of Savile. She argues that

> [Questions] about framing direct our attention to the powers inherent in public articulation of collective memory to influence the private makings of sense. Questions about framing are essentially about limits to the scope of possible interpretations. Their aim is not to freeze one particular 'reading' as *the* correct one, rather, it is to establish the likely range of meanings. (1994: 4)

In Savile's case, the framing of his posthumous image across a range of texts and media sites draws a repeatedly spectral picture of him as a threatening figure, and a figure associated with a form of collective trauma.

Following his death, a number of cultural commentators used the language of haunting to describe the lasting impact of Savile and his crimes: the criminal justice blogger and broadcaster David Jessel described him as a 'ghost come to haunt us, leaving only his grandiose and shattered gravestone behind him like some cackling, demonic Ozymandias' (2016). Journalist Aiden Smith stated that 'I cannot think about *Top of the Pops* now without being reminded of Savile. He haunts the show in memory like he used to stalk its dark recesses when it was a 15 million ratings smasheroo' (2015). Aust and Holdsworth similarly used the language of the supernatural in their analysis of the 'problem' of Savile in the BBC archive, describing him as presenting a 'psychic horror' (2017: 175), which '[lingers], unresolved, as a toxic asset within the corporation and the television archive' (ibid.: 180) and whose 'exorcism' from the archive and from cultural memory remains an 'impossibility' (ibid.: 181). While this language of haunting is frequently applied to Savile and his posthumous image, the significance of the designation of Savile as spectre needs exploring more fully. What does it mean to describe Savile as a spectre, or the archive as an uncanny, haunted space? It is argued here that the documentaries exploring Savile's crimes, and the dramas that depict him, or characters constructed in his image, present him as spectre and the medium as haunted by him, in very explicit ways. If, as Stephen Frosh has argued, 'every generation has something that haunts it' (2013: 1) then maybe Savile, and the terrible crimes he committed, is ours. He haunts our 'collective memory', to use Irwin-Zarecka's phrase to describe 'a set of ideas, images, feelings about the past . . . best located not in the minds of individuals, but in the resources they share' (1994: 4). Irwin-Zarecka cautions us to be modest in our claims about collective memory and recognises that

> Individuals are perfectly capable of ignoring even the best told stories, of injecting their own subversive meanings into even the most rhetorically accomplished 'texts' – and of attending to only those ways of making sense of the past that fit their own. (ibid.)

However, what I show here is the uniformity of the framing of Savile as spectral within our collective remembering of him, and thus offer some reflections on the ways in which we are *being invited* to understand him posthumously as well as his role in television history.

The recycling of Savile's posthumous image and performances is remediated, recontextualised, in a way that often underscores a sense of spectrality. For example, montages of archive images and footage of Savile are frequently manipulated to make his return explicitly, texturally, spectral. In the Channel 5 documentary *Jimmy Savile: Britain's Worst Crimes* (tx. 18/11/15) images of Savile' 'float' over stock images of archival materials (files, tapes, film reels, and so on – see Figure 6.1) as well as props that refer specifically to Savile (a cigar, a union jack, a black-and-white photo of him in a frame), as if he was an apparition who had literally appeared in the archive.

His leering face as spectral image appears as Paul Connew, former editor of the *Sunday Mirror* newspaper, describes the impact of the discovery of Savile's crime on contemporary policing, accompanied by mournful piano music which also demarcates this 'roughly archival' space on screen as haunted. It is easy to read Savile as a kind of malevolent ghost here; the still photograph of his grinning face floats around the screen ethereally as Connew speaks. Later, in the Netflix documentary *Jimmy Savile: A British Horror Story* (2022), this programme's re-examination of the posthumous television archive is also positioned from the outset as a kind of haunting. At the start of the first episode, leading into and through the programme's

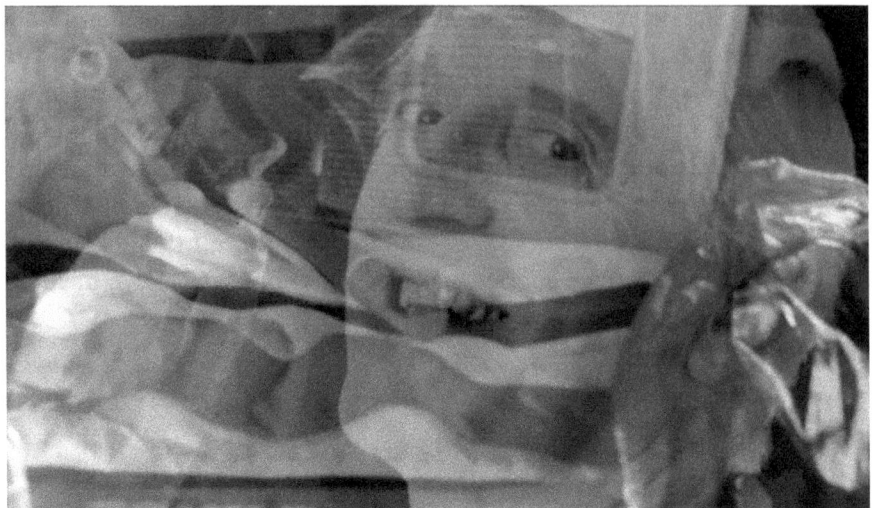

Figure 6.1 Savile as spectre, *Jimmy Savile: Britain's Worst Crimes* (Channel 5, tx. 18/11/15).

credit sequence, the glitching graphics that interrupt archive footage of Savile position him as spectral, with a horror aesthetic that references the 'haunted television' trope explored by Sconce (2000), as if the ghost of Savile was interrupting the streaming of this documentary.

Tom Gunning reminds us that 'As revenants of things past, ghosts make vivid to us the pairing of memory and forgetting' (2013: 232). In Savile's case, no forgetting is allowed, and it is the drive to couple memory with an uncovering of hidden, rather than forgotten, aspects of his life which produces his constant resurrection on our screens.

Many posthumous documentaries about Savile, *Jimmy Savile: Britain's Worst Crimes* included, begin with news footage of his funeral to remind us (and perhaps reassure us) of his death. These are some of the stock images of Savile's story that television returns to time and again. The funeral also stands as a representative moment where masses of people, unaware of his crimes, gathered together to watch Savile 'in the flesh' for one last time, but in the posthumous documentary this scene is the marker of a shift from public mourning to a kind of televisual trauma when presented, repeatedly, with the spectre of Savile. The funeral is a stark representation of *masses* of television viewers who were unaware of his crimes. Repeated resurfacing of his image or the story of his crimes as an abuser via television, not just in the numerous documentaries that explore the abuse that he perpetrated, but also in news programming, current affairs and magazine programmes, television dramas in which he is mentioned or in which characters representing

Figure 6.2 Glitching, 'haunted' title sequence, *Jimmy Savile: A British Horror Story* (Netflix, 2022).

a Savile 'type' appear, even in stand-up comedy shows, does not enable the 'purposeful forgetting' of mourning, but rather promotes a traumatic re-encounter with Savile's spectre. For example, in the two weeks at the end of November and beginning of December in 2016, when a scandal about the historic abuse of young footballers by coaching staff in the UK was revealed, Savile was mentioned and often shown – at least forty-four times on news and current affairs programmes, at all times of the day and night. In October 2017, when the news about the sexual misconduct of Hollywood mogul Harvey Weinstein broke, Savile's crimes resurfaced again on UK TV news, being discussed fifteen times in a ten-day period from 5 to 15 October. Following the initial revelation of Savile's crimes, TV satirist Charlie Brooker described watching the news as 'like riding an endless looping ghost train with a creepy cadaverous monster perpetually leering toward you through the gloom'.[10] These reappearances of Savile within the flow of television programming (not just in programmes explicitly signalled as being 'about' him) might represent what Frosh describes as the 'temporal disturbance' of haunting, where that which ought to be safely in the past is re-materialised repeatedly in the present (2013: 2). Accordingly, Frosh describes haunting as 'something that is supposed to be "past" [being] experienced in the present as if it is both fantastic and real' (ibid.). Writing about the presentation of trauma in the cinema, Köhne et al. argue that film

> [Repeats] and re-enacts the experienced event, causing or actuating 'trauma' again and again on a cultural level . . . Apart from its potentially cathartic effects, the loop of traumatizing events [and] the production

of filmic images and restagings of the past in film may in themselves create recurring patterns of 'trauma'. (2014: 5)

While the authors here think about the re-circulation of traumatic images and events in film, surely the flow of television, and what Amy Holdsworth has called its 'loopiness' (2013), means that the endlessly unfurling loop of trauma, or in the case of Savile, the spectre appearing within the 'endlessly looping ghost train' of television flow, is all the more present, the more invasive, and the more harrowing.

In their analysis of the 'problem' of Savile's posthumous appearances in the archive, particularly in the issues related to re-screening his appearances in the BBC's valuable *Top of the Pops* (BBC1, 1964–2006) back catalogue, and their account of the Corporation's attempt to edit him out of this footage, Aust and Holdsworth argue that it is the press that pore over Savile's image on screen, posthumously searching for clues of his crimes. Indeed, careful searching of this *Top of the Pops* archive has revealed footage of Savile groping a young popstar (Colleen Nolan) and placing his hand up the skirt of Sylvia Edwards, a member of the studio audience, while delivering a link to camera. These terrible discoveries in the television archive bring to mind Iwona Irwin-Zarecka's discussion of 'instant memory' – memory gathered with the 'instant' imperative to remember (for example, diarists in the Holocaust, but also family photography, television news reporting) – in which she argues that traumatic histories lack traces formed by 'instant memorialisation':

> What makes the transition from 'instant memory' to remembrance different – and often difficult – in the case of traumas is that the existence of records is more the exception than the rule. The creation of records is then mostly a work of reconstruction, from a time distance, with all the mnemonic problems that this implies. (1994: 165)

On the contrary, what is horrifying and different about the Savile case, is that the record of his abuse was hidden 'right there' in plain sight. Rowan Deacon's Netflix documentary, *Jimmy Savile: A British Horror Story*, does an outstanding job of 'mining' the posthumous television archive to expose the evidence of Savile 'hiding in plain sight', and edits together clips from the Savile back catalogue that make plain how he seemed to be taunting those around him. For example, in Episode 2 of this documentary, a sequence situated alongside the coverage of the first police and journalist investigations of

Savile's crimes, in which Savile responds to questions across eight different television programmes from a variety of time periods about his sexual predilections by cheekily replying 'My case comes up next Thursday,' emphasises this brazen and taunting behaviour. In addition, Deacon's documentary also shows a number of key figures watching bits of Savile footage back, who now seem incredulous that they had missed what was standing right in front of them. For example, in Episode 1, the TV reporter Martin Young is shown footage of an interview he did with Savile on a sponsored run. The documentary cuts from this footage to shots of Young leaning towards the camera as if peering into this bit of posthumous archive television, and searching for what he had missed. He states 'I hadn't seen that since I did it. Since it went out on air. I'm quite pleased with the script. I worked hard on that. I knew there was something wrong.' He then watches TV journalist Phil Tibernham interviewing Savile and asking whether the physical challenges he puts himself through are some kind of personal punishment, to which Savile replies:

> The only time you punish yourself is when you are with young ladies and then you punish yourself because you are such a villain what as you should be kind to them and you squeeze them and make them go 'ouch' and things like that.

Young's response to this back in the room where he is watching the archive footage is simply an incredulous 'Gosh!' (see Figure 6.3).

These glimpses either of Savile abusing young women on camera, or almost owning up to his crimes in interview, thus stand for a much larger

Figure 6.3 Watching the spectre, *Jimmy Savile: A British Horror Story* (Netflix, 2022).

hidden history of trauma and abuse. However, what Aust and Holdsworth don't really account for in their description of this search through the archive by journalists looking for traces of Savile's crimes is what a televisual encounter, accidental or intentional, might do to his victims or indeed to other victims of historic sexual abuse (arguably, larger viewing groups than the journalists looking for this 'evidence'). While the authors propose that the reframing of archival images of Savile 'produce[s] an unpleasant affective change in response – from familiar nostalgic feeling to the suspicion of culpability just by the act of looking' (2017: 179), they do not account for the feelings of *fear*, rather than guilt, or the re-experiencing of trauma that might be inspired by an encounter with Savile's televisual spectre, both when he was alive and then after his death.

It has been made plain in the press, and in the documentaries in which they appear, that Savile's victims have not been allowed to forget their abuse by his constant resurfacing on television. When footage of him on a rerun of *Top of the Pops* slipped by the BBC's editors, Liz Dux, a lawyer representing a number of Savile's victims, stated: 'You can't underestimate the amount of distress Savile's victims will have suffered if they have seen this. It is a constant reminder of what they have been through . . . Seeing something like this reawakens their suffering' (Anon., 2014). In his *Channel 4 News* blog, the newsreader Jon Snow, himself a survivor of sexual abuse, describes the television appearances of Savile and fellow television presenter-cum-sex offender, Rolf Harris, as 'haunting' their victims (2014), and this was also repeatedly articulated by Savile's victims in many of the documentaries about him. The BBC1 documentary *Abused: The Untold Story*, from April 2016, documents the uncovering of the extent of his crimes following the broadcast of the ITV1 documentary *Exposure: The Other Side of Jimmy Savile* in 2012, when an unprecedented number of victims called a National Society for the Prevention of Cruelty to Children (NSPCC) helpline during and after broadcast. Following the section of the former documentary about this latter programme, over images of blocks of flats at night, we hear a recorded phone message in which a distraught viewer states: 'I watched the documentary and I cried all the way through it because I was physically and sexually abused as a child'. The block of flats is clearly selected here as a visual signifier of collective viewing, or in this case collective viewer trauma. There then follows a shot of a call centre, over which a voiceover goes on to explain that 'as the documentary was going out, helplines were deluged with calls, some revealing details of abuse secret for decades'. Here we see a clear account of television inspiring the return of the repressed via the spectral, posthumous image of Savile and the reporting of his victims' testimony. In the documentary, Kim Thandi of the NSPCC helpline says that this television programme 'started to bring those triggers and those memories back up of [viewers'] own abuse. Our calls doubled, and then tripled', and Thandi's colleague, Louise Exton, goes on to state that 'This documentary going out had . . . ripped something open [for many of its viewers]'. It is clear that this section of the documentary illustrates the validity of Laura S. Brown's feminist revision of trauma theory in which she understands trauma not as a single, cataclysmic event, but rather a cumulative experience of abuse which happens in secret, in private – something which the posthumous surfacing of Savile's crimes via television brings momentarily to light. As Brown writes: 'A feminist perspective [of trauma], which draws our attention to the lives of girls and women, to the secret, private, hidden experiences of everyday pain, reminds us that traumatic events do lie within the range of normal human experience' (1995: 110). This BBC documentary thus attempts to articulate the ways in which television, and specifically the representation of Savile, might be seen as *haunting* people who experienced the 'everyday' pain and trauma of historical sexual abuse.

We also hear an articulation of the position of 'haunted viewer' at the beginning of *Abused: The Untold Story*, when several of Savile's victims are shown in their living rooms, discussing the effect of a chance posthumous encounter with their abuser via television.

- 'I remember the funeral, just not watching it, which was bizarre because you would think that I'd be relieved that he was dead . . .'
- 'It was all Savile here, there, ALL the time. And you thought, 'When's this man going to go off?' Avoid it. That was what we did. Avoid, avoid, avoid.'
- 'I couldn't watch it! I just spent the whole time like "Why is . . . I can't listen to what anybody's saying because that face is there and there and there and there again"'
- 'The legacy of what he did bothers me every day.'

Situating these people in their own living rooms during these interviews serves to emphasise their position *as television viewers* who have repeatedly encountered their abuser via the television archive and the re-broadcast of archive clips and images of the now-dead Savile on TV. Here, the desperation of the repetition of key words ('Avoid, avoid, avoid', 'that face is there and there and there and there again') expresses something of television's cycles of repetition, its endless looping, and the ways in which an experience of this might be linked to the cycles of trauma, for trauma in itself is a serialised experience which keeps on rerunning for those who suffer it, as we saw in the previous chapter. We might question why we would want to see people work through their abuse on television: does this enable a form of televisual 'exorcism' for the people who suffered at Savile's hands, or does this make them the scapegoats of the broadcaster's own 'working through'? This is certainly a question that has been raised by Karen Boyle's work on the Savile case, in which she argues that a 'problematic televisual history is set alongside a redemptive one as the documentaries both narratively and formally reference television's role in exposing Savile' in their focus on victim testimony (2018: 398). Boyle goes on to argue that 'It is right to be sceptical of the self-serving nature of this coverage for the BBC in particular, and there are questions to be asked about whether returning to the same victim/survivors keeps them perpetually trapped in Savile's shadow' (ibid.). To a certain extent, Sam Brown, one of Savile's victims who appears in multiple television documentaries, responds to Boyle's question in the latest television documentary, *Jimmy Savile: A British Horror Story*. Brown's is the last voice to be heard in the final part of this series, and she reflects on the resurfacing of the posthumous Savile archive as both an unwelcome intrusion into her life, and as call to action:

> I knew when this broke with Savile and it was all over the telly screens everywhere. I thought 'Oh no, I'm in trouble'. I was really aware that I had to start talking, and stay talking, and that's what I did . . . I can look at young me with less pain now.

More broadly, the general viewing public, viewers who had not directly experienced abuse at the hands of Savile, reported feeling traumatised by a re-encounter with his spectre, repeatedly articulating their discomfort at encountering Savile on TV as 'haunting' and thus reinforcing the framing idea of spectrality which we have seen in Savile's media representation; this is a discourse that recurs on social media discussions of Savile and his posthumous image.[11] Critical work that thinks about the intersection of trauma and film or TV viewing would account for this as a form of 'secondary trauma', in Shoshana Felman and Dori Laub's terms (1992), or 'shared, cultural trauma' according to Allen Meek (2016: 29), or, for E. Ann Kaplan, 'mediatized trauma' (2005: 2). Kaplan argues that 'viewers of the media, like therapists working with trauma victims, are often vicariously traumatised' (ibid.: 21) and she later states that 'being vicariously traumatised invites members of a society to confront rather than conceal catastrophes' (ibid.: 87). As with the diegetic viewing of archive footage in *Jimmy Savile: A British Horror Story*, the experience of vicarious trauma is dramatised in the first of the Savile documentaries, *Exposure: The Other Side of Jimmy Savile*, when, at the end of the documentary, Esther Rantzen, fellow television presenter and the founder of the charity Childline, is shown watching the interviews with Savile's victims in her kitchen on a laptop, presumably for the first time. As we see her watching the testimonies, she shakes her head, covering her face and averting her eyes, openly performing the trauma of viewing material that she pronounces 'Very painful, very distressing'. While Anne Rothe has warned against the conflation of what we might see as primary trauma (of those who have experienced abuse themselves) and the secondary trauma of those who view or read accounts of this, cautioning against a much wider sense of trauma as a 'floating signifier of the postmodern condition' (2016: 193), we might see Rantzen's actions here as those of a diegetic stand-in, modelling the actions of an imagined viewer in confrontation with the spectre of Savile and his crimes. Savile thus becomes a kind of psycho-cultural projection of the living, and the compulsion to repeatedly return (and return to) this spectre sees us rehearsing our very worst fears.

In exploring why we might want to repeatedly come back to Savile posthumously, we can turn to the work of Barbie Zelizer, whose writing about the news coverage of death reminds us of the multivalence of traumatic images. She explores, via Freud, the fact that

> [Engagement] with memory objects associated with mourning could help ease the trauma and grief involved in loss ... trauma theorists have established that the persistent engagement with a traumatic event in need of resolution can either fix an individual or group in a stage of acting out ... or facilitate the process of working through, by which the individual or group carries on in a posttraumatic stage of development. (2010: 336)

Here we see the collective 'working through' of a community 'memory'. In *Louis Theroux: Savile*, the 2016 BBC1 programme in which the documentarist Theroux returned to his original 2000 Savile documentary, *When Louis Met . . . Jimmy*, and its posthumous rushes, to examine Savile as subject once more, and to ask why the original production had 'missed' the terrible secrets about Savile's past, the presentation of Savile as spectre is quite explicit, and the representation of the documentarist as a haunted figure is made plain.

The opening shot is of Theroux cycling around his own living room, calling out 'Jimmy, what are you up to?' as Savile lurks somewhere off screen in his house. In many ways, this is the perfect visual metaphor for the traumatised documentary filmmaker who is haunted by his association with Savile, and his responsibility for bringing him 'back into the homes' of his viewers, riding in circles as Savile hovers out of shot. The circular motion suggests a form of compulsivity – a visual representation of Theroux's compulsive return to Savile's story as a site of trauma, perhaps? – and speaks of the link shown in psychological research between compulsive behaviours and recovery from trauma.[12] Savile cuts a shady figure in Theroux's house, just as he has done metaphorically in our own. As this sequence ends, and Savile leaves Theroux's house, his taxi is chased down the road by a gaggle of joyful children calling his name, an image which, like much of the footage of Savile in this documentary, is haunted by the 'what might have been'. A seemingly innocent moment in the rushes presumably filmed by Theroux for a future follow-up documentary, this brief sequence captures the everyday occurrence of a predatory paedophile coming into close contact with potential victims who actively seek him out, allured by his famous image.[13] It is, then, in some ways, similar to the CCTV footage with which we become achingly familiar during a criminal investigation, an 'ordinary' moment which is laced with the threat of what is to come next. In the case of a murder, disaster or accident, this CCTV footage is imbued with the frisson of seeing someone transformed into the figure 'about to die', to use Barbie Zelizer's phrase (2010). For example, discussing the CCTV footage of Jill Meagher, an Australian woman who was raped and murdered in 2012, Janine Mary Little considers the 'haunting presence of the woman on screen in "Jill Meagher CCTV" [as] a disembodied subject of representation, a ghostly persona transfigured by the narrative she now inhabits' (2015: 398). Here, the children chasing Savile's taxi are not necessarily about to be abused by him, but this image is haunted by the potential of this happening, and we therefore experience a similar kind of dread watching this posthumous footage as we do when confronted with the CCTV images discussed above.

This documentary continues, like so many ghost stories, with Theroux searching through a box from his attic, searching for clues in order to better understand the particular spectre that haunts him. This is an image which metonymically represents the wider search through the posthumous archive of footage of Savile by Theroux and other filmmakers. Throughout this programme, we get the sense of a filmmaker who is both haunted by his own missed opportunities to confront Savile, as well as being haunted by the spectre of Savile himself. The tone of the music in the sequence in which Theroux pulls the box out of his attic and takes it down into his kitchen to examine it suggests a haunting, as do the selected sequences of Savile which are intercut with this scene. As Louis walks down the stairs with the box into darkness in his own house, Savile opens the door in darkness in his apartment, the match-on image drawing connections between these two domestic spaces and thus suggesting that Savile continues to 'haunt' Theroux's own home. We then cut to footage of Savile expansively performing his 'Sir Jimmy' persona in his own living room. As Theroux asks, 'How are you feeling?', Savile responds, 'Regularly, as it happens', and then continues to say that he is as fit as a butcher's dog, which he describes as a beast that thrives on 'all the scraps, all the bones, all the hair', a grotesque metaphor for a figure we now understand as predatory and repugnant. At the close of this sequence, Savile speaks to Theroux from the other side of his letterbox, and his face hovers at an unexpected angle, behind a closed door. Again, it is hard not to read these sequences as presenting the posthumous Savile as intentionally spectral, as a predatory ghost once 'hiding in plain sight' and now haunting via its televisual reappearance. Later, as Theroux reads an article about their 'strange friendship', audio clips of Savile's gasping laugh and images of him swinging on a chair are intercut with Theroux reading out Savile's denials of inappropriate sexual interest in children. Here, and elsewhere in the documentary, clips from the original documentary and its rushes are haunted by Savile and the knowledge of his crimes; to draw on Caterina Albano's phrase, describing Eva Braun's home movies of Hitler, they offer the 'thorny banality' of a once 'innocuous' image now haunted by, in this case, the potential for abuse (2016: 151).

This documentary forms its narrative around a series of investigations of 'haunted houses' (old footage from Savile's flat, new footage from his secretaries' and victims' homes), and while it never investigates the children's homes, hospitals and television studios which might expose further culpability for Savile's crimes and move this documentary away from being a story about a lone spectre, we do see Savile's spectre 'hang over' a number of domestic spaces (perhaps a metonymic image of the haunting he enacts via television).[14] This is particularly well-illustrated in the final sequence of Theroux's documentary, where we are shown an extended, static exterior shot of the house of Sam Brown, one of the women who was abused by Savile in her teens. Following her interview, the camera lingers on Sam's back garden for nine seconds, as first diegetic noise, and then the haunting, ethereal sound of a vibraphone is heard, playing in a minor key. This music is significant: it lacks harmony, giving it a feeling of emptiness and creating a sense of uneasiness. It thus also draws on a recognisable musical motif from the filmic ghost story, marking this out as a haunted space. The eerie music then extends into the next shot, which is of Savile in his own living room, asking 'What you doing here? Straight punter. Boring! Don't do booze, don't do drugs, don't do none of them foolish things that I see on your programmes'. Here the cut between these two domestic spaces, linked by the dissonant vibraphone music, emphasises their congruence and the horror of Savile's once presence in Sam's everyday life. The documentary thus makes an audio-visual point about the spectre of Savile, via the posthumous television image. As the programme closes on slow motion, and then freeze-framed, footage from Savile's past programming (here *Jim'll Fix It*), we have a clear sense of the uncanny nature of the spectre in the archive, the horror of this spectral return rendering the once familiar, once banal, horrifying, haunting.

In an earlier article on the posthumous representation of Savile, I explore the ways in which Savile is also figured as 'haunting' a variety of television dramas, particularly the BBC-produced *Sherlock* episode 'The Lying Detective' (BBC1, 8/1/17), figuring the Corporation as a haunted institution following the revelation of Savile's crimes (Wheatley, 2020). The rhetoric of the haunted institution is also seen in the news journalism that focuses on Savile, his crimes, and their legacy for the BBC. For example, in 2013, the *Evening Standard* newspaper ran the headline 'The BBC is still haunted by the ghost of Savile' (Anon.) in an article about the Corporation's failure to respond to Freedom of Information requests in a timely way, while Savile is referred to as the 'ghost of Broadcasting House' by the radio industry blogger Paul Bailey (2016). The discourse of the haunted institution is also seen in an episode of *Channel 4 News* (Channel 4, 1982–) from 21 January 2016, in a story about the uncovering of Savile's abuse at the BBC in Dame Janet Smith's review for the BBC Trust.[15] As reporter Paraic O'Brien announces that 'the abuse took place in virtually every one of the BBC premises that Savile worked in', shots of the soon-to-be redeveloped Television Centre are shown, including the inside of Studio One, with various images of Savile's face floating, or 'haunting', over the top of it. The sound of Savile presenting the last episode of *Top of the Pops* is distorted, to make it sound as if his voice is echoing through the studio, and then O'Brien confirms 'Today, the ghost of Savile's twisted legacy returns once again to haunt the Corporation'. This image of the haunted institution is often used to taunt the BBC. However, viewing Savile as a spectre that *can* be exorcised enables us to envisage a future for the BBC in UK broadcasting, though only if its past is confronted and fully explored. The Corporation is caught in something of a double-bind here: posthumous archival footage of Savile (and sometimes its approximation) haunts his victims by its constant reappearance on television, and thus must be handled responsibly. However, Savile's appearance in the archive, across the history of BBC programming, also *must* be worked over, or worked through, to draw on the properly therapeutic understanding of this term, in order to reach some kind of resolution for the Corporation in relation to Savile's role in its troubled past.

While the latter part of this chapter has focused on the singular example of Savile as a posthumous television spectre, his is sadly not the only case of a figure whose televisual presence is associated with forms of trauma. Television companies in the US and the UK have recently had to move swiftly to deal with the archival traces of other on-screen figures associated with trauma and abuse, for fear of producing/broadcasting/streaming programming with the potential to 'haunt', as in the case of Bill Cosby and Kevin Spacey, for example.[16] These are not yet posthumous sounds and images, of course, but still contain within them the ability to disturb and upset viewers. However, what distinguishes Savile's case from these examples is that his posthumous status opens him up to be framed in a more obviously spectral way; on the one hand, this enables him to be more 'safely' presented as monstrously haunting both viewer and broadcaster beyond life. Karen Boyle brings into question the representation of Savile as monstrous because she feels that it disguises the fact of his once popularity and ubiquity (and what this represents about the endemic abuse at the heart of the British broadcasting establishment): 'there is a danger [in depicting him as monstrous] that we forget the cultural conditions which enabled Savile to get away with abusing women, girls and boys for decades – conditions which find a contemporary echo in the Weinstein case' (2018: 400–1). However, the spectrality of Savile's image might also be seen as a visual representation of his status as a classic horror figure *with a purpose*: not the haunting spectre that returns of its own volition to demand justice, to right a wrong, but a more sinister apparition, brought forth via the process of exorcism, to stand accountable for its crimes. As Iwona Irwin-Zarecka acknowledges, collective memory is 'imbued with moral imperatives – the obligations to one's kin, notions of justice, indeed the lessons of right and wrong – that form the basis of normative order' (1994: 9). Here, those producing or framing this collective memory call upon the spectral image of Savile to speak exactly to these moral imperatives.

Savile's spectre is a problem for the BBC as a public service broadcaster which must serve (and, arguably, protect) all elements of its viewing public. In this context, the posthumous television archive's potential to haunt means that there is still a sensitivity around the presentation of this celebrity's image, and archival programmes (and programmes that draw on the TV archive) that feature Savile might rightly be considered as 'in distress, harbouring secrets of which they are unaware', to use Colin Davis's description of the haunted text (2013: 55). If, as Jeffrey Weinstock argues, the ghost is a symptom of 'repressed knowledge' that 'calls into question the possibilities of a future based on avoidance of the past' (2004: 64), then perhaps the constant, even compulsive, return to a spectral Savile, in news, documentary and television drama, on the BBC and elsewhere, represents a productive confrontation with a troubled history and a desire to avoid future repetitions of Savile's awful crimes, particularly via the production of future television.

Viktor Mayer-Schönberger's work has explored what he sees as the unforeseen consequence of the digital age: that '[today], with the help of widespread technology, forgetting has become the exception and remembering the default' (2009: 2). Mayer-Schönberger clarifies: 'because of digital technology, society's ability to forget has become suspended, replaced by perfect memory' (ibid.: 4). The television archive is, in the digital age, increasingly easy to navigate; new programmes can be assembled with sophisticated montages of posthumous images which bring the dead back to life, again and again. Often this resurrection of the dead via the television archive is met with great delight; they are there to entertain us in death as they were in life (as in the case of Victoria Wood, discussed above). But encounters with the dead on television, as with Jimmy Savile, reinforce our inability to forget, even for a moment. The argument has been made here that this inability to forget might be transformed into positive action if it enables either institutional acceptance of failure and change, or recovery for Savile's victims (and, by extension, other victims of abuse).

The majority of examples discussed in this chapter fall into the category of the 'very famous dead' who are frequently 'revived' on television, and therefore never disappear from public view, for better or for worse. But what about other lives, other groups or communities, even, which have a less active/obvious presence on contemporary television via the posthumous archive, but are held within it nonetheless? Returning to the very first example discussed in this chapter, that of the Whiteleys and the 'afterlife' of *Remember All the Good Things*, Vivien Whiteley discussed being glad that their documentary was still held in the BBC archive, but was not immediately accessible to her, given the difficult feelings it might stir up:

> Well, you'll know this if you're a single parent, you can't afford to indulge those feelings because you might not recover and then what would your children do. You've got to hold things together, you've just got to keep going, haven't you? So, sometimes, you know, you just think 'Just let that go then'. I know it's there; I can always go to it if I need it. But just for now . . .

For Vivien, this piece of posthumous archive television was fraught with the possibilities of remembering, rather than forgetting, but for others whose loved ones are held in suspended animation in the television archive, often in spaces and institutions which are inaccessible to the general public, accessing the archive offers the promise of returning the dead to life. In the final chapter of this book, I explore an experimental television archive project, *Ghost Town: Civic Television and the Haunting of Coventry*, which examined precisely how the afterlives of people and places could be brought out of the archive via a collaboration between a television historian, television archivists, and the cultural organisations and people of a city. This project highlighted the power of television as posthumous medium *par excellence* and the following chapter offers some thoughts on the future use and value of the posthumous television archive beyond the production of new TV programming.

Parts of this chapter were first published in Helen Wheatley (2020a) 'Haunted Television: Trauma and the Specter in the Archive', Journal of Cinema and Media Studies, *59: 3, 69–89.*

7

Ghost town: Posthumous television in the city

A news reporter stands on a busy street, reporting on noise levels in a city and a new project to measure, and potentially reduce, the noise produced by traffic. Behind him, cars and buses pass by, as do people who are in the city to shop, or to gather and just 'hang out'. Smart young people rush across the road, paying no attention to the reporter and the camera that is filming him. A couple cross more slowly, turning their heads to see what's happening. A bearded man peers at the camera as he walks by. Two women, one young, one older, walk past pushing a pram and a pushchair, a small boy at their side; as they pass, the young woman and the small boy crane their necks to look at the reporter. As the camera pulls back, we see a line of people of a variety of ages standing behind railings in front of the city's information point over the road, watching the filmed scene unfold. Later, the reporter walks up some stairs in the main shopping precinct of the city. Behind him, dozens of people pass by as they go about their business. An older woman in a hat, holding the arm of a young friend or relative, finds it hard to tear her gaze away from the camera. As the reporter interviews the physicist responsible for this research project on one of the precinct's raised walkways, shoppers continue to pause and pass by behind them: an elderly man checks his shopping list and heads back into a shop, unaware of the filming; some cool-looking young men in shades line up on a balcony behind the reporter, clearly eager to be seen on TV; a young Sikh man runs down the stairs and away from the camera; mothers bustle onwards, attending to their children rather than the report being made on the opposing walkway.

This scene, which took place in Coventry, a city in the West Midlands of the United Kingdom, was televised on the ITV news programme *ATV Today* (1964–1981) on 1 September 1965. On the surface, it is indeed a report about the work of scholars from Lanchester Polytechnic, under the direction of Dr F. J. Pearson, who were researching traffic-based noise pollution in the city. However, this three-and-a-half-minute news item is also a microcosm of Coventry life in 1965, a snapshot of the people of the city at this time, and

Figure 7.1 Posthumous Coventry on television (tx. 1/9/65) *ATV Today* (ATV for ITV, 1964–1981).

as such it is an excellent example of how television captures posthumous images of ordinary people in a specific place and time. Some, though not all, of these shots will be truly posthumous: the people in them (the elderly woman in the hat, the old man consulting his shopping list) will certainly be dead by now. Perhaps they have not been seen going about their daily lives by their friends and family for many years. We might more broadly see this as posthumous television in that it captures a place and time which is irretrievably *past*: as Jeremy Tambling says of the posthumous, it doesn't just refer to a state of 'post death' but is a 'way of thinking about the pastness of the past, and about our own present' (2001: 8). Tambling's understanding of the posthumous is applied throughout this chapter.

The people in this footage will all be fifty-seven years older (at the time of writing) if they are still alive; they will be living very different lives to the ones they were living here, in this moment in time. The city itself is also transformed: shops gone, roads re-routed, buildings raised to the ground and built, the cars and buses that navigate the city entirely different to those seen on this bit of television programming. This posthumous footage sits in the climate-controlled vaults of the Media Archive for Central England (MACE), another archive-mausoleum of the television dead as discussed in the previous chapter, organised around what Jennifer

VanderBurgh describes as 'place-based heritage frameworks for video accumulation projects' – in this case an archive – which 'are often micro-national and regional in scope' (2019: 68). MACE has also made this news item available for the public to view via its website, and it is relatively easy to find for those searching for footage of Coventry in the 1960s, though you would need to be aware of the archive and the excellent work that its staff does to know where to look.[1] As will be shown in this chapter, the opportunity to revisit a city's past lives, even to re-encounter its dead, via the moving image archive is frequently a welcome one, though there are barriers to doing so which range from a lack of awareness of the holdings of television archives to a lack of access for many to many of these valuable collections. We might wonder what viewing the above news item would deliver for a set of viewers in Coventry in 2023. Who misses the woman in the hat or the man with the shopping list? What became of the children in the precinct and how might an encounter with these children on screen resonate for their adult selves? Who wanders the same city centre now and how would it feel to briefly inhabit this 1965 version of Coventry through a (re)encounter with this piece of television history? Who finds themselves absent from this short incursion into the city's past? This brief example thus suggests some possibilities and problems for reconnecting the people of a particular place to the posthumous television archive that I want to explore in this final chapter.

If television is the posthumous medium *par excellence*, and if the television archive is the repository for countless ordinary lives and places now past/lost, how are they to be accessed? What methods and approaches can be applied by archivists, historians, curators and others to open up the posthumous television archive? Why would we want or need to do so? The previous chapter discussed television programming made out of the broadcast archive, and analysed television's recycling of its own posthumous images. It thought about the potential affective power of encounters with the posthumous archive via television, whether as part of the process of mourning public figures, remembering much-loved television performers or being haunted by those on TV with a more problematic past. How else, though, might we encounter posthumous television? In this final chapter of *Television/Death* we shift our focus from (inter)nationally significant posthumous television, edited into new programmes and packages and streamed and broadcast to a wide general public, to the local, the regional, and to thinking about posthumous programming in relation to a specific place and time. This shift in focus raises a set of attendant questions which this chapter will explore. How and why should we take historical (posthumous) television out of archives and universities and into the public realm? What happens when people encounter posthumous television in public spaces, and what is the role of the television historian in these encounters? How should we make sense of what people say at, about, and to screenings of posthumous programmes? And what is the civic value of the television archive – why does television history matter to people of a particular city, a particular place?

All of these questions boil down to a single enquiry: *Who is television history for?* I have never really been that interested in doing work on archival treasures that only I have, or will, ever see, beyond their initial broadcast. Finding ways to bring programmes out of the archive is as important to me as getting into an archive to see them in the first place. In the introduction to my edited collection *Re-Viewing Television History* (2007) I confronted the question of why television history matters, why we should bother doing it at all. At the time of writing that introduction, I was busy exploring why academics should bother to engage with television history, but more latterly I have also been simultaneously interested in the question of why non-academic publics might be interested in television history too. In answering these questions, I frequently return to John Corner's work and his 'utilitarian defence' of history, in which he argues: 'An enriched sense of "then" produces, in its differences and commonalities combined, a stronger, imaginative and analytically energised sense of now' (2003: 275). Corner is talking about television, arguing that we are better able to understand and interrogate contemporary television if we know something of the medium's history, but we might also say the same of history more broadly. If we seek out a better understanding of our past, we might be more prepared to make sense of our present and future. The public-facing television history project I have been running since 2018 has worked on precisely this assumption, bringing the posthumous television archive into the public realm in various ways and contexts to enable the public of the city that I live and work in, Coventry, to interrogate their own pasts (and have conversations about their presents and their futures) through an engagement with the posthumous city on TV.

This project, titled *Ghost Town: Civic Television and the Haunting of Coventry*, has been running out of the Centre for Television Histories at the University of Warwick since the beginning of 2018, up to, and into, the city's stint as UK City of Culture in 2021 and 2022. During this time, I worked with colleagues in various archives and organisations around the UK (the BBC; ITV; MACE; Kaleidoscope, the classic television organisation which runs its own substantial archive; Studio Canal; the British Film Institute) to find programmes made in and about the city of Coventry from the early 1950s to the present day, and bring them back to the city to be shown in a variety of spaces and contexts throughout this period. Through the *Ghost Town* project, I curated screenings and exhibitions in museums, galleries and a number of other places, including an ongoing collaboration with Coventry Cathedral (see Table 7.1 for a full list of *Ghost Town* events).

As explained in relation to the brief example of Coventry-based programming discussed above, I describe this project as enabling encounters with locally significant posthumous television. This is not only because, as we shall see, it provided direct access for the people of the city to friends and relatives who were long dead, but also because the programming I brought out of various archives (with the help of dedicated television archivists) captures the past lives of the city; buildings, businesses, ideas, even people's younger selves, which are irretrievably gone, save for the traces that have been left behind in the television archive (and elsewhere). This chapter draws on data collected at all the above events via a variety of methods (including participant observation, feedback/survey data, voting boxes and semi-structured interviews). It aims to produce a picture of people's interaction with posthumous television at *Ghost Town* events, and to suggest some ways in which other collaborative teams of media historians and archivists might replicate this methodology to increase place-specific access to the posthumous television archive and inspire future conversations about the value of doing so.

I mention collaboration above because it has been so critical for the development of the *Ghost Town* project, both collaborations with key groups and organisations within the city as well as partnerships with various archives. Some of the archives I have worked with have a commitment to engaging the public with their holdings (as well as encouraging them to make further deposits into the archive) which they have been able to partially meet through collaboration on the *Ghost Town* project; this is true for MACE, for example, as explained by Kat Pearson's work on the role of television archives in UK City of Culture years (2023). For other organisations, such as the BBC, enabling access to the archive of posthumous television might be seen as an extension of the broadcaster's public service remit, for, as Helen Piper notes, 'radical privatization and technical evolution [in broadcasting] do not mean the end of public expectations of cultural responsibility, accessibility, regulation, plurality, diversity, public funding and accountability' (2016: 164). In Piper's list, the issue of 'accessibility' might be directly related to public access to a nationally and *locally* significant archive, as is explored below. Graeme Turner confirms that the 'core public function of the national (public or commercial) broadcaster' is 'providing the opportunity for the nation to conduct its conversations with itself, to construct and confirm its national identities, and to populate the symbolic space in which it can play out its "dramas of nationhood"' (2009: 62). While Turner reflects on the opportunities the public service broadcaster provides for the nation to have 'conversations with itself', the BBC's support of the *Ghost Town* project has also enabled more local, place-based conversations to take place in relation to screenings of the posthumous television archive. If, as Stuart Cunningham suggests, public service broadcasters 'typically straddle the boundary between the market and community or civic space' (2009: 85), then contributing to a very local project such as *Ghost Town* delivers some of that commitment to serving the community within a civic space. Enabling media historians – and, through them, the general public – to view the holdings of the posthumous television archive, maintained and made accessible by public service broadcasters, through digitisation and public engagement projects, delivers what Karl Knapskog describes as a commitment to 'making [television archives] culturally productive here and now', arguing that 'public archives should be made available to all citizens for enlightenment and educational purposes' (2010: 20–1).

This project is therefore both interested in the value of the posthumous television archive for the people of the city, understanding it as an asset that enables the public to examine the place they have come from, moved to, or are passing through, provoking thought and discussion about the city's past, present and future, and also values the TV archive as a repository for personal and familial histories. As the above example shows, a news item about traffic in the city might equally be viewed as a piece of family history, capturing a brief moment in the everyday lives of ordinary Coventrians, akin to a piece of family cine film or home movie footage. Viewing it as such places greater emphasis on the *emotional* or sentimental value of the posthumous archive and reminds us that, as Annette Kuhn has said of the interconnectedness of 'private' and 'public' images in photography, 'as far as memory at least is concerned, private and public turn out in practice less readily separable than convention would have us believe' (1995: 4). Kuhn goes on to reiterate that 'personal and collective remembering emerge again and again as continuous with one another' (ibid.: 5). The *Ghost Town* project absolutely confirms this. In the next section of this chapter, then, we consider the role that the posthumous television archive might play in activating 'extended memory' (Hoskins, 2010: 81), in the intertwining of public and private recollections, and in highlighting the relationship between memories and histories.

Table 7.1 *Ghost Town* activities, 2018–2022

Title	Description	Location	Date
Haunting #1: Ghost Town Preview	Screening of *Coventry Kids: People of a Restless City* (BBC, 15/11/60) and *Coventry Cathedral* AKA *An Act of Faith* (BBC, 22/5/62).	Coventry Cathedral	23/3/18
Haunting #2: Remembering Coventry	Exhibition: showing 4.5 hours of Coventry showreels based on the archival holdings of the BBC, ITV, the BFI, Kaleidoscope and MACE.	Shop Front Theatre, City Arcade, Coventry	16–22/4/18
Haunting #3: Ska Town, Ghost Town	Screening of *Arena: Rudies Come Back or the Rise and Rise of 2Tone* (BBC2, 12/3/80) introduced by a Q&A with director Jeff Perks, and *Play For Today: Three Minute Heroes* (BBC1, 26/10/82).	Coventry Cathedral	1/6/18
Coventry Cathedral: Building for a New Britain (BBC4, tx. 9/6/21)	Television documentary. Consultancy work on this programme, written, directed and produced by John Wyver, ran throughout the project, including a public screening of the documentary (with Q&A) at Coventry Cathedral on 17/9/21.	Coventry Cathedral and other locations throughout the city	June 2018– September 2021
Industrial Coventry	Screening of the Industrial Coventry showreel (part of the *Remembering Coventry* exhibition) during the Screening Rights Film Festival.	Herbert Art Gallery and Museum	18–21/10/18
Industrial Coventry	Screening of the Industrial Coventry showreel (part of the *Remembering Coventry* exhibition) at meeting of the Coventry Trades Union Council.	Koco Centre, Spon End, Coventry	15/11/18
Haunting #4: Cathedral of Culture	Screening of *Celebration* (ABC, 10/4/66), a programme of Duke Ellington's performance in Coventry Cathedral, with introduction from producer Brian Tesler and the *Cathedral of Culture* showreel (prepared by MACE for this event).	Coventry Cathedral	29/12/18
Friends of Coventry Cathedral	Illustrated talk for the Friends of Coventry Cathedral on the Cathedral's televisual history.	St Michael's House, Coventry	20/5/19

Title	Description	Location	Date
Coventry Works	Community workshops in local libraries. A collaboration with the Photo Archive Miners on the visual history of Coventry's working life.	Stoke and Tile Hill libraries, Coventry	19–25/7/19
Humans at Work	Community workshop with Photo Archive Miners and Warwick Arts Centre which led to the production of the play 'Humans at Work' at Warwick Arts Centre in February 2020.	Broad Street Community Centre, Foleshill, Coventry	9/10/19
Acts of Faith: Filmmakers in Coventry Cathedral	Screening of *An Act of Faith* (BBC, 22/5/62), restored by MACE, and call-out to local filmmakers to respond to the restored documentary with new works.	Coventry Cathedral	23/1/20
Haunting #5: Acts of Faith: Filming Coventry Cathedral	Screening of *An Act of Faith* (BBC, 22/5/62), and short films made in response to this documentary: *Taffia Cothan* (Adele Mary Reed, 2020), *I have faith in all you blues* (Sherrie Edgar, 2020) and *Phoenix* (Tara Rutledge/Mary Courtney, 2020).	Coventry Cathedral	30/9/20
William Mitchell at Work	Online screening for the Coventry Society of two items from *Tomorrow's World* (BBC1, 1965–2003) about the work of sculptor William Mitchell from 1966 and 1967. Mitchell created significant public art works in Coventry.	Online	12/4/21
Haunting #6: 2Tone Lives and Legacies	Screenings tied into a major exhibition about Coventry's 2Tone music scene, including round table discussion with musicians, historians of popular music and programme makers.	Coventry Cathedral/ Coventry Cathedral Ruins	July–August 2021
Haunting #7: Coventry on TV	Exhibition curated by Kat Pearson/MACE, as a follow-up to *Remembering Coventry* (2018) showing 1.5 hours of Coventry showreels based on the archival holdings of MACE.	Shop Front Theatre, City Arcade, Coventry	14–16/4/22

Activating the archive: memory, history and the uses of posthumous television

In her book *Media and Memory*, Joanne Garde-Hansen proposes, via Henri Bergson's *Matter and Memory* (1991[1896]), that we conceptualise our memory as a kind of archive; 'put simply', Garde-Hansen states, 'Bergson argued that you unconsciously give yourself the impression that your memory-images are remade from a store of memory-images and this orientates you in time, with a past, a present and a future' (2011: 21). We also imagine that our 'memory archive' sits alongside all kinds of other public and private archives, including media archives, and can be cross-referenced with them, to illuminate dusty and forgotten corners of our own 'facilities', or even to add new 'memories' to them. If we are to understand the possibility of triggering or perhaps creating memory through an engagement with posthumous television programming, we must first understand something of the connection between public and private memory, and between memory and history, and the moving image. Particularly, we need to attend to Maurice Halbwach's suggestion that our memories are not individual but collective and formed in relation to the media we consume (2011: 140), or Alison Landsberg's proposal that film and other media create 'prosthetic memories' (2004) whereby we 'remember' things to which we were not witness in real life. Joanne Garde-Hansen summarises:

> Media ... negotiate both history and memory. We understand the past (our own, our family's, our country's, our world's) through media discourses, forms, technologies and practices. Our understanding of our nation's or community's past is intimately connected to our life histories. (2011: 6)

This 'entanglement' of memory and history (see Sturken, 1997: 5), the intertwining of individual and collective memories around media, means that often what we experience and remember from our own lives, and what we know and experience via the media we consume, is hard, if not impossible, to separate. As Landsberg says, 'Prosthetic memories are neither purely individual nor entirely collective, but emerge at the interface of individual and collective experience ... [They] also complicate the distinction between memory and history' (2004: 19). Evoking Eric Hobsbawn's (1987) twilight zone between memory and history, Laura Mulvey argues that 'On celluloid, personal and collective memories are prolonged and preserved, extending and expanding the "twilight zone", merging individual memory with recorded history' (2006: 25).

Archival television is perhaps even more capable than film of delivering us to this twilight zone between memory and history, given its more quotidian relationship to the world. It 'prolongs and preserves' the places of our everyday existence in more vivid detail than the imagined dreamlands of cinema history, and we can therefore draw on posthumous television to intentionally trigger (or create new) memories about our everyday lives. While Garde-Hansen argues that '[most] of the time, our memories are triggered rather randomly in a fleeting and disordered way', she says that sometimes 'we stop and reflect and work through a memory that we have often lived too fast to deal with at the time before we can move forward again' (2011: 15). We might, then, have a memory triggered 'at random' by something we encounter, including via the television programming that we view in our everyday lives, or we might make a more conscious decision to engage with invitations to remember our pasts, perhaps by visiting a museum, or, as in the case discussed in this chapter, by attending an exhibition or screening of historical, posthumous television. Landsberg understands such coincidental and intentional engagements with the past on screen as 'moments of contact' and as direct experiences which suture a person into a wider history (2004: 2). Such conscious engagements as making the decision to attend a screening of archival television based in and about the city you live in, or are visiting, can be seen as undertaking what Kuhn (1995) describes as 'memory work', using TV programming as a mnemonic aid, an invitation to remember, or drawing on the histories and memories that that programming captures to fill in the 'gaps' in your own memory. Andrew Hoskins, via a discussion of Lisa Gitelman's *Always Already New* (2008), considers 'how media, no matter how "old" or "new" are "functionally integral to a sense of pastness" through the "implicit encounters" we have with the past via the media responsible for producing that past' (2010: 77). We therefore find the possibility for an encounter with the past within an engagement with archival television. Garde-Hansen argues that

> Individuals do things to and with media so as to remember, not simply for the sake of personal memory or to contribute to a community's history, but rather to project the multiple and multiplying layers of complex connections between people, places, pasts and possibilities. (2011: 42–3)

This 'doing things to and with media so as to remember' enabled attendees of the *Ghost Town* events described below to retrieve, reconstruct and embellish life histories in the context of the city's history, as will be explained in this chapter. We might be wary of such memory work producing the past as we would *like* to remember it rather than how it actually was, given that, as Andreas Huyssen explains, 'we know how slippery and unreliable personal memory can be: always affected by forgetting and denial, repression and trauma' (1995: 249). Nevertheless, this case study explores, tests and challenges the critical literature on media, memory and history discussed above by considering a very specific, localised example and how television became, in a variety of ways, posthumously significant in the city of Coventry.

Ghost Town: exploring the city through posthumous television

The *Ghost Town* project has shown that the posthumous television archive uniquely gathers together traces of a city's cultural, social and political life, and that bringing these traces out of the archive presents opportunities for exchange, discussion and affective encounters that relate, in a myriad of ways, to the lives of those present. This project has made a case for the importance of the television archive to people and place and proposes a shift away from the conception of the TV archive as being *for* a small number of specialist users (broadcasters, historians) to one which reveals the powerful potential of relationships between television history and people's everyday lives. Over the course of four years, as detailed in Table 7.1, I screened a range of programming in and around the city, from regional news and current affairs programming to episodes and extracts from drama, children's television, documentaries, and music and arts programming. The project has been formed around what Paddy Scannell recognises as television's unique ability to capture everyday life. Scannell writes

> None of these programmes [in the television archive] thought of itself as historic. All are in and of the times in which they were made. That innocence (the guilelessness of not making a gesture toward the future) is what precisely guarantees their status for us today, looking back, as true documents of their own time and thus as genuinely revelatory of that time. (2010: 40)

Similarly, Myra Macdonald suggests that the 'specificity of place' in television has the potential to act as a 'powerful stimulus of memory' (2006: 336). While Macdonald was writing specifically about documentary, the same can be said of many genres of television. If we look to television programming as a historic document that uniquely, and posthumously, captures the everyday life of a particular place and time, then aiding public access to this repository of past lives can help to unlock all kinds of memories and histories that that have otherwise remained partial, inaccessible or unarticulated for many years.

Why does this matter for, in the case of this project, the people of a particular city, though? The *Ghost Town* project is predicated on the fact that cities are haunted places: they are haunted by the ghosts of people, buildings, businesses, ideas, of things which once stood and now no longer remain. Jeffrey Tambling concurs, drawing on Jean Baudrillard's work on the urban environment as 'deathly' (1993: 185–6). 'Urban space is ghostly space', Tambling argues: 'the aggressively modern city, by tearing down what is classed as of the past before it has a chance to be old creates the ghostly as a possibility' (2001: 138). The traces of the haunted city might be slowly lost to the passing of time, but the city is also vividly recalled in another haunted, posthumous place: the television archive. The life of a city then – its big moments, but also its banal, everyday occurrences – are captured by television, across its genres and throughout its schedules. Consider the number of times you have seen the place where you live on television, and the number of different televisual contexts in which it has appeared, over the years. Television brings us a city's landmarks, again and again, but also its back streets and side streets, its factory gates and hospitals, its A-roads and B-roads, its notable sons and daughters, but also its ordinary folk, passing by a camera as they get on with their shopping, take their kids to the park, go to, and from, work. All of these incidental appearances, usually excised from the fiction film by careful crowd control and the placement of paid 'extras', remain in many genres of television. If Demir has called cinema the 'running memory of the city' (2015: 28), then television is this, but more so. In her work on television cities, Charlotte Brunsdon argues that 'paradigms of the cinematic city, which emphasise the relationships between the city, the cinema and modernity, tend to ignore the banal, the mundane, the repetitious, and the complicated relationship between the home and the street' (2018: 6). She proposes that 'It is on this terrain of domestic repetition and everyday life – with all its banality – that the televisual city is constructed, and its cultural invisibility has much to do with attitudes to television and the domestic sphere more generally' (ibid.). The television city, for Brunsdon 'like the television set', was then always 'just there, in the corner' (ibid.).

Brunsdon also asks at the beginning of her book whether the *flâneur*, that figure who navigates the city so deftly, watches television, and Sarah Matheson considers this question in relation to her work on televising Toronto, seeing television itself as a kind of wandering, mobile spectator of the city and proposing that the 'contemporary flâneur is altered by his/her encounter with television' (1997: 2). She is subsequently interested in the ways in which the *flâneur appears on* television, arguing that

> The flaneur, as a figure who revelled in public space, loitering and moving through its streets, seems to be the ideal "mobile" subject through which television could channel Toronto's new bustling street life, albeit in a modified and commodified way (ibid.: 4)

For Matheson, interviews taking place as people walk down the street, or the teenagers 'who scream and mug for the camera, excited by the possibility that they could be caught by television' (ibid.: 6), constitute a new form of televisual *flâneur* who 'no longer desires to be lost in the crowd or hide within a darkened movie theater, but rather strives to make his or her presence unmistakably visible [on television]' (ibid.). The cool young men in shades in our opening example, leaning against the railings behind the interviewer in the city precinct, are precisely this figure. They perhaps imagined the fun of their friends and family spying them on the local evening news, or maybe they even raced home to watch the programme themselves, but did they consider the lasting trace they would leave in the posthumous television archive?

The city, 'just there in the corner', according to Brunsdon, is precisely what I've been exploring with and for the people of Coventry over the last few years. I've engaged with the general public of the city in events which were widely advertised and freely open to all, as well as diverse special interest groups in the city (from the Coventry Trades Union Council and the Coventry Society, a group which campaigns to protect the city's built environment, to Foleshill Women's Training (FWT), an organisation that works with refugee and migrant women newly arrived in the city). Throughout the *Ghost Town* project I have talked to people about the city in relation to the television archive, and about the importance of the archive through an engagement with the city's history. These were not necessarily encounters of recollection for all people: for some, newly arrived in the city, it was a chance to encounter the past lives of the place they now call home or are just visiting. Ultimately, I hope that this research will provide a test case for thinking about the relationship between television archives and particular places, and the methods of this project are described in detail here with the precise hope that people might take them and replicate them elsewhere. The *Ghost Town* project is Coventry focused, but it more broadly reveals how television archives can play a vital role in memory work, in civic place making and in the broader cultural strategies of diverse cities around the world. As Kristyn Gorton and Joanne Garde-Hansen acknowledge, '[All] television memories are really anchored in and around places, people, spaces and buildings, homes (and their interiors), as well as clearly defined networks, organizational relationships, and professional and familial identities' (2019: xii). Through the *Ghost Town* project, I have asked what this means for a city, this encounter with posthumous sounds and images, using the television archive to inspire conversations, thought and action about the city's past, present and future, alongside making a case for the ongoing importance of the archive itself, and for the need for increased and easier public access to it.

Before proceeding to analyse the research data gathered at *Ghost Town* events, it is worth pausing to describe the design of some of our events in more detail. One of the first, and most sustained, events of the *Ghost Town* project was *Remembering Coventry*, a week-long television-based exhibition about the city's past in the Shop Front Theatre in Coventry's City Arcade in April 2018. The arcade, new and modern in the city's post-war development, is now a rather run-down area of the city, scheduled for demolition in 2023, close to the city's market. The theatre, now closed, sadly, was a relaxed and informal space, set up in an old fish and chip restaurant, and was chosen as a location that might entice passers-by, particularly elderly Coventrians, shopping in the arcade and nearby retail market. This exhibition featured a series of curated, themed showreels of programmes made in and about the city, about four-and-a-half hours of archival television in total, that ran on three screens in the exhibition. Themes included Coventry life and people, the city's cultural scene, work and industry, and the built environment and Coventry's post-war redevelopment. Each screen showed the same reel, beginning in a different place, so there were always three different programmes showing in the space; these were on a large screen that enabled audiences to sit in cinema-style seating and often share their recollections about what was on screen with research staff and with each other, and two

Figure 7.2 Remembering Coventry (2018). Author's photograph.

smaller, living-room-style spaces, set dressed with vintage living room furniture, that allowed for quieter viewing for individuals and small groups of up to four people at a time on vintage and retro TV sets, using headphones to 'seal them off' from the hustle and bustle of the room. Some people just dropped in for fifteen minutes or half an hour, but a surprising number of people stayed and watched all of the footage (or came back at a carefully timed juncture in order to 'complete' their viewing). The exhibition ran throughout the week and allowed the general public to drop in and out and have conversations with researchers, and with each other, about what they encountered. The research team[2] also ran some designated sessions for specific groups, including a memory workshop for older Coventrians interested in the city's history, a coffee morning for FWT's group for women newly arrived in the city, and some information sessions for local secondary school teachers. At the exhibition, the *Ghost Town* research team employed multiple techniques to gather data, including asking attendees to fill out surveys and feedback postcards on their experience of the exhibition, undertaking participant observation and writing detailed field notes, and conducting semi-structured interviews with people who had an interesting relationship to the programming we screened, particularly those who recognised themselves, or friends and family, in the material on screen. We made cups of tea and handed out biscuits and chatted to people, creating an environment in which people could stay and talk to us and each other. While the memory workshops at this exhibition invited a particularly sustained set of recollections about the city's past in relation to the television archive, we also saw spontaneous memory sharing throughout the week. *Remembering Coventry* was followed up by a further residency at the Shop Front Theatre, *Coventry on TV*, in April 2022 which utilised many of the same data-gathering techniques.

In addition to these week-long exhibitions, there was also a series of large-scale one-off screenings at Coventry Cathedral, showcasing some of the key archival findings and digitisation and restoration projects of the *Ghost Town* project, from a couple of evenings of programmes about Coventry's 2Tone scene which incorporated guest appearances from programme makers and some of the bands featured in this programming, to the widely attended *Cathedral of Culture* event in December 2018, which featured a digitised and restored screening of *Celebration*, the programme made about Duke Ellington's performance at the Cathedral by ABC television for ITV in 1966. We were also able to document, through screenings at the cathedral, the process of rediscovering and restoring a key television find in the cathedral's own archive: the 1962 BBC documentary *An Act of Faith*, which was an early colour documentary made for the BBC for the cathedral's consecration week about the building's construction, featuring the outstanding work of the fine art documentarist John Read.[3]

The showreel of programmes about Coventry's history of industrial relations produced by MACE for the *Remembering Coventry* exhibition at the Shop Front Theatre was also shown as part of the Screening Rights Film Festival in 2019, and as part of research and development projects with the Photo Miners (a group who curate historic photography exhibitions in the city) on the *Coventry Works* project, and with the Photo Miners and Warwick Arts Centre on the *Humans at Work* project, focusing on developing techniques to work with citizen historians in responding to, documenting and digitising visual material relating to the city's industrial history. All these events have stimulated conversations about the city and have been used to gather data that tells us about the value of the television archive for those diverse groups engaging with it. The project has explored broadcasting history through archival research, but also examined how television constructs, consciously or otherwise, the history of the city,

238 Television/Death

Figure 7.3 Coventry Cathedral (2018–2022). Author's photograph.

largely across the latter part of the twentieth century; in Coventry, this is a history of manufacturing boom and bust, post-war life, a history of social (in)justice and race relations in mid to late twentieth century Britain, a history of gender and familial relations, a history of various musical subcultures, from punk to 2Tone, and so on, for as Asa Briggs tells us 'to write the history of broadcasting in the twentieth century is in a sense to write the history of everything else' (1991: 2).

A number of off-shoot projects and collaborations relating to the *Ghost Town* project have also highlighted the potential re-use and/or creative responses to the re-screening of Coventry via the posthumous television archive. This has included contributing to the research for John Wyver's BBC4 archive-based documentary, *Coventry Cathedral: Building for a New Britain*, which was broadcast in 2021.[4] The documentary drew on some of the holdings uncovered by the project from a number of different television archives, as well as a collection of high-quality amateur films of the building of Coventry Cathedral by the architect Barnard Reyner, brought out of Reyner's daughter's attic as a response to the *Cathedral of Culture* event in 2018 and subsequently lodged with MACE for preservation purposes. Wyver's documentary was screened at Coventry Cathedral after its broadcast, accompanied by a roundtable discussion about the film and about the *Ghost Town* project.⁵ The project also commissioned local filmmakers to creatively respond to the 1962 BBC documentary *An Act of Faith* and screened these films alongside the restored version of the documentary produced for the *Ghost Town* project by MACE in 2020.⁶ Finally, the *Humans at Work* workshops, a collaboration with the Photo Miners and Warwick Arts Centre, took archival TV to people who lived and worked in the Foleshill area of Coventry, and particularly those who worked at the General Electric Company factories in the city in the 1950s, 1960s and 1970s, and fed into the scripting and staging of the play *Humans at Work* at Warwick Arts Centre in February 2020.

In all these events, from large-scale public screenings to long-running exhibitions and creative projects, listening to people's responses to posthumous archive television and what it unlocked in terms of personal, familial and civic memories has been central to this research. As such, these events might be seen as similar in some ways to Rick Prelinger's *Lost Landscapes* series, screenings of loosely assembled archive film, often amateur film, in cities around the United States. As Prelinger describes,

> These barely-plotted events ... leverage public assembly and mass dialogic presence as a means of creating multiple, coequal consensus around historical evidence that can be read in multiple ways, and try to mobilize audiences to produce their own 'narrative of the moment,' on the fly. To speak plainly, I show intricately assembled and lightly edited footage (especially parts of home movies) to audiences who are encouraged to talk to one another in the dark. (2021)

Prelinger's audiences are noisy audiences; his screenings are 'dialogical encounters' with often silent footage in darkened auditoria in which audiences call out to narrate the images on screen, to agree and also disagree with one another, performing as citizen ethnographers in, and in relation to, the contested spaces of the cities at hand. They are there to narrate the posthumous sounds and images on screen for each other. Prelinger sets his screening method of gathering these cities' histories and memories through dialogue and disagreement at his events against the 'simulative power of algorithmic media' of online crowdsourcing which is, in Prelinger's opinion, a 'poor substitute for the affective power of presence and public assembly' (ibid.). Such crowdsourcing projects have indeed enhanced posthumous moving image archive collections with new metadata, described by Knapskog as generating metadata through '*folksonomy* or *social tagging*' (2010: 9) or by Julia Noordegraaf as a shift from authoritative knowledge about an archive's holdings to co-produced knowledge by consensus (2010). However, the focus of such projects has largely been on improving an archive's contextualisation of its holdings rather than enabling audiences to better understand, and have conversations about, their own pasts, presents and futures. Prelinger sees his role in this process as that of 'presenter and scout' rather than 'interpreter and authority' (2021: ibid.); he is there to seek out material of interest from the archive which he then offers to the communities he visits for their engagement and interpretation. He asks, 'Who am I to speak about these cities?' and goes on to say that 'To interpolate oneself as a teller or reteller of histories is to construct one's own pedestal. Usually these are not my own stories to tell' (ibid.). As such, Prelinger's work confirms the assertion of the Popular Memory Group that everyone participates in the social production of memory and history (albeit unequally) and that everyone is therefore in a sense 'a historian' (2011: 254).

So how does Prelinger's account of the *Lost Landscapes* series illuminate the methods and findings of the *Ghost Town* project? I identified strongly with Prelinger's account of the media historian as a kind of scout in, and for, a city, and also with his account of how and why revisiting posthumous urban histories through the moving image archive can be rewarding but also difficult, complicated and emotionally charged for audiences. In many ways the key differences between audience responses at the *Ghost Town* events and those of the *Lost Landscapes* audiences might be seen as cultural differences: *Ghost Town* audiences were (largely) much quieter ones, more likely to share reflections in quiet chat around the edges of the screenings than to call out at the screen (though this also happened). Like Prelinger's participatory and dialogic screenings, audiences at *Ghost Town* events shared knowledge about their city's rich and contested history, acting as ethnographers and cultural geographers, guiding the television historian (me, their scout) through the histories and spaces of their city. Whereas Prelinger relates such exchanges between audiences and historians to a longer history of participatory public entertainments, I understand the 'talking back to television' that took place at our events as also relating to the specificities of television viewing. As Helen Wood's work has shown us, viewers of television have always talked back to the screen; television is a dialogic medium and its co-present audiences frequently talk back to their television sets in response to the medium's simulation of communicability (2009). The posthumous archival television that my collaborators and I found and had digitised was shown in a variety of public spaces, but we also worked hard to transform some of these into 'intimate' and 'domesticated' spaces to enable attendees to 'talk back to television' in a familiar way; at the *Remembering Coventry* and *Coventry on TV* exhibitions, for example, making cups of tea and producing plates of biscuits was the key to enabling chat between our attendees and the researchers. The latter half of this chapter will therefore detail how people responded to the programmes shown through the *Ghost Town* project in these public screening spaces, and what this might tell us about the posthumous resonances of archive television.

Memory explosions and unlocking memory

Scene from Ghost Town #1: A man in a Coventry cap loiters on the back row of seating in the Remembering Coventry *exhibition, watching some local news footage of Coventry city centre on the large screen in front of him. Catching the attention of one of the researchers working in the room, he proceeds to tell them firstly about watching local news on TV, and then his memories of the buildings he can see on screen, but then also about his parents' arrival in the city in the early 1960s, as well as their courtship, their working lives, the places and people in the city that were important to them. Two days later he returns to the exhibition with some family photographs to share with the researcher. He brings his partner with him to watch the footage again, to share with her the stories he shared on first viewing.*

Writing about the association between historical television and the past, Joe Moran proposes that 'A programme that millions once watched but which has now faded into the atmosphere like a dream is a neat encapsulation of the elusive quality of memory itself' (2013: 5). If we see the re-screening of posthumous archive television about the city within the city as the replaying of a (collective) memory of the city, then this goes some way to explain the fact that one of the most common reactions to the *Ghost Town* events and exhibitions has been an expression of memories of the city being 'unlocked' by these encounters in some way. Researchers at the *Remembering Coventry* exhibition described what collectively became known among the research team as 'memory explosions' whereby a discussion of a specific programme or clip would lead to wide sharing of intertwined personal/family/civic posthumous histories: we began by talking to visitors about what they were watching and often learned a great deal about people's family histories, dead relatives, personal histories, health histories, working lives and so on. Amy Holdsworth describes these memory explosions as the production of a 'surplus of feeling that has to be vocalised' in relation to her analysis of visitors to the TV Heaven exhibit at the Bradford-based National Media Museum (2011: 146).[7] Visitors to *Ghost Town* events got particularly animated when they talked to researchers – and each other – about their employment history, and about the boom and bust of a working-class city. We also repeatedly saw people placing importance on the opportunity for intergenerational sharing of memory via an encounter with the television archive (something also documented by Rachel Moseley, Amy Holdsworth and I in relation to our earlier exhibition, a collaboration with the Herbert Art Gallery and Museum in Coventry on *The Story of Children's Television From 1946 to Now* (2019)). People at *Ghost Town* events often noted that watching archival TV had helped trigger memories that they wouldn't have retrieved otherwise; this was frequently said in conjunction with noting that it was important to preserve these programmes for future generations (a visitor to the *Remembering Coventry* exhibition said, for example, 'These films should be shown to young people in schools today, and more [shown] after around the city for everyone to see. [The exhibition] shows they are extremely important for our generation to look back on and especially for future generations').

Engaging with these screenings gave visitors a sense of being able to remember and experience place posthumously ('Seeing the city rebuilt after the war makes me realise how much of what was there has now gone. The city centre is now very shabby'), and also enabled what was perceived as a 'remembering' of the affective experience of place (or the production of prosthetic memory of the 'feel' of the city in the past). Statements such as 'It made me think of what my parents went through as I was too young to understand' suggest that visitors perceived historical television programming as not just accessing posthumous sounds and images of the city, but also enabling them to access the experiences and emotions associated with the past of that place ('It gives a feel of the mood of the city as a whole'). Visitors also talked about the posthumous archive taking them into family histories and experiences to which they had no access, precisely because they related to those who were long dead:

> My dad worked in the car factory so it was really good to see the inside of where he spent so much of his time. And everyone looking so dapper going around town. Very atmospheric. Just good to see the hidden things – his working factory life. I can't talk to him about that now.

People also talked of a longing stirred up by these archival encounters ('I wish I could talk to my mum and dad about what it was like to be here in the 1960s'), so encounters with the posthumous archive also provoked feelings of wistfulness and frustration, as well as creating the sense that the prosthetic memories of place produced by archive television might enable us to understand how the dead once felt.

The *Ghost Town* project saw visitors 'honouring' the fact that we were curating *their* history through these archive-based events by bringing us gifts linked to the city's history: we had hoped that people would bring home recordings of significant bits of Coventry on TV to our events and exhibitions (I had made a call-out for this via local press, radio and television), but what they actually presented us with were treasured newspapers covering the consecration of the cathedral in 1962, a poem about the Locarno ballroom, or sharing family photographs with us (as in the example described above). This seemed to be a recognition of the value being placed on collective memory by the curation of the city's history through the television archive exhibition, offering an exchange of the objects and texts of memory. While our collaborations were mainly with professional media archives, the archive of the city and its broadcast history is also housed in residential homes by what Lynn Spigel calls 'armchair archivists' (2010: 62). Jennifer VanderBurgh's account of collections made up of such material stresses the value of off-air amateur recordings of television broadcasts for capturing the televisual history of a particular place 'since they are more likely to reproduce TV shows along with context-specific broadcast ephemera such as commercials and station identifications that professional recordings tend to lack' (2019: 63). As well as the copies of television programmes that we sourced from legitimate, professional archives for our events, we also frequently saw evidence of home recordings of Coventry on TV circulating online via what Spigel terms 'unintentional archives' (ibid.: 63), primarily on YouTube (and links to that site on local history social media pages). These frequently inspired long lines of reminiscence, online 'memory explosions' that mirrored those moments of extensive sharing at *Ghost Town* events.

To return to the earlier reference to Asa Briggs's work, these 'memory explosions' are precisely an articulation of his point that 'to write the history of broadcasting in the twentieth century is in a sense to write the history of everything else' (1991: 2). In this, and in other television history research and engagement projects I've been involved in, I've found myself having to shift from a position of frustration with what I first saw as a distracted public, unable to focus on talking to me about television history when they wanted to talk to me about that 'everything else', to understanding that to talk about television for most people is to think about the connective tissue between TV and their everyday lives. Television history is thus always entangled in those other histories and memories, and we cannot and should not seek to completely disentangle it.

Posthumous images and the haunting of the city

Scene from Ghost Town #2: A woman in her eighties and her daughter in her sixties wander into the Remembering Coventry *exhibition. 'We've come to see our family history' they tell me, as shown in Philip Donnellan's 1960 BBC documentary* Coventry Kids. *They had seen a clip of this on local news coverage of the exhibition the night before, so they knew they would be able to come and see this today. They sit in front of a small TV, huddled together, and watch intently as the man on screen, Lionel Boddy, directs the work at BMW, a Coventry tool manufacturing business, his back to the camera. The younger woman implores 'Turn around granddad!' as she wills her dead relative to show his face, and then speak to camera. After they watch the programme in its entirety, they turn to me, visibly moved, and say 'It's like he's returned from the dead'. This echoes an encounter at a screening of the same documentary the month before at Coventry Cathedral where an older West Indian Coventrian cried on seeing his long-dead friend play slide guitar in a rhythm and blues band in the upstairs room of the Rose and Woodbine pub on Stoney Stanton Road. Overwhelmed with emotion, he gripped his son's arm, who explained to me: 'He never thought he'd see him again'.*

Later in the week, at the Remembering Coventry *exhibition, local musician Martin Bowes turns up. Friends who have already been in the exhibition have told him that his appearance in 1980 in the BBC2 punk arts programme,* Something Else, *explaining how to edit a fanzine as a teenager, forms a part of the exhibition and he has come to see it for himself. He moves gingerly into the room, laughing nervously and obviously kind of uncomfortable about the encounter he is about to have with his younger self. He leans into his partner, hand over his mouth, as he watches himself on screen. Later, he tells me: 'It was quite emotional actually! . . . I got a bit teary, I don't know, I just got like that . . .'*

What does it feel like to encounter those we have loved and lost on screen? How can the television archive reconnect us with posthumous sounds and images of the dead? This second set of snapshots demonstrate the affective power of an encounter with archive television for the people of a city. They reveal the interweaving of civic stories with familial histories, and the emotional charge of an encounter with the dead, or even with our own younger selves, previously 'lost' to the passing of time, via screenings of old TV. These were not 'memory explosions' as in the first example, but something else; perhaps a haunting in the truer sense, where a specific person is re-encountered through archive TV.

Remembering Emma Wilson's argument, discussed in the previous chapter, that the moving image should be seen 'not as a mausoleum but as a wish-fulfilling, fevered, exotic space in which to live with the dead' (ibid.: 14), how might we understand the encounters above? Again, as we saw in the previous chapter, the ways in which that 'wish-fulfilling space' calls out to the viewer are also addressed by Jacques Derrida and Stiegler, in their discussion of the relationship between television and death. Derrida describes precisely the feelings that I believe were experienced by the woman watching her grandfather on screen in the *Remembering Coventry* exhibition: 'The desire to touch, the tactile effect or affect, is violently summoned by its very frustration, summoned to come back, like a ghost, in the places haunted by its absence' (2007: 115). This haunting is perhaps what also explains the uncanny, 'emotional' experience of people encountering their younger selves on screen, as with the example of Martin Bowes, the musician described in this second snapshot. Throughout the life of the *Ghost Town* project, I regularly spoke to people who 'got' the idea of haunting referred to in the project's title, and who sensed precisely the frustration and the melancholy implied in Derrida's account of watching his friend Pascal Ogier on screen. For example, a woman in her seventies who had recognised the Paralympian and market stall holder Pete McCranor in some ATV news footage in the *Remembering Coventry* exhibition expressed exactly the dual sorrow and joy of this encounter:

> Oh, it was lovely [to see him]! We were very, very close to Pete, and when I watched him laughing, he had a wicked sense of humour did Pete, so it brought back lots of lovely memories of him. Good times. But also sad to see him because I know he's died.

The simultaneous 'there and not there' feelings of encountering the dead via this assemblage of the posthumous television archive might, therefore, be described as bittersweet. People regularly discussed coming to *Ghost Town* events to search the footage for lost loved ones. They repeatedly talked about the desire to pause and pore over crowd scenes in our footage ('I'd like to see the film paused so we could look at the stills and recognise the places and faces. Remember them'), and when John Wyver's documentary *Coventry Cathedral: Building for a New Britain* was broadcast in June 2021, made from many of the same bits of archive footage that had been screened in *Ghost Town* events, local audiences reported doing just that. For example, in a BBC Coventry and Warwickshire radio interview with the DJ Richard Williams on 15 June, in the week after the documentary was broadcast, Williams enthused:

> Now I have watched this documentary *three times* . . . And so many people I know in Coventry are watching and talking about this documentary. Because it tells the story of Coventry Cathedral *but* also because it's got some incredible archive footage in there of Coventry, post-war, when the precinct was built. So, it's got archive of the precinct, people dancing on the dancefloor of the Locarno . . . It's fair to say it's gone absolutely bonkers across Coventry . . . The footage on there! Like you've got the precinct in the 60s and if you pause that screen and you're from Coventry and you've got relations then you might spot them. Then there's two thousand people who are outside the Cathedral for the consecration . . . You can see so many faces and I'm convinced my nan is there at 13 minutes, sitting in the precinct!

In relation to this searching, and the desire to pause and pore over the posthumous image, audiences either reported the bittersweet encounter of seeing but not being able to 'reach' their loved ones, or the frustration of knowing that they 'must have been there, somewhere' but didn't appear on screen, as in the footage of the crowds at the dedication of the Chapel of Unity at Coventry Cathedral in the image below.

A visitor to the *Coventry on TV* exhibition briefly glimpsed their parents queuing to see the Beatles at Coventry Theatre in 1963, but a brief tracking shot afforded a mere glimpse of them as it flew by the crowds. Many people visiting this event also commented on the fact that they themselves 'must be there' in shots of the enormous crowds in Coventry city centre for the celebration of the city's football team's FA Cup final win in 1987. The desire to stop and search the image also highlighted one of the limitations of the *Ghost Town* project, which will be explored at greater length below: while its events and exhibitions provided temporary access to the posthumous television archive, and often created affectively charged encounters with historical television for visitors/audiences, ongoing digital access to the archives represented in this project would ultimately have proved more satisfying for visitors. For example, one visitor to *Remembering Coventry* commented on a feedback card: 'It was totally fascinating and I wish I'd had time to watch it all. Please do this again! A way of navigating it would be

Figure 7.4 Crowds at the dedication of the Chapel of Unity at Coventry Cathedral (tx. 12/6/62) *Midlands News* (ATV for ITV, 1956–1969).

useful – downloadable clips – searchable?' While visitors were frequently directed to MACE's website or a collection of Coventry-related programming on the BBC iPlayer, these open, public access platforms represent only a fraction of the extant programming made in and about the city.

The reactions to the appearance of Lionel Boddy and the musician in the *Coventry Kids* film described in the above scene are clearly examples of the way in which the television archive might offer 'haunting' access to posthumous sounds and images. Whether those encounters are sought out by family members who knew of the presence of a dead relative on screen but who had no easy access to that programme (as in the former example), or whether they are accidentally stumbled upon at a public screening of archive television (as in the latter), these are significant and emotionally charged encounters for the people in question. Also at the *Remembering Coventry* exhibition, the cast and crew of the play *Risky City* (performed at the Belgrade Theatre in 1981 and covered in an episode of the local news programme, *ATV Today*, in the 'Coventry Culture' reel) gathered in small groups throughout the week, partly to see, once more, a friend involved in the production who had died, as well as to re-engage with a significant piece of theatre that they had all worked on. The television exhibition thus sometimes took on the unanticipated role of becoming a memorial space.

These encounters with posthumous images on screen are important. They were deeply moving for the people involved and were enabled by the collaborative efforts of historians and archivists to bring programming made in and about Coventry back to the city. They also make a significant point about the need for better, easier access to broadcast TV archives for the people whose everyday lives are captured in them. A call for better access to the archive was made by John Wyver in 2017, by drawing an analogy between the (largely inaccessible to the public) archive of the BBC and a public library. Wyver eloquently invites us to imagine the holdings of this television archive, the programmes contained within it, as an invaluable collection of books:

> The books were created by many of the best and the brightest of the four nations, and they represent some of the very finest creative achievements by those nation's greatest artists and thinkers and writers. They document what made the peoples of those nations laugh, what made them cry, what made them sad – angry – proud. As a consequence, the library and its books are – or would be, but for one little wrinkle – profoundly and immeasurably valuable to teachers, to school kids, to journalists, to artists, and to all those who want to understand who the peoples of the nations were and are – profoundly, immeasurably valuable indeed to each and every one of us.

Put this way, it is hard to argue with the drive to preserve, protect and make accessible this archive of 'immeasurable value'. In the UK, media historians have joined forces with equally passionate and committed groups of archivists and curators at the BBC and beyond, sometimes in the face of indifference from those who control the key resources necessary to protect this invaluable national asset, to explore it and to protect it; the announcement in 2021 that the BBC's archive was to be opened up to those in educational institutions was therefore a massive, and most welcome, step forward.[8] However, if we imagine the television archive not just as a library of immeasurable public value, but also as set of *family albums or home movies* of enormous *sentimental* value to the loved ones of those held, ghost-like, within, a repository of family memories, then a call for wider public access seems all the more urgent, all the more pressing. Joanne Garde-Hansen (2011) explores what she refers to as communities' 'right to memory', engaging with Anna Reading's work on the right to memory for Gypsy, Roma and Traveller communities (2010). This right, as Reading and Garde-Hansen note, is inscribed in the 2003 *UNESCO Declaration Concerning the Intentional Destruction of Cultural Heritage*[9] and leads Garde-Hansen to argue that 'Those without [an official] history, whose memories are being rediscovered through a variety of media institutions, forms and practices, need a bigger law, the right to remember and be remembered' (2011: 51). This call for 'the right to remember and be remembered' in relation to the television archive is, as Garde-Hansen notes, currently being managed by 'institutions, corporations, commercial organisations and industries that are heavily involved in recording, producing, archiving, creating and making accessible memories of local, national, and global significance' (ibid.). Drawing on Nancy van House and Elizabeth F. Churchill's work (2008), she stridently appeals for the BBC to open up their archive of 'digital treasures' to a general public that relies on this access to reactivate memory and reclaim its own pasts:

> [If] 'both personal and collective memory rely in part on the records of the past and on our technologies and practices of remembering' and the BBC has produced and houses those records with the means to technologise and practise them on behalf of UK citizens, then it is incumbent on the broadcaster to make its archive as accessible as possible. That does not mean simply using its archive for the production of more content to be archived further. Rather it means that, as a national archivist [sic], the BBC's archives ought to be opened up to the licence-fee payer to be used creatively and educationally. (ibid.: 102)

To this list of potential re-use, I would also add the ability to access posthumous sounds and images of those who are dead, lost or gone, contained within the archive, not just for creative and educational use but simply to reflect and remember. Although the last chapter began with the case of the Whiteleys, who chose not to return to their own posthumous programming, the *Ghost Town* project has revealed a widespread public desire to access precious recordings in the BBC and other archives that contain the dead of a particular community, and a desire to 'repatriate' posthumous family to that community via the archive.

This is our history: remembering past lives through the television archive

Scene from Ghost Town #3: *A woman in her seventies bustles in one afternoon, accompanied by her grown up daughter who says, 'We've come to see what's going on – we're on your poster!'. A now-retired trade union activist who spends her days looking after her disabled husband, she sees her history of protest and activism in the city captured on screen in montages of news and current affairs footage, the lives of her friends and family and colleagues frozen in a pivotal moment in the city's history, as well as her own. Her daughter says: 'We want to stay and see it all. It's no surprise we saw ourselves – this is our history' (she is the baby in a pram which has a placard propped against it that appears on our publicity materials for the exhibition, a screen-grab from an ATV news bulletin). Later in the week, the older woman comes back on her own and talks to me about how important the exhibition has been for her, to have the space to reflect on her past in relation to our screenings. She says 'I don't get chance, looking after my husband every day. I'm normally caring for him and doing the housework on a Sunday. I feel quite emotional, thinking about my life.'*

Later in the year, in the middle of a busy Trades Union meeting, I am invited to play our Coventry Industry showreel which gathers together local news footage of the history of industrial action in the city in the late twentieth century. The TUC are considering how they will engage with Coventry's City of Culture year and welcome this opportunity to look at how Coventry's trade unions have been represented on television, historically. There is lots of lively banter throughout this screening – people call out when they see themselves and their friends and comrades on screen. They scoff at some of the reporting of the actions of the unions: 'It wasn't like that at all!'. As the lights go up, Dr Kindy Sandhu, Labour Councillor for Coventry's Earlsdon ward, is visibly angry. She tells me that this compilation of television news is incomplete, inadequate. She asks why the trade unionists on screen were all white and recounts her parents' roles as important figures in the city's trade union history. I flounder through an explanation of the partiality of news reporting and try to explain how and why this history might be missing from the archive. I later resume the hunt for any representation of black and Asian trade unionists in Coventry in a variety of television archives. I find fragments of this history, but this encounter continues to challenge and reframe the work that I do in the city, and what I say to people about it.

As discussed above, television histories are always stories about place, and the *Ghost Town* project sought directly to inspire talk and thought about a particular place – the city of Coventry – through an engagement with the posthumous television archive. The stories and interpretations of that place that emerge through an engagement with television history can be ones of civic pride and a greater sense of understanding of the city's history, but they also might be contested histories or stories that illuminate absences in the archive, missing figures, and the significance of these absences.

Over a third of the visitors to *Ghost Town* exhibitions and events talked about increased feelings of wellbeing and civic pride as a result of their encounter with the archive of programmes made in and about the city. This was particularly significant, given that Coventry's City of Culture Trust developed a Theory of Change for 2021 and beyond that highlights increased civic pride as one of the key desired outcomes of the city's City of Culture year.[10] It is clearly demonstrable through the *Ghost Town* project that bringing footage out of the television archive frequently has a positive impact on people's feelings about the city. For example, visitors to our events and exhibitions reported the following:

- 'It's made me feel more connected to the place of my birth.'
- 'I had a feeling of nostalgia from watching the archives even though I didn't live in the city for most of the period covered, and I'm not from Coventry! It's made me feel pride in the city which wasn't there before. I have to admit I have struggled in the past to feel love or passion for Coventry – this has inspired it!!'
- 'Reinforced, really, my pride in this city of reconciliation, diversity, inspiration and radical vision.'
- 'We were more multinational than I ever knew. Never realised that people moved from all over to find work in Coventry. Younger people should see this archive to see the struggles this city has been through.'

This latter comment is important; it would be hard to see all the programming curated for *Ghost Town* events as 'nostalgic'. The television archive also documents some of the more difficult histories of the city: the racial tensions in Coventry in the early 1980s, and the economic downturn caused by the decline in the city's motor industry, for example. As Viktor Mayer-Schönberger has noted, the archive does not allow us to forget such difficult and painful histories: 'because of digital technology, society's ability to forget has become suspended, replaced by perfect memory' (2009: 4). The woman at the start of this third snapshot was visiting the exhibition, with and without her daughter, to see the role that she played in a series of industrial actions that were ultimately unsuccessful, and yet she still took pride in remembering, via posthumous archive television, this important moment of conflict, division and collective action in the city. In discussion with me, she gave the sense that while this was a 'difficult' history, it was still important because it was *her* history and the greater, 'direct' access that the archive television exhibition gave to this history which she had, to some extent, 'lost' was therefore extremely valuable to her.

Sometimes what was important to participants in *Ghost Town* events were the ways in which the television archive portrayed the city as resilient and improving. Some of the women from FWT Women's Health and Wellbeing Coffee Morning, invited to the *Remembering Coventry* exhibition, were newly arrived in the city and offered an interesting perspective on the stories about Coventry and its people in the exhibition. They were keen to discuss what might have happened to the young Muslim women in one of the programmes in the Coventry People reel which focused on a women's group in the area in which their own group was based, but in the early 1980s, and to track the story of the people on screen from migrant to settled. They also noted that some of the problems facing young Muslim women in Coventry in the 1970s and 1980s as shown in the showreel were still problems that they faced today (for example, difficulties associated with leaving the home and their families to attend support groups). For these women, and for other people commenting on the comparative state of the built environment of the city in the mid-twentieth century and now, the television archive doesn't always reveal a story of progress for the city: it also marks stagnation, a lack of progress, and decline in some areas. These events thus engendered some difficult conversations about the city's past, present and future, as well as evoking (sometimes simultaneous) feelings of civic pride.

Some of the *Ghost Town* events also made the research team acutely aware of the gaps and absences in the media archive and brought to light moments that the project failed to represent or open up in the past lives of the city. Lynn Spigel describes in her writing on the architectures of the television archive that,

> The archive contains traces of its own absences. The undocumented past, and even intentions not acted upon are inscribed there . . . It is not just a holding place where one discovers the past through the empirical materials left there, but also a venue for imagination, or, in Derrida's view, a 'spectral' space haunted by ghosts neither fully absent nor present in material terms. (2010: 53)

She later goes on to describe the television archive as a 'house with a two-sided edifice where the spectral and the speculative coexist' (ibid.).

In relation to the *Ghost Town* project, these absences show the city's histories to be contestable, and riddled with problems and difficulties; they fail to adequately reflect or animate Coventrians' memories of the past, for as Mayer-Schönberger states, 'For some, such limited diversity of information upon which the people form their memories of events is prohibitively confining' (2009: 44). Whereas for some in the TUC meeting described above the encounter with the archive brought about a welcome opportunity to both nostalgically reminisce about a particular moment in the history of the city's industrial relations and to jovially critique television's coverage of this history, for others this brought up (*and replicated*) more problematic and painful gaps and absences in public knowledge about the Black and Asian trade unionists in the city. These absences reveal much of the inherently racist attitudes in television reporting at the time as well as in the employment practices of the companies whose histories were gathered on screen.

This moment at the Coventry TUC meeting also brings to mind Rick Prelinger's reflections on the diverse ways in which different publics receive and relate to the *Lost Landscapes* screenings:

> Audience reactions make clear that there is no single takeaway. I've found that Black and white Detroiters watching *Lost Landscapes of Detroit* often see very different films. Younger and older San Franciscans don't always regard their urban history in the same way. Presenting urban history to public audiences almost inevitably foregrounds contradictions that demand collective conversation . . . Many residents of cities . . . might think of them as places of extreme contestation: cities in which battles were fought to maintain racialized power and control, cities filled with zones where bodily safety was contingent on race, class, gender and age. (2021)

When we bring compilations of place-specific programming out of the archive in projects such as *Ghost Town* or Prelinger's *Lost Landscapes* series, we have to be ready to surface the stories about place that these potentially posthumous archives do not tell and have not captured, for, as Caterina Albano states, 'the archive – not unlike the unconscious – is governed by loss, by something that has never been forgotten but whose amnesia is however haunting' (2016: 147). The idea that the television archive can capture the life of a city *in its entirety* is, therefore, a fantasy. This acknowledgement, to some extent, undermines my earlier assertion that the television archive captures all aspects of the city's past lives.

We also need to face the fact that sometimes what the television archive captures are 'difficult', problematic histories. This was explored in the previous chapter, of course, in relation to the archival traces left behind by the spectre of Jimmy Savile. Others – Joshua Hirsch (2004), Allen Meek (2016) – have also reflected on the ways in which traumas associated with particular places are revisited through the moving image archive. Prelinger notes that for many of his *Lost Landscapes* audiences, it was easier to focus on the granular detail of other aspects of urban histories – particularly associated with spaces of leisure and pleasure – rather than focusing on 'uncomfortable structural issues' (like racism) which might evoke anger or trigger conflict (2021). The *Ghost Town* project has challenged me not to shy away from these 'difficult histories' in the city's past life when bringing television out of the archive – difficult histories which include racist violence and murder, widespread discrimination, corruption, and the failure to protect people from abject poverty – but I remain sensitive to the need to better frame these screenings with some contextualisation of the times and broadcasting contexts in which programmes were made. As Anette Kuhn proposes,

> [The] democratic quality of memory work makes it a powerful practical instrument of 'conscientization', the awakening of critical consciousness through [participants'] own activities of reflection and learning, among those who lack power; and the development of a critical and questioning attitude towards their own lives and the lives of those around them. (1995: 490)

Ultimately, I return to the fact that, like Prelinger, I feel that these are not my histories or stories to tell, though my role as scout or presenter *for* the city is an important one. Prelinger ends his article on his own project by pondering:

> What if *Lost Landscapes* evolved into a community project whose work happened mostly at the neighbourhood level? What if younger makers, for instance, connected with elders to find images, explicate them and identify people pictured, and edit presentations that would happen first locally? Shifting the emphasis from putting on a one-time event to enabling a process of local connection and discovery would relocate historical agency from a single filmmaker [or historian] to an entire community, and perhaps be an opportunity for media training as well. (2021)

He also wonders, 'What more could we do with an assembly of people gathered in a room than simply screen a movie? Could we stimulate audiences to take on greater agency and new responsibilities?. . . Could we model a new commons?' (ibid.). Similarly, Alison Landsberg proposes that prosthetic memory – that is, memory which, in this case, is produced by an engagement with the posthumous television archive – 'creates the conditions for ethical thinking precisely by encouraging people to feel connected to, while recognizing the alterity of, the "other"' (2004: 9). In light of these challenges and proposals, we might ponder what action, or change in thinking, might be inspired by an engagement with place-specific posthumous programming. This could lead to at least two sets of actions for media historians:

1. To set activities, opportunities, and resources in place, alongside other collaborators (such as archivists, curators), to empower communities to do their own television history research.
2. To provide opportunities for people who gather for screenings of historical television to respond to these screenings by taking on 'greater agency and new responsibilities' in their communities.

The former is not easy; it requires collaborative work between academic media historians, archivists, broadcasters, museums, galleries and libraries and a willingness to keep opening up this significant historical resource. The latter call to enable audiences to develop agency and new responsibilities might range from audiences creating new opportunities for television history appreciation themselves – sharing with other people, perhaps other generations or other groups of interest, the great riches of the television archive – to taking action on current social problems or injustices when confronted with those of the past via the television archive.

Taking posthumous television programming out of the archive *always* brings new discoveries of its cultural importance, revealing things that are captured on screen (or are missing from that capture) that the broadcaster, archivist and historian had not anticipated, even. Vana Goblot writes that the 'reproduction and reuse of the televisual, and audio, archives . . . can lead to rediscoveries of the archive's new cultural purposes and contribute towards television's complexity as a rich cultural form' (2015). As we have seen, archival television takes on different meanings for different audiences, powered by connections that range from a recognition of the presence of past lives, lost loved ones, or even buildings and businesses that no longer stand in the city, or by a more generalised sense of connection to the past of a particular place. This has led to a greater appreciation of the television archive's importance for the people of the city of Coventry in the case of the *Ghost Town* project. Over two-thirds of attendees at 'Remembering Coventry' discussed their increased knowledge of, or reaffirmation of, the importance of the television archive. Twenty-three per cent of visitors didn't previously know about the existence of television archives, and said that they now realised its value, and at all *Ghost Town* events people talked about wanting better/more open/continual access to the archives we had drawn on in curating our exhibition. People said things like:

- 'I feel it is very important and should be made available offline for the world to view.'
- 'It should be viewed as a resource in the same way as books. A visual/living history archive.'
- 'It should be available on permanent display at the Herbert [Coventry's civic museum] for all to see.'
- 'I really enjoyed seeing the city as it was as I grew up. I hope that eventually more archive will be digitised and made available.'
- 'Television archive is very important as it mirrors actual people [and] events without it being sanitised by history books.'
- 'It's so important to know that this archive exists and can be opened to the public.'
- 'I have always believed in the importance of preserving our past and cultural heritage and the exhibition was a lovely reminder of the reasons why.'
- 'I probably haven't valued television archives much, and certainly not given it much thought. Being able to view the history of the city today from 'everyday' TV broadcasts has changed my perspective.'

These sentiments are quoted at length here because they represent one of the most significant findings of the project. Public access initiatives relating to the television archive have previously privileged and prioritised highly popular television genres (drama and comedy particularly) with wide national appeal (particularly through various attempts to 'monetise' the extant TV archive through platforms such as Britbox, Netflix and Amazon Prime), as well as programming with a kind of 'quirky' retro appeal (via the BBC Archive website, for example). The *Ghost Town* project, however, demonstrates that there is clear cultural value in being able to access the television archive in a way that emphasises its significance in relation to place, the construction of civic identity, and the power of posthumous sounds and images for families and individuals, particularly through television's most 'ordinary' of genres: local news and current affairs programming, children's television, arts broadcasting, and so on.

Television brings us up close to the dead in many different ways. From its attempts to represent experiences of death, dying and the afterlife, to its often sensitive portrayals of the impact of death on others, and finally to its reanimation of the dead via the posthumous archival image, television has brought the dead back into the rooms from which they might otherwise have been absent, and will continue to do so. As this chapter has shown, our dead remain with us via the television archive, and new initiatives to make that archive more accessible, more easily searchable and viewable by a wide range of people, will allow us to continue to make contact with those posthumous lives captured on TV. New programming relating to the history of particular places might deliver this, but so might other collaborative public access projects and initiatives that take place at a more local level. The story told in this chapter is one of a specific place – a medium-sized city in the middle of England with a diverse population and a history of booming industries and their subsequent decline – but a similar story about people's affective connections to archive television and the histories it contains might be told anywhere in the country or in the world. People will always search crowds on screen for their lost loved ones or their equally lost younger selves, hunting across the archival image for a brief glimpse into their own pasts. The thrill of recognising a street that you have walked down, or a factory that you worked at, on television is not a thrill that is specific to Coventry, although the rebuilding of the city and its subsequent decline made it a particularly interesting subject for late twentieth-century television. Ghostly traces of many towns and cities, and the people that populated them, sit waiting for rediscovery in the television archives. The fact that the medium continues to surface these ghosts, and to work through the subject of death, dying and bereavement for its viewers, is perhaps, ironically, evidence of the continuing liveliness of a medium which has so often been pronounced 'dead' itself.

Notes

Introduction

1 According to Wright et al. (1989), 25% of 5–8 year olds, 48% of 9–13 year olds and 31% of 14–17 year olds in the US watched this broadcast live. A BBC website captures some of the memories of viewers watching this tragic disaster being broadcast in the UK and US: <http://news.bbc.co.uk/onthisday/hi/witness/january/28/newsid_2643000/2643109.stm> (last accessed 31 August 2023).
2 Senna's death was broadcast on multiple television channels all around the world, shot from overhead helicopter, on 1 May 1994.
3 *Christine* (2016) and *Kate Plays Christine* (2016).
4 See <https://www.judiciary.senate.gov/imo/media/doc/Parker%20Testimony1.pdf> (last accessed 31 August 2023).
5 The nature of this controversy, and the ethical issues raised by the production of the documentary in question, will be explained at greater length in Chapter 2 of this book.
6 For example, Emily Bishop (Eileen Derbyshire), a member of this congregation, first joined *Coronation Street* in 1962.
7 *Coronation Street* was awarded the 2014 BAFTA for Best Soap and Continuing Drama and a National Television Award (NTAs) for Best Serial Drama in the same year. In the British Soap Opera Awards (BSOAs) for 2014, the programme won awards for Best Storyline in relation to Hayley's cancer, Best Single Episode for the episode covering Hayley's death, as well as a string of performance awards for Julie Hesmondhalgh and David Neilson at the BSOAs and NTAs.
8 During the last month of her life, for example, we saw, across multiple episodes, Hayley's move from hope in her treatment; her acceptance of palliative care; her anger at her shortened life; her talking through her relationship with Roy; her telling close friends about her impending death; her speaking to a Humanist celebrant about her funeral plans; Hayley's friends and husband struggling to feed her as her appetite and energy waned; and her decision to take her own life.
9 The Queen's body was not visible during this broadcast, though her coffin and the various members of her family that stood guard around it were. My thanks to Leanne Weston for alerting me to this programming.
10 See my comments on the representation of the AIDS/HIV crisis in the following chapter, for example.

Chapter 1

1. For example, *Horizon: When is a Body Dead?* (BBC2, tx. 31/1/67); *Matters of Life and Death* (BBC1, 4/3/69); *The Body in Question: Perishable Goods* (BBC2, tx. 12/2/79); *Jaywalking: Is Life Still Precious?* (ITV, tx. 29/4/79); *Medical Ethics: A Matter of Life and Death* (ITV, tx. 29/5/80); *Horizon: Death of the Working Classes* (BBC2, tx. 1/2/88); *Horizon: Sudden Death* (BBC2, tx. 7/1/91); *Why Men Die Younger* (BBC2, tx. 25/2/96); *Horizon: Death by Design* (BBC2, tx. 4/3/96); *The Chemistry of (Almost Everything)* (BBC2, tx. 8/10/96).
2. For example, *Panorama: Transplants – are the donors really dead?* (BBC1, tx. 13/10/80); *Panorama: The Brain Death Debate* (BBC1, tx. 24/11/80).
3. For example, *The Immortalists* (BBC1, tx. 11/11/79); *Heart of the Matter: The Frozen Few* (BBC1, tx. 4/11/90); *Short Circuit: Frozen to Death* (BBC2, tx. 3/6/93); *Here and Now* (BBC1, tx. 17/3/97).
4. For example, *Meeting Point: Death Before Birth* (BBC1, tx. 25/2/68).
5. For example, *Measure of Conscience: And Death is All* (BBC2, tx. 19/4/72); *The Man Alive Report: A Life for a Life* (BBC2, tx. 5/4/77); *Old Sparky* (BBC2, tx. 30/7/83); *Deathwatch* (BBC2, tx. 6/8/83); *Execution* (BBC2, tx. 13/8/83); *Fourteen Days in May* (BBC1, tx. 11/11/87); *The Journey* (BBC1, tx. 14/9/88); *Everyman: Lifeline* (BBC1, tx. 2/2/92); *Crime and Punishment Open Space: The Final Scream* (BBC2, tx. 26/5/93); *Crime and Punishment: Just Desserts* (BBC2, tx. 5/6/93); *Human Rights, Human Wrongs: Death Penalty/Capital Punishment* (BBC2, tx. 15/12/94); *East: A State of Intolerance* (BBC2, tx. 18/4/95); *Everyman: Not Too Young To Die* (BBC1, tx. 14/5/95); *Fine Cut: Raising Hell* (BBC1, tx. 20/5/95); *Correspondent* (BBC2, tx. 3/6/95); *Everyman: Angel of Death Row* (BBC1, tx. 1/10/95); *Hollywood Angel* (BBC1, tx. 31/3/96).
6. For example, *Everyman: AIDS – The New Lepers* (BBC1, tx. 9/11/86); *Remember Terry* (BBC2, tx. 17/12/87); *Brass Tacks: A Sentence of Death?* (BBC2, tx. 20/9/88); *Inside Story: AIDS in the Family* (BBC1, tx. 24/4/91); *Fighting Back: Arthur Ashe* (BBC2, tx. 10/6/93); *Over the Edge: Remember Me* (BBC2, tx. 17/9/93).
7. For example, *Meeting Point: Things They Say – 'When you're dead, you're dead'* (BBC, tx. 1/11/56) *Out of Step: Spiritualism* (ITV, tx. 23/10/57); *About Religion: Eternal Life: Is there a Life after Death* (ATV/ITV, tx. 19/1/58); *The Sunday Break: Is there life after death?* (ABC/ITV, tx. 27/10/63); *Whicker's World: Is there anybody there?* (BBC2, tx. 30/7/66); *Looking for an Answer* (ABC/ITV, 1967–1968), *Meeting Point: Is Death the End?* (BBC1, tx. 12/3/67); *The Other Side* (BBC2, tx. 5/9/69); *Through Darkness to Light* (BBC1, tx. 2/4/72); *Simple Faith: Is there life after death?* (BBC2, tx. 24/3/78); *40 Minutes: The Happy Medium* (BBC2, tx. 8/11/84); *Is there something after death?* (BBC2, 1988); *40 Minutes: Many Happy Returns* (BBC2, tx. 19/3/90); *In Search of the Dead* (BBC2, 1992); *Everyman: The Happy Medium* (BBC1, tx. 27/3/94).
8. For example, *The Glory that Remains* (BBC2, tx. 6/4/70); *Ceremony and the Citizen* (BBC2, tx. 11/6/77).
9. Hitchens died of oesophageal cancer in 2011.
10. This grew out of the Sunday Committee, established by John Reith (Viney, 1999).
11. Viney's source for this is Central Religious Advisory Committee (1975).

12 The psychiatrist was unnamed because General Medical Council rules meant that until 1973 (Potts, 2019), medical practitioners were not supposed to be named in the media for fear of being seen as advertising their services, 'a practice deemed ungentlemanly and likely to bring the profession into disrepute' (Loughlin, 2005: 200).
13 *Lifeline: Moment of Truth* (tx. 6/1/60, 10.15 pm, BBC); a panel programme about those facing death.
14 *Perspective: How Should We Face Death?* (tx. 15/2/62, 1.30 pm, BBC); a panel programme featuring Dr L. Colebrook, F.B.S., a doctor doing clinical research on pain, Russian Orthodox Bishop Anthony Bloom, philosopher and atheist J. P. Corbett and anthropologist Francis Huxley.
15 See <https://lifemoving.org> for Aaron's own filmmaking project, a collaboration between researchers, a filmmaker and hospice patients that explores the power of film to communicate the meaningful and honest experiences of those affected by terminal illness (last accessed 1 September 2023).
16 Sadly, this episode no longer exists.
17 Recalled in interview with the author, 7/6/22.
18 Vivien Whiteley-Toyn, interview with the author, 7/6/22.
19 A black and white video copy was eventually passed on to the family by friends, some years later, but Vivien did not own a VCR until the early 1990s.
20 The Whiteleys' later viewing of *Remember All The Good Things* is returned to in Chapter 6 of this book.
21 Vivien Whiteley-Toyn, interview with the author, 7/6/22.
22 Vivien also received a letter from the retired journalist and broadcaster Frank Gillard, which she described to me in the following terms: 'He said [the film] was moving, he thought we were very brave, and it was a lovely film, it was beautifully done. And it made a very important point, something like that. It was really, really nice. I thought: "Oh my God, Frank Gillard! My hero".'
23 Both quotes from Vivien Whiteley-Toyn, interview with the author, 7/6/22.
24 Vivien Whiteley-Toyn, interview with the author, 7/6/22.
25 'Testimony' (tx. 17/7/68), 'It Comes to Us All – In Time' (tx. 3/12/68), 'Death in Holland' (tx. 2/9/69), 'A Good Place to Die . . .' (tx. 3/12/72), 'Death on the Road' (tx. 30/8/73) and 'Suicide in Germany' (tx. 23/4/74).
26 See the listing on <https://genome.ch.bbc.co.uk/5edf2a05741240babd40bde661258296> (last accessed 1 September 2023).
27 This episode is particularly affecting to watch today, given that we are now aware that Dando would be murdered just over a year after the programme was made (see Part III of this book for a discussion of the posthumous image on television), and thus her discussion of the impact of sudden death with her participatory audience carries extra weight and significance.

Chapter 2

1 The term 'post-broadcast' television refers here to programming that is not broadcast as part of a schedule or 'flow' of programmes on 'regular' television, but rather is streamed, downloaded or watched online outside of a planned schedule.

2   See Wilson (2003) for a thorough history of the Catholic church's opposition to assisted dying in the twentieth century.
3   *Whose Life is it Anyway?* was produced by Granada and broadcast on ITV on 12 March 1972.
4   See Henderson (2019) for a detailed history of the development of *Open Door*.
5   It was partnered with a film about the Auxiliary Fire Service.
6   Dr Henderson Smith from the Voluntary Euthanasia Society.
7   Dr Ciceley Saunders (outspoken opposer of assisted dying and hospice pioneer from St Christopher's Hospice, London); Dr Michael Barnet (consultant anaesthetist from Guy's Hospital), Dr Jack Norell and Dr Fraser (both GPs who were respectively against and for euthanasia).
8   Canon Hugh Melinsky, an Anglican Minister from Norwich.
9   Professor Glanville Williams (Cambridge-based Professor of English Law); David Napley (a solicitor representing the Law Society).
10 Mrs Kay Webber, Mrs Jill Raikes and Mrs Jean Drewery, who all took different positions in the debate relating to their own experience of their parents' deaths.
11 She was given a one-week suspended jail sentence and twelve months' probation.
12 The panel was made up of Ludovic Kennedy (as Vice President of the Voluntary Euthanasia Society), Melanie Phillips (anti-euthanasia journalist), Dame Cicely Saunders (St Christopher's Hospice), Dr Nigel Sykes (also from St Christopher's), Dr Nigel Jack (an anesthetist working and practicing euthanasia in the Netherlands) and Dr Van Oijen.
13 Either Albert van der Wildt or Deodaat Visser.
14 See Shacklock (2017, 2021) for an expansion of television's kinesthetic intimacies.
15 All quotes from Charlie Russell come from an interview conducted with him by the author in London on 21/6/16.
16 All quotes from Rowan Deacon come from an interview conducted with her by the author in London on 21/6/16.
17 See Part III of this book for a discussion of posthumous television sounds and images.
18 Agnese Sile's discussion of the photograph of hands in Briony Campbell's *The Dad Project* (2020), as well as the image of the hand on the arm that is evoked in both Paul Sutton's (2020) and Andrew Kötting's (2020) contributions to Holdsworth, Lury and Tweed's edited collection, *Discourses of Care*, also attest to the power of this image.

Chapter 3

1   In the following episode, Sansa is also traumatically forced by her fiancé to look at her father's severed head, her eyes red raw from crying, in an extension of this horror in viewing the television dead.
2   'Sweeps week' (something of a misnomer as the period lasts for nearly a month) is the critical period in US broadcasting when Nielsen Media Research takes its regular survey of TV viewing habits. It is known as a time where plot lines get feverishly outlandish in the hope of attracting peak viewing figures.

3 This practice continues. For example, the journalist Naomi Elias also noted the hyper-presence of death during 'sweeps weeks' in 2018.
4 Michael-Fox refers here to the anthropologist Geoffrey Gorer, whose article 'The pornography of death' in *Encounter* in 1955 initiated the logics of the 'death denial' thesis.
5 Foltyn is referring to *Quincy, ME* (NBC, 1976–1983).
6 Here, Weissmann refers to Isabel Christina Pinedo's work (1997) and the link she draws between hard-core pornography and hard-core horror through this term.
7 Chris Albrecht was then HBO president of original programming, soon to be CEO and Chair of HBO.
8 This visual effect is rendered through a head and torso recreation of the actor Peter Krause by MastersFX.
9 It should be acknowledged that for the purpose of this analysis I watched this sequence multiple times trying to figure out how the creators of *Six Feet Under* had made Krause look as if he was dead and had had his eyes and internal organs removed. While my interest in this scene is of course heightened by the fact that I am writing about death in this series, I can equally imagine that a regular viewer of *Six Feet Under* might have been similarly curious and baffled, enthralled and appalled.
10 Alice Bennett notes that the hotel has been a particularly recurrent image for contemporary imaginings of the afterlife as a 'particularly potent and multivalent symbol because of its potential to represent any aspect of the afterlife' (2012: 6). Luxury hotels feature prominently as afterlife locations in both *Upload* and *Forever*.
11 This trope perhaps mirrors what J. G. Ballard described as the 'organisational structures' and 'presiding bureaucracy of demons and supernatural gauleiters' present in the visions of hell in Wyndham Lewis's The Human Age trilogy in the mid-twentieth century: *The Childermass* (1928), *Monstre Gai* (1955) and *Malign Fiesta* (1955).
12 As Eleanor exclaims in 'Michael's Gambit' (S1, E13) 'We've been torturing each other since the moment we arrived!'
13 This is a fascinating episode which is beyond the scope of this chapter, given that it was produced for the UK broadcaster Channel 4. Neal Kirk (2017) offers an excellent analysis of this episode and how it relates to the concept of 'networked spectrality' in an era where the digital afterlife feels an uncertain, but near, future possibility.

Chapter 4

1 See <https://deathcafe.com> (last accessed 1 September 2023).
2 From Garland's last MGM musical, *Summer Stock* (1950).
3 As with Austerlitz's rewatching of *Six Feet Under* discussed above (2021), *The Leftovers* has been a particularly hard watch during the pandemic in its depiction of worldwide grief and bereavement.

Chapter 5

1 In the 'Making of *The Living and the Dead*' featurette in the 2016 BBC Worldwide DVD release of *The Living and the Dead*.

2 Ibid.
3 See in particular 'Tree with sheep, Alcomden, Yorkshire' (1977), 'Path and reservoir above Lumbutts, Yorkshire' (1977), and 'Top Withens, near Haworth, Yorkshire' (1977)).
4 Arguably the very final scene of the serial undercuts this sense of peace and equilibrium once more, with the suggestion of further haunting to come at Shepzoy.
5 The ghost drama that perhaps most chillingly demonstrates Johnston's point here is the French series *Marianne* (Empreinte Digitale/Federation Entertainment for Netflix, 2019), which employed the dark corners of a complex frame to contain (almost) unseen spectres to dramatic effect.
6 Perhaps like the excessively detailed *mise-en-scène* of contemporary television drama described by Johnston above.
7 See Link (2020) for a discussion of subjective time in the Netflix drama *The Haunting of Hill House*.
8 See Melanie Robson for a discussion of character projections in *The Haunting of Hill House* (2019: 9).
9 *The Innocents* is an adaptation of Henry James's *Turn of the Screw* (1898), as is Mike Flanagan's follow-up to *The Haunting of Hill House*, *The Haunting of Bly Manor*.
10 Virgil's name is surely significant here. In Dante's *Inferno*, Virgil is the author's guide through heaven, hell and purgatory, a nod to the journey that his request will take Dan on in investigating the deaths at the Visser and examining his own death-related trauma. Purgatory is also referred to in the title of the opera which is composed by one of the Visser's cult members, and might be seen as a reference to the way in which the Visser becomes space between life and death by the end of the serial.

Chapter 6

1 Vivien Whiteley-Toyn, interview with the author, 7/6/22.
2 Ibid.
3 Arnell Group ad for Chanel No. 5, 1994. Penfold-Mounce and Smith describe Monroe as 'the first and only woman to feature in the first eight years of the publication of the [Forbes Dead Rich List]' (2020: 45).
4 AMV BBDO London and Framestore ad for Mars Galaxy, 2013.
5 Falls ad for Dirt Devil, 1997. As Penfold-Mounce and Smith note of this ad, 'Astaire's widow Robyn agreed to the commercial deal, but it led his daughter Ava to claim she was "saddened that after his (Fred's) wonderful career he was sold to the devil"' (2020: 42).
6 This was re-broadcast in 2012 before her death, and in 2021 after it.
7 BBC2 rebroadcast *Victoria Wood: Seen on TV* the night after she died.
8 For example, Gold showed all of Series 1 of her sitcom *Dinnerladies* (BBC1, 1998–2000) and *Victoria Wood's Midlife Christmas* (BBC1, 24/12/09) on the weekend of her death, and BBC2 replaced episodes of *Antiques Road Trip* (2010–) and *Natural World: Nature's Perfect Partners* (2016) with episodes of *Victoria Wood: As Seen on TV* (1985–1987).

9 For example, the BBC's tribute night on 18 December 2016, which included the *Victoria Wood: As Seen on TV Special* (BBC2, 18/12/87), the documentary *Best of British: Victoria Wood* (BBC1, 11/11/98), *Victoria Wood's Midlife Christmas*, and *Victoria Wood: At It Again* which was performed at the Royal Albert Hall in 2001 and first shown on television on this night.
10 In *Charlie Brooker's 2012 Wipe* (BBC2, tx. 1/1/13).
11 For example, one Twitter user said, in November 2014: 'Must the media show his pic whenever there's an item on Jimmy Savile in the news? It's as if he still has to haunt everyone #JimmySaville', and another worried: 'Watching a programme about jimmy savile and getting scared he will haunt me in my sleep.'
12 See Huppert et al. (2005) for a discussion of the relationship between trauma and compulsive behaviours.
13 They were shot after the 2000 documentary was broadcast.
14 Karen Boyle has pointed out that this lack of focus on the institution, and the emphasis placed on his female victims rather than the men that supported Savile and his career for so long, at the BBC and elsewhere, is highly problematic in this new Theroux documentary (2016).
15 Dame Janet Smith, 'The Dame Janet Smith Review', *BBC Trust Website*, <http://www.bbc.co.uk/bbctrust/dame_janet_smith> (last accessed 4 January 2023).
16 Karen Boyle has called for an examination of the connections between the Savile case and the representation of men like Harvey Weinstein, Kevin Spacey, Johnny Depp or Dustin Hoffman, or in a British TV context, with convicted celebrity sex offenders including Max Clifford, Stuart Hall and Rolf Harris (2018).

Chapter 7

1 This news item can be viewed on MACE's website here: <https://www.macearchive.org/films/atv-today-01091965-noise-levels-coventry> (last accessed 1 September 2023).
2 The research team across the week was Eddie Charles, Joanne Garde-Hansen, Cat Lester, Rachel Moseley, Daisy Richards, Bryony Salisbury, Zoë Shacklock, Rick Wallace, James Waterhouse and Helen Wheatley.
3 Restoration of the cathedral's copy, particularly of the colour on their faded print, was undertaken by the Media Archive for Central England on behalf of the *Ghost Town* project.
4 This research was done alongside our jointly supervised collaborative doctoral award student, Kat Pearson.
5 The roundtable involved John Wyver, Dr Nirmal Puwar from Goldsmiths University, and the author.
6 These films were *Taffia Cothan* (Adele Mary Reed, 2020), *I have faith in all you blues* (Sherrie Edgar, 2020) and *Phoenix* (Tara Rutledge/Mary Courtney, 2020).
7 Now the National Science and Media Museum.
8 See the following press release for this announcement: <https://www.bbc.com/mediacentre/2021/bbc-100> (last accessed 1 September 2023).

9 See <https://international-review.icrc.org/sites/default/files/irrc_854_unesco_eng.pdf> (last accessed 1 September 2023).
10 See <https://warwick.ac.uk/research/partnerships/place-based-research/impact-value/researchresources/uk_coc_2021_interim_report_-_january_2022_web.pdf> (last accessed 1 September 2023).

References

Aaron, M. (2007) *Spectatorship: The Power of Looking On*. London: Wallflower.
—— (2014) *Death and the Moving Image: Ideology, Iconography and I*. Edinburgh: Edinburgh University Press.
—— (2019) 'Sharing in *Winter*: Film, participatory practice and the art of dying', in S. Banham, S. Hunter, M. Brady and R. O'Shea (eds) *Summer. Autumn. Winter. Spring – Staging Life and Death*. Manchester: Manchester University Press, pp. 125–34.
—— (2020) 'Love's revival: Film practice and the art of dying', *Film-Philosophy*, 24(2), pp. 83–103.
Abbott, S. (2016) 'Loss is part of the deal: Love, fear and mourning in TV horror', in A. N. García (ed.) *Emotions in Contemporary TV Series*. Basingstoke: Palgrave Macmillan, pp. 155–71.
Adorno, T. (2011) 'From "Valéry Proust Museum" and from "In Memory of Eichendorff"', in J. K. Olick, V. Vinitzky-Seroussi and D. Levy (eds) *The Collective Memory Reader*, Oxford: Oxford University Press, pp. 110–12.
Akass, K. and McCabe, J. (2005) 'Introduction: "Why do people have to die?" "To make contemporary drama important, I guess"', in K. Akass and J. McCabe (eds) *Reading Six Feet Under: TV to Die For*. London: I.B. Tauris, pp. 1–15.
Albano, C. (2016) *Memory, Forgetting and the Moving Image*. London: Palgrave.
Allen, B. (2020) 'Wait, haven't I already seen Amazon's afterlife comedy *Upload*?', *GQ*, 1 May. Available at: <https://www.gq-magazine.co.uk/culture/article/upload-amazon-prime-review> (Accessed: 1 September 2023).
Anon. (1959) 'Legalised "mercy killing" would be most "retrograde step", British TV panel told', *National Catholic Welfare Council Newsfeed*, 27 April. Available at: <https://thecatholicnewsarchive.org/?a=d&d=cns19590427-01.1.154&e=-------en-20--1--txt-txIN--------> (Accessed: 4 January 2023).
—— (1966) 'Briefing: Television', *The Observer*. 27 November, p. 22.
—— (1976) 'TV Guide: Briefing', *The Observer*. 11 April, p. 30.
—— (2004) 'Bringing *Six Feet Under* corpses to life', *Today*, 9 June. Available at: <https://today.com/popculture/bringing-six-feet-under-corpses-life-wbna5174672> (Accessed: 4 January 2023).
—— (2012) 'BBC criticised for *Newsnight* axed Jimmy Savile report', *BBC News Online*, 19 December. Available at: <https://www.bbc.co.uk/news/uk-20778261> (Accessed: 4 January 2023).

—— (2013) 'The BBC is still haunted by the ghost of Savile', *Evening Standard*, 24 June. Available at: <https://www.standard.co.uk/news/londoners-diary/the-bbc-is-still-haunted-by-the-ghost-of-savile-8671077.html> (Accessed: 4 January 2023).

—— (2014) 'BBC apologises for Jimmy Savile clip', *The Guardian*, 22 September. Available at: <https://www.theguardian.com/media/2014/sep/22/bbc-apologises-jimmy-savile-clip> (Accessed: 4 January 2023).

—— (2022) 'Six times the Queen made us laugh', *BBC News Online*, 9 September. Available at: <https://www.bbc.co.uk/news/uk-62849166> (Accessed: 4 January 2023).

Ang, I. (1989) *Watching Dallas: Soap Opera and the Melodramatic Imagination*. London and New York: Routledge.

Appleyard, B. (1995) 'An unjustified death on the box', *The Independent*, 15 March, p. 19.

Arav, D. (2016) 'Television: A traumatic culture', in Y. Ataria et al. (eds) *The Interdisciplinary Handbook of Trauma and Culture*. New York: Springer, pp. 39–49.

Ariel (1974) 'Poignant subject makes brilliant TV documentary', *Liverpool Echo*, 13 November, p. 2.

Ariès, P. (1994) *Western Attitudes Toward Death: From the Middle Ages to the Present* (trans. P. M. Ranum). London and New York: Marion Boyars.

—— (2000) 'Death denied', in D. Dickenson, M. Johnson and J. Samson (eds) *Death, Dying and Bereavement* (2nd edition). London/Thousand Oaks: Sage, pp. 10–13.

Armitt, L. (2017) 'Haunted landscapes', in S. Brewster and L. Thurston (eds) *The Routledge Handbook to the Ghost Story*. London and New York: Routledge, pp. 291–300.

Atkins, W. (2014) *The Moor: A Journey into the English Wilderness*. London: Faber and Faber.

Atkinson, N. (2014) '*Remember Me*: Creator of BBC1 drama hit is Slaithewaite writer Gwyneth Hughes', *Huddersfield Daily Examiner*, 5 December. Available at: <http://www.examiner.co.uk/news/west-yorkshire-news/remember-me-creator-bbc1-drama-8232955> (Accessed: 4 January 2023).

Aust, R. and Holdsworth, A. (2017) 'The BBC archive post-Jimmy Savile: Irreparable damage or recoverable ground?', in J. Boyce Kay, C. Mahony and C. Shaw (eds) *The Past in Visual Culture: Essays on Memory, Nostalgia and the Media*. Jefferson, NC: McFarland, pp. 170–84.

Austerlitz, S. (2021) 'Twenty years later, *Six Feet Under* lives on', *New York Times*, 5 June. Available at: <https://www.nytimes.com/2021/06/04/arts/television/six-feet-under-20th-anniversary.html> (Accessed: 4 January 2023).

Azoulay, A. (2001) *Death's Showcase: The Power of Image in Contemporary Democracy* (trans. R. Danieli). Cambridge, MA: MIT Press.

Baer, U. (2013) 'To give memory a place: Contemporary holocaust photography and the landscape tradition', in M. del Pilar Blanco and E. Peeren (eds) *The Spectralities Reader: Ghosts and Haunting in Contemporary Cultural Theory*. London, UK: Bloomsbury, pp. 415–44.

Bailey, P. (2016) 'The ghost of Broadcasting House', *Radio Survivor*, 14 June. Available at: <http://www.radiosurvivor.com/2016/06/14/ghost-broadcasting-house> (Accessed: 4 January 2023).

Ballard, J. G. (1966) 'Visions of Hell', *New Worlds*, March, 49(160), pp. 148–54.

Barnard, P. (1995) 'Last rights?', *Radio Times*, 11–17 March, p. 4.

Barthes, R. (1981) *Camera Lucida: Reflections on Photography* (trans. R. Howard). Hill and Wang: New York.
Baudrillard, J. (1993) *Symbolic Exchange and Death* (trans. H. H. Grant). London: Sage.
Bazin, A. (1960) 'The ontology of the photographic image' (trans. H. Gray). *Film Quarterly*, 13(4), pp. 4–9.
—— (2003) 'Death every afternoon' (trans. M. A. Cohen), in I. Margulies (ed.) *Rites of Realism: Essays on Corporeal Cinema*. Durham, NC: Duke University Press, pp. 27–31.
BBC (2016) '*The Living and the Dead*: Press Pack', 9 June. Available at: www.bbc.co.uk/mediacentre/mediapacks/livinganddead (Accessed: 4 January 2023).
Benjamin, W. (1996) 'The task of the translator [1921]' in M. Bullock and M. W. Jennings (eds) *Selected Writings Volume 1 1913–1926*. Cambridge, MA and London: The Belknap Press of Harvard University Press, pp. 253–63.
Beesley, S. (1995) 'MPs "misled" over euthanasia claim', *The Guardian*, 16 March, p. 4.
Belsey, Andrew (1992), 'Privacy, publicity and politics', in A. Belsey and R. Chadwick (eds) *Ethical Issues in Journalism and the Media*. London and New York: Routledge, pp. 77–92.
Bennett, A. (2012) *Afterlife and Narrative in Contemporary Fiction*. Basingstoke: Palgrave Macmillan.
Bergson, H. (1991[1896]) *Matter and Memory* (trans. N. M. Paul and W. S. Palmer). New York: Zone Books.
Bernico, M. (2020) 'It's coming from inside the house: Houses as bodies with organs', in Kevin J. Wetmore Jr (ed.) *The Streaming of Hill House: Essays on the Haunting Netflix Adaptation*. Jefferson, NC: McFarland & Co., pp. 39–49.
Boddice, R. (2019) 'Hysteria or tetanus: Ambivalent embodiments and the authenticity of pain', in D. Martín-Moruno and B. Pichel (eds) *Emotional Bodies: The Historical Performativity of Emotions*. Urbana: University of Illinois Press, pp. 19–35.
Boltansky, L. (1993) *Distant Suffering: Morality, Media and Politics*. Cambridge: Cambridge University Press.
Bowring, J. (2016) *Melancholy and Landscape: Locating Sadness, Memory and Reflection in the Landscape*. London and New York, Routledge.
Boyle, K. (2016) 'Louis Theroux's new Jimmy Savile documentary is a horrible misstep', *The Conversation*, 3 October. Available at: <https://theconversation.com/louis-therouxs-new-jimmy-savile-documentary-is-a-horrible-misstep-66421> (Accessed: 4 January 2023).
—— (2018) 'Television and/as testimony in the Jimmy Savile case', *Critical Studies in Television*, 13(4), pp. 387–404.
Bramesco, C. (2020) '*Upload* review – Amazon's afterlife comedy is the less good place', *The Guardian*, 30 April. Available at: <https://www.theguardian.com/tv-and-radio/2020/apr/30/upload-review-amazon-afterlife-comedy-less-good-place> (Accessed: 4 January 2023).
Breese, E. (2022) 'People are sharing their favourite clips of the Queen's most heartwarming moments', *The Big Issue Online*, 9 September. Available at: <https://www.bigissue.com/news/people-are-sharing-videos-queen-heartwarming-moments> (Accessed: 4 January 2023).
Brennan, Mhairi. (2020) *Archiving the Referendum: BBC Scotland's Television Archive and the 2014 Scottish Independence Referendum*. Unpublished thesis. University of Glasgow.

Brennan, Michael. (2018) 'Christopher Hitchens' public dying: Toward a secular-humanist ars morendi?', *OMEGA: Journal of Death and Dying*, 77(2), pp. 99–132.
Briggs, A. (1991) *The Collected Essays of Asa Briggs: Volume 3*. Brighton: Harvester.
Bronfen, E. (1992) *Over Her Dead Body: Death, Femininity and the Aesthetic*. Manchester: Manchester University Press.
—— (2009) 'The power of death in life', in A. Blackwell and D. MacKay (eds) *Power*. Cambridge: Cambridge University Press.
Brooks, R. (1995) '"Sick" BBC to screen Dutch mercy killing', *The Observer*, 29 January, p. 5.
Brown, C. G. (2012) '"The Unholy Mrs Knight" and the BBC: Secular humanism and the threat to the "Christian Nation", c.1945–60', *English Historical Review*, 127(525), pp. 345–76.
Brown, L. S. (1995) 'Not outside the range: One feminist perspective on psychic trauma', in C. Caruth (ed.) *Trauma: Explorations in Memory*. Baltimore: Johns Hopkins University Press, pp. 100–12.
Brunsdon, C. (2018) *Television Cities: Paris, London, Baltimore*. Durham, NC: Duke University Press.
Buonnano, M. (2008) *The Age of Television: Experiences and Theories* (trans. J. Radice). Bristol: Intellect.
Burton, T. I. (2018) 'The (secular) gospel according to *The Good Place*', *Vox*, 5 December. Available at: <https://www.vox.com/2018/9/27/17888310/the-good-place-religion> (Accessed: 4 January 2023).
Cadava, E. (1997) *Words of Light: Theses on the Photography of History*. Princeton, NJ: Princeton University Press.
Caldwell, J. T. (1995) *Televisuality: Style, Crisis and Authority in American Television*. New Brunswick, NJ: Rutgers University Press.
Caruth, C. (1995a) 'Introduction: Trauma and experience', in C. Caruth (ed.) *Trauma: Explorations in Memory*. Baltimore and London: The Johns Hopkins University Press, pp. 3–11.
—— (1995b) 'Recapturing the past: Introduction', in C. Caruth (ed.) *Trauma: Explorations in Memory*. Baltimore and London: The Johns Hopkins University Press, pp. 151–7.
Caughie, J. (2000) *Television Drama: Realism, Modernism, and British Culture*. Oxford: Oxford University Press.
Central Religious Advisory Committee (1975) *Evidence to the Committee on the Future of Broadcasting under the Chairmanship of Lord Annan*. London: BBC/IBA.
Chapman, J. (2015) *A New History of British Documentary*. Basingstoke: Palgrave MacMillan.
Chilton, L. (2021) '"Make it more f***ed up": The story of *Six Feet Under*, 20 years on', *The Independent*, 3 June. Available at: <https://www.independent.co.uk/arts-entertainment/tv/features/six-feet-under-alan-ball-b1857686.html> (Accessed: 4 January 2023).
Christie, I. (1995) *The Last Machine: Early Cinema and the Birth of the Modern World*. London: BFI/BBC.
Corner, J. (2003) 'Finding data, reading patterns, telling stories: Issues in the historiography of television', *Media, Culture and Society*, 25(2), pp. 273–80.

Cunningham, S. (2009) 'Reinventing television: The work of the "innovation" unit', in G. Turner and J. Tay (eds) *Television Studies after TV: Understanding Television in the Post-Broadcast Era*. London and New York: Routledge, pp. 83–95.

Curtis, B. (2008) *Dark Places: The Haunted House in Film*. London: Reaktion Books.

Daniel, A. (2020) 'Ghosts of future past: Spatial and temporal intersections', in K. J. Wetmore Jr (ed.) *The Streaming of Hill House: Essays on the Haunting Netflix Adaptation*. Jefferson, NC: McFarland & Co., pp. 142–51.

Davies, A. (2021) 'Channel 4 backlash: Prince Philip death snubbed as viewers brand schedule "disgusting"', *The Express*, 10 April. Available at: <https://www.express.co.uk/showbiz/tv-radio/1420992/Channel-4-backlash-Prince-Philip-death-schedule-Come-Dine-with-Me-video> (Accessed: 4 January 2023).

Davies, D. (2005) *A Brief History of Death*. Oxford: Blackwell.

Davis, C. (2013) 'État Présent: Hauntology, spectres and phantoms', in M. del Pilar Blanco and E. Peeren (eds) *The Spectralities Reader: Ghosts and Haunting in Contemporary Cultural Theory*. London, UK: Bloomsbury, pp. 53–60.

Davis, T. (2004) *The Face on Screen: Death, Recognition and Public Memory*. Bristol: Intellect.

Deacy, C. (2012) *Screening the Afterlife: Theology, Eschatology and Film*. London and New York: Routledge.

DeGroot, J. M. and Leith, A. P. (2018) 'R.I.P. Kutner: Parasocial grief following the death of a television character', *OMEGA: Journal of Death and Dying*, 77(3), pp. 199–216.

Del Pilar Blanco, M. (2012) *Ghost-Watching American Modernity: Haunting, Landscape, and the Hemispheric Imagination*. New York: Fordham University Press.

Del Pilar Blanco, M. and Peeren, E. (2013) 'Introduction: Conceptualizing spectralities', in M. del Pilar Blanco and E. Peeren (eds) *The Spectralities Reader: Ghosts and Haunting in Contemporary Cultural Theory*. London: Bloomsbury, pp. 1–28.

Demir, S. (2015) 'The city on screen: A methodological approach on cinematic city studies', *CINEJ Cinema Journal*, 4(1), pp. 21–36.

Dempsey, D. (1976) 'The dead speak for themselves on a TV special', *New York Times*, 25 April, pp. 1 and 29.

Denison, R. and Jancovich, M. (2007) 'Introduction', *Intensities: The Journal of Cult Media*, 4. Available at: <https://intensitiescultmedia.files.wordpress.com/2012/12/jancovich_intro.pdf> (Accessed: 4 January 2023).

Derrida, J. (1994) *Specters of Marx: The State of the Debt, the Work of Mourning, and the New International* (trans. P. Kamuf). London and New York: Routledge.

Derrida, J. and Stiegler, B. (2007) *Echographies of Television*. Cambridge: Polity.

Dickinson, G. E. (2018) 'State of the field of death in the United States', in C. K. Cann (ed.) *The Routledge Handbook of Death and the After Life*. London and New York: Routledge, pp. 10–19.

Dilman, J. C. (2014) *Women and Death in Film, Television, and News: Dead But Not Gone*. New York and Basingstoke: Palgrave Macmillan.

Doka, K. J. (2018) 'Understanding grief: Theoretical perspectives', in C. K. Cann (ed.) *The Routledge Handbook of Death and the After Life*. London and New York: Routledge, pp. 30–9.

Dollimore, J. (2001) *Desire and Loss in Western Culture*. London and New York: Routledge.

Downing, L. and Saxton, L. (2010) *Film and Ethics: Foreclosed Encounters*. London and New York: Routledge.

D'Rozario, D. (2016) 'Dead celebrity (Deleb) use in marketing: An initial theoretical exposition', *Psychology and Marketing*, 33(7), pp. 486–504.

Edemariam, A. (2018) 'Agoraphobia and an unhappy marriage: The real horror behind *The Haunting of Hill House*', *The Guardian*, 22 October. Available at: <https://www.theguardian.com/books/2018/oct/22/pure-fear-how-the-haunting-of-hill-house-opened-a-new-chapter-in-horror-netflix> (Accessed: 4 January 2023).

Egner, J. (2017) 'Michael Schur on *The Good Place*: Ted Danson and Kantian ethics', *New York Times*, 18 January. Available at: <https://www.nytimes.com/2017/01/18/arts/television/michael-schur-on-the-good-place-ted-danson-and-kantian-ethics.html> (Accessed: 4 January 2023).

—— (2020) '*The Good Place* finale finds the meaning of life: "Yep, nailed it"', *New York Times*, 28 January. Available at: <https://www.nytimes.com/2020/01/28/arts/television/the-good-place-michael-schur.html> (Accessed: 4 January 2023).

Elias, N. (2018) 'How the shows of 2018 reckoned with grief and nailed it', *Film School Rejects*. Available at: <https://filmschoolrejects.com/tv-shows-grief-2018> (Accessed: 4 January 2023).

Ellis, J. (1999) *Seeing Things: Television in the Age of Uncertainty*. London: I.B. Tauris.

—— (2012) *Documentary: Witness and Self-Revelation*. London and New York: Routledge.

Feldman, L. (2019) 'A note on *Dead to Me's* origins', *Glamour.com*, 7 May. Available at: <https://www.glamour.com/story/dead-to-me-netflix-liz-feldman> (Accessed: 4 January 2023).

Feller, M. (2019) 'Grief is messy and hard. These TV shows make it feel beautiful and real', *Elle.com*, 18 July. Available at: <https://www.elle.com/culture/movies-tv/a28377363/2019-tv-shows-about-grief-loss-death> (Accessed: 4 January 2023).

Felman, S. and Laub, D. (1992) *Testimony: Crises of Witnessing in Literature, Psychoanalysis, and History*. London and New York: Routledge.

Fishman, S. (2022) '*Archive 81* showrunner unpacks complex and terrifying first season', *TV Insider*, 17 January. Available at: <https://www.tvinsider.com/1028179/archive-81-season-1-finale-explained-season-2/> (Accessed: 1 September 2023).

Fiske, J. and Hartley, J. (1978) *Reading Television*. London: Methuen.

Foltyn, J. L. (2009) 'Dead sexy: Why death is the new sex', in S. Earle, C. Bartholomew and C. Komaromy (eds) *Making Sense of Death, Dying and Bereavement: An Anthology*. Maidenhead: Open University Press, pp. 47–51.

Freud, S. (1957 [1917]) 'Mourning and melancholia', in J. Strachey (ed. and trans.) *The Standard Edition of the Complete Psychological Works of Sigmund Freud: Volume 14 (1914–16) On the History of the Psychoanalytic Movement: Papers on Metapsychology and Other Works*. London: The Hogarth Press and the Institute of Psychoanalysis, pp. 243–58.

Frosh, S. (2013) *Hauntings: Psychoanalysis and Ghostly Transmissions*. Basingstoke: Palgrave Macmillan.

Fryers, M. (2015) 'There's always water – water that shouldn't be there. *Remember Me* (2014) and the haunted seascapes of British television', *CST Online*, 1 May. Available at: <http://cstonline.net/theres-always-water-water-that-shouldnt-be-there-remember-

me-2014-and-the-haunted-seascapes-of-british-television-by-mark-fryers> (Accessed: 4 January 2023).

Fulton, R. and Owen, G. (1987–8) 'Death and society in twentieth century America', *OMEGA: Journal of Death and Dying*, 18(4), pp. 379–95.

Fuss, D. (2013) *Dying Modern: A Meditation on Elegy*. Durham, NC: Duke University Press.

Garde-Hansen, J. (2011) *Media and Memory*. Edinburgh: Edinburgh University Press.

Garrett, G. (2015) *Entertaining Judgement: The Afterlife in Popular Imagination*. Oxford: Oxford University Press.

Gibbs, A. (2014) *Contemporary American Trauma Narratives*. Edinburgh: Edinburgh University Press.

Gibson, M. (2011) 'Death and community', in S. Conway (ed.) *Governing Death and Loss: Empowerment, Involvement, and Participation*. Oxford: Oxford University Press, pp. 15–25.

Gilbert, S. M. (2006) *Death's Door: Modern Dying and the Ways We Grieve*. London: W.W. Norton.

Giles, D. (2017) 'The immortalisation of celebrities', in M. Hviid Jacobsen (ed.) *Postmortal Society: Multidisciplinary Perspectives on Death, Survivalism and Immortality in Contemporary Culture*. London and New York: Routledge, pp. 97–113.

Gitelman, L. (2008) *Always Already New: Media, History and the Data of Culture*. Cambridge, MA: MIT Press.

Goblot, V. (2015) 'The television archive on BBC Four: From preservation to production', *View: Journal of European Television History and Culture*, 4 December. Available at: <https://viewjournal.eu/articles/10.18146/2213-0969.2015.jethc095> (Accessed: 4 January 2023).

Godwin, F. (1985) *Land*. London: Heinemann.

Gorer, G. (1955) 'The pornography of death', *Encounter*, 5, pp. 49–52.

Gorton, K. and Garde-Hansen, J. (2019) *Remembering British Television: Audience, Archive and Industry*. London: Bloomsbury.

Granek, L. (2017) 'Is grief a disease? The medicalisation of grief by the psy-disciplines in the twenty-first century', in N. Thompson and G. R. Cox (eds) *Handbook of the Sociology of Death, Grief and Bereavement*. London and New York: Routledge, pp. 264–77.

Greene, S. (2020) '*Upload* review: A forced futuristic rom-com that's more artificial than reality', *Indiewire*, 1 May. Available at: <https://www.indiewire.com/2020/05/upload-review-amazon-prime-video-comedy-1202227640> (Accessed: 4 January 2023).

Grindstaff, L. (2002) *The Money Shot: Trash, Class, and the Making of TV Talk Shows*. Chicago: University of Chicago Press.

Gripsrud, J. (2004) 'Broadcast television: The chances of its survival in a digital age', in L. Spigel and J. Olsson (eds) *Television after TV: Essays on a Medium in Transition*. Durham, NC: Duke University Press, pp. 210–23.

Gross, R. (2015) *Understanding Grief: An Introduction*. London and New York: Routledge.

Gunning, T. (2013) 'To scan a ghost: The ontology of mediated vision', in M. del Pilar Blanco and E. Peeren (eds) *The Spectralities Reader: Ghosts and Haunting in Contemporary Cultural Theory*. London: Bloomsbury, pp. 207–44.

Gunther, B. and Viney, R. (1994) *Seeing is Believing: Religion and Television in the 1990s*. London: John Libbey & Co.

Hadadi, R. (2022) 'Beneath the clichés, *Archive 81* is a slow-burning horror scorcher', *Vulture*, 12 January. Available at: <https://www.vulture.com/article/archive-81-netflix-series-review.html> (Accessed: 4 January 2023).

Halbwach, M. (2011) 'From *The Collective Memory*', in J. K. Olick, V. Vinitzky-Seroussi and D. Levy (eds) *The Collective Memory Reader*. Oxford: Oxford University Press, pp. 139–49.

Hamilton, I. (1975) 'Life after death', *Radio Times*, 27 March–2 June, pp. 11–14.

Hampson, R. (2017) 'Sites of death in some recent British fiction', *New Formations: A Journal of Culture/Theory/Politics*, 89–90, pp. 212–29.

Hancock, S. (2021) 'BBC has "lessons to learn" over coverage of Prince Philip's death, admits director-general', *The Independent*, 20 August. Available at: <https://www.independent.co.uk/arts-entertainment/tv/news/bbc-prince-philip-death-coverage-b1906268.html> (Accessed: 4 January 2023).

Heath, S. and Skirrow, G. (1977) 'Television: a world in action', *Screen*, 18(2), 7–59.

Henderson, J. (2019) *Documents of Ordinariness: Authority and Participation in the BBC Video Nation Project, 1994–2011*. Unpublished thesis. University College London.

Hendy, D. (2018) 'One of us? Opening doors', *BBC 100*. Available at: <https://www.bbc.com/historyofthebbc/100-voices/people-nation-empire/opening-doors> (Accessed: 4 January 2023).

Henley, J. (1995) 'John Henley talks to a widow with no regrets', *The Guardian*, 15 March, p. 8.

Hesmondhalgh, D. and Baker, S. (2008) 'Creative work and emotional labour in the television industry', *Theory, Culture and Society*, 25(7–8), pp. 97–118.

Hills, M. (2005) *The Pleasures of Horror*. London/New York: Continuum.

—— (2021) 'Streaming Netflix original horror: *Black Mirror, Stranger Things*, and datafied TV horror', in E. Falvey, J. Hickibottom and J. Wroot (eds) *New Blood: Critical Approaches to Contemporary Horror*. Cardiff: University of Wales Press, pp. 125–42.

Hinson, H. (2004) 'Plots that work in mysterious ways', *New York Times*, 28 March, p. 1.

Hirsch, J. (2004) *Afterimage: Film, Trauma and the Holocaust*. Philadelphia: Temple University Press.

Hobsbawm, E. (1987) *The Age of Empire 1875–1914*. New York: Pantheon Books.

Hodkinson, J. (2020) 'Returning again: Resurrection narratives and afterlife aesthetics in contemporary television drama', *Poetics Today*, 41(3), pp. 395–416.

Hodkinson, J. and Horstkotte, S. (2020) 'Introduction to the postsecular: From conceptual beginnings to cultural theory', *Poetics Today*, 41(3), pp. 317–26.

Holdsworth, A. (2011) *Television, Memory and Nostalgia*. Basingstoke: Palgrave Macmillan.

—— (2013) 'French and Saunders are a girl's best friend', unpublished paper presented at *Television for Women: An International Conference*, University of Warwick, 16 May.

—— (2021) *On Living With Television*. Durham, NC and London: Duke University Press.

Holdsworth, A. and Lury, K. (2016) 'Growing up and growing old with television: Peripheral viewers and the centrality of care', *Screen*, 57(2), pp. 184–96.

Holdsworth, A., Lury, K. and Tweed, H. (2020) *Discourses of Care: Media Practices and Cultures*. London and New York: Bloomsbury.

Holdsworth, A., Moseley, M. and Wheatley, H. (2019) 'Memory, nostalgia and the material heritage of children's television in the museum', *VIEW: Journal of European Television History and Culture*, 8(15), pp. 111–22.

hooks, b. (1994) 'Sorrowful black death is not a hot ticket', in K. Gateward and M. Pomerance (eds) *Sugar, Spice and Everything Nice: Cinemas of Girlhood*. Detroit: Wayne State University Press, pp. 91–102.

Horne, J. (2015) 'Screening the dying individual: Film, mortality and the ethics of spectatorship', in M. Blanco and R. Vidal (eds) *The Power of Death: Contemporary Reflections on Death in Western Society*. New York and Oxford: Berghahn Books, pp. 126–41.

Hoskins, A. (2010) 'New memory', in A. Brøgger and O. Kholeif (eds) *Vision, Media and Memory*. Liverpool: Liverpool University Press, pp. 72–82.

Hoskins, W. G. (1954) *The Making of the English Landscape*. London: Hodder and Stoughton.

Hudson, M. (2017) *Ghosts, Landscapes and Social Memory*. London and New York: Routledge.

Hughes, S. (2015) 'Good grief! Why has TV become so obsessed with bereavement?', *The Guardian*, 6 November. Available at: <http://www.theguardian.com/tv-and-radio/2015/nov/06/good-grief-why-tv-so-obsessed-with-bereavement-river-mr-robot-unforgotten-leftovers-returned> (Accessed: 4 January 2023).

Huppert, J. D. et al. (2005) 'The relationship between obsessive-compulsive and post-traumatic stress symptoms in clinical and non-clinical samples', *The Journal of Anxiety Disorders*, 19, pp. 127–36.

Hutchings, P. (2004) 'Uncanny landscapes in British film and television', *Visual Culture in Britain*, 5(2), pp. 27–40.

Huyssen, A. (1995) *Twilight Memories: Marking Time in a Culture of Amnesia*. London and New York: Routledge.

Irwin-Zarecka, I. (1994) *Frames of Remembrance: The Dynamics of Collective Memory*. New Brunswick and London: Transaction Publishers.

Jacobsen, M. H. (2016) '"Spectacular death" – Proposing a new fifth phase to Philippe Ariès's admirable history of death', *Humanities*, 5(2), 19.

Jessel, D. (2016) '*Proof* magazine: Salem comes to Salisbury', *The Justice Gap*, 19 January. Available at: <https://www.thejusticegap.com/salem-comes-to-salisbury> (Accessed: 4 January 2023).

Johnston, D. (2015) *Haunted Seasons: Television Ghost Stories for Christmas and Horror for Halloween*. Basingstoke: Palgrave Macmillan.

—— (2017) 'Ghosts and television', in S. Brewster and L. Thurston (eds) *The Routledge Handbook to the Ghost Story*. London and New York, Routledge, pp. 378–87.

Jowett, L. and Abbott, S. (2013) *TV Horror: Investigating the Darker Side of the Small Screen*. London: I.B. Tauris.

Kaplan, E. A. (2005) *Trauma Culture: The Politics of Terror and Loss in Media and Literature*. New Brunswick, NJ: Rutgers University Press.

Kearl, M. C. (1989) *Endings: A Sociology of Death and Dying*. Oxford: Oxford University Press.

Keller, D. J. (2020) '"A house is like a body": Processes of grief and trauma', in K. J. Wetmore Jr (ed.) *The Streaming of Hill House: Essays on the Haunting Netflix Adaptation.* Jefferson, NC: McFarland & Co., pp. 95–104.

Kelly, S. (2003) 'Dead bodies that matter: Toward a new ecology of human death in American culture', *Journal of American Culture*, 35(1), pp. 37–51.

Kennedy, L. (1995) 'Letter', *The Times*, 21 March, p. 17.

Kerekes, D. and Slater, D. (1993) *Killing for Culture: An Illustrated History of the Death Film from Mondo to Snuff.* London: Annihilation Press.

Kilborn, R. and Izod, J. (1997) *An Introduction to Television Documentary.* Manchester: Manchester University Press.

Kirk, N. (2017) '"I'm not in that thing you know . . . I'm remote. I'm in the cloud"', in C. M. Davison (ed.) *The Gothic and the Dead.* Manchester: Manchester University Press, pp. 218–32.

Kitzinger, J. (1999) 'The moving power of moving images: Television constructions of Princess Diana', in T. Walter (ed.) *The Mourning for Diana.* London: Bloomsbury Academic, pp. 65–76.

Knapskog, K. (2010) 'Archives in public service', *Critical Studies in Television*, 5(2), pp. 20–33.

Kornhaber, S. (2020) '*The Good Place* felt bad in the end', *The Atlantic*, 31 January. Available at: <https://www.theatlantic.com/culture/archive/2020/02/good-places-finale-made-heaven-look-hopeless/606001> (Accessed: 4 January 2023).

Köhne, J. B., Elm, M. and Kabalek, K. (2014) 'Introduction: The Horrors of Trauma in Cinema', in M. Elm, K. Kabalek and J. B. Köhne (eds) *The Horrors of Trauma in Cinema: Violence Void Visualization.* Newcastle Upon Tyne: Cambridge Scholars Press, pp. 1–30.

Kötting, A. (2020) 'B is for . . . Body' in A. Holdsworth, K. Lury and H. Tweed (eds) *Discourses of Care: Media Practices and Cultures.* New York and London: Bloomsbury, pp. 231–44.

Kübler-Ross, E. (1969) *On Death and Dying.* London and New York: Routledge.

Kübler-Ross E. and Kessler, D. (2014) *On Grief and Grieving: Finding the Meaning of Grief Through the Five Stages of Loss.* New York: Scribner.

Kuhn, A. (1995) *Family Secrets: Acts of Memory and Imagination.* London and New York: Verso.

Lacan, J. (1977) 'Desire and the interpretation of desire in *Hamlet*', *Yale French Studies*, 55/56, pp. 11–52.

Laderman, G. (2005) *Rest in Peace: A Cultural History of Death and the Funeral Home in Twentieth Century America.* Oxford: Oxford University Press.

Lambert, S. (1995) 'Another view: Filming the last taboo', *Independent*, 17 March. Available at: <https://www.independent.co.uk/voices/another-view-filming-the-last-taboo-1611573.html> (Accessed: 1 September 2023).

Landsberg, A. (2004) *Prosthetic Memory: The Transformation of American Remembrance in the Age of Mass Culture.* New York: Columbia University Press.

Laredo, J. A. (2020) 'Some things can't be told: Gothic trauma', in K. J. Wetmore Jr (ed.) *The Streaming of Hill House: Essays on the Haunting Netflix Adaptation.* Jefferson, NC: McFarland & Co., pp. 63–73.

Lavery, D. (2005) '"It's not television, it's magic realism": The mundane, the grotesque and the fantastic in *Six Feet Under*', in K. Akass and J. McCabe (eds) *Reading Six Feet Under: TV to Die For*. London: I.B. Tauris, pp. 19–33.

Ledbetter, M. (2012) 'Do not look at y/our own peril: Voyeurism as ethical necessity, or to see as a child again', in A. Grønstad and H. Gustafsson (eds) *Ethics and Images of Pain*. London and New York: Routledge, pp. 3–14.

Lim, B. C. (2009) *Translating Time: Cinema, the Fantastic and Temporal Critique*. Durham, NC and London: Duke University Press.

Link, A. (2020) 'Where the heart is', in K. J. Wetmore Jr (ed.) *The Streaming of Hill House: Essays on the Haunting Netflix Adaptation*. Jefferson, NC: McFarland & Co., pp. 118–27.

Little, J. M. (2015) 'Jill Meagher CCTV: Gothic tendencies in narratives of violence and gender justice', *Feminist Media Studies*, 15(3), pp. 397–410.

Livingstone, S. and Lunt, P. (1994) 'The mass media, democracy and the public sphere', in S. Livingstone and P. Lunt (eds) *Talk on Television: Audience Participation and Public Debate*. London: Routledge, pp. 9–35.

Loughlin, K. (2005) 'Spectacle and secrecy: Press coverage of conjoined twins in 1950s Britain', *Medical History*, 49(2), pp. 197–212.

Luckhurst, R. (2002) 'The contemporary London Gothic and the limits of the "spectral turn"', *Textual Practice*, 16(3), pp. 527–46.

—— (2008) *The Trauma Question*. London and New York: Routledge.

—— (2017) 'Why have the dead come back?: The instance of photography', *New Formations: A Journal of Culture/Theory/Politics*, 89–90, pp. 101–15.

Lyons, M. (2018) 'Tele-theology: God is again the co-star', *New York Times*, 16 September, p. 112.

McCort, J. R. (2020) 'Flipping Hill House: The Netflix renovation of Shirley Jackson's landmark novel', in J. E. Anderson and M. R. Anderson (eds) *Shirley Jackson and Domesticity: Beyond the Haunted House*. London and New York: Bloomsbury, pp. 223–42.

Macdonald, M. (2006) 'Performing memory on television: Documentary and the 1960s', *Screen*, 47(3), pp. 327–45.

McFarland, M. (2017) 'How-to-be-good TV: *The Good Place*', *Salon*, 9 December. Available at: <https://www.salon.com/2017/12/09/how-to-be-good-tv-the-good-place> (Accessed: 4 January 2023).

Macfarlane, R. (2012) *The Old Ways: A Journey on Foot*. London: Hamish Hamilton.

—— (2015) 'The eeriness of the English countryside', *The Guardian*, 10 April. Available at: <https://www.theguardian.com/books/2015/apr/10/eeriness-english-countryside-robert-macfarlane> (Accessed: 4 January 2023).

McIlwain, C. D. (2005) *When Death Goes Pop: Death, Media and the Remaking of Community*. Oxford: Peter Lang.

McInerney, F. (2014) 'Ladies' choice? Requested death in film', in N. Carpentier and L. van Brussel (eds) *The Social Construction of Death: Interdisciplinary Perspectives*. Basingstoke: Palgrave Macmillan, pp. 92–113.

McNally, R. J. (2004) 'Conceptual problems with the DSM-IV criteria for posttraumatic stress disorder', in G. M. Rosen (ed.) *Posttraumatic Stress Disorder: Issues and Controversies*. Chichester: John Wiley and Sons Ltd., pp. 1–14.

Magid, R. (2002) 'Family plots', *American Cinematographer*, November. Available at: <https://theasc.com/magazine/nov02/six/index.html> (Accessed: 4 January 2023).

Malkowski, J. (2017) *Dying in Full Detail: Mortality and Digital Documentary*. Durham, NC and London: Duke University Press.

Matheson, S. (1997) 'Televising Toronto: The construction of urban space in CITY-TV', *Spectator – The University of Southern California Journal of Film and Television*, 18(1), pp. 70–81.

May, T. (2009) *Death*. London and New York: Routledge.

—— (2020) '*The Good Place* asks "Are you the worst thing you've ever done?"', *New York Times*, 28 January. Available at: <https://www.nytimes.com/2020/01/09/opinion/good-place-season-4.html> (Accessed: 4 January 2023).

Mayer-Schönberger, V. (2009) *Delete: The Virtue of Forgetting in the Digital Age*. Princeton and Oxford: Princeton University Press.

Mayes, I. (1995) 'Near unbearable intimacy in near unthinkable situation', *The Guardian*, 16 March, p. 4.

Mayward, J. (2020) '*The Good Place* finds meaning in the end', *Christianity Today*, 3 February. Available at: <https://www.christianitytoday.com/ct/2020/february-web-only/good-place-tv-show-finale-afterlife-comedy-meaning-in-death.html> (Accessed: 4 January 2023).

Medhurst, A. (2016) 'English comedy as we know it died with Victoria Wood', *The Conversation*, 22 April. Available at: <https://theconversation.com/english-comedy-as-we-know-it-died-with-victoria-wood-58305> (Accessed: 4 January 2023).

Meek, A. (2016) 'Cultural trauma and the media', in Y. Ataria et al. (eds) *The Interdisciplinary Handbook of Trauma and Culture*. New York: Springer, pp. 27–37.

Mercer, J. and Shingler, M. (2004) *Melodrama: Genre, Style, Sensibility*. London and New York: Wallflower.

Merck, M. (2005) 'American Gothic: Undermining the uncanny', in K. Akass and J. McCabe (eds) *Reading Six Feet Under: TV to Die For*. London: I.B. Tauris, pp. 59–70.

Michael-Fox, B. P. (2019) *Present and Accounted For: Making Sense of Death and the Dead in Late Postmodern Culture*. Unpublished thesis. University of Winchester.

Millard, P. H. (1995) 'Public deaths, private doubts', *British Medical Journal*, 310, 18 March, pp. 746–7.

Miller, L. S. (2016) 'Tribeca: *Six Feet Under* creator Alan Ball reveals just how personal the HBO drama was for him', *Indiewire*, 19 April. Available at: <https://www.indiewire.com/2016/04/tribeca-six-feet-under-creator-alan-ball-reveals-just-how-personal-the-hbo-drama-was-for-him-289680> (Accessed: 4 January 2023).

Millerson, G. (1972) *The Technique of Television Production*. New York: Hastings House.

Mittell, J. (2006) 'Narrative complexity in contemporary American television', *Velvet Light Trap*, 58, Fall, pp. 29–40.

—— (2015) *Complex TV: The Poetics of Contemporary Television Storytelling*. New York and London: New York University Press.

Moran, J. (2013) *Armchair Nation: An Intimate History of Britain in Front of the TV*. London: Profile.

Mulvey, L. (2006) *Death 24x a Second: Stillness and the Moving Image*. London. Reaktion.

Munro, B. (2018) 'Everything is fine: Is *The Good Place* TV's best looking show?', *BBC Front Row Website*, 13 December. Available at: <https://www.bbc.co.uk/programmes/articles/bd5vThsRBN2lnsMxdVb7vp/everything-is-fine-is-the-good-place-tvs-best-looking-show> (Accessed: 4 January 2023).

Murray, K. A. (2016) 'The last laugh: Dark comedy on US television', in C. Bucaria and L. Barra (eds) *Taboo Comedy: Television and Controversial Humour*. Basingstoke: Palgrave Macmillan, pp. 41–59.

Naughton, J. (1995) 'Killing with kindness', *The Observer*, 19 March, p. 97.

Newcomb, H. M. and Hirsch, P. M. (1983) 'Television as cultural forum: Implications for research', *Quarterly Review of Film Studies*, 8(3), pp. 45–55.

Nichols, B. (1991) *Representing Reality*. Bloomington and Indianapolis: Indiana University Press.

Noonan, C. (2011) '"Big stuff in a beautiful way with interesting people": The spiritual discourse in UK religious television', *European Journal of Cultural Studies*, 14(6), pp. 727–46.

—— (2013) 'Piety and professionalism: The BBC's changing religious mission (1960–1979)', *Media History*, 19(2), pp. 196–212.

Noordegraaf, J. (2010) 'Who knows television? Online access and the gatekeepers of knowledge', *Critical Studies in Television*, 5(2), pp. 1–19.

Oakley, G. and Lee-Wright, P. (2016) 'Opening doors: The BBC's Community Programme Unit, 1973–2002', *History Workshop Journal*, 82(1), pp. 213–34.

O'Kane, M. (1995) 'When the hardest choice is death', *The Guardian*, 11 March, p. 25.

O'Neill, K. (2016) *Internet Afterlife: Virtual Salvation in the Twenty First Century*. Santa Barbara and Denver: Praeger Digital.

Paxton, B. (2018) *At Home with Grief: Continued Bonds with the Deceased*. London and New York: Routledge.

Pearson, A. (1995) 'Euthanasia: the video diary', *The Independent*, 19 March, p. 20.

Pearson, K. (2023) *'Always Nice to See Cov on Telly': Television, Placemaking, and UK Cities of Culture*. Unpublished thesis. University of Warwick.

Penfold-Mounce, R. (2018) *Death, The Dead and Popular Culture*. Bingley: Emerald.

Penfold-Mounce, R. and Smith, R. (2020) 'Resisting the grave: Value and the productive celebrity dead', in M. Hviid Jacobsen (ed.) *The Age of Spectacular Death*. London and New York: Routledge, pp. 36–51.

Piatti-Farnell, L. (2021) 'As raw as flesh: Consuming humans in TV horror', in L. Jowett and S. Abbott (eds) *Global TV Horror*. Cardiff: University of Wales Press, pp. 139–56.

Pinchevski, A. (2011) 'Archive. Media. Trauma.', in M. Neiger, O. Myers and E. Zandberg (eds) *On Media Memory: Collective Memory in the New Media Age*. Basingstoke: Palgrave Macmillan, pp. 253–64.

Pinedo, I. C. (1997) *Recreational Terror: Women and the Pleasures of Horror Film Viewing*. Albany, NY: SUNY Press.

Piper, H. (2016) 'Broadcast drama and the problem of television aesthetics: Home, nation, universe', *Screen*, 57(2), pp. 163–83.

Plunkett, J. (2016) 'Victoria Wood as seen on TV: From *Acorn Antiques* to *Let's Do It*', *The Guardian*, 20 April. Available at: <https://www.theguardian.com/media/2016/apr/20/victoria-wood-as-seen-on-tv-acorn-antiques-lets-do-it-clips> (Accessed: 4 January 2023).

Popular Memory Group (2011) 'From "Popular Memory: Theory, Politics, Method"', in J. K. Olick, V. Vinitzky-Seroussi and D. Levy (eds) *The Collective Memory Reader*. Oxford: Oxford University Press, pp. 254–60.

Potts, H. W. W. (2019) 'Caroline Deys', *British Medical Journal*, 367. Available at: <https://doi.org/10.1136/bmj.l5761> (Accessed: 4 January 2023).

Prelinger, R. (2021) 'Assembly over algorithm: Resisting overnarrativization', *World Records*, 5. Available at: <https://worldrecordsjournal.org/assembly-over-algorithm-resisting-overnarrativization> (Accessed 4 January 2023).

Pryluck, C. (2005) 'Ultimately we are all outsiders: The ethics of documentary filming', in A. Rosenthal and J. Corner (eds) *New Challenges for Documentary*. Manchester: Manchester University Press, pp. 194–208.

Reading, A. (2010) 'Mobile and static memories in Gypsy, Roma, and Traveller communities', unpublished paper presented at *Media, Memory and Gypsy, Roma and Traveller (GRT) Communities* symposium, University of Gloucestershire, 22 June.

Renov, M. (2004) *The Subject of Documentary*. Minneapolis and London: University of Minnesota Press.

Richards, N. (2013) 'Rosetta Life: Using film to create "bearable fictions" of people's experiences of life-limiting illness', in M. Aaron (ed.) *Envisaging Death: Visual Culture and Dying*. Newcastle Upon Tyne: Cambridge Scholars Publishing, pp. 190–204.

Riesman, A. J. (2016) 'The existence of Christine Chubbuck's suicide video has been confirmed', *Vulture*, 8 June. Available at: <https://www.vulture.com/2016/06/christine-chubbuck-suicide-video-exists.html> (Accessed: 4 January 2023).

Robson, M. (2019) 'Five shots, twice disappeared: Staging memory through the long take in the *Haunting of Hill House*', *Mise-en-scene*, 4(1), pp. 1–17.

Roe, M. (1995) 'House of Commons Debate: Euthanasia', *Hansard*, 19 April, 258, Col. 160. Available at: <https://hansard.parliament.uk/Commons/1995-04-19/debates/7465285f-6c2b-4701-a4ec-55bffb7ca419/Euthanasia> (Accessed: 4 January 2023).

Rothe, A. (2016) 'Irresponsible nonsense: An epistemological and ethical critique of postmodern trauma theory', in Y. Ataria et al. (eds) *The Interdisciplinary Handbook of Trauma and Culture*. New York: Springer, pp. 181–94.

Sartre, J. P. (1945) *Huis clos*. Paris: Gallimard.

Scannell, P. (2010) 'Television and history: Questioning the archive', *The Communication Review*, 13(1), pp. 37–51.

Schaefer, E. (1999) *'Bold! Daring! Shocking! True!' A History of Exploitation Films 1919–1959*. Durham, NC: Duke University Press.

Schiappa, E., Gregg, P. B. and Hewes, D. E. (2010) 'Can a television series change attitudes about death? A study of college students and *Six Feet Under*', *Death Studies*, 28(5), pp. 459–74.

Schultz, N. W. and Huet, L. M. (2001) 'Sensational! Violent! Popular! Death in American movies', *OMEGA: Journal of Death and Dying*, 42(2), pp. 137–49.

Sconce, J. (2000) *Haunted Media: Electronic Presence from Telegraphy to Television*. Durham, NC: Duke University Press.

Seale, C. (1998) *Constructing Death: The Sociology of Dying and Bereavement*. Cambridge: Cambridge University Press.

Shacklock, Z. (2017) *The Kinaesthetics of Serial Television*. Unpublished thesis. University of Warwick.

—— (2021) 'You are no longer just you: Netflix, *Sense8* and the evolution of television', in D. Shaw and R. Stone (eds) *Sense8: Transcending Television*, New York and London: Bloomsbury, pp. 41–56.

Sharkey, A. (1995) 'The doctor prescribes death', *The Independent*, 1 February, p. 1.

Shattuc, J. M. (1997) *The Talking Cure: TV Talk Shows and Women*. London and New York: Routledge.

Sile, A. (2020) 'Gestures of care in Briony Campbell's *The Dad Project*', in A. Holdsworth, K. Lury and H. Tweed (eds) *Discourses of Care: Media Practices and Cultures*. New York and London: Bloomsbury, pp. 38–57.

Smith, A. (2015) 'Jimmy Savile too big a demon for *Top of the Pops* to overcome', *The Scotsman*, 7 December. Available at: <https://www.scotsman.com/news/opinion/columnists/aidan-smith-jimmy-savile-too-big-demon-top-pops-overcome-1487657> (Accessed: 4 January 2023).

Smith, J. (2016) 'The Dame Janet Smith Review', *BBC Trust Website*. Available at: <http://www.bbc.co.uk/bbctrust/dame_janet_smith> (Accessed: 4 January 2023).

Snow, J. (2014) 'How Savile and Harris must have haunted their victims', *Channel 4 News Blog*, 1 July. Available at: <https://www.channel4.com/news/by/jon-snow/blogs/savile-harris-haunted-victims> (Accessed: 4 January 2023).

Sobchack, V. (1984) 'Inscribing ethical space: Ten propositions on death, representation, and documentary', *Quarterly Review of Film Studies*, 9(4), pp. 283–300.

Sontag, S. (1977) *On Photography*. London and New York: Penguin.

—— (2002) 'Looking at war: Photography's view of devastation and death', *The New Yorker*, 9 December. Available at: <https://www.newyorker.com/magazine/2002/12/09/looking-at-war> (Accessed 4 January 2023).

—— (2003) *Regarding the Pain of Others*. London: Hamish Hamilton.

Spigel, L. (1992) 'Introduction', in R. Williams, *Television: Technology and Cultural Form*. Hanover and London: University Press of New England and Wesleyan University Press, pp. ix–xxxvi.

—— (2010) 'Housing television: Architectures of the archive', *The Communication Review*, 13(1), pp. 52–74.

Stanley, A. (2003) 'And word was given unto the networks', *New York Times*, 22 September, p. 1.

Steinhart, E. (2017) 'Digital afterlives', in Y. Nagasawa and B. Matheson (eds) *The Palgrave Handbook of the Afterlife*. Basingstoke: Palgrave Macmillan, pp. 255–73.

Sterne, J. (2003) *The Audible Past: Cultural Origins of Sound Reproduction*. Durham, NC: Duke University Press.

Stoeckl, K., Rosati, M. and Holton, R. (2012) *Global Connections: Multiple Modernities and Postsecular Societies*. London and New York: Routledge.

Sturken, M. (1997) *Tangled Memories: The Vietnam War, the AIDS Epidemic and the Politics of Remembering*. Oakland, CA: University of California Press.

Sutcliffe, T. (1995) 'Taking pains to produce a tranquil end', *The Independent*, 16 March, p. 25.

Sutton, P. (2020) 'Care, illness and television spectatorship', in A. Holdsworth, K. Lury and

H. Tweed (eds) *Discourses of Care: Media Practices and Cultures*. New York and London: Bloomsbury, pp. 58–65.

Tait, S. (2006) 'Autopic vision and the necrophilic imaginary in *CSI*', *International Journal of Cultural Studies*, 9(1), pp. 45–62.

Tambling, J. (2001) *Becoming Posthumous: Life and Death in Literary and Culture Studies*. Edinburgh: Edinburgh University Press.

Tanner, L. E. (2006) *Lost Bodies: Inhabiting the Borders of Life and Death*. Ithaca and London: Cornell University Press.

Tate, G. (2022) 'Cheer up! There's lots to laugh about', *Radio Times*, 24 December–6 January, p. 47.

Thompson, N. (2017) 'Existentialism', in N. Thompson and G. R. Cox (eds) *Handbook of the Sociology of Death, Grief and Bereavement*. London and New York: Routledge, pp. 128–40.

Thomson, D. (1994) 'Death and its details', *Film Comment*, 29, September–October, pp. 12–18.

Todorov, T. (1975) *The Fantastic: A Structural Approach to a Literary Genre*. Ithaca, NY: Cornell University Press.

Turner, G. (2009) 'Television and the nation: Does this matter anymore?', in G. Turner and J. Tay (eds) *Television Studies after TV: Understanding Television in the Post-Broadcast Era*. London and New York: Routledge, pp. 54–64.

Turnock, R. (2000) *Interpreting Diana: Television Audiences and the Death of a Princess*. London: British Film Institute.

—— (2005) 'Death, liminality and transformation in *Six Feet Under*', in K. Akass and J. McCabe (eds) *Reading Six Feet Under: TV to Die For*. London: I.B. Tauris, pp. 39–49.

Twycross, R. et al. (1995) 'Letter', *The Times*, 16 March, p. 17.

VanArendonk, K. (2020) '*Upload* is bleak as hell', *Vulture*, 7 May. Available at: <https://www.vulture.com/2020/05/upload-amazon-review.html> (Accessed: 1 September 2023).

Van Brussel, L. (2014) 'A discourse-theoretical approach to death and dying', in N. Carpentier and L. van Brussel (eds) *The Social Construction of Death: Interdisciplinary Perspectives*. Basingstoke: Palgrave Macmillan, pp. 13–33.

VanderBurgh, J. (2019) 'Grounding TV's material heritage: Place-based projects that value or vilify amateur videocassette recordings of television', *VIEW Journal of European Television History and Culture*, 8(15), pp. 59–78.

VanDerWerff, E. (2016) 'TV is killing off so many characters that death is losing its punch', *Vox*, 1 June. Available at: <https://www.vox.com/2016/6/1/11669730/tv-deaths-character-best> (Accessed: 4 January 2023).

VanDerWerff, E., Wilkinson, A. and Matthews, D. (2020) '*The Good Place* was groundbreaking TV. Did it's finale measure up?' *Vox*, 31 January. Available at: <https://www.vox.com/culture/2020/1/31/21116261/the-good-place-series-finale-recap-whenever-youre-ready-season-4-door> (Accessed: 4 January 2023).

Van House, N. and Churchill, E. F. (2008) 'Technologies of memory: Key issues and critical perspectives', *Memory Studies*, 1(3), pp. 295–310.

Villarejo, A. (2014) *Ethereal Queer: Television, Historicity, Desire*. Durham, NC: Duke University Press.

Viney, R. (1999) 'Religious broadcasting on UK television: Policy, public perception and programmes', *Cultural Trends*, 9(36), pp. 1–28.
Walker, M. (2017) *Modern Ghost Melodramas: 'What Lies Beneath'*. Amsterdam: Amsterdam University Press.
Walter, T. (1994) *The Revival of Death*. London and New York: Routledge.
—— (2009) 'Jade's dying body: The ultimate reality show', *Sociological Research Online*, 14(5), pp. 105–15.
Waterson, J. (2021) 'BBC's Prince Philip coverage breaks UK TV complaints record', *The Guardian*, 12 April. Available at: <https://www.theguardian.com/media/2021/apr/12/bbcs-prince-philip-coverage-breaks-uk-tv-complaints-record> (Accessed: 4 January 2023).
Watson, J. C. and Arp, R. (2011) *What's Good on TV? Understanding Ethics through Television*. Chichester: Wiley-Blackwell.
Weatherhead, L. (1965) *The Christian Agnostic*. Abingdon/Nashville: Festival Books.
Weber, T. (2011) *Drop Dead Gorgeous: Representations of Corpses in American TV Shows*. Frankfurt: Campus Verlag.
Weinstock, J. A. (2004) 'Introduction: The spectral turn', in J. A. Weinstock (ed.) *Spectral America: Phantoms and the National Imagination*. Madison: University of Wisconsin Press, pp. 3–17.
Weissmann, E. (2007) 'The victim's suffering translated: *CSI: Crime Scene Investigation* and the crime genre', in *Intensities: The Journal of Cult Media*, 4. Available at: <https://intensitiescultmedia.files.wordpress.com/2012/12/weissmann-victims-suffering-translated.pdf> (Accessed: 4 January 2023).
Wheatley, H. (2006) *Gothic Television*. Manchester: Manchester University Press.
—— (2007) 'Introduction: Re-viewing television histories', in H. Wheatley (ed.) *Re-Viewing Television History: Critical Issues in Television Historiography*. London: I.B. Tauris, pp. 1–12.
—— (2012) 'Uncanny children, haunted houses, hidden rooms: Children's Gothic television in the 1970s and 80s', *Visual Culture in Britain*, 13(3), pp. 383–97.
—— (2016) *Spectacular Television: Exploring Televisual Pleasure*. London: I.B. Tauris.
—— (2020a) 'Haunted television: Trauma and the specter in the archive', *Journal of Cinema and Media Studies*, 59(3), pp. 69–89.
—— (2020b) 'Signs of care: Assisted suicide on television', in A. Holdsworth, K. Lury and H. Tweed (eds) *Discourses of Care: Media Practices and Cultures*. New York and London: Bloomsbury, pp. 21–37.
Whiston Spir, A. (1998) *The Language of Landscape*. New Haven and London: Yale University Press.
White, M. (1992) *Tele-Advising: Therapeutic Discourse in American Television*. Chapel Hill and London: University of North Carolina Press.
—— (1999) 'Television liveness: History, banality, attractions', *Spectator*, 20(1), pp. 39–56.
Wijfjes, H. B. M., Blom, J. C. H. and Wieten J. (eds) (1996) *Van geloof, hoop en liefde: Vijftig jaar interkerkelijke omroep in Nederland 1946–1996*. Kampen/Hilversum: Kok/IKON.
Wilson, E. (2012) *Love, Mortality and the Moving Image*. Basingstoke: Palgrave Macmillan.
Wilson, J. (2003) *Abortion, reproductive technology, and euthanasia: Post-concolliar responses*

from within the Roman Catholic Church in England and Wales 1965–2000. Unpublished thesis. Durham University.

Winston, B. (2000) *Lies, Damn Lies and Documentaries.* London: BFI Publishing.

—— (2005) 'Ethics', in A. Rosenthal and J. Corner (eds) *New Challenges for Documentary.* Manchester: Manchester University Press, pp. 181–93.

Wood, H. (2009) *Talking with Television: Women, Talk Shows, and Modern Self-Reflexivity.* Urbana: University of Illinois Press.

Wright, J. C., Kunkel, D., Pinon, M. and Huston, A. C. (1989) 'How children reacted to televised coverage of the space shuttle disaster', *Journal of Communication*, 39(2), pp. 27–45.

Wyver, J. (2017) 'Imagine a library . . .', *Illuminations Blog*, 22 February. Available at: <https://www.illuminationsmedia.co.uk/imagine> (Accessed: 4 January 2023).

Zelizer, B. (2010) *About to Die: How News Images Move the Public.* Oxford: Oxford University Press.

Index

Aaron, M., 29, 35, 40, 79, 81, 99, 133, 139–40, 148–9, 260n
abjection, 101, 103–7, 171
Abbott, S., 133, 161, 166, 175
About Religion, 36, 259n
abuse, 21, 164, 181, 195, 204–20, 264n
Abused: The Untold Story, 212–14
Acts of Faith: Filmmakers in Coventry Cathedral, 229
Admiraal, P., 72
Adorno, T., 195
advice programming, 50
afterlife, 15, 18–19, 22–3, 30, 91, 95–6, 102–3, 107–29, 184, 187, 189, 195–6, 220–1, 221, 257, 259n, 262n
Against Legalised Euthanasia – Research and Teaching (ALERT campaign), 74
AIDS/HIV, 30, 53, 258–9n
Akass, K., 102–3
Albano, C., 217, 253
Albrecht, C., 102, 262n
Alighieri, D., 263n
Allen, B., 123
Alldin, J., 38
American Academy of Pediatrics, 98
A Monster Calls, 158
An Act of Faith (aka *Coventry Cathedral*), 228–9, 237, 239
Ang, I., 19, 136
angels, 113–14, 118, 120, 198
Annan Committee, 36–7
Antiques Road Trip, 263n
Appleyard, B., 75–6
Arav, D., 205
archives, 3–5, 13–15, 20–3, 25, 30–1, 44, 65, 68, 91, 146, 178, 184, 187–9, 192–257, 264n
as mausoleum, 21, 194–6, 223–4
Archive 81, 20, 153, 165, 174–83
Arena, 228
Ariès, P., 29–30, 100
Armchair Theatre, 2
Armitt, L., 156, 159

arts programming, 228–9, 232, 244, 257
A Short Stay in Switzerland, 66
assisted dying, 5–7, 17–18, 30, 33, 53, 61, 66–91
Assisted Dying Bill (2015), 66
Astaire, F., 193
A Suitable Case for Killing, 72–3, 261n
A Time to Live, 16–7, 64–5
Atkins, W., 159
Atkinson, N., 159
ATV Today, 222–3, 247–8
Austerlitz, S., 131–2, 262n
Aust, R., 205–6, 210, 212
Austin, G., 75
autopathography, 16–7, 31–2, 40–68, 73–91
Azoulay, A., 100–1

Baer, U., 167
Bailey, P., 218
Baker, S., 86
Ball, A., 108, 131
Ballard, J.G., 262n
bardic television, 33, 59
Bargain Hunt, 13
Barnard, P., 75
Barnet, M., 261n
Barthes, R., 20, 35, 190–1, 194
Baudrillard, J., 233
Bazin, A., 4, 20, 122,190–1
BBC Archive 14–15, 30–1, 44, 187–9, 198–201, 205–6, 210, 212, 214, 218–21, 225–9, 238, 248–9, 256, 264n
BBC Community Programme Unit, 16–17, 29, 34, 51–4, 68, 71–2
BBC iPlayer 13, 247
Beatles, 246
Before I Die, 53, 55
Belsey, A., 80
Bennett, A., 109, 113, 115, 125, 262n
Bergson, H., 230
Best of British: Victoria Wood, 264n
Betjeman, J., 37

Index   285

Bezos, J., 125
Big Little Lies, 130
Binner, S., 81–6, 88–90
Bishop, D., 116
Black Mirror, 123, 262n
Bloom, A., 38, 260n
Boddy, L., 244, 247
body horror, 101–2
Body in Question, The, 259n
Boltansky, L., 147
Bourne, S., 64–5
Bowes, M., 244–5
Bowring, J., 158, 162
Box of Broadcasts, 91
Boyle, K., 214, 219, 264n
Brady, I., 159
Bramesco, C., 120
Brass Tacks, 259n
Braun, E., 217
Brennan, Mhairi, 14–15
Brennan, Michael, 31, 40, 43, 47, 84–5, 201
Breslin, J., 38
Bridge, T., 38
Briggs, A., 238, 243
Bright, P., 38
British Association of Cancer United Patients, 38
Broad Street Community Centre, 229
Bronfen, E., 60–1, 132
Brooker, C., 209, 264n
Brunsdon, C., 233–4
Brown, C. G., 35–6
Brown, L. S., 213
Brown, S., 214, 217–18
Buckman, R., 55–6
Buddhism, 39, 111, 114, 128
Build a New Life in the Country, 199
Buonnano, M., 90–1

Cadava, E., 190–1
Caldwell, J. T., 101–2, 104
Cameron, J., 41
Campbell, B., 261n
cancer, 9, 17, 38, 42–50, 53, 56, 81, 187, 201, 258–9n
care, 17–18, 31, 39–40, 52, 54–5, 62, 64, 67–74, 76–81, 85–91, 189, 198, 258n
Caruth, C., 153, 167–8, 172, 180
Catholicism, 69–70, 75, 261n
Caughie, J., 57
Causse, M., 79
Celebration, 228, 237
Central Religious Advisory Committee, 36–8, 259n
Ceremony and the Citizen, 259n
Challenger disaster, 2, 258n
Chapman, J., 41
Chapman, S., 53
Charcot, J., 138

Charles, E., 264n
Charlie Brooker's 2012 Wipe, 264n
Chemistry of (Almost Everything), The, 259
Childline, 215
children, 2, 7, 11, 25, 37, 42–4, 46–9, 51–4, 56, 62, 81, 97–8, 127, 134. 137–8, 143–4, 155, 161–2, 164, 168–71, 173–4, 176, 180–1, 187–8, 198, 203–5, 212, 215–17, 221–2, 224, 232, 242, 257, 258n
children's television, 25, 37, 138, 203, 232, 242, 257
Chilton, L., 103
Choices, 38–40
Christianity, 36–8, 69–70, 75, 108, 111–15, 120, 122, 126; *see also* Catholicism
Christie, I., 191
Christine, 258n
Chubbuck, C., 2–3, 4–5
Churchill, E. F., 249
cinema, 4, 41, 79, 126, 133, 147, 152, 156, 168, 172, 191–2, 196–8, 204, 209, 231, 233, 235; *see also* film
cities, 21–2, 154, 171, 175, 182, 221, 222–9, 231–57
civic television, 21–2, 225, 227, 235, 239, 241–2, 244–5, 251–2, 256–7
Clark, B., 71
Clark Dilman, J., 18
Clayton, J., 176
Clement Jones, V., 38
Clifford, M., 264n
Colebrook, L., 260n
Colley, R., 42
Coltraine, R., 16
comedy, 1–2, 15–16, 18, 95–6, 110–30, 137, 201–3, 209, 256
community, 7–8, 9–12, 22, 25, 32–3, 35, 40, 47–8, 51–2, 59, 61–5, 97, 132, 146–50, 162, 249, 255
Connew, P., 207
consent, 33–4, 78–80
consumer programming, 50
Cooper, T., 1–2, 4, 15–16
Corbett, J. P., 260n
Corner, J., 225
Coronation Street, 9–12, 66, 199, 258n
Correspondent, 259n
Cosby, B., 219
Counterblast, 72
Couples Come Dine with Me, 199
Courtney, M., 229, 264n
Coventry Cathedral, 226, 228–9, 237–9, 244, 246–7, 264n
Coventry Cathedral: Building for a New Britain, 228, 238, 246
Coventry Kids: People of a Restless City, 228, 244, 247
Coventry Society, 229, 234
Coventry Theatre, 246
Coventry Trades Union Council, 228, 234, 250, 253
Coventry Works, 229, 237

Covid-19 pandemic, 19, 131–2, 149
Crime and Punishment, 259n
Crime and Punishment Open Space, 259n
crowdsourcing, 239–40
CSI: Crime Scene Investigation, 101
cultural forum, 29, 33, 35, 39, 61, 68, 70, 90–1, 132
Cunningham, S., 227
Currie, C., 71–2
current affairs television, 8, 17, 30, 41, 50, 53, 55, 59, 70, 205, 208–9, 232, 250, 257
Curtis, B., 155, 164

Dallas, 136
Dando, J., 55, 260n
Daniel, A., 167
Daniels, G., 123
Davies, D. J., 32, 122, 191
Davis, C., 220
Davis, M., 120
Davis, T., 198, 201
daytime television, 13, 29, 50, 199
Deacon, R. 80, 83, 86–91, 210–11, 261n
Deacy, C., 98, 110–11, 113, 126
Dead Like Me, 110, 118–20
Dead to Me, 19, 130, 133, 136–7, 141, 145–9
death denial thesis, 18, 98–9, 262n
death education, 5, 8–9, 17, 25, 31, 40, 46–8, 61–2, 64–6, 72, 90–1, 95–6, 125–6, 132, 139–40, 147
death film, 4
Death on the Street, 11–12
death penalty, 30
Death Scenes, 4
Death Today, 56–60
Deathwatch, 259n
debate programmes, 35–7, 40, 66, 69–73, 76, 90, 259n, 261n
DeGroot, J. M., 11
del Pilar Blanco, M., 19, 151, 154, 162, 165, 203
Demir, S., 233
Dempsey, D., 48
Denison, R., 101–2
Depp, J., 264n
Derrida, J., 192, 203, 245
Diamond, A., 55
Diana, Princess of Wales, 197–200
Dibnah, F., 56
Dickinson, G. E., 131, 149
Dignitas – la mort sur ordannance, 17–18, 67, 79–80
Dilman, J. C., 18, 97, 100, 131
Dinnerladies, 263n
Direct Cinema, 41
Disneyland, 116
documentary, 5–8, 11–12, 14, 16–8, 23, 29, 30–5, 40–68, 70–91, 95, 187–90, 194–5, 197, 199–221, 228–9, 232–3, 237–9, 244, 246, 258–61n, 263–4n

Dodds, N., 62
Doka, K. J., 54, 140–1
Dollimore, J., 99
Donnellan, P., 244
Dood op Verzoek (Death on Request) 17, 73–8, 81, 89–90, 258n, 261n
Downing, L., 35, 78–9, 147
dramedy, 8, 18, 95, 110–29, 137
Drewery, J., 261n
D'Rozario, D., 193–4
Dux, L., 212
Dwyer, G. P., 69–70
Dying, 48–50

East, 259n
Eastenders, 66, 200
Edemariam, A., 169
Edgar, S., 229, 264n
Edwards, S., 210
Egner, J., 113, 126
Einaudi, L., 63
Elias, N., 132, 262n
Ellington, D., 228, 237
Ellis, J., 34, 55, 82, 194
Elm, M., 172, 209
Emmerdale, 66
emotional realism, 19–20, 25, 136–9, 141, 150, 166–7
empathy, 46, 50, 76, 88, 171, 189
Esther, 55, 260n
ethics, 8, 17–18, 23, 30, 33–5, 39, 66–7, 73, 78–80, 113, 126–7, 147, 189, 203, 255, 258n
ethnography, 239–40
Europa, 50, 260n
Europeans, 50
Euthanasia Society, 69–70
Everyman, 68, 71, 259n
Execution, 259n
existentialism, 53, 108, 119, 126–7, 149
Exposure: The Other Side of Jimmy Savile, 205, 212, 215
extinction, 25, 149
Exton, L., 213

Facebook 123, 145–6
Faces of Death, 4
Feldman, L., 136
Feller, M., 131, 136
Felma, S., 214
Fieger, G., 71
Fighting Back, 259n
film, 1, 3–4, 6, 15, 34–5, 40–1, 45, 48–9, 66, 78–9, 81, 85–6, 98, 109, 111, 113, 121, 130, 133, 138, 147–9, 153, 158, 163, 167, 172, 174, 176–9, 183, 189–94, 196–7, 204, 207, 209–10, 214, 218, 227–31, 233, 237–9, 253–4, 260n; *see also* cinema
Fine Cut, 259n

Finlay, I., 72
Fishman, S., 176
Fiske, J., 33, 59
Flanagan, M., 167–8, 263n
flaneur, 234
flashbacks, 127, 134–5, 145–6, 162–4, 167, 170–5, 179–81, 198
flow, 2, 23, 91, 193, 204–5, 209–10, 260n
Foleshill Women's Training (FWT), 234, 236, 252
Foltyn, J. L. 98, 100–1, 262n
forensic drama, 101
Forever, 18–19, 96, 109, 115–18, 120–2, 126–8, 262n
40 Minutes, 259n
found footage, 183–4
Four Corners: My Own Choice, 17–18, 67, 91
Fourteen Days in May, 259n
Francis, D., 51
Freud, S., 140, 154, 160, 162, 168, 180, 215
Friends of Coventry Cathedral, 228
Frosh, S., 207, 209
Fry, T., 72
Fryers, M., 159
Fulton, A., 38
Fulton, R., 54, 135–6
funerals, 9–14, 50, 55–61, 81–2, 102, 104, 106, 128, 174, 200–1, 208, 213, 258n
Funny Women: Victoria Wood, 202
Fuss, D., 191

Gabriel, P., 63
Game of Thrones, 96–7, 261n
Garde-Hansen, J., 197, 230–1, 235, 249, 264n
Garland, J., 137, 262n
Garrett, G., 108–10, 112–13, 118
General Electric Company, 239
General Medical Council, 260n
ghost dramas, 19–20, 110, 132–3, 151–84, 203, 218
ghosts *see* haunting
Ghost Town project, 21–2, 221, 225–9, 232–57, 264n
Gibbs, A., 153–4, 168
Gibson, J., 51
Gibson, M., 146, 196
GIFs, 195
Gilbert, S. M., 85, 145, 190, 204
Giles, D., 193
Gillard, F., 260n
Gitelman, L., 231
Glory that Remains, The, 259n
Goblot, V., 255
Godwin, F., 159, 263n
Gogglebox, 200
Good Place, The, 18–19, 96, 109, 111–20, 122, 125–8, 262n
Goody, J., 31, 201
Gorer, G., 100, 262n
Gorton, K., 235

Gothic, 20, 24, 59, 121, 157, 165, 181–2
Grand National, 25
Granek, L., 148
Gray, A., 22
Gray, M., 155
Gregg, P. B., 98, 103–4
Greene, S., 110
Grevelink, M., 72–3
grief, 8, 10–12, 18–20, 22, 25, 29, 45, 49, 53–6, 58–61, 64, 81, 86, 88–9, 96, 102–3, 107, 110, 130–50, 152, 157–71, 173–4, 179–82, 188, 197–8, 200, 203, 215, 262n
parasocial, 11–12
Grindstaff, L., 86
Gripsrud, J., 90
Gross, R., 147
Grout, J., 38
Gunning, T., 152, 160, 208
Gunther, B., 40
Gypsy community, 249

Hadadi, R., 180
Halbwach, M., 230
Hall, S., 60
Hamilton, I., 43–4
Hampson, R., 101
Hardy, T., 157
Harris, R., 212, 264n
Harrison, T., 60
Hart, D., 59
Hartley, J., 33, 59
Hartstra, A., 50
haunting, 19–21, 103, 122–3, 151–84, 189–90, 192–5, 203–10, 212–21, 224–5, 228–9, 233, 244–5, 247, 252–3, 263–4n
Haunting of Bly Manor, 263n
Haunting of Hill House, The, 20, 153, 165, 167–75, 179–80, 263n
Haworth, D., 56–7
Heart of the Matter, 259n
Heath, S., 8, 32–3, 64
heaven, 108, 112–16, 118, 120, 122, 125, 263n
hell, 112–16, 118, 120, 122, 262n, 263n
Henderson, J., 51, 71, 261n
Hepburn, A., 193–4
Herbert Art Gallery and Museum, 228, 242
Here and Now, 259n
Hesmondhalgh, D., 86
Hewes, D. E., 98, 103–4
Hills, M., 165–6
Hindley, M., 159
Hinduism, 36, 111
Hinson, H., 113
Hirsch, J., 179, 254
Hirsch, P., 33, 39, 90
Hitchens, C., 31, 201, 259n

Hitler, A., 217
Hobsbawn, E., 230
Hodkinson, J., 110, 112, 114
Hoffman, D., 264n
Hoggart, R., 37
Holdsworth, Amy, 45, 55, 67–8, 188, 195–6, 201, 205–6, 210, 212, 242, 261n
Holdsworth, Angela, 41
Hollywood Angel, 259n
Holton, R., 112
home shopping, 4
home movies, 85, 145–6, 204, 217, 227, 239, 248
home recording technologies, 3–5, 21, 43–4, 145–6, 174–5, 177, 187, 189, 191–4, 223–4, 243, 260n
Honderich, T., 39
hooks, b., 95, 130, 133
Horizon, 48, 259n
Horne, J., 41, 61
horror, 8, 101–2, 105–7, 116, 119, 133, 138, 144, 153, 156, 165–6, 182–3, 205–8, 218–19, 261–2n
Hoskins, A., 227, 231
Horstkotte, S., 112
Hoskins, W. G., 156
Hostel of God (Clapham), 41
How to Die in Oregon, 67
How to Die: Simon's Choice, 17–18, 67, 80–90
Hudson, M., 20, 152, 154–5, 159, 162, 165, 181–2
Huet, L. M., 130
Hughes, G., 158–9
Hughes, S., 131, 149
Humanist Society, 50
Human Rights, Human Wrongs, 259n
Humans at Work, 229, 237, 239
Huppert, J. D., 163, 264n
Huston, A. C., 258
Hutchings, P., 156–7
Huxley, F., 260n
Huyssen, A., 232
hyper presence of death, 18, 95, 97–9, 262n

I have faith in all you blues, 229, 264n
Immortalists, The, 259n
In Loving Memory, 60
Innocents, The, 176, 263n
In Search of the Dead, 259n
Inside Story, 259n
In the Flesh, 158
In the Midst of Life, 57, 59–60
intimacy, 5–8, 17, 25, 33, 41–2, 45–6, 48–50, 52–3, 62–5, 74, 76–9, 85–6, 100, 166, 230, 241, 261n
Irwin-Zarecka, I., 206–7, 210, 219
Islam, 36, 111, 252
Is There Something After Death?, 259n
Izod, J., 52

Jack, N., 261n
Jackson, S., 168
Jacobsen, M. H., 100
Jancovich, M., 101–2
James, H., 263n
James, J., 70
Jaywalking, 259n
Jessel, D., 206
Jim'll Fix It, 204, 218
Jimmy Savile: A British Horror Story, 207–8, 214–15
Jimmy Savile: Britain's Worst Crimes, 207–8
Johnston, D., 165–6, 177, 263n
Jones, G., 2
Journey, The, 259n
Judaism, 111

Kabalek, K., 172, 209–10
Kaleidoscope, 225, 228
Kaplan, E. A., 214–15
Kate Plays Christine, 258n
Kearl, M. C., 98
Kempton, L., 87
Kennedy, L., 72, 74, 261n
Kessler, D., 140
Kettlety, C., 52
Kevorkian, J. 71
Kidding, 19, 130, 137–9, 145, 149
Kilborn, R., 52
kinaesthesia, 77, 161, 163, 171, 261n
Kirk, N., 262n
Kitzinger, J., 198
Knapskog, K., 227, 239
Köhne, J. B., 172, 209–10
Koko Centre, 228
Koole, T., 50
Kornhaber, S., 128
Kötting, A., 261n
Kübler-Ross, E., 19, 54, 140–1
Kuhn, A., 227, 231, 254
Kunkel, D., 258n

Laderman, G., 18
Lambert, S., 74, 76
Landsberg, A., 230–1, 255
landscape, 19–20, 60, 118, 151–65, 167, 182
Laredo, J. A., 167, 169, 173
Late Show, The, 76, 90
Laub, D., 214
Lavery, D., 104, 108
League of Gentlemen, The, 158
Ledbetter, M., 35
Leeder, M., 176
Lee Flanagan II, V., 3
Leftovers, The, 19, 130, 141–2, 146, 149, 262n
Leith, A. P., 11
Leibovitz, A., 45

Index   289

Lester, C., 264n
Let's Do It: A Tribute to Victoria Wood, 202
Lewis, M., 50
Lewis, W., 262n
Lifeline, 38, 69–70, 260n
light entertainment, 1–2, 4
Lightfields, 20, 152, 154–5, 157, 162–3
Lim, B. C., 168
Link, A., 263n
Little, J. M., 216
Louis Theroux: Savile, 215–17, 264n
Lumière brothers, 191
Live from Her Majesty's, 1–2, 16
Live from Two, 187–9
liveness, 1–5, 13, 55, 72, 20–1, 187–9, 192–4, 197–8, 199, 210, 258n
Living and the Dead, The, 20, 152, 155–7, 161–2, 164, 262–3n
Livingstone, S., 39
Living with Dying, 50
Long, B., 53
long duration, 11–12, 19
Looking for an Answer, 259n
Looking for Dad, 88
Lost, 110
Loughlin, K., 260n
Luckhurst, R., 97, 153–4, 156, 167, 172, 181
Lunt, P., 39
Lury, K., 55, 67–8, 261n
Lynch, D., 167
Lyons, J., 110, 118

McAuliffe, C., 2, 4
McCabe, J., 102–3
MacDonald, C. K., 69–70
MacDonald, M., 233
McFarland, M., 113, 126
MacFarlane, R., 156–7
McIlwain, C. D., 7–8, 18, 99, 111, 126, 149
McInerney, F., 66
McNally, R. J., 172
McRanor, P., 245
Mad Men, 116
magazine programmes, 36
Malikowski, J., 48–9, 99
Man Alive, 41, 48, 68, 70
Man Alive Report, The, 259n
Marchlands, 20, 152, 154–5, 157, 160–1, 163–4
Marianne, 263n
Marshall, R., 87–8
Martys, P., 42
Martys, T., 41–2
MasterChef, 200
MastersFX, 105, 262n
Matheson, S., 234
Matters of Life and Death, 259n

May, T., 122, 127–8
Mayer-Schönberger, V., 220, 251, 253
Mayes, I., 76
Mayward, J., 122
Meagher, J., 216
Measure of Conscience, 259n
Medhurst, A., 30, 202–3
Media Archive for Central England (MACE), 223–6, 228–9, 237, 247, 264n
Medical Ethics: A Matter of Life and Death, 259n
Meek, A., 214, 254
Meeting Point, 38, 259n
melancholia, 140, 144, 149, 158–62, 164, 245
Melinsky, H., 261n
melodrama, 62–3, 136, 153
memento mori, 43–4, 46, 52, 82, 89
memorialisation, 21, 43–5, 84, 123, 132, 191, 195–203, 210, 247–8
memory, 43–5, 146, 151–4, 158, 162–3, 167–83, 187, 204–20, 227, 230–57
    collective, 206–7, 219, 230–1, 241, 243, 249
    explosions, 241–5
    prosthetic, 230, 255
    work, 231–2, 236–7
Mercer, J., 153
Merck, M., 103
Michael-Fox, B., 99, 110, 122, 126, 194, 262n
Millard, P., 75
Millarini, L., 199
Miller, L. S., 131
Miller, T., 159
Millerson, G. 32
Miracle Workers, 18–19, 96, 109, 118, 120
Mitchell, W., 229
Mittell, J., 12, 133, 167
Modern Times, 17, 74, 76
mondo film, 4
Monroe, M., 193
Moran, J., 241
Moseley, R., 242, 264n
motor neurone disease, 6, 17, 63, 74, 81, 90
mourning, 14, 19–21, 45, 54–7, 103, 130–3, 140–50, 152, 160–84, 190, 195–8, 201–2, 208–9, 215, 224
Mulvey, L., 15, 20–1, 189–91, 193, 196–7, 230–1
Munro, A., 62
murder, 3
Murgatroyd, A. 42, 45, 47
Murray, K. A., 98, 110, 137
museums, 195–6, 226, 228, 231, 242, 255–6, 264n
music programming, 229, 232
My Last Summer, 16–7, 61–4

Napley, D., 261n
narrative complexity, 12, 19, 133–5, 145, 152, 154, 167, 172–3

National Catholic Welfare Conference News Service, 70
National Institute of Mental Health, 98
National Science and Media Museum, 196, 242, 264n
National Society for the Prevention of Cruelty to Children, 212–13
Natural World, 263n
Naughton, J., 76
Nederhost, M., 74
Negative Space, 196
Network, 42
Neuberger, J., 38–9
Newcomb, H., 33, 39, 90–1
news, 2–4, 13–15, 50, 53, 66, 70, 98, 183, 193, 196–202, 205, 208–10, 212, 215, 218, 220, 222–4, 227, 232, 234, 241, 244–8, 250, 257, 264n
Newsnight, 53, 205
Newsround, 2
Nichols, B., 78–9, 85–6, 189
Nock, S., 82–3
Nolan, C., 210
Noonan, C., 36
Noordegraaf, J., 239–40
Norrell, J., 261n
nostalgia, 16, 157, 193, 212, 251, 253

Oakley, G., 52–3
O'Brien, P., 218
Ogier, P., 245
O'Kane, M., 74
Old Sparky, 259n
O'Neill, K., 109–10, 116, 122–3
One Show, The, 14
Open Door, 71, 261n
Open University, 90
Origen, 126
Other Side, The, 259n
Our Friend Victoria, 202
Out of Step, 259n
Over the Edge, 259n
Owen, G., 54, 135–6

palliative care, 17, 38–40, 54, 62, 64, 72, 80–1, 258n
panel shows, 16, 37–41, 65, 68–73, 76, 260–1n
Panorama, 56, 71, 259n
Paramedics on Scene, 199
Parents Television Council, 98
Parker, A. 3–4
Paxton, B., 146
Pearson, A., 76
Pearson, F. J. 222
Pearson, K., 226, 229, 264n
Peeren, E., 162, 203
Penfold-Mounce, R., 122, 193, 263n
Perks, J., 228
Perrotta, T., 142

Perspective, 38, 260n
Petit, C., 196
Pharoah, A., 157
Phillips, M., 261n
Phoenix, 229, 264n
Photo Archive Miners, 229, 237, 239
photography, 1, 10, 13, 15–16, 34–5, 45, 51, 85, 142–3, 159, 167, 172, 177, 180, 189–92, 194, 198, 207, 210, 227, 237, 241, 243, 261n
Pinchevski, A., 196
Pinedo, I. C., 262
Pinon, N., 258n
Piper, H., 90, 226
Play for Today, 228
Plunkett, J., 202
Pope, A., 59
Popular Memory Group, 240
pornography of death, 95, 100–1
post-broadcast television, 13–14, 61, 67, 90–1, 95, 125, 133, 146–50, 153, 165–84, 200–1, 207–8, 260n
posthumous television, 7, 13–16, 20–2, 24–5, 65, 184, 187–257, 261n
Postma, G., 72–3
postsecular television, 18, 112–15
Potter, D., 201
Poul, A., 105
Pratchett, T., 6, 80, 89
Prelinger, R., 239–40, 253–5
Prince Philip, 14, 199–200
Proust, M., 195
Pryluck, C., 34, 80
public service broadcasting, 8, 25, 29–30, 34–5, 55–6, 61, 66–9, 73, 90–1, 95, 220, 226–7
Pushing Daisies, 110
Puwar, N., 264n

Queen Elizabeth II, 13–15, 200–1, 258n
Question Time, 39
Quincy, ME, 100, 262n

Raikes, J., 261n
Rantzen, E., 215
Read, J., 237
Reading, A., 249
reality television, 62–3, 86
Reaper, 110
Reed, A. M., 229, 264n
Reith, J., 259n
religious programming, 16–17, 29–30, 35–40, 69
Remember All the Good Things, 16, 42–8, 187–9, 220–1, 260n
Remember Me, 20, 152, 157–9, 161
Remember Terry, 259n
Renov, M., 45, 192
Reyner, B., 238

Index

Rhode, S., 187
Richards, D., 264n
Richards, N., 81–2
Risky City, 247–8
Robin, K., 132
Robson, M., 172–4, 263n
Roe, M., 74–5
Roemer, M., 48, 50
Roma community, 249
Rosati, M., 112
Rothe, A., 215
Russell, C., 80, 84, 86–9, 261n
Russian Doll, 110
Russian Orthodox Church, 38
Rutledge, T., 229, 264n

St Michael's House, 228
Salisbury, B., 264n
Sandhu, K., 250
Sartre, J., 120, 122
Saunders, C., 261n
Savile, J., 21, 195–6, 204–20, 254, 264n
Saxton, L., 35, 78–9, 147
Scannell, P., 232
Schiappa, E., 98, 103–4
schools programming, 29
Schultz, N. W., 130
Schur, M., 113, 115
Screening Rights Film Festival, 228, 237
Sconce, J., 122–3, 177, 184, 192–3, 208
Seale, C., 147
Secret of Crickley Hall, The, 20, 152, 154–5, 161, 164
secularisation, 35–6, 96, 109, 112, 115
Seeing and Believing, 38
Senna, A., 2, 4, 258n
seriality, 12, 19–20, 132–4, 137–8, 141, 152, 154, 163, 166–7, 201, 214
Shacklock, Z., 163, 261n, 264n
Shattuc, J., 56
Shen, M., 126
Sherlock, 218
Shingler, M., 153
Ship, C. 199
Shopfront Theatre, 228–9, 235
Short Circuit, 259n
Sikhism, 36, 222
Sile, A., 261n
Simple Faith, 259n
Six Feet Under, 18, 96, 102–8, 131–2, 262n
Skirrow, G., 8, 32–3, 64
Smedley, C., 6, 86, 89
Smedley, P., 6–7, 84, 86, 89
Smith, A., 206
Smith, H., 261
Smith, J., 218, 264n
Smith, R., 263n

Snow, J., 212
snuff film, 4, 74
soap opera, 9–12, 66
Sobchack, V., 6, 29, 34, 78
social media, 91, 123, 133, 145–6, 200–3, 206, 214, 243, 264n
Something Else, 244
Sonnenshine, R., 176
Sontag, S., 34–5, 45, 147, 190
Soper, D., 72
Sorry for Your Loss, 19, 130, 133–5, 145–6, 149
soul, 96, 108, 110–11, 114–15, 118, 122–3
South Bank Show Revisited: Victoria Wood, The, 202
Spacey, K., 219, 264n
spectacle, 3–4, 18, 24, 41, 61, 65, 75, 95, 97, 100–1, 104, 130–2, 162
spectres *see* haunting
Spence, J., 51
Spigel, L., 196, 243, 252
Split Screen, 71
sports broadcasting, 2, 4
Steinhart, E, 123
Sterne, J., 20, 191–2
Steyger, T., 51
Stiegler, B., 192, 245
Stoeckl, K., 112
Story of Children's Television from 1946 to Now, 242
streaming platforms, 13–14, 61, 67, 90–1, 95, 133, 146–50, 153, 165–84, 200–1, 207–8, 219, 260n
Studio Canal, 225
Sturken, M., 230
suicide, 2–3, 4–5, 9, 11, 56, 70, 72, 86, 120, 168, 171; *see also* assisted dying
Suicide Tourist, The, 67, 85–6
Summer Stock, 262n
Suncoast Digest, 2–3
Sunday Break, The, 259n
Sunday Committee, The, 259n
Sutton, P., 188, 261n
Swallow, N., 11–12
Sykes, N., 261n

Taffia Cothan, 229, 264n
Tait, S., 3
talent shows, 4, 86
talk shows, 2–3, 36, 55–6, 65, 86, 187–9
Tambling, J., 15, 20, 189–92, 194, 223, 233
Tanner, L. E., 18, 96, 104, 130
Taylor, L., 71
television for women, 37–8, 56
Terry Pratchett: Choosing to Die, 5–7, 17–18, 67, 80, 84, 86–9
Tesler, B., 228
Thandi, K., 213
Theroux, L., 204, 215–17, 264n
This England, 12

This is Us, 19, 130, 133–4
This Morning, 199
Thomas, D., 38
Thomas, K., 41
Thompson, N., 141
Thomson, D., 98
Through Darkness to Light, 259n
Tibernham, P., 211
Todorov, T., 175–6
Tomorrow's World, 229
Tonight, 56, 59
Top of the Pops, 206, 210, 212
trauma, 8, 11–12, 19–20, 97, 138–9, 145, 152–6, 160–5, 167–82, 196, 203, 205–20, 232, 263–4n
traveller communities, 249
Tru Calling, 110
Turner, G., 90, 226–7
Turn of the Screw, 263n
Turnock, R., 102–3, 197–8
Tweed, H., 67–8, 261n
Twin Peaks, 167

UK City of Culture, 225–6, 250–1, 264n
uncanny, 122, 143, 157, 175, 177, 181, 193–4, 196, 206, 218, 245
UNESCO Declaration Concerning the International Destruction of Cultural Heritage, 249, 264n
Upload, 18–19, 96, 109, 114–18, 122–7, 262n

Valéry, P., 195
VanArendonk, K., 125
Van Brussel, L., 66
VanderBurgh, J., 223–4, 243
VanDerWerff, E., 97–8, 128
van der Wildt, A., 261n
van House, N., 249
van Oijen, W., 73–7, 261n
Van Roijen, J-H., 75
van Wendel de Joode, A., 73–7
van Wendel de Joode, C., 73–7, 81
VCR *see* home recording technologies
Victoria Wood: A BAFTA Tribute, 201, 263n
Victoria Wood: As Seen on TV, 263n
Victoria Wood: As Seen on TV Special, 264n
Victoria Wood: At It Again, 264n
Victoria Wood: A Tribute, 202
Victoria Wood: In Her Own Words, 202
Victoria Wood: Seen on TV, 201–2, 263n
Victoria Wood: Short Term Memories, 202
Victoria Wood's Midlife Christmas, 263–4n
Victoria Wood: The Secret List, 202
Video Diaries, 51, 55
Villarejo, A., 201

Vimeo, 91
Viney, R., 36–8, 40, 259n
Vivien Whiteley: On Her Own, 16, 47–8, 55
Visser, D., 261n
Voluntary Euthanasia Society, 39, 71–2, 74, 261n
voyeurism, 34–5, 75–6

Walker, M., 153, 158, 162–4
Wallace, R., 264n
Walter, T., 31, 40, 147, 201
Ward, A., 3
Warwick Arts Centre, 229, 237, 239
Waterhouse, J., 264n
Waterson, J., 200
Way to Go, 66
Weatherhead, L., 69–70
Webber, K., 261n
Weber, T., 18, 100–1, 131, 193
Weinstein, H., 209, 219, 264n
Weinstock, J. A., 153, 162, 220
Weissman, E., 101, 262n
West, T., 38–9
Wheatley, H., 7, 18, 22–4, 30, 95, 100, 157, 162, 165, 181, 203, 218, 225, 242
When Louis Met… Jimmy, 204, 264n
Where There's Life, 55
Whicker's World, 259n
White, M. 4, 56
Whiteley, T., 16, 42–7, 187–9, 220, 249
Whiteley, V., 16, 20, 42–8, 187–9, 220–1, 249, 260n
Who Do You Think You Are?, 45
Whose Life is it Anyway?, 71, 261n
Why Men Die Younger, 259n
Wilkins, R., 89
Williams, G., 261n
Williams, Raymond, 51
Williams, Richard, 246
Wilson, E., 45, 81, 184, 191, 196, 204, 245
Wilson, J., 261n
Winston, B., 34, 90, 189
Woman's Hour, 64
Wood, H., 240
Wood, V., 201–3, 220, 263–4n
World in Action, 8
World Trade Center attack (2001), 2, 103, 113, 149
Wright, J. C., 258n
Wyver, J., 228, 238, 246, 248, 264n

Young, M., 211
YouTube, 3–4, 91, 123, 202, 243

Zelizer, B., 215–16
zombies, 110, 194

EU representative:
Easy Access System Europe
Mustamäe tee 50, 10621 Tallinn, Estonia
Gpsr.requests@easproject.com

www.ingramcontent.com/pod-product-compliance
Lightning Source LLC
Chambersburg PA
CBHW071620170426
43195CB00038B/1496